NATIONAL
PARKS
and Reserves of Western Europe

ERIC DUFFEY

NATIONAL PARKS

and Reserves of Western Europe

Macdonald
Macdonald & Company
London

CONSULTANTS

NORWAY
Arne Gjellan and Atle Hage
Ministry of Environment, Oslo

ICELAND
Dr Arni Reynisson
Náttúruvernadarrad, Reykjavik

SWEDEN
Dr Torsten Larsson
National Environment Protection Board, Solna

FINLAND
Anja Finne
Office for National Parks, National Board of Forestry, Helsinki
Dr Pekka Borg
Department of Botany, University of Helsinki

DENMARK
Claus H. Ovesen
National Agency for the Protection of Nature, Copenhagen
Dr and Mrs Jon Buttenschøn
Nature Protection Department, Ribe Local Authority Tecnical Section, Ribe

WEST GERMANY
Professor W. Erz
Institute for Nature Protection and Animal Ecology, Bonn

AUSTRIA
Dr Stefan Plank
Institute for Environmental Science and Nature Protection, Graz

SWITZERLAND
Dr Dieter Burckhardt and Dr J. Röhner
Swiss League for the Protection of Nature, Basle

NETHERLANDS
Drs S. W. F. van der Ploeg
Free University of Amsterdam
Mr P. H. Goossens
Research Institute for Nature Management, Leersum (Utrecht)

BELGIUM
Professor Jan Hublé
Laboratory of Animal Ecology, Zoogeography, and Nature Protection, University of Gent
Professor A. Noirfalise
Laboratory of Plant Ecology, Gembloux

UNITED KINGDOM
Sir Hugh E. I. Elliott
Nature Conservancy Council, London
J. S. Furphy
Department of the Environment (NI), Belfast

EIRE
Dr Alan J. Craig
Office of Public Works, National Parks and Monuments Branch, Dublin
Dr Martin Speight
Forest and Wildlife Service Research Branch, Bray, Co. Wicklow

FRANCE
Dr J.-P. Raffin
Laboratory of General and Applied Ecology, University of Paris
Professor J.-C. Lefeuvre
National Museum of Natural History, Paris

SPAIN
Professor M. G. de Viedma
Polytechnic University of Madrid

PORTUGAL
Professor C. M. L. Baeta Neves
Institute of Agronomy, Entomology, Agriculture and Forestry, Lisbon

ITALY
Avv. Dr Fabio Cassola
Italian World Wildlife Fund
Professor Franco Tassi
Abruzzo National Park Autonomous Authority, Rome

YUGOSLAVIA
Dr Stane Peterlin
Slovenian Nature Conservancy, Ljubjana
Dr Ljerka Godicl
University of Maribor

GREECE
Dr Byron Antipas
Hellenic Society for the Protection of Nature, Athens
Dr C. Cassios
National Parks Section, Ministry of Agriculture, Athens

First published in Great Britain in 1982 by
Macdonald & Company (Publishers) Limited, London & Sydney
Holywell House
Worship Street, London EC2A 2EN

ISBN 0 356 08586 4

Edited, designed and produced by
Harrow House Editions Limited
7a Langley Street, Covent Garden, London WC2H 9JA

Phototypeset in Times by Tameside Filmsetting Ltd., Ashton-u-Lyne, England
Illustrations originated by Reprocolor Llovet S.A., Barcelona, Spain
Printed and bound by Arnoldo Mondadori Editore, Verona, Italy

CONTENTS

FOREWORD

Man's relationship with the rest of nature has always been equivocal. We admire the landscape – and drive heavy machinery through it. We extol the beauty of wild animals – then destroy their habitat and thus their chances of survival. The National Parks and Reserves of Western Europe, which this book so ably describes, are a conscious though comparatively recent attempt (the oldest was created less than a century ago) to restore some part of the balance we have so very recently begun to understand.

The poetic harmony of all nature has been recognised throughout history, from the Greek philosophers to the lakeland poets, yet the inexorable pressures of "civilisation" have brought man increasingly into conflict with the wild world. From the moment his first plough turned a furrow, thousands of years before Christ, the primeval habitat was disturbed; confrontation between man and the rest of nature had begun.

The process continued throughout the Middle Ages. Forests were cleared, swamps and marshes were drained. Man altered rapidly and forever the ecological equilibrium and condemned to extinction many other species of animals – and plants – which had once formed part of a relatively harmonious whole.

The Industrial Revolution in Europe, with its accompanying growth of population, provided a devastating acceleration of the process, which still continues. It was not simply a matter of landscapes and habitats permanently destroyed. Rivers and coasts were polluted, fertilisers, pesticides and atmospheric pollution, played havoc with the natural environment.

But now a new spirit seems to have emerged which accepts that the care and maintenance of our small planet could be in the best interests of its human inhabitants, materially, aesthetically and ethically. People have begun to accept that we have a responsibility at least to keep the options open for our children and grandchildren. The National Parks and Reserves of Western Europe are not merely recreation areas or open-air laboratories for naturalists. They are a tangible acknowledgement, at the highest level, that the planet is more than a work place or playground for man. A wild marsh, a stretch of heathland, or a scene of mountain gradeur, deserves as much protection as a great cathedral, or a famous painting.

Slimbridge
January 1982

Sir Peter Scott CBE, DSc, LL.D
Chairman of the World Wildlife Fund
Honorary Director of The Wildfowl Trust, Slimbridge

INTRODUCTION

Travel for pleasure either at home or abroad is much more interesting and rewarding than it was even a generation ago: so many more places are open to us than were available to our parents before. For the nature lover this is especially true. Increased awareness of the importance of nature conservation by governments in the last few decades has stimulated the establishment of large numbers of protected areas, conserving those parts of the countryside that are scenically or biologically outstanding. This book is about these places – what they look like, what they contain and how to reach them.

Throughout Western Europe there are several thousands of parks and reserves, a number far in excess of what can be encompassed within a single volume. The 344 described here are a mere sample of what the continent has to offer. They have been chosen with expert help to reveal the range of landscapes that exists and to give a selection of the finest examples in the hope of exciting the reader's interest in Europe's natural heritage.

In its efforts in preserving Europe's plants and animals in their natural surroundings the work of European conservation organizations has both increased our knowledge and understanding of natural history and provided us with an opportunity of experiencing nature free of man's interference.

Throughout the book two particular features have been incorporated to give guidance to the potential visitor and to help the reader wishing to discover more about a particular park or reserve.

Information Panels
The grey-tinted panel at the side of each right-hand page gives practical information about all the areas described on that page and the one facing.
The panels are divided into four sections:
Information An address from which further information can be obtained.
Access The best or easiest route by which the area can be reached. The place name printed in CAPITAL LETTERS can be found on the route map at the beginning of each chapter.
Open Opening times, where applicable. "Unrestricted" here implies that, as far as is known, the area can be entered at any time. It does *not* mean that there are no restrictions to what the visitor can do or where he can go. Every area has its own rules and regulations and these should be consulted before entering. Advice can be had from the addresses given under "Information".
Facilities Amenities provided for the general public, including such things as information centres nature trails and accommodation.

Route Maps and Summary Charts
On the second double page in each country chapter a short summary of the areas described in that section is given in chart form. The map references within the chart refer to the adjacent route map, which shows the location of the areas in relation to the country's major road network.

Throughout we have given the names of the parks and reserves in the language of the country to help the traveller find the areas on local maps and signposts. However English equivalent names are used for the Greek sites and for those in Yugoslavia where the Cyrillic alphabet is in use.

CONSERVATION IN ACTION

Since man first started to study and record the flora and fauna of natural habitats he has become aware of changes and fluctuations in both the numbers and distribution of certain animals and plants from one year to the next. In the majority of cases he has simply put the matter down to the inevitable course of nature, thereby failing to realize that, more often than not, he was the direct cause. It was only in the course of the last century, after many species of animals and plants had been made extinct, that man started to make a determined effort to stem the devastating advance of civilization. Among conservation measures he has since taken are the prohibition of the hunting and trapping of animals and the collecting of plants in areas where their populations are declining; the reintroduction of species that were formerly resident in a region; the restriction of the use of land for farming or settlement; and, more recently, the prevention of the spread of pollutants. The story of the conservation of nature, however, is one of mixed fortunes. Among the case histories described below, some reflect success, others failure. Not all measures have been taken in time and neither have they always been successful.

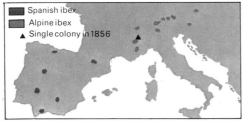

Spanish ibex
Alpine ibex
▲ Single colony in 1856

IBEX *Capra ibex*

A naturalist visiting the Alps in the mid-nineteenth century would have looked in vain for this striking mountain goat with its imposing horns of some 75 centimetres in length, because excessive hunting had almost wiped it out in the eighteenth or early part of the nineteenth century. Not only was the head a much prized trophy and the flesh good to eat, but many parts of its body were supposed to have remarkable medicinal properties. No wonder this fine animal almost reached the point of extinction in Europe. However, about sixty ibex survived in the western Italian Alps, where a royal hunting reserve had been established in 1856 by King Victor Emmanuel II.

The surviving Italian population of the mid-nineteenth century steadily recovered once poaching had been stopped, and the numbers had reached several hundreds when King Victor Emmanuel III gave the hunting reserve to the nation in 1922. It then became the Gran Paradiso National Park, one of Italy's finest wildlife areas. By 1958 the Italian ibex population had increased to over 3000, and colonization of other parts of the Alps was beginning to take place. This process was speeded up by a series of reintroductions, particularly into the Swiss Alps, where there are now about forty separate colonies. The ibex was also reintroduced in Germany, Austria and France. Although the alpine ibex is now safely reestablished and completely protected, poaching is still a serious problem. During the Second World War, when the wardening system in the Gran Paradiso National Park broke down, illegal hunting reduced the population to a few hundreds, and in recent years a strike by park guards gave poachers another chance to hunt in this protected area, and a large proportion of the ibex population was slaughtered. Throughout central and western Europe there are several subspecies of *Capra ibex*. The Spanish population, however, is regarded by most experts as a separate species – *Capra pyrenaica*. It is now extremely rare in the Pyrenees, but other races of *C. pyrenaica* are holding their own in the sierras of northern, central and southern Spain, such as the Sierra de Alba, the Sierra de Gredos and the Sierra Nevada.

THE SAXIFRAGE *Saxifraga florulenta*

About fifty species of saxifrages are known to live in the Alps, but many are now rare because of collecting and habitat destruction by man. The larger and more striking the plant the more likely it is to be removed to someone's garden, and this has often been the fate of *Saxifraga florulenta*. It occurs only in the Maritime Alps on the borders of France and Italy. Most of the known localities are at altitudes of between 2000 and 2500 metres and have a north or northwest aspect. Generally, the plant grows in small isolated groups of ten or more plants. It lives almost exclusively on steep rock faces, often inaccessible to the climber. Formerly it grew in less remote places, but it was too easy for the plant collector to reach and soon disappeared. *S. florulenta* is a very slow-growing plant and often takes as much as ten to twelve years to flower. Having produced its magnificent flowers the plant dies, and the next generation depends on the successful germination of seeds. Being very difficult to cultivate, its collection for horticultural purposes will only hasten its extinction. It is fully protected on the Italian side of the Maritime Alps.

LARGE COPPER BUTTERFLY
Lycaena dispar

There are about 380 species of butterflies throughout Europe, nearly a third of which are found only in certain restricted localities. In other cases, a subspecies may be rare, and this is so with the large copper. The largest and the finest of the coppers was the race *Lycaena dispar dispar,* which was first described in 1795 from the East Anglian fens in England. It survived for only a short time due to the drainage of the marshes and the attentions of collectors, and after 1851 no further specimens were seen. In 1915 an almost indistinguishable race was discovered in the fens of Friesland and Overijssel in the Netherlands, where it still survives.

Although a rare insect, its single foodplant is the relatively common great water dock, *Rumex hydrolapathum,* which grows along the edges of dykes, rivers and lakes and in marshy ground. The female large copper lays her eggs on the leaves of the water dock in July and August, and after hatching, the small larvae feed for only a short time before descending to the base of the plant, where they hibernate on dead leaves until the following spring. Once the larvae are in hibernation flooding does no harm, but if the water level rises in late April or early May when they have reemerged to feed on the fresh new leaves, they may be drowned. It may be for this reason that the female generally avoids laying eggs on dock plants growing in standing water. This tends to restrict the butterfly to the scarce marshy vegetation away from the water's edge. Like many caterpillars, those of the large copper are readily eaten by insects, mice, small birds and by the grubs of parasitic flies. Even so this is not the main reason for the rarity of this butterfly; man's destruction of much of its natural habitat is more important.

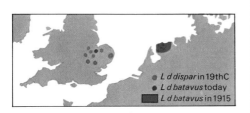

- ● *L d dispar* in 19thC
- ● *L d batavus* today
- ■ *L d batavus* in 1915

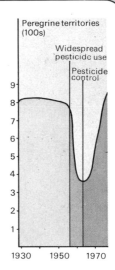

Peregrine territories (100s)

Widespread pesticide use

Pesticide control

9
8
7
6
5
4
3
2
1

1930   1950   1970

PEREGRINE FALCON *Falco peregrinus*

In the Middle Ages this hawk was a great favourite with the nobility for falconry and was protected by severe penalties, but later it was regarded as an enemy of the gamekeeper and often shot on sight. Nevertheless, it was able to maintain a safe population level, helped by its particularly wide distribution throughout Europe. In Britain during the Second World War, it was accused of killing homing pigeons, which were used for carrying military communications. Because of this, some 600 adult peregrines were destroyed. Ten years after the war its numbers had recovered again, but in the mid-1950s a serious decline was recorded, which was eventually shown to be due or organochlorine pesticides that reached the peregrine through poisoned prey. At this time only about 16 per cent of the nesting birds were successfully rearing young. By 1971 a slow recovery was recorded, and this has continued among birds nesting inland but not among those on the coast. It seems that sea pollution levels have remained high, mainly due to PCBs (polychlorinated biphenyls), which originate from industrial processes and reach the sea via the rivers. Today the pergrine is protected in most countries of Europe. However, this has greatly increased the black market price of these birds, so that more eggs and young are being stolen than ever before.

BEAVER *Castor fiber*

Before man began to clear the forests of temperate Europe for cultivation, one of its most wide-spread animals was the beaver. As trees made way for the plough and hunting pressures increased. Europe's largest rodent rapidly declined in numbers. In the whole of the Palaearctic region the only remaining populations by the 1920s were in Norway, the Rhône Valley of France, the Elbe in Germany and certain localities in Poland and Russia.

It was in Russia that early attempts were made to protect and manage the beaver, and today there are 60,000 animals compared with a total population of about 1000 in the 1920s. In 1922 the beaver was brought back to Sweden and to Finland, although in the latter case the Canadian beaver was imported as well as native Scandinavian animals. In 1956 it was established in Switzerland and now eleven small populations are known. The Rhône Valley colony has grown from about 300 in 1940 to over 5000 today and new groups have been started in Belgium, Germany, and Austria. An attempt is now being made to reintroduce it to Britain.

Beavers live along rivers and streams. In well-wooded areas they live in harmony with the environment and the trees that they fell for food or dam-building do not exceed the capacity of the forest to replace them. Where they are numerous, the populations can be cropped without danger to produce meat and the much-coveted fur.

THE SPIDER *Eresus niger*

Spiders are not a popular group of animals, even with keen naturalists, but nevertheless they have a place in our environment, even if it is only in keeping down the hoards of insects which plague us in summer. Although not many European spiders are as brilliantly coloured as are, for instance, the tropical jumping spiders, there is one spider, or at least the male of the species, which is an exception, and that is *Eresus niger*. Although the female is entirely black the male's abdomen has a brilliant red dorsal surface with four black spots, and its legs are conspicuously ringed with alternate black and white bands.

Eresus lives in a silk-lined tube. At the entrance to the tube there is a tangle of silk threads, stretching along the ground and up into the vegetation. When a passing beetle gets its legs tangled in this web the spider rushes to the surface to seize and drag it down into its lair. The adult males are usually seen in May when they leave their own burrows in search of those of females.

Because its powers of dispersal seem to be very limited the spider depends for survival on its habitat being undisturbed. Once the ground in which it has made its burrow has been ploughed or planted with trees which produce a dense shade, the colony will die. In Europe it is most common in the south and often lives in semidesert areas that are too poor for cultivation: sometimes a colony is found in a very small site, perhaps only a few metres square. The spider is greatly helped by the preservation of archaeological sites such as Roman ruins, which provide a ready-made protected habitat. Farther north it is much more scarce, partly for climatic reasons and partly because more efficient agriculture and forestry have disturbed the land and left the spider with few habitats suitable for colonization.

In Britain it lived on a south coast heath near Bournemouth, Dorset, until the early years of this century, when the site disappeared under a housing development. It was then thought to be extinct until it was rediscovered in 1979 occupying a small site in an altogether completely different part of the country.

OLM *Proteus anguinus*

The caverns of the limestone karst country of Yugoslavia have the most interesting cave fauna of any country in western Europe. Although only a few of the creatures have been studied thoroughly there is little doubt that one of the strangest must be the olm, a long, thin amphibian, which reaches 25 centimetres in length. The olm has external gills like a tadpole and is morphologically in a permanently immature state even when ready to breed. It prefers water of about 10°C, at which temperature it lays eggs, but if the temperature falls the eggs are retained within the animal's body and the young are born alive.

The olm is restricted to the Adriatic side of Yugoslavia and to one place in northern Italy. It is probably safe at present in the darkness of its cave habitat, but some of its best sites are now visited by growing numbers of tourists. It is not known whether this disturbance of its habitat will affect the population.

LADY'S SLIPPER ORCHID *Cypripedium calceolus*
Perhaps no other plant provides such a fine example of decline due to the destructive attentions of man as the lady's slipper orchid. Many other plants which have become rare in the last thirty years have declined because of habitat changes due to farming, forestry or urban development. The lady's slipper orchid, preferring limestone soils, has however a fairly secure habitat and is usually found growing in woodland clearings. It is often associated with mountains, except in Scandinavia where it can occur at low altitudes. In some cases, even though the ground where it grew was too rocky to be ploughed, the orchid was eliminated by the dense uniform planting of conifers. The plant grows to 50 or even 70 centimetres tall, has broad oblong leaves and a flower – usually one but sometimes two – which may be 9 centimetres in diameter. With reddish maroon sepals and a large yellow pouch-shaped lip it is the most impressive of all European orchids. In Britain it is very scarce and flowers between May and June. It is found mainly in woodland and mountain districts.

In the past people could not resist digging it up and transferring it to their gardens, where unfortunately it almost certainly died. Orchids have a close and intimate relationship with the micro-organisms in the soil, so that removal to a completely different site from which they are most probably absent often results in death.

Today the lady's slipper is carefully protected by law in nearly all countries, particularly in National Parks and nature reserves. The public are now persuaded by posters and literature that such attractive plants should be left for all to see and enjoy.

EUROPEAN LYNX *Felis lynx*
The lynx, the largest wild cat in Europe, was formerly widespread wherever there was forested land, particularly in mountains.

In the breeding season the female seeks out a hollow tree or rock cleft where she can hide her young. She and her mate hunt rabbits, hares, squirrels, rodents

and ground-nesting birds. However, with the fragmentation of forests, the disappearance of old trees as breeding sites and more particularly with the activities of hunters who shot them as vermin, the lynx disappeared from nearly the whole of western and central Europe and even vanished entirely from the Alps. It remained in Norway, Sweden and Finland, eastern Europe and parts of the Balkans, and also in southwest Spain and parts of Portugal, where a distinct subspecies, known as the pardel lynx, occurs.

In the last twenty years attempts have been made to reintroduce the lynx to several of its old haunts, particularly in the Alps and in Germany. It is too early to say how successful these reintroductions have been.

LAMMERGEIER *Gypaetus barbatus*
This magnificent bird, with its distinctive wedge-shaped tail and long, narrow wings, was once a familiar sight over the Alps and other European mountain ranges. It feeds principally on bones, which it breaks open by dropping them from a height onto stones to get at the marrow. Even the young are fed on bone fragments. However, as it was mistakenly thought to kill lambs it became a prime target for the hunter's gun and because of its large size it probably found it difficult to withstand the onslaught. It was perhaps easier to shoot than, for instance, the griffon vulture, which is still widespread in Iberia, the Mediterranean islands, in the Balkans and elsewhere in southern Europe. A falling food supply may also have been partly responsible for the decline.

In 1923 the last lammergeier was shot in the Alps, by which time it had already become scarce in other mountain ranges. Although only a few pairs still breed in the Pyrenees, Sardinia, Corsica and the Balkans, the vulture is widespread in Africa, and proposals have been made to reintroduce it to parts of the Alps using zoo stock.

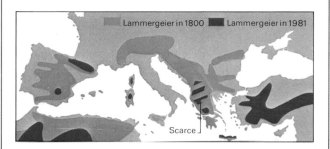

Lammergeier in 1800 ■ Lammergeier in 1981

Scarce

MONK SEAL *Monachus monachus*

Only one seal, the Monk seal, brown in colour with a white patch on its underparts, lives in the Mediterranean. Its range extends also to a few areas on the coast of northwest Africa and to parts of the Black Sea. It haunts rocky coasts and breeds in caves or on small secluded beaches. It is now very rare and as close to extinction as any European mammal.

Formerly it bred on all the Mediterranean islands, but its range has been contracting eastwards and in the last few years its population has declined catastrophically. In the middle 1970s it still bred in a few places in the Adriatic, and Yugoslavia featured it on a postage stamp to draw attention to its endangered state. However, by the time the stamp appeared the seal had already become extinct along its shores.

A few years ago it was still found on the coasts of Corsica and Sardinia, but by 1980 breeding records had ceased. It survives today only on a few Greek islands, and recent studies predict that at the present rate of decline the Monk seal will be extinct in the Mediterranean by the year 2000.

Its decline is another sorry tale of conflict with man. Although protected by law, fishermen regard it as a competitor and shoot it on sight. The second and perhaps the more serious reason for its decline is the growth of the tourist industry. All sandy Mediterranean beaches are now accessible to the tourist, if not by road then by boat. Caves which used to be monk seal breeding sites are now tourist attractions for pleasure boats. Its habitat is not destroyed, as has happened in other cases, but has been taken over by crowds who scare the seal away. With nowhere left for it to breed there is urgent need for positive action to save this interesting species.

FRITILLARY *Fritillaria meleagris*

A member of the lily family, the fritillary is one of the most charming of European wild flowers. Buds appear in the early spring and in early April the first flowers begin to open. The blooms appear singly and form large pendulant bells, typically mauve with reds and pinks; however the colour is very variable and even a pure white form exists. Unfortunately it has become very rare because the valley meadows of permanent grassland, which are its typical habitat, have been largely drained and reclaimed for agriculture, or else "improved" by the use of herbicides and pesticides. The fritillary flourishes best where the meadow is managed by taking a hay crop followed by grazing; the plant has time to grow, flower and set seed before the hay is cut.

The decline of the fritillary in Britain since the Second World War has been dramatic and it survives only on nature reserves where the conditions it needs are preserved. It has also declined on the continent of Europe, although not to the same extent, because there are more places where traditional farming without modern chemicals has survived.

WOLF *Canis lupus*

For centuries the wolf has been a traditional enemy of man and is still destroyed at every opportunity. It is therefore remarkable that the species has survived as long as it has. The last British wolf was killed in the mid-eighteenth century, whereas it survived for over a hundred years longer in France. It is surprising that it has almost disappeared from the vast forests and wilderness areas of Norway and Sweden but has survived in Spain and Italy. In Scandinavia it was regarded as an enemy of the reindeer by the Lapps, who are still allowed to kill it today, even in National Parks. In Italy, where about 100 wolves still live in the Apennines, it is in actual fact legally protected, albeit by a law which is widely disregarded. In Spain, however, it has no protection.

The Apennine and Spanish wolves are small animals and seem to be quite harmless to man, although they will attack sheep from time to time.

Although conservationists in many countries are working to protect the animal public prejudice dies hard and in some countries this shy animal may not survive much longer.

LARGE BLUE BUTTERFLY *Maculinea arion*

The blue butterflies of the family Lycaenidae are among the most beautiful insects in western Europe. Most are rather small and their larvae feed mainly on plants of the family Leguminosae. Many are known to have some association with ants during their life cycle – the larvae produce a sweet sticky substance which the ants eat in return for giving the caterpillar some protection from predators.

The large blue is one of the most striking of the blues and very careful study of its life history has shown that their relationship with ants is both complicated and essential, and is usually with one particular species. This means that not only must the butterfly's habitat have the right conditions for the growth of the food plant – wild thyme in the case of the large blue – but it must also be suitable for the ant species in whose nests the large blue larvae pass the winter. This balance is very delicate, and a modest change in land use which discourages the ant but not the food-plant would be sufficient to cause the extinction of the population. Such changes can be brought about by a cessation in grazing, which allows the vegetation to grow taller and cover the ground. In Britain the large blue has always been a scarce insect, but for the last thirty or forty years there has been a sharp decline in the type of heathland it prefers and in 1980 only one breeding site was known. In 1981 the insect became extinct in Britain.

Very rare

Although suitable heaths are widespread in some countries it occurs only locally in Europe. Why its status should be so local is, however, not known.

GREAT BUSTARD *Otris tarda*

A ground-nesting bird as large as a turkey and good to eat is bound to have a hard time surviving in the highly populated countries of western Europe. Two hundred years ago the great bustard was widespread all over the continent and even bred in England, where the last birds were shot in 1832.

The great bustard continues to decline in western Europe and now survives only in the North German Plain, in East Germany, where it is scarce; in Portugal and Spain, where it breeds in many parts of the southwest, and in eastern Austria, where there are still a few pairs. In Hungary and elsewhere in central and eastern Europe it is much more numerous.

Its natural breeding habitats would seem to be grassy plains and heathlands, but in its remaining localities in western Europe it has adapted to breed on cultivated land, particularly in areas where there are no hedges or walls to obstruct its view of an approaching enemy. It is a shy bird and takes flight long before it can be approached closely.

In most countries the bird is now protected by law, but its numbers continue to decline. In recent years a small stock has been kept in captivity on Salisbury Plain in Hampshire with the object of releasing them some time in the future.

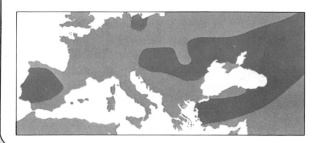

CONSERVATION IN EUROPE

Wildlife conservation in Europe began several centuries ago with the creation of royal hunting reserves. However, the first true nature reserves, formed mainly by private organizations, did not come into being until the late nineteenth century and Western European governments did little for nature conservation until after 1872, when the first National Park in the world was established at Yellowstone, USA. This magnificent example was followed by many countries. The first in Europe was Sweden, where five parks were established in 1909.

The different categories of parks and reserves and their functions are sometimes confusing because each country interprets them in its own way. Most people are familiar with National Parks and their aim of preserving large wilderness areas in their natural state. This magnificent concept is followed in most countries where wilderness still survives, but in smaller and more densely populated regions the landscape everywhere has been modified by man and the term National Park, if used, has a different meaning. In Great Britain, for example, it is applied to large areas of attractive countryside – with towns, agriculture, forestry and even industry – which in other countries would probably be called Nature or Regional Parks. But even within the wilderness category, management and effectiveness of protection vary considerably.

The visitor to a National Park in Scandinavia, Switzerland, France and Italy will find explanatory notices, signed footpaths, information centres, wardens and other evidence of their park status, but in Greece he will have difficulty in finding even a notice with a National Park's name; the Samaria Gorge National Park in Crete is a notable exception. This does not mean that the Greek National Parks are any less beautiful than others; they are magnificent, but the government has not yet found the resources to staff and manage them.

In some parks visitors may be surprised at the amount of organized tourist activity. This is because in most countries the authorities believe that parks are as much for people as for wildlife. The Swiss National Park is a rare exception; wildlife has priority and the visiting public must regard themselves as guests. In France, National Parks are zoned with the inner part for wildlife and the outer developed for tourism. In Yugoslavia about 10 per cent of each park is set aside for tourist development. In Italy there is no zoning and the park managements face considerable difficulties in maintaining a balance between tourism and preservation.

National Parks are without doubt one of the most important types of protected area in Europe, mainly because they generally cover very large areas. However, they are few in number – only six in France, one in Switzerland, and five in Italy (one is a park in name only). Finland, with twenty-five, easily tops the list in Western Europe. The wilderness-type park is typically situated in mountainous regions where human settlement is localized or even absent. In the area covered by this book, they form two complexes, one in Scandinavia, mainly comprising remote areas, sometimes without access roads; and a second in the Alps, where, from the Vanoise in France, through Switzerland, northern Italy, Bavaria and into the Julian Alps of Yugoslavia, there are eight magnificent mountain parks rich in wildlife, blessed with glorious summers, and easily accessible to the public.

When defined as wilderness areas, it is virtually impossible to have National Parks in the extensive lowlands of Europe. In those regions, agriculture, forestry, industry and urban development are powerful competitors for land and space for wildlife is limited.

However, much can be done for nature conservation by the creation of nature reserves, which are generally small areas and may include man-made as well as semi-natural environments. Throughout Western Europe nature reserves are extremely variable, not only in size and ownership but also in administration, management, the resources available for effective care and the amount of research conducted to understand the needs of the fauna and flora. In some countries there are large numbers of nature reserves, for example in Sweden there are over 2000, in West Germany 1262, in the Netherlands over 800 and in Britain 166 state reserves and 1000 private reserves. On the other hand in most Mediterranean countries, nature reserves are relatively few. State resources to create them are inadequate or not available, and private organizations, if they exist, are not strong enough to establish more than a few.

An important category of protected area, with the main object of providing rural amenities for the public, is the Regional or Nature Park. They now exist in several countries and consist of attractive countryside, often with distinctive traditional characteristics, containing towns and villages, and have normal agricultural and forestry activities. Administration is by the local authorities. The term Regional Park is used in France, which has fourteen, many with wildlife habitats of considerable interest. The name Nature Park was first used by the German Federal Republic, which now has forty-two. The main benefit derived by wildlife from this category of protected area is that the character of the landscape is preserved; some have nature reserves established within them.

Mention must also be made of protected landscapes and the many types of private land properties, where wildlife is able to survive in peace. Perhaps the best European example of an organization controlling land in this category is the National Trust in Britain, which owns and protects from development 630 kilometres of coastline and 167,000 hectares of semi-natural land throughout the country.

Public support and interest in nature conservation continues to expand and there is a growing realization that parks and reserves are as much part of our natural heritage and culture as are works of art. But too many visitors may sometimes ruin the very thing we all wish to preserve. We need more parks and reserves, better management and regulation and a much improved information service for the public.

International efforts to pursue these ends and to find a common policy throughout Western Europe are concentrated within the International Union for the Conservation of Nature supported by the World Wildlife Fund. The Council for Europe and the EEC are also working towards improving nature conservation in Europe, and although progress is slow national governments are responding.

VOLCANS D'AUVERGNE The wonderfully varied countryside of the Regional Park lies at the heart of the Massif Central in France.

THE FACE OF EUROPE

Europe's political boundaries frequently reflect the physical geography and vegetation zones of the Continent. Physical barriers are in many instances the forerunners of political boundaries; the Alps separating Switzerland from Italy, the Baltic dividing Norway and Sweden from the North European Plain. The natural vegetation of Europe, zoned in east–west belts across the Continent, is determined largely by climate and varies from tundra in the far north to Mediterranean scrub in the south. Apart from the modifying influence of altitude, its present distribution is entirely due to man's interference as farmer and industrialist.

1 Norway and Iceland (pages 18–35), situated on the northwestern extremity of Europe, have many features in common – a heavily idented coastline and extensive ice fields.

2 Sweden (pages 36–51) lies on land sloping eastwards from the Norwegian mountains to the Baltic coast. Almost half the country is covered by forest, both of natural origin and commercially planted.

3 Finland (pages 52–61), with over sixty thousand lakes, is called by the Finns, Suomi – the land of lakes. Its chaotic landscape, the result of haphazard deposition, is a legacy of the last ice age.

4 Denmark (pages 62–75), although culturally part of Scandinavia, is geographically properly a part of the North European Plain.

5 West Germany (pages 76–99) can be divided into three distinct areas – the northern plain, the Hercynian Massif and the southern Alpine uplands. The northern region is the most heavily cultivated and thoroughly urbanized.

6 Austria (pages 100–111). highly mountainous to the south and west, extends northwards across the heavily cultivated Danube Plain.

7 Switzerland (pages 112–127), aptly called the roof of Europe, straddles the Continent's highest mountain range – the Alps, an area of great floral interest.

8 Netherlands (pages 128–143) lies largely on alluvial deposits laid down by the rivers Maas and Rhine and have been reclaimed from the North Sea.

9 Belgium and Luxembourg (pages 144–157), although occupying one of the most densely populated corners of Europe, have large tracts of undisturbed woodland.

10 United Kingdom and Eire (pages 158–181) have been intensively cultivated for centuries. Even the vegetation of the upland areas has been heavily modified and impoverished by sheep grazing.

11 France (pages 182–205) was in the past completely covered by forest except for the highest mountains. In most areas the woodland has now given way to agricultural land.

12 Spain (pages 206–223) is an area of high plateau walled off from the rest of Europe by the Pyrenees. It is a land of high contrast, ranging from desert to coniferous forest.

13 Portugal (pages 224–233) is an area of river-dissected uplands on the western coast of the Iberian Peninsula.

14 Italy (pages 234–249) forms a peninsula extending south along the backbone of the Apennine Mountains into the Mediterannean. Some deciduous woodland remains in highland areas.

15 Yugosavia (pages 250–261) has one of the most diverse vegetations in Europe, varying from chalky scrub on the summits of the Dinaric Alps to coniferous forest and deciduous woodland on the lower slopes.

16 Greece (pages 262–271) consists mainly of the Balkan Peninsula and the islands of the northern Aegean. The natural vegetation is predominantly scrubby woodland.

NORWEGIAN SEA

White Sea

NORWAY

SWEDEN

FINLAND

Gulf of Bothnia

Onega

Ladoga

Gulf of Finland

Vanern

UNION OF SOVIET SOCIALIST REPUBLICS

Skagerrak

Kattegat

DENMARK

Dvina

B A L T I C   S E A

Elbe

NETHERLANDS

Vistula

WEST GERMANY

EAST GERMANY

POLAND

Rhine

Ore Mts. (Erzgebirge)

Oder

Sudeten Mts.

Dnieper

Volga

LUXEMBOURG

Beskidy Mts.

Carpathian Mountains

Dniester

Vosges

Black Forest

Bohemian Forest

CZECHOSLOVAKIA

Sea of Azov

Jura

Danube

SWITZERLAND

AUSTRIA

Tauern

HUNGARY

ROMANIA

Crimea

P S L

Transylvanian Alps (Carpatii Meridionali)

BLACK SEA

Po

YUGOSLAVIA

Apennines

Adriatic Sea

Dinaric Alps (Dinarske Planina)

Stara Planina

BULGARIA

Corsica

ITALY

Rodopi Planina

ALBANIA

TURKEY

Sardinia

Tyrrhenian Sea

Aegean Sea

Ionian Sea

GREECE

Sicily

Peloponnese

Crete

- ● Urban areas
- Cultivated land
- Grassland
- Forest and woodland
- Montane vegetation and tundra
- Semi-desert
- Permanent snow
- Marshland

0   200   400 kms

NORWAY AND ICELAND

Penetrating over 500 kilometres beyond the Arctic Circle and with a length of 1750 kilometres, Norway forms a defensive mountain wall on the western side of the Scandinavian countries. It has one of the most impressive and beautiful coastlines in Europe, characterized by many fjords extending deep into the mountains and fringed by thousands of islands, of which the most important are the Lofoten. The large island of Spitzbergen, lying to the north of North Cape, and the smaller Jan Mayen and Bear Islands, are also Norwegian territory.

From the coast the land rises steeply to alpine plateaux and mountain ranges, reaching nearly 2500 metres on Galdhöpiggen, the highest peak. The nearby Jostedalsbreen, the largest ice-field in continental Europe, feeds several glaciers. Although the country spans the Arctic Circle the climate is unusual in the mildness of its winters, and the coast remains ice-free throughout the year.

Apart from the Norwegians themselves, about 20,000 Lapps live in the north, depending largely on reindeer husbandry for their needs. Forests, which are mostly coniferous, cover about 30 per cent of the land and provide a valuable raw material.

Norway's rich water resources and their utilization have been one of the factors responsible for arousing greater public interest in conservation; as more and more waterfalls and rivers disappeared into extensive tunnel systems as part of the construction of hydroelectric schemes, it became clear that in a few years' time virtually no important river or large watershed would be unaffected by hydrological and ecological changes.

Today there are thirteen National Parks, twenty-one Protected Landscapes, about 192 Nature Reserves, most relatively small, and 215 Nature Monuments. Additionally in Spitzbergen there are three National Parks, fifteen bird sanctuaries and two nature reserves, including one of the largest in the world, with an area of 1.5 million hectares.

In common with other Scandinavian countries Norwegian policy relating to open-air recreation is based on the traditional right of Norwegians to enter all land regardless of its ownership. Norway is fortunate in still having large forests and unspoilt wilderness areas, which even with increased pressure from industry and urban expansion provide a magnificent open-air environment for its people.

The legislation for the protection of flora and fauna outside National Parks is not as strong as in some countries, for example only one plant is protected – the mistletoe. With regard to the fauna, all birds of prey are protected by law as well as the brown bear and the wolf. However, a new law will protect all wild animals except those specifically listed as game.

The most active voluntary society in Norway is the Norwegian Union for Nature Protection, established in 1914. It now has 36,000 members in eighteen local associations and, although supported in part by government funds, it is completely independent.

ICELAND occupies a central position in the North Atlantic, just south of the Arctic Circle. It lies only 280 kilometres from the east coast of Greenland and is the most westerly country in Europe. In the south its extensive low grassy coastline is indented with many fjords and bays and in the north by deep valleys cut into the highlands. The interior is a high plateau with mountains, lakes, glaciers and rivers and is largely devoid of human settlement.

The flora of Iceland includes one endemic species, and thirty-one plants which now have legal protection. In some protected areas, traditional use by farmers for grazing and cultivation is only excluded where the protection of the flora is of special importance.

Scarcely any forest remains in the country and it is believed that extensive sheep grazing on the

coastal lowlands rather than the adverse climate was responsible for destroying the woodland that once existed. The newly established Forestry Service is at present attempting to redress this balance.

The main nature conservation legislation in Iceland is the Nature Conservation Act of 1971, which is administered by the Ministry of Culture and Education through its executive body, the Náttúruverndarráð. Each major town and county also has a Nature Conservation Committee, which advises the national body.

Voluntary organizations play an important part in Icelandic nature conservation; the most influential is the Landvernd – the Icelandic Environment Union – which was established in 1969. This organisation has many different interests, covering travel, sport, youth activities and soil conservation, as well as environmental matters.

There are three National Parks, which are open to the public and are widely used in the summer, as well as seven landscape reserves, fifteen biotope reserves, sixteen natural monuments and the large and complex Mývatn and Laxá River area, which is designated by a special law. The Inventory of Icelandic Sites of Conservation Interest (1981) also contains 215 sites which the Náttúruverndarráð has

ICELAND A combination of glaciation and sea-level changes are responsible for Norway and Iceland's characteristic coastlines.

declared worthy of protection in the future. Special attention is given to the Reykjavik area, because intensive urban development demands a high priority for the conservation of natural sites for education and recreational purposes.

The bird fauna is not rich compared with elsewhere in Europe; a total of 260 birds has been recorded, of which 80 breed or have bred in the country. Some of the protected island bird colonies are closed to the public. Perhaps the most important is the island of Eldey, which although only 1.5 hectares in area, has the largest gannet colony in Iceland – 11,000 nests. Historically it is of great interest as the last refuge and breeding site of the now extinct great auk.

All birds are protected during the breeding season, but a few may be hunted from August to May. In addition local people retain the traditional right to take the eggs and young of some protected species when these are important to their livelihood. The bird protection law also contains provisions to regulate the photography of rare species, such as eagles, gyr falcons and little auks, near their nests.

19

Impressive though they undoubtedly are, the mountains of Norway are really no more than the eroded stumps of a much grander range, uplifted and faulted, then relentlessly attacked by water and more recently ice – the latter having left its unmistakeable imprint on the landscape in the form of ice-scoured surfaces, hanging valleys, magnificent fjords and a low coastal platform, broken in many places into island remnants.

The range reaches its highest in the middle of the southern massif, in the Jotunheimen area, where Glittertind (2472 metres) and Galdhøppigen (2469 metres) vie for the honours. The interior of the plateau is wild and desolate, little used but for some scattered farms in the more sheltered valleys, but the fjords of the west are surprisingly productive. However, barely 3 per cent of the land area is cultivated and most of that is in the coastal plains of the southeast and in the Oslo fjord.

The prevailing westerly wind systems produce a typically maritime climate in the west, while the eastern regions experience more continental influences with greater extremes and lower temperatures.

Some 1000 kilometres out to the west lies Iceland. For the most part it is a 600- to 1000-metre high barren, unpopulated desert plateau of lava fields and glaciers, notable mainly for Europe's largest ice-sheet, the 3,400-square mile Vatnajökull. Large areas are bare rock and sand, sparsely colonized by mosses, lichens and stunted shrubs, though dwarf willow, birch and mountain ash manage to survive in the more sheltered lowland valleys.

SKAFTAFELL The Svartifoss cataract is one of several waterfalls found in the park. The cliff behind is a magnificent example of columnar basalt and appears almost to be the work of a stone mason.

PARK/RESERVE	SIZE (km²)	DESCRIPTION	MAP REF	PAGE NO
NORWAY				
ÅNDERDALEN	68.0	National Park. Mountainous region with coastal forest. Several orchid species and interesting bird fauna.	C1	22
STABBURSDALEN	97.0	National Park. Most northerly pine forest in the world with trees up to 500 years old. Variety of tree-hole nesting birds and raptors. Elk and reindeer grazing.	D1	22
ØVRE ANARJÅKKA	1400	National Park. Largest Norwegian park in remote region. Bogs and treeless areas interspersed with birch and relict pine forest. Many small-mammal species.	D1	22
ØVRE PASVIK	63.0	National Park. Primeval forest with extensive swamps and lakes lying between the borders of Finland and the Soviet Union. Typical mammal fauna including reindeer, bears and wolverines.	D1	23
ØVRE DIVIDAL	750	National Park. Region of extensive plateaux, valleys and lakes. Rich flora with hundreds of flowering plants.	C1	24
RAGO	171	National Park. Rugged, rock-covered terrain with many lakes and sharp mountain ridges.	C2	24
BØRGEFJELL	1065	National Park. Mountainous landscape with high forest cover in the south and west. Varied flora of heath and snow-bed plants. Rich bird fauna of raptors, waders, ducks and owls.	B2/B3	26
GRESSÅMOEN	180	National Park. Forest and mountain terrain on mainly poor soils, derived from the region's granitic rocks.	B3	26
FEMUNDSMARKA	386	National Park. Wild mountain area of particular geological interest. Evidence of Stone Age settlement.	B3	27
GUTULIA	19.0	National Park. Region of morainic ridges, forests and lakes dominated by the peak of Gutulivola.	B3	27
DOVREFJELL	265	National Park. Mountainous region of great botanical interest. Rich and varied flora on calcareous soils in the east. Notable for the only population of musk ox in Norway.	B3	28
FOKSTUMYRA	75.0	Nature Reserve. Marshy land in the valley of the Foksåi River. Remarkable birdlife.	B3	28
RONDANE	572	National Park. Dramatic landscape created during the last ice age. Sparse alpine and subalpine vegetation. Typical northern mammal fauna and some wild reindeer.	B3	29
ORMTJERNKAMPEN	9.0	National Park. Created to protect the eastern spruce forest. Interesting flora in western birch woodlands.	B4	30
HARDANGERVIDDA	3400	National Park. High plateau of granitic rocks and schists. Rich flora and bird fauna. Largest population of wild reindeer in Europe.	A4	30
NORDRE ØYEREN	69.0	Nature Reserve. Lake with interesting aquatic flora and fish fauna. Important feeding area for migrant birds.	B4	31
ORA	12.0	Nature Reserve (Proposed). Shallow brackish-water area in delta of River Glomma. Large number of migrating and wintering waterfowl. Unusual fish fauna and amphibian species.	B4	31
ICELAND				
MÝVATN OG LAXÁ	4400	Protected Area. Lake in volcanic region fed by warm and cold springs. Luxuriant plant growth. Important breeding locality for wild ducks. A conservation area for over 200 years.	A1/B1	32
HORNSTRANDIR	580	Landscape Reserve. Wilderness area of steep inland valleys and cliffs facing the Arctic Ocean.	A1	34
JÖKULSÁRGLJÚFUR	151	National Park. Spectacular canyon with unique waterfalls, sheer cliff walls and grassy plains.	A1/B1	34
THINGVELLIR	40.0	National Park. Lake with remarkable volcanic landscape on northern shore.	A1	35
SKAFTAFELL	5000	National Park. Region of matchless scenery, partly glaciated. Wide variety of flowering plants. Of particular ornithological interest for nesting colonies of skuas.	A1	35

ICELAND inset map:
HORNSTRANDIR
Súðavik · Húsavik · JÖKULSÁRGLJÚFUR
Blönduós · Akureyri · Grimsstaðir
Stykkishólmur · MÝVATN & LAXÁ · Egilsstaðir
Dalsmynni
REYKJAVIK · THINGVELLIR · SKAFTAFELL
Keflavik · Hella · Hof
Kirkjubaejarklaustur
0   100

Conservation area
Motorway
Main road
0   100   200km

A   B   C   D

21

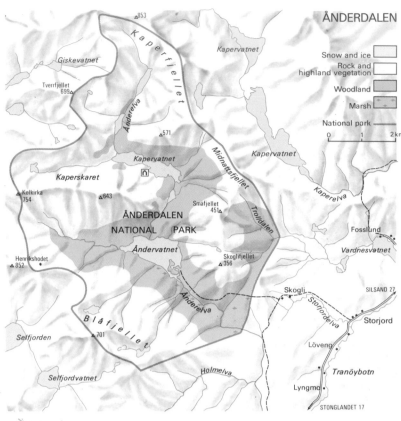

ÅNDERDALEN

Snow and ice

Rock and
highland vegetation

Woodland

Marsh

National park

0   1   2 km

NORWAY LEMMING
A large vole confined to
Scandinavia and usually
found in tundra or birch
and willow scrub.
Lemming numbers
fluctuate and when the
population is high, mass
migrations to new
habitats occur.

Ånderdalen National Park

South of Tromsø on the island of Senja,
Ånderdalen National Park forms a large area
of undisturbed pine and birch forest on the
sheltered inland side of the island. Two-thirds
of the park is mountainous and lies above the
tree line, which in this region is about 300
metres above sea level. The mountains are
granitic with rounded contours; the highest
point reaches 853 metres.

On the south side of Åndervatnet the landscape has been eroded into several deep
ravines, the largest of which reaches the
lakeside. The wild Trolldalen, on the east
side of the park, narrow and overgrown with
virgin forest, is rather difficult to penetrate.
Some of its ancient pine trees have curiously
twisted trunks and are at least 500 years old,
and many are beginning to die.

Several interesting orchids, such as the
ghost and the coralroot, are found in the
park and the common spotted orchid is
abundant on the moorlands, where the large
white flowers of *Diapensia lapponica* are a
common sight.

Large predators, such as bears and wolves,
were exterminated at the end of the last
century; elks, however, have colonized the
area in recent times and there is also a herd
of domestic reindeer. The smaller mammals
include the fox, otter and stoat as well as the
mountain hare.

As the whooper swan, golden and sea
eagles all breed in the area the birdlife is
particularly interesting. The more common
birds include the raven, brambling, meadow
pipit, reed bunting, willow warbler, redstart
and cuckoo. The abundant trout and char
found in the rivers provide splendid sport
fishing. Although there are no permanent
settlements in Ånderdalen itself, coastal Lapp
families use the area for reindeer grazing.

Stabbursdalen National Park

As trees do not normally grow north of 70°
of latitude because of the severe climate and
very short growing season, the pine forest of
Stabbursdalen at 70° 10′N is exceptional,
and is in fact the most northerly anywhere
in the world.

The park also lying farther north than any
other in Scandinavia is, like Øvre Pasvik
National Park, a real wilderness. It consists
of a broad valley whose river empties into
Porsanger fjord. The lower end of the valley
is wide and flat, but higher up it narrows into
a mighty chasm with steep sides and rock-
strewn slopes. At the highest point it broadens
out again into a wide rolling landscape with
small lakes and many streams.

The park's remarkable pine forest covers
about 1000 hectares on both sides of the
valley and in places the conifers are mixed
with birch. As the winters are long and
summers short the trees grow very slowly;
the largest and finest are said to be 500 years
old. Apart from the forest and the belts of
myrtle-leaved willows along the river sides,
the flora is not very rich, with mare's-tail,
the alternate water-milfoil and pond crowfoot. However, in one part of the valley,
where the river is very wide, with many bays,
islands, inlets and promontories, there are
several plants not found elswhere in the park;
the rarest is a species of Jacob's ladder
Polemonium acutiflorum.

Partly because the forest has numerous
hollow trees birdlife is surprisingly abundant.
The most widespread tree-hole nesting waterbirds are the goldeneye and goosander; the
brambling and redstart are the most commonly found small birds. The rarest species
is the little bunting, a Siberian bird which is
here on the edge of its range in arctic Norway.
The osprey and the merlin are the most
frequently seen predators.

The elk is present, in increasing numbers
each year, and domesticated reindeer also
graze here. The Stabburs River is rich in
fish, particularly salmon, and specimens
of up to 19.8 kilograms have been caught.

Øvre Anarjåkka National Park

Lying in the heart of the Lapp country with
its boundary on two sides running along the
Finnish border, Øvre Anarjåkka National
Park sits on a plateau between 300 and 500
metres above sea level where lie scattered
areas of birch (*Betula odorata*) forest and an
alpine flora dominated by dwarf birch,
willow scrub and lichens. About half the
park consists of bogs and treeless areas.

The rocks are of two main types: granitic
with soils lacking in nutrients on the west
side and more basic rocks in the east derived

1 ÅNDERDALEN
Information : TTK Troms, Boks 1077, 9001 Tromsø
Access : by track from Storjord 28km SW of SILSAND
Open : Unrestricted
Facilities : Lapp hut available

2 STABBURSDALEN
Information : Vest-Finnmark Statens Skog Distrikt, Boks 108, 9501 Alta
Access : from LAKSELV
Open : Unrestricted
Facilities : Camp site at Stabbursnes (outside the park boundary) has cabins available

3 ØVRE ANARJÅKKA
Information : Vest-Finnmark Statens Skog Distrikt, Boks 108, 9501 Alta
Access : by track from Iskuras, 40km S of KARASJOK
Open : Unrestricted
Facilities : Lapp huts and reindeer herdsmen's cabins available in the summer

4 ØVRE PASVIK
Information : Øst Finnmark Statens Skog Distrikt, Boks 90, 9901 Kirkenes
Access : from Gjøkåsen, 100km SW of KIRKENES
Open : Unrestricted
Facilities : Reindeer herdsmen's cabins available. Marked footpath within the park

from past volcanic activity. There are small deposits of gold in many parts of the plateau and also in some of the rivers. However, insufficient has been found to warrant commercial exploitation.

Although birch is the commonest tree, there are several areas with Scots pine. Some of these are relict areas of old forest and have large trees, 70 to 80 centimetres in diameter. The regeneration of pine and Norway spruce is hindered in many places by elk, which eat the tops out of the small trees. In more open areas are found typical heathland plants such as crowberry, heather, bilberry, juniper, and a species of lichen known as reindeer moss. Cloudberry grows everywhere in boggy areas and there is also an interesting species of cotton-grass, *Eriophorum russeolum*.

Many small mammals have been recorded, particularly Norway lemmings, ground voles, short-tailed voles, rat-headed voles and northern red-backed voles. When these important prey species are numerous rough-legged buzzards, hawk owls and short-eared owls often appear in considerable numbers. The commonest passerine birds are willow warblers, bramblings, redstarts, tree pipits, pied flycatchers and wheaters. Among the other interesting species are the whooper swan, arctic warbler, jack snipe, bar-tailed godwit, spotted redshank, bean goose, golden-eye and goosander.

Øvre Pasvik National Park

Northern Norway penetrates far beyond the Arctic Circle into the White Sea and shares part of its frontier with the Soviet Union and

ØVRE PASVIK Lakes cover roughly one quarter of the National Park's surface area.

Finland. Øvre Pasvik National Park is situated in this region on a tongue of Norwegian territory which extends between these two neighbouring countries.

At this high latitude the winters are long and severe, with temperatures falling to 45°C. However, in summer temperatures may in some years rise to over 29°C.

The area, varying between 92 and 202 metres altitude, is relatively flat, and supports a fine primeaval forest, forming the western-most extension of the Siberian taiga: the commonest trees are Scots pine and the birch *Betula odorata*. This region was settled by man only comparatively recently – the first farms were established in the 1930s by Norwegian and Finnish settlers – and the forest has not suffered exploitation.

Being so far north the flora is not particularly rich, although 192 vascular plants have been found within the park. Some of the most widespread species are ledum, the sedge *Carex tenuiflora*, the cottongrass *Eriophorum russeolum*, the sandwort *Moehringia lateriflora* and *Ranunculus lapponicus*. One of the most characteristic plants is the cloud-berry, which in favourable years produces enormous quantities of fruit: the rarest plant is the snowy cinquefoil.

Elk and semi-domesticated reindeer graze within the park boundary and wolverines and bears are the only large beasts of prey which remain permanently within the region. Two rare birds, the whooper swan and the great grey owl, breed in the area.

23

Øvre Dividal National Park

Situated on the Swedish border southwest of Tromsø, Øvre Dividal is an area of extensive plateaux separated by broad valleys with gently sloping sides and one of the finest National Parks in Norway. The region comprises several mountain ridges and rocky peaks, the highest being Mount Jerta at 1428 metres. The many lakes both large and small, and the red granite boulders that have come from the Swedish side of the frontier are evidence of past glacial activity.

About 10 per cent of the area is woodland, containing mainly the birch *Betula odorata*, which forms the limit of tree growth in most parts of Norway, and although coniferous forest is not extensive there are some very old pine trees. The area's alder forests are the home of the interesting ostrich fern.

The park's rich flora, known to contain 315 species of flowering plants, includes the glacier crowfoot, the arctic mouse-ear chickweed and the alpine hair-grass. Extensive bogs have developed at between 600 and 700 metres altitude.

Lapps find this region favourable for grazing their herds and large numbers of domesticated reindeer can be seen in the park. There are also predators such as the brown bear, wolverine and lynx.

The most commonly occurring small birds are bramblings and lesser redpolls, and Tengmalm's owl and hawk owls can be seen in forested areas. In the birch forests song thrushes, fieldfares and redwings nest and the most widespread bird of prey is the rough-legged buzzard.

Above 900 metres, in the treeless alpine zone, the most typical birds are the snow bunting, wheatear, ptarmigan and willow grouse. As it prefers heathlands with willow, birch and juniper scrub, the willow grouse is found at lower altitudes than the ptarmigan.

Rago National Park

The most inaccessible of the Norwegian National Parks, Rago is situated along the Swedish border adjacent to the three largest National Parks in Europe – the Swedish Padjelanta, Sarek and Stora Sjöfallet areas. These four parks, with the adjacent Sjaunja bird reserve, form the most extensive wilderness region in the whole of Europe.

The landscape is magnificent, with numerous lakes, swamps, ravines, and mountains – three exceeding 1000 metres in height. The limit of tree growth is between 400 and 450 metres and large areas of the park are open and treeless. Below this altitude the forest is not extensive and consists mainly of pine, with some birch, rowan and alder.

In and around the boggy areas common purple moor-grass grows with cotton-grass, two species of whitlow-grass *Draba alpina* and *Draba crassifolia*, arctic mouse-ear chickweed, the snow buttercup and the Carpathian catsfoot, a plant of central Europe.

STOAT In Northern regions the stoat's fur turns completely white during the winter months, except for the black tip to its tail, giving it the advantage of camouflage in snowy landscapes.

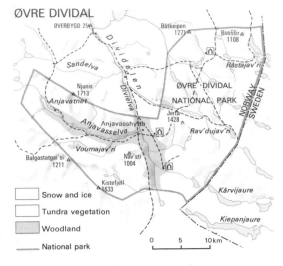

ØVRE DIVIDAL

Snow and ice
Tundra vegetation
Woodland
National park

0   5   10km

LAPLAND RHODODENDRON *right* A native of Scandinavia, this low-growing evergreen shrub is probably Øvre Dividal's most characteristic plant.

The birdlife is not very rich. The best area for birdwatching is Ragoelva, where the song thrush, fieldfare, redwing, willow warbler and garden warbler can be seen. The waterbirds include the common gull, red throated diver, and goldeneye; birds of prey are few and only the merlin has been recorded. At Bevervatn a fairly large population of beavers has grown from a few specimens introduced in 1968. There are also otters and mink.

Bears have not been seen in the Rago area for many years. However, as they do occur on the Swedish side of the border, they may possibly recolonize the park eventually. The fox, pine marten and stoat are common and there are a few elk and the occasional reindeer. In the past the human population has used the area for trapping fur-bearing animals and there has also been a certain amount of tree felling. During the First World War attempts were made to work deposits of silver, but mining ceased in 1918.

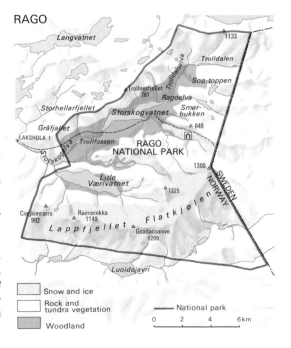

RAGO

Snow and ice
Rock and tundra vegetation
Woodland
National park

0   2   4   6km

1 ØVRE DIVIDAL
Information: TTK Troms, Boks 1077, 9001 Tromsø
Access: by track from Gambekken 85km S of STORFJORD
Open: Unrestricted
Facilities: Cabins available. Footpaths within the park, including some marked specifically for tourists

2 RAGO
Information: TTK Nordland, Boks 434, 8001 Bodø
Access: by track from Lakshola, 30km NE of FAUSKE
Open: Unrestricted
Facilities: Cabin available. Marked footpath from Lakshola to Storskogvatnet. Visitors should note that walking is particularly difficult in this park

GREENSHANK *above*
This wader nests on
northern moorlands,
migrating to the
south in winter.

OSPREY *right* A large
fish-eating eagle which
dives onto its prey from
heights of up to 30m
above the water surface.

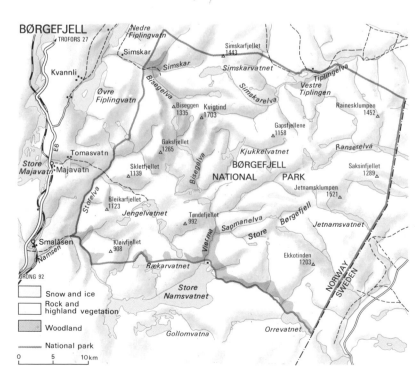

Børgefjell National Park

The wild and beautiful mountain landscape
of Børgefjell, the third largest protected area
in Norway, became a National Park in 1963.
Situated adjacent to the Swedish border, it
has many impressive peaks, the highest
reaching 1703 metres, and a vast number of
streams and lakes. The park's numerous
rivers are wide and swift-flowing and may be
difficult or even dangerous to cross by the
inexperienced. There are many waterfalls,
and although none is particularly high, some
are very beautiful.

Less than 5 per cent of the area below the
tree line, which here lies at about 600 metres,
is wooded, a bareness which adds to the
park's wild and deserted appearance. Most
of the remaining forest is birch *Betula
odorata,* but there are also some conifers
in the south and southwest. Elsewhere the
park is covered with a heathy vegetation of
sedges, grasses and bilberry, as well as many
typical snow-bed plant species. About 295
species of flowering plants have been recorded.

The park is probably best known for its
fauna, which includes some species of great
interest. The lesser white-fronted and bean
goose, for instance, both nest in the park, as
well as the osprey and golden eagle.

Around the lower end of the Simskar River
and in Vestre Tiplingen many smaller
passerine birds, waders and ducks, particularly bluethroats, red-necked phalaropes,
long-tailed ducks and Temminck's stints can
be seen during the long summer days. On
the hills above the lakes the snow bunting
and ptarmigan are the characteristic species.
The rough-legged buzzard is probably the
most common bird of prey.

For hundreds of years Lapps have raised
reindeer herds in the region of the park and
these can still be seen today. The most
common wild mammals are the hare, red deer
and elk. There is a small population of
wolverines and lynx and brown bears
are occasionally seen.

Gressåmoen National Park

At the beginning of the century the spruce
forests of Gressåmoen were renowned as one
of the best elk-hunting areas in Norway. The
park's name comes from an ancient farm
which, when established many years ago, was
important as a stopping place for travellers
journeying through the region. Today the
farm lies outside the National Park, but is
still an important meeting place for visitors.

The region's rock formations are mainly
pre-Cambrian; a rough reddish granite,
frequently marked with lines made by ice
during the last glaciation, is the most widespread type. Topographically the National
Park can be divided into three parts: a broad
valley in the north, a barren mountain area
in the south and west, where lies Bugvassfjell
(1009 metres), Gressåmoen's highest point,
and a lakeland landscape in the south and east.

The ancient spruce forests, found at Gamstuhaugane and in the south of the park, are on average about 150 years old: the oldest trees, however, are thought to be about 530 years. On the dry barren ridges, where scattered pines grow, the soils, derived from the granite rocks, are generally poor and are not rich in flowering plants.

In the last century wolves, bears and wolverines were common, but the wolf is now extinct and the others are very rare. Today the largest predator, the lynx, is still common, and fox, pine marten and mink are also numerous.

There are many marshy areas around the lakes and the most characteristic bird in this habitat is the whimbrel. The golden eagle and gyrfalcon are well established, as are Siberian jays, common jays, bluethroats and bramblings in the forested areas.

Femundsmarka National Park
Lying between the Swedish border and Lake Femund, this park is a wild mountain area dotted with hundreds of lakes, and has a history that dates from its first human settlement in the Stone Age. In the early seventeenth century it was colonized by Lapps, and in the eighteenth century the forests were exploited for charcoal needed in copper smelting.

For the most part, the area consists of a level mountain plateau between 800 and 900 metres in altitude, moulded by glacial action, and with large numbers of erratics, kettle holes, moraines and other features that make it of particular interest to the geologist. The rocks are mainly quartzite and sparagmite, which weather to form a poor mineral soil and on which only a few plants can grow.

More than half the park consists of bare rock with very little vegetation, and between 10 and 15 per cent is covered by lakes and rivers. The region's scattered areas of forest consist of pine and the birch *Betula odorata*, which grow at altitudes up to 960 metres. In the northern and central part of the park moonwort, together with many species of lady's mantle, form part of a meadow-like vegetation; moor-king grows close to Femund Lake. Rarer plants, such as strange sedge, the cotton-grass *Eriophorum brachyantherum* and the sedge *Carex parallela*, can be seen in the marshes around Røvollen.

In the older pine forests the three-toed woodpecker nests in rotten and dying stumps. Over the lakes common and arctic tern hunt for small fish and on the higher moorlands the snow bunting, ptarmigan, golden plover and dotterel breed. The domestic reindeer is the commonest animal, and wolverine and lynx are occasionally seen. Beavers and pine martens are in the process of repopulating the park and there are mink around the lakes.

Gutulia National Park
Lying at a fairly high altitude, between 615 and 948 metres, Gutulia National Park, consisting mostly of sandstones, is geologically rather homogeneous. As a result of glacial action in the past, moraines of several different types are found throughout the area, and around Valsjøen there is a landscape of long morainic ridges separated by deep depressions. Farther east towards the Swedish border the countryside is flat with open pine forests, marshes and small lakes. In the region of Gutuli Lake spruce forest covers the mountainsides, and although the limit of tree growth in this district is around 950 metres birch scrub reaches 1100 metres in places. The centre of the park is dominated by Gutulia's highest peak, Gutulivola.

Although few species of mammals are found, tame reindeer, the most southerly group of Lapp-owned herds in Norway, graze in most areas. The badger, a species which is seldom found as far north, is also known to occur, and during the summer of 1964 evidence of beavers was discovered for the first time in more than 200 years. The park does not have any rare birds, but there are many bramblings, tree pipits, willow warblers and redstarts in the forests, and in the wetter parts, reed buntings, greenshanks and wood sandpipers are found. Three birds of prey have been recorded breeding – the goshawk, sparrowhawk and merlin; golden eagles and ospreys although not nesting are also sometimes seen.

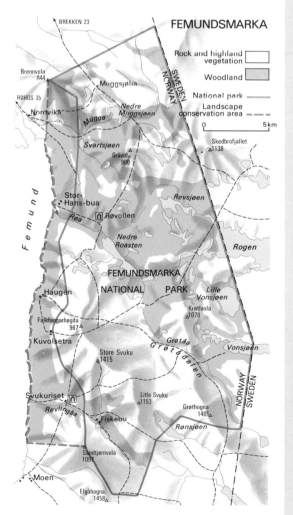

1 BØRGEFJELL
Information: TTK Nordland, Boks 434, 8001 Bodø
Access: from MAJAVATN
Open: Unrestricted
Facilities: Reindeer herdsmen's cabins available

2 GRESSÅMOEN
Information: Nord-Trøndelag Reiselivslag, Boks 186, 7701 Steinkjer
Access: from Myrset (north of Agle station) 30km SE of GRONG
Open: Unrestricted
Facilities: Accommodation available at the Gressåmoen farm during the summer.

3 FEMUNDSMARKA
Information: TTK Hedmark, Boks 318, 2301 Hamar
Access: from Jonasvollen, 21km NE of BRENNA
Open: Unrestricted
Facilities: Tourist cabins available. Marked footpaths within the park

4 GUTULIA
Information: TTK Hedmark, Boks 310, 2301 Hamar
Access: from BRENNA
Open: Unrestricted
Facilities: Cabins previously used by dairy farms at Gutulivollen available, but in poor repair

MUSK OX *right* When threatened, musk oxen often form a protective circle, the adults constantly turning to face the predator.

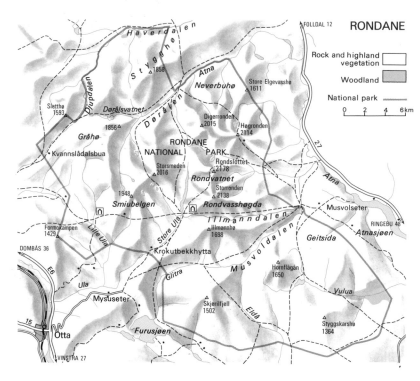

RONDANE

Rock and highland vegetation

Woodland

National park

0 2 4 6km

FOKSTUMYRA

Grassland

Marsh

Woodland

Nature reserve

0   1   2 km

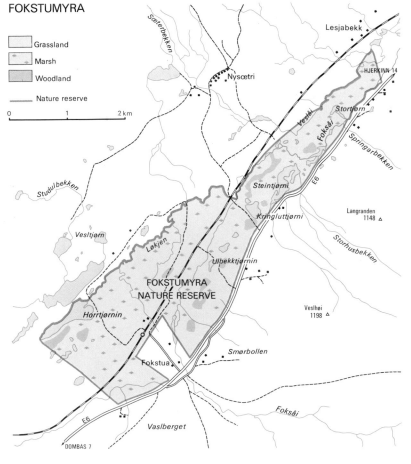

Dovrefjell National Park

In ancient times the Dovrefjell formed a barrier between the north and the south of Norway and many of the ancient sagas describe journeys that took place over the mountains. Today the main road and rail routes to Trondheim pass through Dovrefjell, via the Driva Valley. This valley although with the status of a landscape protection zone, lies outside the National Park area and effectively divides the park into two separate eastern and western parts, which differ both geologically and floristically.

It is claimed that almost all the mountain plants known in Norway occur at Dovrefjell, and the mountains have excited botanists for more than 200 years. Collecting became such a problem that in 1911 many species were protected by law, although it was only with the establishment of the National Park in 1974 that this law became effective.

Only a small part of the park is forest-covered. The forest is mainly composed of the birch *Betula odorata*, associated with rowan and bird cherry. In marshy areas there is a luxuriant scrub of willows, herbs and ferns. The open grassland has several interesting plants such as northern wolfsbane, red campion, whorled Solomon's seal, Jacob's ladder, wood forget-me-not, as well as a species of valerian and the blue sow-thistle, which is an important food plant for red deer, elk and reindeer. Common cotoneaster grows in warmer, sunnier places, and higher up, above the birch forest, mountain avens are common. Here they are found growing with Norwegian mugwort, spring anemone, snow buttercup, a species of whitlow-grass and many orchids, particularly the fragrant orchid, small white orchid and false musk orchid.

The park is notable for being the only place in Norway where the wild musk ox is found. There are about 40 individuals, all descendants of animals brought from Greenland. The musk ox used to be native to Norway, but the last animals were killed by the Vikings many centuries ago. There are also herds of wild reindeer, and elks are common. The rodents found in the park include a rather rare species, the northern birch mouse. It has a very long tail and a distinguishing dark mark down the spine.

Fokstumyra Nature Reserve

Close to the Dovrefjell and Rondane National Parks lies an area of marshy land in the valley of the Foksåi River, which has been a bird sanctuary since 1923. Its rich birdlife first attracted ornithologists as early as 1816 and by the middle of the nineteenth century foreign collectors of bird skins and eggs had almost eradicated some of the rare wader species. In 1916–17 a railway was constructed through the wettest parts of the marsh, reducing the area bird-breeding habitat.

During most of the nineteenth and the early part of the twentieth century the number of bird species found in the reserve steadily declined. Whereas in 1816 there were forty-one species breeding in the area, in 1917 there were only nineteen. However, protection enabled a recovery to take place, and in 1966 fifty-four species were found breeding and another thirty-three were observed.

Regular breeding species include red-necked phalaropes, bluethroats, Lapland buntings, common cranes and grey-headed wagtails. The ruff has returned to breed and is steadily increasing, and the great snipe, absent from 1916 to 1958, has been heard "drumming". The hen-harrier has bred each year since 1938. New breeding species include the whimbrel, common gull and lesser white-fronted goose.

Rondane National Park

Rondane, whose magnificent mountain scenery attracted the attention of a mountain inspector in 1956, became Norway's first National Park in 1970. With many glaciated cirques, moraines and canyons, and ten peaks rising to over 2000 metres, the scale of the landscape is dramatic. There are also many steep rock faces such as the precipice on the north face of Rondslottet, which has a drop of 700 metres. This topography was sculpted during the last glaciation by ice movement, which also gave rise to widespread large terraces of sand and gravel.

Within the park boundaries only about 1000 hectares are forested, and the principal species is the birch *Betula odorata*. The rest is covered with sparse subalpine and alpine vegetation, lichens and mosses, or else by glaciers. In the highest parts there is a scrub of dwarf willow and in wetter places glacial crowfoot grows with *Saxifraga stellaria*.

The park's larger vertebrates include wild reindeer, wolverine, red fox, stoat, weasel, and mountain hare. Along the watercourses are found otters and mink, and elk are often seen near the park boundary. As Rondane is situated west of the Lapp country, no tame reindeer are kept for pasturing. However, about 3000 wild reindeer are found in the area and there is a long history of hunting. A number of pitfall traps and hunting settlements have been found dating from the Nordic Iron Age, around 300 BC.

Rough-legged buzzards and kestrels frequently nest inside the park and gyrfalcons have been found in years when lemmings and other small rodents are plentiful. Golden eagles enter the park on hunting forays, but they probably breed outside the protected area. The scarce red-necked phalarope nests by the southern lakes, and on the higher alpine moorlands there are dotterels and golden plovers. Of the smaller birds, the Lapland bunting and the bluethroat are well established and in the higher mountains the typical birds are the ptarmigan, snow bunting, meadow pipit and wheatear.

DOVREFJELL *below* Spring melt-water rushes down the Stolodalen in the northern part of the park. The Dovrefjell has a reputation as one of the finest areas for mountain plants in the whole of Norway.

1 DOVREFJELL
Information: TTK Oppland, Kirkegt. 74, 2600 Lillehammer
Access: from DOMBÅS or OPPDAL
Open: Unrestricted
Facilities: Tourist cabin available. Marked footpaths within the park

2 FOKSTUMYRA
Information: TTK Oppland, Kirkegt. 74, 2600 Lillehammer
Access: from Fokstua, 10km NE of DOMBÅS
Open: July 8 to April 30 although marked trail is open all year between 0700–2300
Facilities: Marked trail which may be altered before June 10 to avoid disturbing nesting cranes

3 RONDANE
Information: TTK Oppland, Kirkegt. 74, 2600 Lillehammer
Access: from DOMBÅS or OTTA
Open: Unrestricted
Facilities: Tourist cabins and stone huts available. Marked footpaths within the park

29

Ormtjernkampen National Park

In the central part of southern Norway, west
of the town of Lillehammer, lies the Ormtjernkampen National Park. At the heart of the
park, the 1128-metre Ormtjernkampen mountain towers above a long, narrow lake which
lies at the high altitude of 774 metres and is
situated along the eastern border. Owing to
the relatively high elevation, summer temperatures, varying between 9.5°C and 12°C,
are low and the winter is long and cold. The
fairly high summer rainfall, falling mainly in
July and August, has encouraged the widespread formation of bogs, a characteristic
feature of the landscape.

The forests of spruce, birch and pine,
including remnants of ancient forest, are of
special scientific interest as they are relatively
undisturbed. Their flora, however, is generally
poor and is dominated by bilberry and ferns.
The most interesting plant life occurs in the
extensive areas of birch forest on the eastern
and southern sides of Dokkampen and on
the south side of Snareskampen, at the
extreme westerly edge of the park. Here one
can see the white buttercup, large white
buttercup, meadow-sweet, blue sow-thistle,
northern wolfsbane, yellow mountain saxifrage, purple moor-grass, alpine cinquefoil
and cloudberry. At higher altitudes crowberry,
heather and lichens grow beneath dwarf birch,
and on the south-facing slopes, lily-of-the-
valley, whorled Solomon's seal, wild straw-
berries, field gentians, the rush *Juncus castanius*
and moor-king are favoured by the warmer
conditions. One of the most interesting plants
in the region is the bearded bellflower, which
is confined to this part of Norway.

The elk, red deer and roe deer are the
commonest larger mammals – bears also
occurred up to about 1950. The fox, mink,
lynx, wolverine and pine marten all live in
the park and there are many rodents. The
bird fauna includes many typical Norwegian
mountain species such as the willow grouse,
capercaillie and black grouse – the rough-
legged buzzard, merlin, sparrowhawk and
goshawk are the birds of prey. The golden
plover nests in open plateau regions and in
boggy areas there are several species of wild
duck, snipe and redshank.

Hardangervidda National Park

Located in southern Norway, close to the
Bergen-Oslo road, the extensive high plateau
of Hardangervidda, varying from 1200 metres
to 1700 metres in height, has long been famous
as the home of the largest population of wild
reindeer in Europe and attracts many tourists
each year.

The whole plateau, approximately 10,000
square kilometres in area, consists mainly
of granitic rocks and schists, in which
steep-sided valleys were cut after the rocks
were uplifted during the Tertiary. Although
the average height of the land is modest, it
lies mostly above the tree line. The reindeer
find their food chiefly in the areas of lichens,
mosses, dwarf birch and cowberry.

The park has a rich flora, with Lapland
rhododendron, purple saxifrage, mountain
avens, several species of lady's mantle as
well as many other arctic and subarctic
plants. In sheltered valleys are found pine
and birch woods.

As many species more typical of the true
arctic nest here, at the most southerly part of
their range, Hardangervidda is a favourite

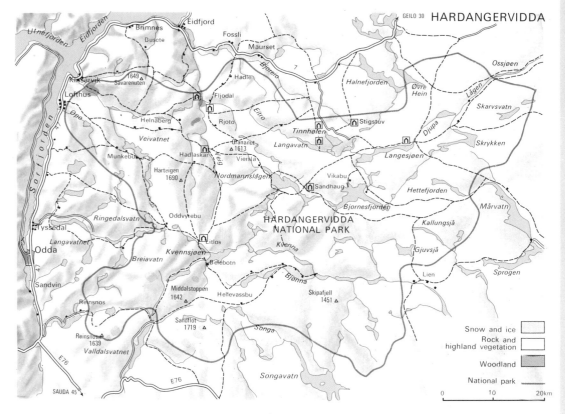

Snow and ice
Rock and highland vegetation
Woodland
National park

0   10   20km

1 ORMTJERNKAMPEN
Information: TTK Oppland, Kirkegt. 74, 2600 Lillehammer
Access: by track from Ormtjernsetrene, 50km W of LILLEHAMMER
Open: Unrestricted

2 HARDANGERVIDDA
Information: TTK Buskerud, Storgt. 2, 3500 Hønefoss
Access: from ODDA or KINSARVIK
Open: Unrestricted
Facilities: Huts available. Marked footpaths within the park

3 NORDRE ØYEREN
Information: Oslo RTF, Radhusgt. 19, Oslo 1
Access: from Lillestrøm, 15km E of OSLO
Open: Unrestricted

4 ORA
Information: TTK Østfold Turistsenteret, 1600 Fredrikstad
Access: from FREDRIKSTAD
Open: Unrestricted

place for the birdwatcher. Species typical of temperate Europe also occur, so it is possible to see willow warblers, cuckoos, wheatears, ringed plovers and white wagtails in the same area in which are found the purple sandpiper, dotterel, great snipe and Temminck's stint. As snow lies late on the plateau and ice may remain on the lakes until midsummer, the breeding season is often short.

In the forests the pygmy and Tengmalm's owl occur and also three-toed and black woodpeckers. On the lakes are ducks such as scaup, goldeneyes and velvet scoters.

Birds of prey are few. The most frequent species is probably the merlin. However, ospreys sometimes come to catch trout and arctic char, and the golden eagle is occasionally seen; merlin is the most common species. Fishing is a popular sport with summer tourists and in the autumn and winter the reindeer are hunted. At present their numbers, around 1400, are too high for the amount of food available.

Nordre Øyeren Nature Reserve

Because the Nitelva and Leirelva rivers meander through depositis of Pleistocene marine clay, their waters are rich in nutrients by the time they enter the shallow northern end of Lake Øyeren. This enrichment of the lake waters has encouraged the development of interesting plant communities of sedges and water plants. The dominant species are the slender spiked sedge, the slender spiked-ruch, the three-stamened waterwort, the creeping spearwort, the pond crowfoot and the perfoliate pondweed.

The rich nutrient content and algal flora support a fish fauna of twenty-three species, several of which migrate at certain times of the year between the deep southern and shallower northern regions of the lake. There is an interesting birdlife and the lake is of particular importance as a feeding and roosting area during the migration seasons and in winter. It is the most important site for whooper swans in Norway, as many as 550 having been recorded overwintering.

Ora Nature Reserve (Proposed)

On the eastern shore of the entrance to Oslofjord, Ora Nature Reserve, a shallow brackish-water area lying in the delta of the River Glomma and covered with lush vegetation, forms an important site for birds, mammals and fish. The birdlife breeding in the reserve includes the greylag goose, wigeon, pintail, shoveler, water rail, dunlin, ruff, curlew and the Caspian tern. It is also an important resting and feeding area for migrating and wintering waterfowl.

The fish population is unusual in that there are many fresh and saltwater species present that are more typical of the fauna of the Gulf of Bothnia than of the North Sea. There are several mammals of interest, although most are infrequently seen. They include the northern water vole, the short-tailed vole, the fox, badger and the introduced American mink. The otter occurs from time to time and also the common seal. Four out of the five amphibian species occurring in Norway have been seen here – smooth newt, common toad, common frog and moor frog. The last occurs only at the southern tip of Norway and although it is similar to the common frog it has shorter legs, a more pointed snout and a distinctive muted voice.

MÝVATN OG LAXÁ

In the volcanic region of northeast Iceland, 42 kilometres from the coast, lies a lake of 3800 hectares amidst a vast area of marshes and smaller lakes with a rich vegetation. The area's remarkably hilly landscape is formed of old volcanic cones and is punctuated by a large number of small pseudo-craters, formed when steam burst through a lava field which had flowed over the marshes.

Water entering Lake Mývatn, mainly at its eastern shore from both cold and warm springs brings with it an abundance of nutrients, which with the high insolation and summer temperature makes possible a luxuriant plant growth, particularly of blue-green algae. This vegetation in turn supports enormous swarms of midges, which are an important link in the food chain of trout, char and wild duck – and eventually man.

The area around Lake Mývatn has been settled by farmers for many centuries and is unique in having been managed as a nature conservation area since the beginning of the eighteenth century or even earlier. Since that time it is known that no wildfowl have been shot because the local people attached more importance to a regular supply of eggs.

The lake and surrounding ponds and marshes form one of the most important breeding places for wild ducks in northern Europe, having as many as sixteen species, both European and North American – the entire European population of Barrow's goldeneye (about 1000 pairs), a large population of Slavonian grebes, several thousand red-necked phalaropes and a hundred or so pairs of the remarkably coloured harlequin duck, which nest along the Laxá River. Other breeding birds include the scaup, tufted duck, pochard and common scoter.

Some years ago work began to turn the lake into a reservoir for the generation of hydro-electric power, but strong opposition from both the local people and conservationists persuaded the government to carry out a study into the scientific interest of the area, even though some of the power-plant buildings had already been constructed. As a result of the investigation the Icelandic government agreed in 1974 to grant, by a special Act of Parliament, nature reserve status to no less than 440,000 hectares.

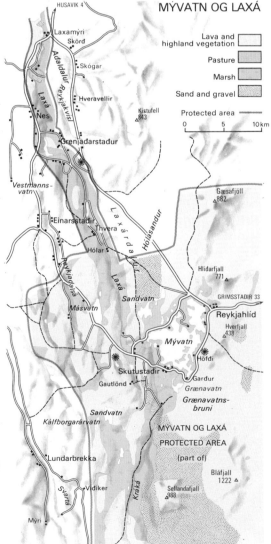

MÝVATN OG LAXÁ

Lava and highland vegetation

Pasture

Marsh

Sand and gravel

Protected area

0   5   10 km

HARLEQUIN DUCK
below A small diving duck which in Europe is restricted to Iceland. It breeds on mountain streams or near waterfalls and winters by the sea, on bleak rocky coasts.

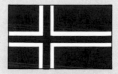

MÝVATN OG LAXÁ
Information: Náttúruverndarráð
(Nature Conservation Council),
Hverfisgötu 26, 101 Reykjavík
Access: from HÚSAVÍK or
GRÍMSSTAÐIR
Open: Unrestricted except
during the period May 15 to
July 20 when access to the NW
shore is prohibited to safeguard
nesting birds
Facilities: Hotels within the
park and camp sites near the
boundary at Reykjahlíð and
Skútustaðir. Marked footpaths.
Observation points. Wardens
on site

HVERFJALL *above* An explosive eruption about 2500 years ago was responsible for the creation of this volcanic crater, standing just east of Lake Mývatn.

PSEUDO CRATERS *below* Now largely grass-covered, Mývatn's low craters were formed by steam erupting through molten volcanic rock.

HORNSTRANDIR

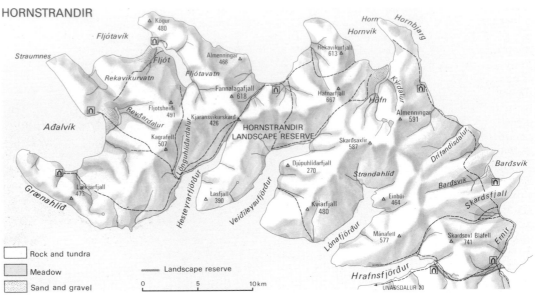

POLAR BEAR *above*
Confined to the arctic the polar bear hunts mainly seals. It was formerly shot for its valuable fur but is now protected nearly everywhere.

SKAFTAFELL *below*
Hot springs occur where underground water comes into contact with hot volcanic rocks.

Rock and tundra
Meadow
Sand and gravel

Landscape reserve

0   5   10 km

SKAFTAFELL

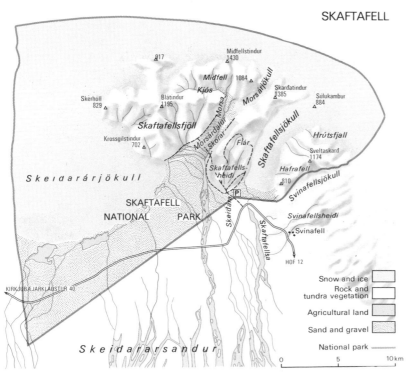

Snow and ice
Rock and tundra vegetation
Agricultural land
Sand and gravel
National park

0   5   10 km

Hornstrandir Landscape Reserve

In the rocky northernmost peninsula of the Icelandic Westfjords is a remarkable wilderness area facing the Arctic Ocean, with impressive cliffs and ravines full of nesting seabirds during the summer. The winters are longer here than in other parts of Iceland and the heavy snow fall remains lying for many months. In the early part of the year drift ice often comes close to the coast and may form a bridge for the polar bear.

Hornstrandir has no roads or resident population and is of considerable interest to the biologist for the many thousands of razorbills, puffins and fulmars inhabiting the cliffs, which rise some 500 metres above sea level. Inland the landscape forms a series of steep U-shaped valleys with rapid streams of clear water teaming with arctic char, brown trout and sometimes the Atlantic salmon. The valleys are called "viks", a word which may have the same origin as "Viking". They occur all around the coast of Iceland, but are particularly numerous at Hornstrandir.

Jökulsárgljúfur National Park

The Jökulsá canyon in northeast Iceland, some 25 kilometres in length, about half a kilometre wide and over 100 metres deep in many places, is the largest in the country, and was created a National Park in 1973. On the south side the park begins at the Dettifoss waterfall, 45 metres high and 100 metres wide and regarded by many as the most impressive in Europe. There are two other waterfalls downstream from Dettifoss, and the three form a series unique to Iceland. In the central part of the canyon, the valley is broader with a luxuriant vegetation and many spring-fed streams and rivers. In the north, in the valley of the Vesturdalur, the park has a very different scenery, with sheer cliff rock walls perforated by many caves which tower over the grassy plain below.

The canyon, with a relatively low rainfall and an average July temperature of about

10°C, has a more continental climate than most parts of Iceland. The winters are rather long, with snow lying on the ground from October until May or even June, and frosts may occur at almost any time of the year. The vegetation varies from sedge communities in the waterways, mostly the bottle sedge, to scrub woodlands of downy birch with two species of willow *Salix phylicifolia* and *S. lanata*. On the cliffs and scree slopes scattered rowan trees occur.

The hill slopes are covered with dwarf shrub communities, particularly of bilberry, cowberry, and bearberry, but dwarf willows, dwarf birch and the common juniper are also found. In sheltered hollows a number of interesting flowering plants occur, particularly the wood cranesbill, angelica, the wood millet, broad-leaved willowherb, wild strawberry and, perhaps the most typical plant of all, the serrated wintergreen. Some species are characteristic of the east Icelandic flora and do not penetrate farther west, for example the harebell and a species of lady's mantel *Alchemilla faeroensis*. The rarer plants include herb Paris, the rosebay willowherb and the meadow vetchling.

Apart from the area's magnificent scenery, the feature most attractive to the visiting naturalist is the birdlife. On the moorlands and heathlands there are golden plovers, meadow pipits, redwings, ptarmigans, snow buntings, redpolls, wheatears, wrens and snipe; merlins and gyrfalcons haunt the cliffs and the raven is common everywhere. Near the lake and ponds redshanks, red-necked phalaropes and various species of ducks and geese are found.

The sandy stretches towards the sea in the northern part of the park form one of the most important nesting areas for the great skua, and the fulmar has recently established itself on the Asbyrgi cliffs. Although there are few mammals the occasional arctic fox and mink can be seen.

Thingvellir National Park

The largest lake in Iceland, the Thingvalla-vatn, together with a remarkable volcanic landscape on its northern shore, has been a National Park since 1928. The original idea behind the creation of the park was to protect this historic spot where the Icelandic chiefs first met in council in the year AD 930. It is a great tourist attraction and easily accessible, the capital Reykjavik is only 50 kilometres away.

The area consists of a tectonic trench overlain by successive lava flows and split by numerous fissures. On the west it is bounded by a fault which, with a displacement of no less than 40 metres, has created the famous falls of the River Oxara. The level ground between the faults is largely covered by dwarf birch, and the woolly fringed moss, characteristic of open exposed areas, is widely distributed. The waters feeding the lake originate from cold springs, and the shores are steep and rocky.

There is only one common fish, the arctic char, the brown trout having declined following the construction of a hydroelectric station.

Skaftafell National Park

For centuries the Skaftafell region has been famous throughout Iceland for its scenery and natural beauty – splendid waterfalls, impressive ravines and a luxuriant and varied vegetation. Even so it was not until 1960 that a proposal was made by the famous geologist Sigurdur Thorarinsson to create a National Park in the area. In his case to the Icelandic government, he maintained that as well as containing the highest peak, the biggest glacier and the widest expanse of sandplain in Iceland, few other places had scenery of such grandeur or such matchless views.

The landscape, deeply dissected by glacial and fluvial erosion, is highly reminiscent of alpine regions, even though the highest point is only 1430 metres. There are three glaciers lying partly or wholly within the boundaries of the National Park, one of which, covering about 1600 square kilometres, is the largest valley-glacier in Europe. Elsewhere hot springs with water temperatures of about 80°C rise from the basaltic rocks.

About 210 species of flowering plants have been recorded in Skaftafell, including many characteristic of eastern Iceland, for example the harebell, which grows on woody and grassy slopes, the yellow mountain saxifrage found on stony ground, and the pyramidal saxifrage which grows on cliff ledges and in rock cracks. Some of the park's species are rather rare, notably the twayblade, the maidenhair spleenwort and the valerian *Valeriana officinalis*. An extensive scrub of downy birch grows on the mountain slopes up to about 260 metres and some stunted trees reach 600 metres. On the slopes below the farms birch trees grow to a height of 6 to 7 metres and there is a luxuriant ground vegetation with the wood cranesbill, harebell, lady's bedstraw, wild angelica, sweet vernal-grass and the common bent-grass. In some parts there are many rowan trees growing with the birch, and above the tree line are found heaths, moorland bogs and partially vegetated gravel flats.

Redwings nest in the birch woodland and in open areas there are snipes, meadow pipits and the Icelandic wren – a particular sub-species confined to this country. In the last few years the brambling, which in other parts of Iceland is known only as an irregular autumn and winter visitor, has bred.

The most thrilling experience for the birdwatcher is to see the nesting colonies of great skuas, arctic skuas and greater black-backed gulls. Skeidararsandur sand-plain has about 3000 breeding pairs of skuas and is therefore one of the most important localities for these two species.

1 HORNSTRANDIR
Information : Náttúruverndarráð (Nature Conservation Council) Hverfisgötu 26, 101 Reykjavík
Access : by track from Unaðsdalur, 140km by road. NE of SUÐAVIK
Open : July and August
Facilities : Emergency shelters within the reserve. Warden on site

2 JÖKULSÁRGLJÚFUR
Information : Náttúruverndarráð (Nature Conservation Council) Hverfisgötu 26, 101 Reykjavík
Access : from the valley of Vesturdalur, 45km NW of GRÍMSSTAÐIR
Open : June 15 to September 1
Facilities : Camp sites within the park. Wardens on site

3 THINGVELLIR
Information : Fedaskrifstofa Ríkisins (Iceland State Tourist Office), Reykjanesbraut 6, Reykjavik
Access : from Thingvellir, 52km NE of REYKJAVÍK
Open : Unrestricted
Facilities : Marked hiking trails within the park

4 SKAFTAFELL
Information : Náttúruverndarráð (Nature Conservation Council), Hverfisgötu 26, 101 Reykjavík
Access : 15km NW of HOF
Open : June 1 to September 15
Facilities : Camp site within the park. Marked footpaths

SWEDEN

One of the largest countries in Europe, Sweden has a surface area of 449,964 square kilometres and a total length from north to south of about 1600 kilometres. It has a low population density of about 20 per square kilometre and 82 per cent of its inhabitants live in urban areas. There are therefore large expanses of countryside with few or no people – beautiful wilderness areas of forest, lake and mountain. About 56 per cent of the country is forest-covered, a further 9 per cent is made up of lakes and another 9 per cent is agricultural land – a low figure compared with most other Western European countries.

Stretching as it does from well north of the Arctic Circle down to the same latitude as Copenhagen and the Scottish Lowlands, the climatic variation is enormous. Long, cold winters are followed by cool, short summers in the north, and although there is a milder regime in the south, nowhere does the mean February temperature exceed freezing point, and all the northerly sea ports are closed for some time during winter. In general the climate is transitional between the milder oceanic regime of Norway and the more continental type of Finland.

The vast coniferous forests of pine and spruce are an important natural resource, particularly for the paper-making industry. The mills required to produce the pulp are often situated beside or on the outlets from freshwater lakes, which in many cases have been polluted by toxic chemicals used in processing timber. Sweden's water resources are also used for hydroelectric power and very few rivers, even in the far north, have been left unmodified. The need to conserve some rivers in their natural state is of great importance, and conservationists have managed to save four water courses of special interest.

Sweden does, however, take a broad and enlightened view of nature protection. The rural environment is regarded as a natural resource to be used wisely, carefully and fairly, so that recreational activities, regulated exploitation and nature conservation interests are all catered for. As in other Scandinavian countries, the Swedish public enjoys the "allemansratten" – everyman's right – to walk, picnic or camp on private land, or to swim or boat on private lakes. This is in marked contrast to countries outside the region, where the owner's permission must be sought before entering private land.

The National Environment Protection (SNV) Board, which is an independent agency under the Ministry of Agriculture, deals with all aspects of the environment, one department being concerned with landscape protection, game management and rural activities for the public, including sports, and policy, planning, administration and funding of conservation work.

The Forest Service also has an important role in nature conservation in Sweden, as it is responsible for the management of all protected areas on Crown Land. It is also responsible under the supervision of the SNV for the sixteen National Parks, all of which are owned by the State. As National Parks can only be established by Act of Parliament, a slow and complicated procedure, it seems likely that few will be formed in the future.

On the other hand, nature reserves are relatively easy to create, as most of the work is done by the county administrations. There are 1007 nature reserves; 447 Wildlife Sanctuaries; 1321 Natural Monuments, which are very small sites, perhaps only a single tree or a rock; and about 800 Crown Reserves, mostly forest sites protected for their interesting fauna and flora. The work of the county administrations in creating nature reserves is

greatly helped by the SNV Board, which is empowered by the government to pay up to 50 per cent of the costs, according to the importance of the site.

Animals and plants in National Parks and nature reserves are, of course, protected, but the traditional right of Lapps to hunt and fish is now causing problems. This right is acknowledged by the government, and applies to all land, whether or not it is important for wildlife. In other respects the law protects all animals and birds except those regarded as game or vermin. Illegal hunting of the bear wolf, lynx and wolverine is known or suspected to occur in several northern parts of the country. The wolf which is totally protected was known recently to have been reduced to six specimens and is now thought to be extinct; lack of effective protection in Lapp territory is most probably the reason why the population failed to recover.

Sweden collaborates with the other Nordic countries in preserving representative and exceptional Nordic biotopes. Eleven examples have so far been designated in Sweden.

Concern for the environment goes beyond the establishment of National Parks and nature reserves. The Environment Protection Act of 1981 requires that any person intending to engage in any activity likely to have detrimental effects on the environment must take all reasonable precautions to prevent their occurrence. Also as an expression of State commitment, the long-established Swedish Society for the Conservation of Nature, which has 75,000 members, receives a substantial annual grant from the government to help it in its work.

STORA SJÖFALLET The peak of Kallaktjåkkå seen from the side of Lake Akkajaure. This is one of Europe's wildest corners.

The major part of the country consists of a broad, high plain sloping eastwards from the Caledonian mountain range – the Kjölen hills – which form the spine of the peninsula. The highest point in the range, just over 2000 metres, is in the north, close to the border with Norway, but most of this very heavily eroded ancient plateau is between 250 and 500 metres above sea level.

The high plateau of Norrland is cut into a series of blocks by deeply incised streams, many of which have become dammed by moraines to create lakes and areas of swamp. Most of the region, however, is a vast tract of spruce, pine and birch forest with occasional patches of bare rock: and one of the last refuges for the larger European mammals – bear, wolverine and lynx.

Much of southern Sweden comprises a low, undulating plateau containing the huge lakes of Vänern, Vättern and Mälaren, in addition to scores of smaller lakes. Soils here are more fertile than in the north and the area is part farmed and part mixed deciduous and coniferous forest. Almost the entire coastline is skirted by a broad fertile plain, but the most intensive farming occurs in a very small area in the extreme south, where thick boulder-clay deposits overlie the older geology.

The high ridge of the peninsula shields northern Sweden from maritime influences, and strong seasonal variations are accentuated, particularly in the far north, by the enormous difference between daylight hours in summer and winter. Temperatures drop in October and remain low until February, when all Sweden is below 32°F.

PADJELANTA A bleak and snowy landscape. The National Park forms part of a vast protected region on the Swedish-Norwegian border and lies between 60 and 150 km north of the Arctic Circle.

PARK/RESERVE	SIZE (km²)	DESCRIPTION	MAP REF	PAGE NO
ABISKO	75.0	National Park. Mountain region of barren rock and birch scrub. Rich flora. Rare orchid species.	C2	40
VADVETJÅKKO	24.5	National Park. Remote high arctic area with alpine meadows and sub-alpine birch forest.	C1	41
PADJELANTA	2010	National Park. Region of wide plains, mountains, scattered lakes and some glacial features.	C2	41
SAREK	1940	National Park. Impressive mountain landscape of rocky peaks, gorges and glaciers.	C2	41
STORA SJÖFALLET	1380	National Park. Wilderness area of waterfalls and primeval pine and spruce forest. Rich bird fauna.	C2	41
MUDDUS	492	National Park. Vast area of forests, mires and watercourses. Main valley exhibits many glacial features. Park includes three bird sanctuaries. Lapps retain rights to graze herds and cut timber.	C2	42
PELJEKAISE	146	National Park. Established to protect mountain-birch woods. Varied flora of herbaceous plants.	C2	43
TÄRNASJÖN	118	Nature Reserve. Unspoilt lake of special interest to conservationists. Important nesting site for ducks.	C2	43
GAMMELSTADSVIKEN	4.40	Nature Reserve. A wetland of international importance near the Gulf of Bothnia. Diverse range of breeding water birds. Resting place for birds during spring and autumn migration periods.	D2	43
SONFJÄLLET	27.0	National Park. Upland massif with lower zones of birch and coniferous forest. Famous brown-bear population.	B3	44
TÖFSINGDALEN	13.7	National Park. Wild forested area of considerable geological interest close to Norwegian border.	B3	44
HAMRA	0.27	National Park. Remarkable primeval forest in central Sweden. Particularly rich flora of lichens and mosses.	B4/C4	44
GARPHYTTAN	1.08	National Park. Chosen to preserve a traditional man-made agricultural landscape. Ash and hazel coppices.	B4/C4	46
HJÄLSTAVIKEN	7.9	Nature Reserve. Popular bird reserve with open water, rushes and reeds, meadows and grasslands. Rare bird breeding species. Important resting place for migrants, especially in spring.	C4	46
ÄNGSÖ	0.75	National Park. Green landscape of meadows and wooded hills. Old farming methods still practised. Beautiful display of spring flowers. Important grebe colony.	C4	46
BULLERÖ & LÅNGSKÄR	46.3	Nature Reserves. Offshore area containing about 900 islands. Created principally to protect birdlife. Many species of waterfowl.	C4	47
NORRA KVILL	0.27	National Park. Primeval forest near Småland highlands dominated by Norway spruce and Scots pine. Well-formed shrub layer, many flowering plants. Fallen trees provide ideal habitat for numerous insect species.	C5	48
BLÅ JUNGFRUN	0.66	National Park. Dome-shaped rocky island of red granite. Unusual rock formations and remarkable caves.	C5	49
RONE YTTERHOLME-LAUS HOLMAR	15.9	Nature Reserve and Bird Sanctuary. Gravel-covered limestone islands, attracting many species of wildfowl. Large numbers of brent and greylag geese.	C5	49
OTTENBY	9.95	Nature Reserve. Island reserve of sandy coves, beaches and spits. Birch woods in north, with meadowland to east. Interesting birds seen throughout the year. Area first studied in 1741 by Linnaeus.	C5	49
TÅKERN	56.0	Nature Reserve. Area of shallow water, partly covered by man-made reed beds. Breeding site for all 5 European grebes. Large number of bean geese in winter.	B5/C5	50
GETTERÖN	3.4	Nature Reserve. Coastal bay on spring and autumn migration routes.	B5	50
KÄVSJÖN & STORE MOSSE	74.5	Nature Reserve. Remarkable raised bog, attracting divers, waders and cranes. Soon to become a National Park.	B5	51
DALBY SÖDERSKOG	0.36	National Park. Area of mixed deciduous forest. Particularly attractive in spring before tree canopies develop.	B5	51

ABISKO

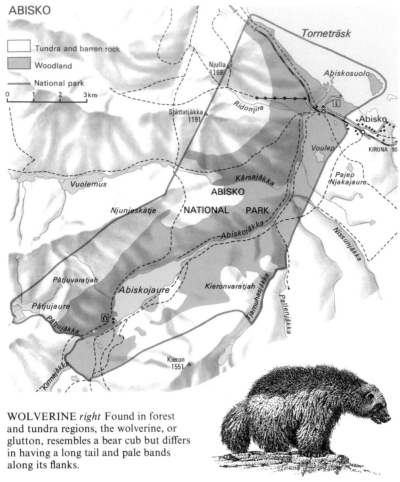

Tundra and barren rock

Woodland

National park

0   1   2   3km

Abisko National Park

One of the most northerly and the best known of Swedish parks to the tourist, Abisko is, unlike other National Parks in Swedish Lapland, easily accessible and is visited by about 10,000 people each year. The park consists of the Abiskojåkka Valley, whose river flows through a canyon-like formation and, on the north side, contains some of the shoreline of Lake Torneträsk and the island of Abiskosuolo.

About a third of the area is barren rock. On the greater part birch scrub covers the lower slopes, with an alpine zone of dwarf willow, alpine meadows and boulder-fields lying above.

Abisko has a rich flora, very similar to that found in the other Lapland parks, and is famous for the ghost orchid and the butterfly orchid *Platanthera oliganthe.*

Among the many species of birds found in the park is the arctic warbler, which here breeds on the slopes of Mount Njulla. The mammal fauna is typical of the northern area – bear, lynx, elk, wolverine, arctic fox, lemmings and other rodents.

The park's accessibility has made it possible to build a natural sciences research station, which has served as a base for visiting scientists and student parties for over thirty years, and has made the Abisko area the best researched mountain region in Sweden.

WOLVERINE *right* Found in forest and tundra regions, the wolverine, or glutton, resembles a bear cub but differs in having a long tail and pale bands along its flanks.

PADJELANTA, SAREK & STORA SJÖFALLET

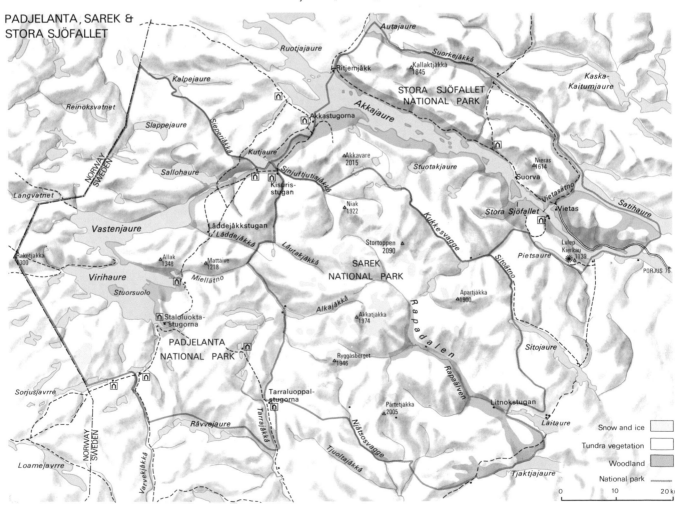

Snow and ice

Tundra vegetation

Woodland

National park

0   10   20km

Vadvetjåkko National Park

Although situated not far from Abisko, which is easily reached, Vadvetjåkko is virtually inaccessible. It is the most northerly of the Swedish National Parks, and is situated at 68° 30′N, on the northwest side of Lake Torneträsk close to the Norwegian border. It takes its name from Mount Vadvetjåkko (1250 metres), to the south of which lies a plain with lakes, willow thickets and marshes. Alpine meadows cover the greater part of the park and there is a small area of subalpine birch forest. The prevailing humid westerly winds and the presence of calcareous rocks have enabled a rich flora to develop, with dwarf birch and blue mountain heath among the more usual plants in this region of high arctic terrain.

Although the Lapps retain their rights to hunt, fish and graze herds of reindeer, they make only occasional visits to the park. The bird and mammal life is similar to the other National Parks in Swedish Lapland, but, in addition, the lake with its delta provides a refuge for large numbers of water birds at certain times of the year.

Padjelanta National Park

Padjelanta, Sarek and Stora Sjöfallet are all names evocative of the arctic wilderness of northern Sweden. They are all vast territories, much larger than most other European National Parks and share common borders. Together their combined area of 533,000 hectares makes them the largest area of protected wilderness in Europe.

Established in 1962, Padjelanta, the largest National Park in Sweden, consists of a wide plain with mountains and scattered lakes, the most famous of which, Virihaure and Vastenjaure, form the nucleus of the park. Although glacial phenomena, such as soil polygons, which are typical of arctic regions, are common, many parts of the park's landscape are green with alpine meadows, dwarf willow scrub and grass heath. In places where the soils are calcareous, three plants occur which grow nowhere else in Sweden – the gentian *Gentianella aurea*, the sandwort *Arenaria humifusa* and the cinquefoil *Potentilla hypartica*.

The mammal and birdlife, similar to that of the Sarek National Park, also includes the rough-legged buzzard and the scarce lesser white-fronted goose. Hunting rights are preserved for the Lapps, who have a summer camp in the area.

Sarek National Park

The remoteness and inaccessibility of Sarek ensures that the park is visited by only the most adventurous; consequently there is little danger of its wildlife being disturbed by tourists as happens elsewhere in Europe.

In no other part of Sweden are there such impressive mountains, rocky peaks – ninety over 1800 metres – gorges and glaciers, of which there are nearly one hundred. Lying entirely north of the coniferous-forest zone the principal constituents of the park's vegetation are subalpine birch forest, a lower alpine zone of dwarf-willow scrub and, above 1200 metres, an upper alpine zone dominated by lichens. The plants found growing among the birch and willow are typical of those that can tolerate arctic conditions, and include the blue mountain heath and the three-leaved rush *Juncus trifidus*. In summer the alpine zone is speckled with the white flowers of mountain avens.

Most of the large Scandinavian mammals occur in the park; the rarest is the wolf, which is now virtually extinct in Sweden. Of the others, the lynx, bear and wolverine are all very secretive and are not likely to be seen. The elk and arctic fox are however less shy and are more easily observed.

Golden eagles and gyrfalcons hunt the mountainsides, the purple sandpiper nests where there is cover in the vegetation, and the long-tailed skua breeds in scattered colonies on stony ground and in the region of the high tundra.

Stora Sjöfallet National Park

The series of natural arctic and subarctic lakes, cascades and waterfalls that lies within this National Park were at one time its most impressive feature. Unfortunately in 1920 1200 hectares were taken to build two hydroelectric power stations; the rivers were regulated, roads were built and gravel was excavated, seriously damaging the park's unspoiled character. As a result the Great Waterfall, or Stora Sjöfallet, lying in the centre of the park and after which the area is named, is now completely devoid of water for most of the year.

Around Lake Akkajaure is a fine mountain range dominated by the well-known silhouette of Akkavare (2015 metres). In the east the park's altitude is generally much lower and in some places is less than 400 metres. In these areas there are magnificent primeval forests of Scots pine and Norway spruce – the haunts of bears, lynxes, wolverines and elk. The lemming, the commonest rodent, is an important prey species of most of the predatory birds and mammals. In the birch scrub (*Betula tortuosa*) and dwarf willow heath of the subalpine zone, are found many birds which are seldom seen in breeding plumage in more southerly parts of Europe – wood sandpiper, brambling, fieldfare, redwing and the bluethroat, which Linnaeus called the Swedish nightingale. These are all widespread species and are found in this habitat throughout much of Swedish Lapland. In the alpine zone, snow buntings, dotterels and snowy owls occur. The lakes and marshes have an equally fascinating birdlife and are the habitat of the purple sandpiper, red-necked phalarope and Temminck's stint among others.

1 ABISKO
Information: Statens Natur vårdsverk, Nature Conservation Division, Box No. 1302, 171 25 Solna
Access: from ABISKO
Open: Unrestricted but best visited between June and September
Facilities: Information and tourist centre with accommodation available. Marked trails. Cable car to Mt Njulla

2 VADVETJÅKKO
Information: Statens Naturvårds verk, Nature Conservation Division, Box No. 1302, 171 25 Solna
Access: from Bjorkstugan or Koppardsen, 110km NW of KIRUNA
Open: Unrestricted but best visited between July and August
Facilities: Mountain hut within the park

3 PADJELANTA
Information: Domänverket, Nationalparksförvaltningen, V Torggatan 8, 960 40 Jokkmokk
Access: by track from KVIKKJOKK
Open: Unrestricted but best visited between July and September
Facilities: Tourist lodges with overnight accommodation available. Marked trails

4 SAREK
Information: Domänverket, Nationalparksförvaltningen, V Torggatan 8, 960 40 Jokkmokk
Access: by track from KVIKKJOKK
Open: Unrestricted but best visited between July and September

5 STORA SJÖFALLET
Information: Domänverket, Nationalparksförvaltningen, V Torggatan 8, 960 40 Jokkmokk
Access: from VIETAS
Open: Unrestricted but best visited between July and September
Facilities: Tourist lodges with overnight accommodation available. Marked trails

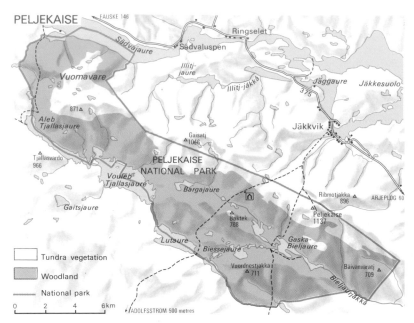

PELJEKAISE

Tundra vegetation

Woodland

National park

0   2   4   6km

Muddus National Park

Situated in the centre of Swedish Lapland, this vast area of forests, mires and watercourses has been a National Park since 1942. Lying between 160 and 661 metres, it occupies a plateau transected by a valley, which is broad and shallow in its upper parts but narrows to the south to form gorges and waterfalls. Glacial action in the past has deposited moraines and eskers in the lower parts of the valley.

Forest covers over 53 per cent of the park. It is mainly of spruce and Scots pine, but there are also many broad-leaved trees, particularly birch and willow. Peatlands and marshes extend over 43 per cent of the area, and the remaining 2 per cent is high fjeld – a

MUDDUS *below* The peat and marshland that cover nearly half the area of the park have their origin in the chaotic drainage bequeathed the region by haphazard glacial deposition during the last Ice Age.

tundra zone of stony ground and low plants.

Some 115 species of bird have been seen in the park, including whooper swan, crane, golden eagle, eagle owl and capercaillie. There are three bird sanctuaries within its boundaries, totalling 9700 hectares, to which access is forbidden in the breeding season.

The area's mammals are just as interesting as its birds – brown bears, elk, pine martens, wolverines, otters, lemmings and several other arctic rodents such as rat-headed voles, red-backed voles, as well as water voles and water shrews, which are more widespread.

Although the park is protected, the Lapps retain certain rights, particularly to graze their reindeer herds and to cut mature timber.

Peljekaise National Park
Of the seven large National Parks in Swedish Lapland, Peljekaise is the most southerly. Established in 1909 and originally covering

no more than 200 hectares, it was greatly enlarged four years later. It was chosen primarily to protect the undisturbed mountain birch woods that cover about one-third of the area. The park also contains lakes, marshes and moorland, and includes the south and west slopes of Mount Peljekaise and the lakes of Tjallasjaure and Lutaure.

Beneath the birch trees, the woodland vegetation varies from heather to a herbaceous flora which includes *Lactuca alpina*, northern wolfsbane angelica and the wood cranesbill. The fauna, with elk, fox, stoat, blue or mountain hare, is typical of Scandinavian forested mountains. Even the rare wolverine is said to occur regularly.

In the summer a small Lapp community of about thirteen families camps in the park to hunt, fish and pasture their reindeer herds.

Tärnasjön Nature Reserve
In north central Sweden near the Norwegian border lies Tärnasjön, a long, narrow lake in the upper part of the River Ume, which has so far escaped the attentions of hydroelectric schemes and is therefore of special scientific interest for conservation and research. The lake's marshy shores, fringed with reeds and birch woods, which flood in the winter, are of great botanical interest in summer. At its southern end parallel moraines and drumlins form an archipelago which constitutes an important nesting area for ducks and waders, such as wigeons, teal, scaup, velvet and common scoters, red-necked phalarope, ruff and whimbrel.

In addition to the mammals usually found in this part of Sweden are the brown bear and the beaver, which has recently been introduced, but is still rare.

Gammelstadsviken Nature Reserve
Near the head of the Gulf of Bothnia, north-west of Luleå, is a 4-kilometre-long bay which was established as a nature reserve by the regional authority in 1969. The bay, which is shallow and overgrown with vegetation, is very close to the town, and a certain amount of urbanization is taking place close to its shores. Despite this, Gammelstadsviken is still of major importance for wildlife and is included in the Swedish List of Wetlands of International Importance.

All the Swedish duck species apart from the gadwall breed here and there are numerous wading birds, particularly little ringed plovers, greenshanks, wood sandpipers, ruffs, curlews and occasionally the jacksnipe. Other species of water birds breeding on the reserve are great crested, red-necked and Slavonian grebes, and little gulls. Short-eared owls and marsh harriers are common predators.

During the spring and autumn migration periods, it is possible to see many other species, such as the smew, broad-billed sandpiper, curlew-sandpiper, spotted redshank and black-tailed godwit.

1 MUDDUS
Information: Domänverket, Nationalparksförvaltningen, V Torggatan 8, 960 40 Jokkmokk
Access: from Ligga, 20km N of JOKKMOKK
Open: Unrestricted except for central bird sanctuary where entry is prohibited between March 15 and July 31. Best visited between June and September
Facilities: Cabins with overnight accommodation available. Hiking trails. Observation tower

2 PELJEKAISE
Information: Domänverket, Arjeplogs revir, Fack 63, 930 90 Arjeplog
Access: by track from JÄCKVIK
Open: Unrestricted but best visited between June and September
Facilities: Marked trails with resting places and Lapp cabins, one of which is equipped for overnight accommodation

3 TÄRNASJÖN
Information: Statens Naturvårdsverk, Nature Conservation Division, Box No. 1302, 171 25 Solna
Access: from TÄRNABY
Open: Unrestricted

4 GAMMELSTADSVIKEN
Information: Statens Naturvårdsverk, Nature Conservation Division, Box No. 1302 171 25 Solna
Access: from LULEÅ
Open: Unrestricted except during the breeding season when entry to some areas is prohibited

Sonfjället National Park

The largest of the three National Parks in the uplands of central Sweden, Sonfjället consists of a massif which ranges in altitude from 430 to 1278 metres and is isolated from the southern end of the Scandinavian mountain chain. The highest regions are above the timber line. Lower down there is a zone of birch scrub which merges into coniferous forest. The park has a rather curious shape, having boundaries of straight lines, except in the east, instead of ones following the natural contour of the landscape.

Sonfjället is famous in Sweden for its population of brown bears, which is isolated from those in Swedish Lapland and from those in the rest of Jämtland Province. Normally the only hope of seeing the bears is to spend hours patiently watching during the early morning or evening. Other animals that might be seen are the lynx and wolverine, although both are scarce. The birdlife is typical of the Scandinavian mountains – dotterel on areas of alpine pastures, snow bunting in rocky regions and rough-legged buzzard over forests.

Töfsingdalen National Park

The central part of Sweden, close to the Norwegian border, where lies Töfsingdalen National Park, is a wild forested area, intersected by a system of ridges and varying in altitude from 660 to 892 metres. Geologically it is of considerable interest on account of its areas of barren ground strewn with gigantic boulders and its old moraines, both relics from past periods of glaciation. Three zones of vegetation are found in the park – coniferous forest with spruce and pine trees, subalpine birch-scrub and alpine grasslands. In the sheltered valley of Töfsingån, however, the vegetation is able to grow more luxuriantly. The park is at times used by nomadic Lapps to pasture reindeer and to hunt and fish.

Few animals are found in the park: elk and mountain hare are, however, relatively common, and the brown bear and wolverine are occasionally seen. The ptarmigan and raven are characteristic birds of the region. The golden eagle also occurs.

Hamra National Park

In the northern part of Orsa-Finnmarken in central Sweden lies the Hamra State Forest, covering about 37,000 hectares. Conifers grow on the plateau lands of the north and east and on the hills to the south, which in places exceed 600 metres in height. The soils are fertile and the trees are often large.

The National Park, a small remnant of primeval forest surviving in the centre of the area on the south side of Lake Svansjön, is claimed to be one of the most remarkable areas in Sweden. The oldest pines date from an extensive forest fire in the 1690s, during which all the spruce trees were killed. It is thought that the pines, having thicker barks were able to survive.

About 100 species of higher plants have been recorded in the park. The plant life is typically northern, with May lily, spotted orchid, golden rod, lily-of-the-valley and twinflower. The flora is particularly rich in lichens and mosses – 130 species of lichens and 149 species of mosses are known to grow in the park. Typical of the area's large mammals are the elk and roe deer. In the forest are found capercaillie, black grouse and several species of owl – the hawk, tawny, pygmy, Ural and eagle owls. The common crane can be seen on passage and black-throated divers and goldeneyes can be found on the lake. Ospreys nest in the nearby trees.

HAMRA The park's virgin forest, lying south of Lake Svansjön, dates from the late 17th century. It is one of Sweden's prime natural sites.

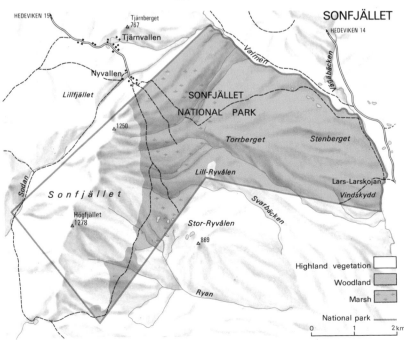

Highland vegetation
Woodland
Marsh
National park

0   1   2 km

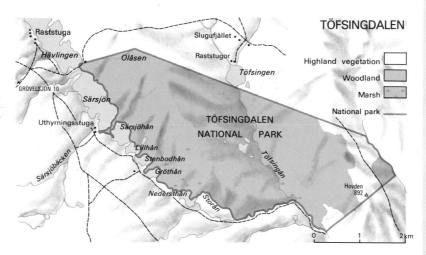

TÖFSINGDALEN

Highland vegetation
Woodland
Marsh
National park

TÖFSINGDALEN
NATIONAL PARK

Hovden
892

0   1   2 km

MOUNTAIN HARE
above Its coat changes
from grey-brown to white
in winter.

SONFJÄLLET *below*
The magnificent 1278m
peak of Högfjället lies in
the western part.

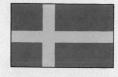

1 SONFJÄLLET
Information: Domänverket,
Östersundsförvaltningen,
Storgatan 16, 831 00
Östersund
Access: from Nyvallen, 17km
SW of HEDEVIKEN
Open: Unrestricted but best
visited between June and
September
Facilities: Marked trails

2 TÖFSINGDALEN
Information: Domänverket,
Älvdalens revir, 790 80
Älvdalen
Access: by track from
Grövelsjon, 60km NW of
SÄRNA
Open: Unrestricted but best
visited between June and
September

3 HAMRA
Information: Domänverket,
Informationssektionen, 791 81
Falun
Access: from FÅGELSJÖ
Open: Unrestricted but best
visited between June and
October
Facilities: Marked trails

45

Garphyttan National Park

In 1909, when Sweden established its first National Parks, Garphyttan was one of the earliest to be chosen. Situated in the lowland region of southern Sweden it is unusual in that its main objective is to preserve a traditional landscape which has been developed by man over the centuries. This contrasts with the typical Western European National Park, which is generally an extensive wild area of rugged mountain country.

Until the early part of this century, Garphyttan had three farms or "manses", each with its hay meadows and plot of land for cereal cultivation. The greater part of the area however consisted of a stretch of open deciduous forest, situated on the southern slope of Mount Kilsbergen.

Beneath the open canopy of this ash and hazel woodland lay meadowland, which provided grazing for cows and goats owned by local people. The leaf-fall from the deciduous trees returned nutrients to the grassland so that the whole system was in balance and the area's fertility was preserved. Garphyttan provides a good example of how man lived in harmony with nature before industrialization changed the countryside.

In the spring and summer the meadows are bright with wild flowers – mezereon, hepatica, cowslips, lilies-of-the-valley, globe flowers, wood anemones and many others.

Hjälstaviken Nature Reserve

One of Sweden's best known and most frequently visited bird reserves, Hjälstaviken occupies a shallow bay in Lake Mälaren not far from Uppsala. The area, which has been a nature reserve since 1948, consists of open water, rushes, reedmace and a 200 to 300-metre-wide stretch of reed bed bordering the shore. On the landward side the reed merges into wet meadows, giving way to drier grasslands on higher ground. On one side of the bay the shores rise steeply with exposed rocks and coniferous trees.

Hjälstaviken has a fine record in the introduction of new species. In the year of its foundation bitterns bred on the reserve – the first record of this species breeding anywhere in Sweden – and it was from here that the mute swan spread to colonize the whole of central Sweden. Among the area's other important breeding species are marsh harrier, spotted crake, gadwall, Slavonian grebe, tufted duck, pochard, osprey, water rail, and possibly also the little crake. Hjälstaviken is popular with birdwatchers because it is easily accessible and there is always the chance of seeing something rare or unusual; a great many waders, swans, geese, duck and cranes pass through during migration.

The pastures are grazed to maintain the best conditions for the birdlife. However, lack of sub-aquatic vegetation and increased overgrowth have brought about a deterioration in conditions in recent years.

HJÄLSTAVIKEN

Hjälstaviken
HJÄLSTAVIKEN
NATURE RESERVE

☐ Agricultural land ▨ Woodland
Marsh subject to flooding — Nature reserve
Marsh

0   1km

SEA EAGLE *left* A large broad-winged eagle found in marine and freshwater habitats, it is now considered an endangered species.

RAZORBILL *right* The stocky razorbill breeds on coastal cliff ledges from Brittany to the Arctic in colonies often numbering several thousand.

Ängsö National Park

In the northern part of the Stockholm archipelago lies Ängsö, the finest of the region's islands. A mosaic of meadows and wooded hills with both coniferous and deciduous trees, this island's lovely green landscape, typical of the traditional Sweden of the last century, has been preserved since 1909 as part of the country's national heritage of nature. Old farming methods are still practised in some areas, helping to maintain the fine display of spring flowers which exist in the island's meadows. The most notable flowering plant is the elder-flowered orchid, which has two colour forms – yellow and pink. It flowers between March and June and is extremely abundant in places. Among the other flowers found in the area are wood anemones, bird's-eye primroses, cowslips, marsh marigolds, hepaticas, Solomon's seals, lilies-of-the-valley and the yellow star of Bethleham, a low-growing herb with six-petalled flowers.

1 GARPHYTTAN
Information: Domänverket,
Västra Naturvårdsförvaltningen,
462 00 Vänersborg
Access: from OREBRO
Open: Unrestricted but best
visited between April and
October
Facilities: Marked trails

2 HJÄLSTAVIKEN
Information: Statens
Naturvårdsverk, Nature
Conservation Division, Box No.
1302, 171 25 Solna
Access: from UPPSALA or
ENKÖPING
Open: Unrestricted

3 ÄNGSÖ
Information: Domänverket,
Stockholms revir, 171 93 Solna
Access: by boat from
Vättershaga, 60km NE of
STOCKHOLM
Open: Unrestricted except for
some areas which are closed to
visitors between March 1 and
August 15. Best visited between
May and August
Facilities: Marked trails

4 BULLERÖ & LÅNGSKÄR
Information: Domänverket,
Stockholms revir, 171 93 Solna
Access: from Stavsnäs, 40km
E of STOCKHOLM
Open: Unrestricted except for
three bird sanctuaries where
entry is prohibited between
March 1 and August 15
Facilities: Field centre on
Bullerö open from May to
September. Nature trail

The sea eagle and the osprey are often seen in the vicinity of the park and one of the largest colonies of great crested grebes in Sweden is found in Hamviken Bay. Foxes, badgers and roe deer can also be seen.

Bullerö and Långskär Nature Reserves

Not many capital cities have nature reserves on their doorsteps, but with the Bullerö and Långskär reserves only 35 kilometres away, Stockholm can claim to be an exception. Containing about 900 of the thousands of islands, rocks and skerries that lie where Lake Mälaren has its outlet to the Baltic Sea, the reserves comprise approximately 4200 hectares of water and 400 hectares of grass-land, scrub, rock and coastal wetland. On the outer islands there are a few pine, birch and rowan trees, but in the central region, trees such as spruce are more common, and there are also a few boggy areas with willows, bilberry, crowberry, cloudberry and species of cotton-grass. In some parts of the archi-

pelago junipers are common – the former inhabitants brewed "tea" from its berries. The locally growing heather, as well as providing valuable forage, was also used as a dye, and for making baskets and brooms. The farms of Bulleron and Ragskar have long been abandoned: the bushes that invaded the old meadows are now being cleared and the primroses are now returning.

The principal purpose of the reserve is to protect birdlife: many species of waterfowl nest on these small islands away from disturbance by man. The characteristic species are eider and tufted duck, velvet scoter, the beautiful long-tailed duck and the goosander. The razorbill and black guillemot nest in crevices and sheltered ledges on the low rock-outcrops along the island coasts and, where there are trees and bushes, the black grouse and a number of common birds, such as the tree pipit and lesser whitethroat, also breed. The wheatear and white wagtail nest in holes in stone walls and sheltered crevices.

SPRING PASQUE-FLOWER *above*
Delicately flowered with ever-green leaves, it grows in alpine meadows, often near melting snow.

Norra Kvill National Park

Primeval forests are rare in Europe, even in Sweden which has 55 per cent of its land surface covered with trees. Usually they survive only in areas such as steep mountain slopes and inaccessible gorges, where it is difficult for man to exploit the timber. Norra Kvill National Park is an ancient forest of this type but is unusual in that it is easily accessible and can in fact be reached by car. It is situated on the eastern edge of the Småland highlands between 165 and 230 metres and can best be seen by approaching it from the north.

The forest, dominated by Norway spruce and Scots pine, has many trees between 250 and 350 years old, a great age for a conifer. In addition there are many fallen trees – forest giants which have decayed or been blown down in storms. This is a typical feature of many ancient forests, which, because the process of decay is slow, sometimes have more dead wood than living. Fallen trees make it difficult to walk through the forest, but the decaying timber provides a habitat for many insects, particularly beetles, and for fungi giving the forest-fauna an extra dimension.

BLÅ JUNGFRUN
The area's red-granite rocks are patterned by lichen and weathered by wind and rain into fantastic shapes.

At least 200 species of flowering plants have been found in the park, including the lovely spring pasque-flower, *Viola mirabilis*, bloody cranesbill, twin-flower and the poisonous baneberry. There is a well-formed shrub layer of guelder rose and hazel, and the ground vegetation consists mainly of cowberry and bilberry. Although the park is not large, several interesting mammals can be seen. Elk sometimes wander in from the surrounding forests and there are roe deer, foxes and pine martens. Of the many birds recorded in this area, the eagle owl is perhaps the most striking.

Blå Jungfrun National Park
In the northern part of the Kalmarsund, between the large island of Öland and the Swedish mainland, lies the dome-shaped rocky island of Blå Jungfrun which has been a National Park since 1926. During the summer it attracts many visitors to its curious rock formations and remarkable caves. The low cliffs and huge boulders found along the south coast are of interest to geologists. Much of the island is bare rock on which grow lichens and mosses, but in sheltered crevices and in the lower regions there is a woodland of pine, spruce and birch, and dense oak forest grows on the south-facing slopes. The forests also contain small-leaved limes and Norway maples.

The island's granite rocks weather to produce a poor acid soil, on which only heather and crowberry grow. The gorges in the south central part of the island – the Jungfrukammaren (the Virgin's Chamber) and Kyrkan (the Church) – are favourite places for visitors. The highest point in the National Park is a bare rocky dome only 86.5 metres high, where a scanty vegetation can be found growing in the rock fissures.

Rone Ytterholme–Laus Holmar Nature Reserve – Bird Sanctuary
Off the east coast of Gotland in the Baltic Sea lie several gravel-covered limestone islands which are flat and low-lying, and used traditionally for sheep, cattle and horse-grazing. The grassy sward which has resulted attracts large numbers of wildfowl not only as a breeding site but also during migration periods and in the winter months.

Laus Holmar consists of three of these islands lying close together and is separated by a few kilometres from Rone Ytterholme and nearby Grötlingboholme. These last two areas are usually considered together and treated as one reserve.

Grötlingboholme is a rich breeding ground for several species of birds, especially for colonies of black-headed gulls and sandwich terns. Both islands are also important resting places for brent and greylag geese. About 3000 of each species have been counted and the area is regarded as the most important moulting ground for the greylag in Sweden.

The large, shallow expanses of water with projecting banks, found within the reserve, provide the shelter needed for the protection of these birds during the moulting period, when they are unable to fly.

Two of the three islands in the Laus Holmar group are not grazed, the third, Storholmen, has a herd of cattle and consequently the grass here is much shorter. All three islands have a remarkable bird fauna. About thirty-five species breed in the protected areas, a number which inclues many pairs of greylag geese, eiders, dunlins, little terns, avocets and turnstones.

Ottenby Nature Reserve
Natural history observations have been made at Ottenby ever since 1741, when the famous Swedish naturalist Linnaeus went there to record plants and birds.

The reserve is located at the tip of the island of Öland, which is nearly 150 kilometres long and 10 kilometres broad, and is itself of interest to the naturalist. It is also very popular as a holiday resort and the new bridge connecting the island to the mainland has made it most accessible.

The reserve's coastline has sandy beaches, sandspits, shingle banks, sheltered coves and half-submerged boulders. Here many wading birds find an abundant food supply of sand hoppers, flies and their larvae, small beetles and spiders in the thick belt of seaweed, many metres wide, which is washed up on the shore.

North of the promontory lies Ottenby-lund, an isolated wood of birch, aspen and oak which is of great importance as a shelter for migrating passerine birds. To the east is an extensive area of sheep-grazed meadow-land, which also attracts many birds, and although the area is best known for the concentration of birds found there in the autumn, birds can be seen flying over the reserve at most times of the year. One of the most interesting nesting species is the avocet, a waterfowl which breeds in very few other parts of Sweden.

1 NORRA KVILL
Information: Domänverket, Vimmerby revir, Box 7, 598 00 Vimmerby
Access: from Ydrefors, 18km NW of VIMMERBY
Open: Unrestricted but best visited between April and September
Facilities: Marked trails

2 BLÅ JUNGFRUN
Information: Domänverket, Kalmar revir, Kaggensgatan 30, 392 32 Kalmar
Access: by boat from OSKARSHAMN and BYXELKROK
Open: Unrestricted but best visited between May and September
Facilities: Marked trails

3 RONE YTTERHOLME-LAUS HOLMAR
Information: Statens Naturvårdsverk, Nature Conservation Division, Box No. 1302, 171 25 Solna
Access: by boat from Ronehamn, 26km N of BURGSVIK
Open: Entry to both groups of islands is restricted

4 OTTENBY
Information: Statens Naturvårdsverk, Nature Conservation Division, Box No. 1302, 171 25 Solna
Access: from Ottenby, 85km S of BORGHOLM
Open: Unrestricted except for some areas which are closed to visitors between spring and autumn
Facilities: Marked footpaths

49

AVOCET *below*
An elegant wader, the
avocet has long blue-grey
legs and a delicate,
upturned bill.

Tåkern Nature Reserve

In a region of exposed Cambrian–Silurian rocks and cultivated plains, to the east of Lake Vättern in southern Sweden, lies Tåkern Nature Reserve, an area of shallow water bordered by a 250-metre strip of land. The reserve is of considerable ornithological interest due to man's interference with the lake in the past. In the last century the water level was permanently lowered, allowing the

development of vast reed beds, which now cover a third of the area. In this shallow water stoneworts and water-milfoil grow, providing food for large numbers of duck.

Tåkern is remarkable in having all five European grebes as breeding species – the little, great crested, Slavonian, black-necked and red-necked. There are about forty pairs of marsh harriers; the little crake has been recorded breeding, and six species of waders nest regularly, including dunlins and ruffs. Large numbers of water birds of many different species visit during the spring and autumn migrations. Between 35,000 and 40,000 bean geese visit the area in November.

Getterön Nature Reserve

On the shores of the Kattegat, the busy sea route separating the west coast of Sweden from Denmark, is situated the Getterön Nature Reserve. It occupies a coastal bay north of Varbeg which has become partly enclosed and desalinated following the construction of embankments in the 1930s. Since then it has gathered importance as a wintering area for large numbers of brent geese and as a resting place for many ducks, geese and waders during the spring and autumn migrations. Many other interesting species are found in the area, notably ruffs, black-tailed godwits, short-eared owls, dunlins and shelducks, and the reserve is also a

TÅKERN

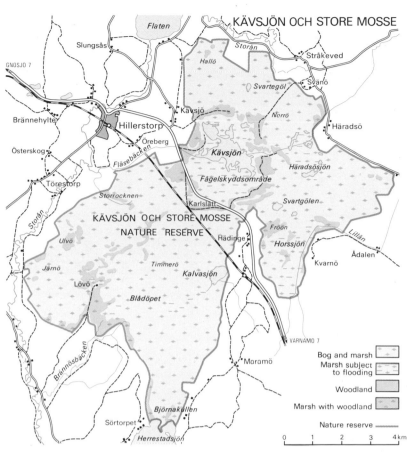

Bog and marsh

Marsh subject to flooding

Woodland

Marsh with woodland

Nature reserve

0   1   2   3   4 km

TÅKERN *left* The lake, which occupies almost the entire area of the reserve, is seen here from its southern shore. As a consequence of the low water level, one-third is covered by fringing vegetation.

1 TÅKERN
Information: Statens Naturvårdsverk, Nature Conservation Division, Box No. 1302, 171 25 Solna
Access: from LINKÖPING or MOTALA
Open: Unrestricted
Facilities: Between April and June access allowed only to bird towers and along marked trails

2 GETTERÖN
Information: Statens Naturvårdsverk, Nature Conservation Division, Box No. 1302, 171 25 Solna
Access: from VARBERG
Open: Unrestricted, except during breeding season

3 KÄVSJÖN OCH STORE MOSSE
Information: Statens Naturvårdsverk, Nature Conservation Division, Box No. 1302, 171 25 Solna
Access: from VÄRNAMO
Open: Unrestricted

4 DALBY SÖDERSKOG
Information: Domänverket, Kristianstads revir, Föreningsgatan 5, 291 33 Kristianstad
Access: from Dalby, 27km E of MALMÖ
Open: Unrestricted but best visited between April and October
Facilities: Marked trails

breeding site for the avocet, a bird which is rare in Sweden.

Getterön, which became a nature reserve in 1970, is now threatened by the proposed extension of a nearby airfield. The Swedish Ornithological Society has carried out bird census work and ringing here for many years.

Kävsjön och Store Mosse Nature Reserve

In the central part of Småland, in one of Sweden's southern provinces, lies a remarkable raised bog, which is said to be the best in the country. Raised bogs usually occur in high rainfall areas and are formed of dead plant material which cannot rot away in the acid waters and instead gradually accumulates as lens-shaped deposits of peat. Lake Kävsjön and two small meres provide areas of open water within the reserve. Away from the bog, where the peat is drier and firmer, there are scattered groups of Scots pine and dwarf shrubs.

The birdlife is an ornithologist's dream. On the pools and lakes are found red-throated and black-throated divers, red-necked grebes, wigeon, garganey, pintail, shovelers, water rails and spotted crakes, and the marshy ground is the nesting area for what is probably the largest colony of cranes in Sweden. Dunlins, golden plovers and short-eared owls also breed in the area and nests of whooper swans and jack snipes,

which are normally confined to Lapland, have been found. The bog also attracts greylag and bean geese on migration. It has been decided that because this area is so important it is to become a National Park.

Dalby Söderskog National Park

In the extreme south, only 12 kilometres from Lund, lies Dalby Söderskog, an area of mixed deciduous forest which has developed on land that formerly consisted of grazed meadows. Declared a National Park in 1918, Dalby Söderskog is particularly attractive in the spring, when the white flowers of the wood anemone and the lovely flowers of the yellow wood anemone and the lesser celandine carpet the ground. The purple-flowered *Corydalis bulbosa* and *C. solida* are also common. The summer-flowering plants include the yellow star of Bethlehem, lungwort and the Solomon's seal.

The burst of colourful flowers in spring is all the more vivid because the trees are not yet in leaf and the sunshine penetrates to the forest floor. Later, dark canopies of beech, wych elm, ash and pedunculate oak shade the ground and the herbaceous vegetation becomes dominated by dogs mercury, which prefers these conditions. Many common passerine birds nest in the woodland and both roe and red deer may be seen. The latter, however, is scarce.

FINLAND

A country of water and forests, Finland has 62,000 lakes and two-thirds of its land surface is tree-covered; over 30,000 islands lie along its idented coastline, which extends well beyond the Arctic Circle. The population, 4.75 million, is fairly low, and, with a density of only 13.7 per square kilometre, the country gives the general impression of a beautiful, unspoilt landscape, with little or no evidence of human occupation or activity.

National Parks form the main category of protected area. There are nine, all freely accessible to the public and most with such facilities as nature trails, camp sites, and accommodation huts. The fifteen strict nature reserves – usually called Nature Parks in Finland (but here referred to as nature reserves to prevent confusion with the largely recreational areas of other countries) – can only be visited in the company of the warden.

In addition to 1557 nature monuments, usually small areas of less than one hectare, there are 650 other protected areas, including peatlands, nature management areas, forest conservation areas and virgin forests, all of which are the responsibility of the National Board of Forestry. There are also twenty-four areas protected and managed by the Finnish Forest Research Institute and some private areas which are protected at the owners' request in accordance with the act of 1923.

As might be expected, Finland has a large number of wetlands of international importance, and forty-five separate sites are listed in the Directory of Western Palaearctic Wetlands. But in spite of this, protection of lake shores and rivers is not extensive, and less than 5000 hectares are listed as fully protected. The same is true for the thousands of off-shore islands, in such demand for summer cottages that land prices are high and the total area where wildlife is protected is less than 150 hectares.

The protection afforded to wildlife is also sometimes uncertain. Although the hedgehog, flying squirrel, arctic fox, weasel, freshwater pearl mussel and all bats are protected by law, the lynx and the bear may be hunted with special permission from the Ministry of Agriculture and Forestry, and in the whole of the Lapp region, including the National Parks, reindeer herdsmen are permitted to kill carnivores such as wolves, bears and wolverines. The golden eagle is also still shot by the herdsmen, although illegally. Most other non-game birds are legally protected, including birds of prey, except for the goshawk, which outside the nesting season may be killed by gamekeepers, or taken by falconers. Several bird species such as the garganey and scaup are endangered or rare and the sea eagle has declined because of pesticide use.

VESIJAKKO Lakes and coniferous forests are perhaps Finland's most characteristic landscape features.

FINLAND

Suomi – "land of fens and lakes" – is a geologically very ancient land. Formerly a mountain area, it is now greatly reduced by erosion and overlain by vast areas of thick glacial deposits, notably the long sinuous sand and gravel "eskers" left by the retreating ice-sheets. Since the withdrawal of the enormously heavy ice mass, the land has risen by about 200 metres in the northwest and this elastic readjustment continues today at a rate of about one metre in a hundred years along the northern shore of the Gulf of Bothnia.

In the far north a remnant highland arc forms a watershed to the north and east with its highest point, Haltiatunturi (1328 metres), at its westernmost end. The greater part of the country consists of a vast undulating plateau, 100 metres above sea level, densely clothed in spruce, pine and birch forest and littered with tens of thousands of lakes, including Saimaa, Paijanne and Oulujärvi – so large that they are really lake-systems rather than clearly defined individual lakes. One-third of Finland's land surface is occupied by lakes, bogs and marshes.

Stretching from the head of the Gulf of Bothnia all the way round the coast to Lake Ladoga across the border with the USSR, is a broad, fertile plain. Cereals, root crops and even fruit trees are cultivated in the south, but only hardy crops can be grown in the restricted, 30-day growing season of the far north. Sub-zero temperatures are common in winter on the southern coast, but maritime influences make the climate less severe than might be expected. Summers are warm though short, spring and autumn characteristically brief, and winter long and cold, but the overall climate is less extreme than any country of comparable latitude anywhere in the world, with the exception of neighbouring Norway and Sweden. Average precipitation is about 50 millimetres, much of it occurring in winter as snow.

PARK RESERVE	SIZE (km²)	DESCRIPTION	MAP REF	PAGE NO
MALLA	30.0	Nature Reserve. High fell with alpine vegetation. Rich flora on limestone crags.	A1	56
KEVO	339	Nature Reserve. Canyon in north Finland with wide range of habitats. Large population of breeding birds.	C1	56
LEMMENJOKI	1720	National Park. Remote wilderness region with forests, "aapa" fens and open fell country. Striking glacial features. Traditional Lapp grazing area with ancient hunting pits still intact.	B1	56
PALLAS-OUNASTUNTURI	500	National Park. Mountain plateau largely above tree line, impressive canyons to the south. Varied flora, including insectivorous plants. Unusual mixture of northern and southern bird species.	B1/B2	57
MALTIO	147	Nature Reserve. Landscape of hills, fells and peat bogs, typical of region. Wide variety of birds.	C2	58
PYHÄTUNTURI	31.0	National Park. Part of conservation forest containing high peaks, pine and spruce woodland and "aapa" fens.	C2	58
PISAVAARA	50.0	Nature Reserve. Area of forest and peat bogs lying south of the Arctic Circle, along west side of the Kemijoki River. Rich flora and variety of interesting rodent species.	B2	58
OULANKA	107	National Park. Unique landscape of deep valleys, heathland, peat bogs and riverside meadows. Lady's slipper orchid found in valleys. Bird species typical of high north.	C2	59
ROKUA	4.2	National Park. Area consisting of the Rokuanvaara ridge and sandy heathlands. Lichen ground cover.	C3	60
PYHÄHÄKKI	10.1	National Park. Largest natural forest in Finland. Interesting bird fauna and rare insect species.	B4	60
LINNANSAARI	8.0	National Park. Group of islands in Saimaa Lake with varied topography and vegetation. Noted as a breeding area for relict population of ringed seals.	C4	60
PETKELJÄRVI	6.3	National Park. Rugged region of glacial deposits and lakes. Mammal fauna typical of northern regions.	D4	61
LIESJÄRVI	1.5	National Park. Sparsely populated, infertile area of forest, peat bogs and offshore islands.	B5	61

KEVO The birch trees growing in this nature reserve, deep inside Finnish Lapland, are among the most northerly in western Europe.

MALLA

NORWAY

KEVO

LEMMENJOKI

PALLAS-
OUNASTUNTURI

MALTIO

PYHÄTUNTURI

PISAVAARA

OULANKA

SWEDEN

*Gulf of
Bothnia*

ROKUA

FINLAND

U.S.S.R.

PYHÄHÄKKI

PETKELJÄRVI

LINNANSAARI

LIESJÄRVI

Conservation area

Motorway

Main road

0   50   100km

HELSINKI

*Gulf of
Finland*

*Ladozhskoye
Ozero*

Leningrad

A   B   C   D

PALLAS-OUNASTUNTURI *above* Lakes, marsh, bogs and birch woodland are typical elements of the National Park's landscape. This area lies at the foot of Mount Taivaskero, in the centre of the region.

CREEPING AZALEA *left* An evergreen undershrub with tiny leaves and flowers, this alpine azalea forms a low-growing mat of vegetation.

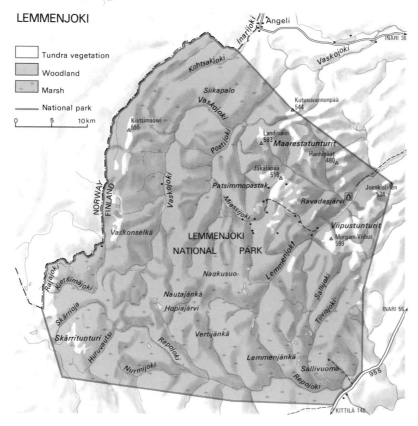

Malla Nature Reserve

In the extreme northwest, where Finnish territory projects into Norway and Sweden as a tongue of land no more than 35 kilometres across, sits Malla Nature Reserve at the farthest point.

A region of high fell with alpine vegetation, there are local outcrops of limestone, and the calcareous soils derived from them support a rich and interesting flora. In one part, where there is a rocky ravine with cliffs, several pairs of house martins nest in the crevices – an unusual nesting site for this bird, which is almost always found on buildings.

The mammal fauna is interesting, with elk and reindeer, and among the smaller animals, the northern red-backed vole, short-tailed vole, rat-headed vole and Norway lemming. On the alpine headland the golden plover, shore lark and snow bunting breed, and in the dwarf scrub the willow grouse occurs. The forest fauna includes the redwing, brambling and willow warbler; the main predator is the rough-legged buzzard.

Kevo Nature Reserve

In the north of Finland, deep inside Lapland, lies the great canyon known as Kevojoki. Although it is situated beyond the limits of spruce and pine forests, some pine woodland occurs along the margins of the Kevo River. The most characteristic tree is birch, which here, at its most northerly point in Scandinavia, is reduced to a scrubby plant.

The most conspicuous mammal is the reindeer, and a large number of birds breed in the reserve's wide range of different habitats. There are rough-legged buzzards, ptarmigan and golden plovers on the open heathlands, and where there is more cover for nesting, the whimbrel breeds.

In the scrubby birch the arctic warbler, one of the most northerly of warblers, is found as well as the bluethroat, redwing, Lapland bunting, snow bunting, brambling and redpoll. The arctic fox is sometimes seen in the open tundra.

Lemmenjoki National Park

High in northern Finland adjacent to the Norwegian border, Lemmenjoki National Park is situated in a large roadless wilderness close to the limit of tree growth and extends into the fell regions of Lapland. The central part of the park is a broad plain on which birch and pine forest alternate with long stretches of northern "aapa" fens. The eastern part is dominated by mountains reaching nearly 600 metres in height. The northern growing limit of pine and spruce runs through the park and both trees are found, particularly spruce, which occurs in small groves in the southern half of the protected area.

The area's most important topographic feature is the Lemmenjoki Valley, which has high precipitous rock walls in places and is bordered by open fell country on either side. The valley has several narrow lakes with margins of high gravel terraces and eskers formed during the last Ice Age. Small streams forming torrents and waterfalls rush down through deep gorges and canyons.

On the lower slopes of the Lemmenjoki Valley grow pine trees reputed to be over 600 years old. Higher up is found a birch zone, above which is an area of mountain heath and boulder fields. The typical plants of the area are mountain heath and the attractive creeping azalea, which has a dense mat of pink flowers. In some places there are ancient hunting pits erected for reindeer, and the area is still important to the Lapps for grazing their herds. The brown bear and the wolf, both scarce, occur in the park and among the smaller mammals is the locally found grey-sided vole. The birdlife is typical of these northern regions and includes the rough-legged buzzard, hawk owl, willow grouse, golden plover, whimbrel, shore lark, waxwing, bluethroat, redwing, Lapland bunting, brambling, snow bunting, Siberian jay and whooper swan.

Pallas-Ounastunturi National Park

In northwest Finnish Lapland, a vast tract of mountain plateau lying largely above the tree limit with lakes, meres, peat bogs, spruce and pine forests, has been a National Park since 1938. It lies along part of the beautiful Ounasselka hills and extends as far as Mount Keimiötunturi in the south.

The plateau, part of the Pallas range, is dominated by Taivaskero (807 metres), the highest point. To the south lie three impressive canyons with clear, cold water tumbling down their steep slopes, and at the foot of the fells there are imposing sand hills deposited during the last Ice Age by glacier meltwater.

The park lies in the coniferous forest zone and about 60 per cent of the southern part is covered by pines. Spruce reaches its northern limit in the park and although the trees are generally of small size some fine specimens grow in a wet valley area overlying basic rocks to the west of Suaskuru. In these groves are found several interesting plants, notably coniferous bedstraw, Lapland buttercup, long-leaved stitchwort, the ostrich fern *Struthiopteris filicastrum* and blue sow-thistle.

In lowland areas towards the north of the park a number of colourful plants grow among the trees, particularly the globe flower, melancholy thistle, northern marsh violet and red baneberry. On wet ground and damp rocks near springs three insect-eating plants can be found, the sundew, common butterwort and the much rarer white-flowered alpine butterwort.

Between 400 and 550 metres altitude, depending on the exposure, coniferous forest can no longer grow, and is replaced by the birch *Betula odorata*. In these areas the

ground vegetation consists of heath with bilberry, crowberry, heather, arctic bearberry, mountain heath, *Diapensia lapponica*, mountain avens, three-leaved rush and polar willow. The birch soon gives way to open alpine fells, where on rocky terraces the plants, although dwarf or creeping, are often very attractive, for instance, the arctic saxifrage and the creeping azalea.

The larger mammals include the bear, which is a regular inhabitant and the elk, wolf and wolverine, although the last two are rare. In the summer, herds of domestic reindeer roam the alpine meadows. The fox and its prey, the hare and lemming, are common.

One of the interesting features of the birdlife is the surprising mixture of southern and northern species – on the one hand robins, chiffchaffs, hedge sparrows, song thrushes and bullfinches and on the other, snow buntings, shore larks, ptarmigan, long-tailed skuas and Lapland buntings. The roseate tern, ruff and whimbrel are common birds in marshy places. The rough-legged buzzard breeds on the rocky cliffs and there are two to three pairs of golden eagles. The park was at one time the only inland nesting locality for the sea eagle in Finland – a bird of prey which is in decline throughout Europe.

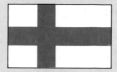

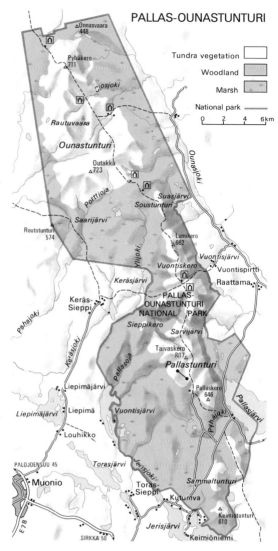

PALLAS-OUNASTUNTURI

Tundra vegetation
Woodland
Marsh
National park ⎯⎯⎯
0   2   4   6km

1 MALLA
Information: Office for National Parks, National Board of Forestry, Box 233, 00121 Helsinki 12
Access: from KILPISJÄRVI
Open: Strict reserve. Permission to enter must be obtained from the Office for National Parks. Hikers using the trail must inform the warden, Kilpisjärvi centre or the hotel in advance
Facilities: Hiking trail

2 KEVO
Information: Office for National Parks, National Board of Forestry, Box 233, 00121 Helsinki 12
Access: from Kevo, 18km S of UTSJOKI or by track 11km E of KARIGASNIEMI
Open: Strict reserve. Permission to enter must be obtained from the Office for National Parks.
Facilities: Hiking trails

3 LEMMENJOKI
Information: Office for National Parks, National Board of Forestry, Box 233, 00121 Helsinki 12
Access: from Lemmenjoki, 50km SW of INARI
Open: Unrestricted
Facilities: Marked paths with camp sites within the park. Fell cabins

4 PALLAS-OUNASTUNTURI
Information: Office for National Parks, National Board of Forestry, Box 233, 00121 Helsinki 12
Access: from ENONTEKIÖ or MUONIO
Open: Unrestricted
Facilities: Hiking trails with camp sites and fell cabins within the park. Nature trails

FINLAND

Maltio Nature Reserve

In northern Finland, northeast of the Pyhä-tunturi National Park, lies Maltio Nature Reserve, a picturesque area of wooded hills, fells and peat bogs. Although it is situated close to the southern border of Lapland, the landscape is typical of the country.

On the park's lakes are found such northern bird species as the black-throated diver, as well as mallard, pintail and wigeon, which are more widely distributed. The wood sandpiper is common and nests on boggy areas around the lakes. In the forests, Siberian tits, bramblings, redpolls, song thrushes and mistle thrushes are found, together with a number of common species more typical of temperate regions, such as the willow warbler, tree pipit and spotted flycatcher. The mammals include the elk, reindeer, mountain hare, red squirrel, fox and stoat.

Pyhätunturi National Park

The southernmost of Finland's northerly mountains, a magnificent scenic area rising to a height of 540 metres from a surrounding lowland region of forests and peat bogs, forms the Pyhätunturi National Park.

The mountain has a most distinctive form with steeply sloping sides and bare stony valleys separating its five peaks and is famous for its fine panoramic views.

Vegetation is scarce, due mainly to the hard quartzite rock which forms a poor and relatively infertile soil. On the low-lying land at the foot of the fells, there are pine and spruce forests and extensive "aapa" fens. The park includes the long fell ridge of Luosto and extensive peat-lands, and is managed by the State Forest Service. The vegetation in the pine forests is limited to heather, crowberry and lichens, while in areas where there are stands of spruce the dominant species are bilberry and the moss *Hylocomium splendens*. On the "aapa" peatlands cranberry is found with many sedges and *Sphagnum* species.

The mammal life, although not particularly rich, includes elk, reindeer, red squirrel and the Norway lemming. The birdlife, rather surprisingly, does not contain many alpine species, despite the alpine character of the park. There are, however, rough-legged buzzards, Siberian tits, bramblings and redwings. The willow grouse and Siberian jay are also typical species.

Pisavaara Nature Reserve

In the western part of northern Finland, just south of the Arctic Circle, Pisavaara Nature Reserve lies on the west side of the Kemijoki River, southwest of the Pyhätunturi National Park. The region, consisting mainly of the slopes of Pisavaara hill, rising to 220 metres, has an interesting topography containing evidence of ancient raised sea beaches. Much of the forest, mostly pine and spruce, is said to be primeval and the nature reserve has extensive peat bogs, which are of considerable

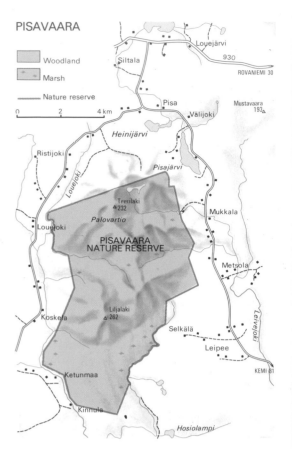

PISAVAARA

Woodland

Marsh

Nature reserve

58

interest to both the botanist and geographer. It has a rich flora, particularly of plants which grow along the banks of steams.

The mammal fauna is noted for its number of interesting rodent species, including the masked or Laxmann's shrew and the wood lemming. Reindeer and elk are well established and among the commonest breeding birds in the reserve are bramblings, siskins and Siberian jays.

Oulanka National Park

Situated north of 66° latitude and just south of the Arctic Circle, Oulanka National Park presents a unique landscape of geological, biological and scenic interest.

There are deep valleys, which in places have vertical-walled chasms, and others with thick gravel layers into which rivers have cut deep, steep-sided banks. The many rivers, of which the Oulankajoki is the most important, flow northeast into the White Sea. The park also has many rapids and waterfalls, a great attraction to visitors.

Most of the forest land is pine-dominated heath, typical of the far north. In the northern part there are large wet peat bogs which are difficult or even dangerous to cross. Elsewhere there are beautiful meadows, full of flowers, bordering the river banks. The barren pine heath has a ground cover of heather, bilberry, crowberry, wavy hair-grass and common cow-wheat. Flowering plants in the valleys include the incomparable lady's slipper orchid, arctic saxifrage, yellow marsh saxifrage, mountain avens, globe flower and many others.

The park's mammals include the reindeer, red squirrel, mountain hare, fox, bank vole and several species usually found farther north, such as the rat-headed vole and grey-sided vole. The birdlife has a range of species characteristic of alpine heathlands, peat bogs and woodlands. On the lakes are found black-throated divers, goldeneye, mallard, wigeon and pintail; in open wooded heath-land, the wood sandpiper nests and in the forests there are Siberian tits, bramblings and redpolls. The rough-legged buzzard and Tengmalm's owl are common birds of prey, and the honey buzzard is also seen.

Several bird species occur that are more typical of temperate regions, such as the tree pipit, meadow pipit, yellow wagtail, willow warbler, spotted flycatcher and song thrush. Among the rarer species found in the park are the whooper swan, smew, golden eagle and the eagle owl.

1 MALTIO
Information: Office for National Parks, National Board of Forestry, Box 233, 00121 Helsinki 12
Access: from Martti 26km N of SAVUKOSKI
Open: Strict reserve. Permission to enter must be obtained from the Office for National Parks

2 PYHÄTUNTURI
Information: Office for National Parks, National Board of Forestry, Box 233, 00121 Helsinki 12
Access: 50km N of KEMIJÄRVI
Open: Unrestricted
Facilities: Tourist lodge. Hiking trails with camp sites within the park

3 PISAVAARA
Information: Office for National Parks, National Board of Forestry, Box 233, 00121 Helsinki 12
Access: from Pisa, 40km SW of ROVANIEMI
Open: Strict reserve. Permission to enter must be obtained from the Office for National Parks

4 OULANKA
Information: Office for National Parks, National Board of Forestry, Box 233, 00121 Helsinki 12
Access: from KÄYLÄ
Open: Unrestricted
Facilities: Marked trails with camp sites and fell cabins within the park. "The Bear's Trek" hiking trail runs through the park

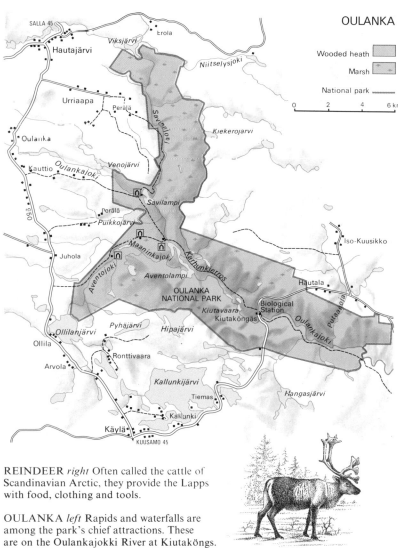

OULANKA

Wooded heath

Marsh

National park

0   2   4   6 km

REINDEER *right* Often called the cattle of Scandinavian Arctic, they provide the Lapps with food, clothing and tools.

OULANKA *left* Rapids and waterfalls are among the park's chief attractions. These are on the Oulankajokki River at Kiutaköngs.

LINNANSAARI

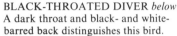

Woodland

National park

0 1 2km

BLACK-THROATED DIVER *below*
A dark throat and black- and white-
barred back distinguishes this bird.

PYHÄHÄKKI *right* Coniferous
forest covers about two-thirds of
the National Park.

Rokua National Park

Situated in central Finland, fairly close to
the Gulf of Bothnia, Rokua National Park
consists of a long, level ridge known as
Rokuanvaara, which rises from the peatland plains of northern Ostrobothnia and was
formed since the Ice Age by the action of sea
and wind.

Apart from old coastal dunes which are
now fully stabilized with vegetation and
stand out sharply in the rather featureless
landscape, there are flat sandy heathlands
and deep kettle holes containing little tarns
or bogs. The small pools have crystal-clear
water and date from the period when ice, left
by the retreating glaciers, began to melt. The
forests of pine growing in the park's rather
barren heathland landscape have a ground
cover mainly of lichens, which in dry weather
become almost white: the main species are
Cladonia alpestris and *Cetraria nivalis*. Other
typical plants are heather, wild thyme and
relict species such as creeping willow and the
elder-leaved valerian *Valeriana sambucifolia*
subsp. *salina*. This latter plant recalls a time
when the area was part of the sea shore.

Pyhähäkki National Park

In south central Finland, Pyhähäkki, the
largest natural forest in the country, has
been protected as a National Park since 1912.
About a third of the area is covered by old
dense spruce forest with a ground flora
dominated by bilberry, wavy hair-grass,
hairy woodrush, twinflower, heather and
cowberry. Another third is more open and

predominantly pine forest, much of which is
250 years old with some trees thought to be
at least 450 years old. There are bogs and
small ponds scattered throughout the forest
and in open peatland areas the flora includes
ledum, bog wortleberry, dwarf birch and
many *Sphagnum* species.

The park is a fine refuge for wildlife, and
red squirrel, mountain hare, fox and elk are
widespread. There are many birds in the
forest, notably pied and spotted flycatchers,
common redstarts, siskins and redbreasted
flycatchers. Among the commonest are the
spotted woodpecker and Tengmalm's owl;
the waxwing and Siberian jay breed here and
the hazelhen and capercaillie are very common. The forest's old timber is well known as a
habitat for rare insects such as the unusual
beetles *Ips longicollis* and *Carphobrus minimus*.
The woodland has also many interesting
species of butterfly.

Linnansaari National Park

In the great lake of Saimaa in the Finnish
lakeland region lies the Linnansaari National
Park. It consists of a group of islands of
varied topography and coastline, with deep,
narrow coves, rocky outcrops, ravines, glens
and forests ranging from pines to broad-
leaved trees. The largest island is no more
than 4 kilometres long and there are dozens
of smaller islands and rocky outcrops. Pine,
spruce, birch, alder and lime are common
trees, and are associated with bilberry, cowberry, fly honeysuckle, mezereon, baneberry
and bearberry.

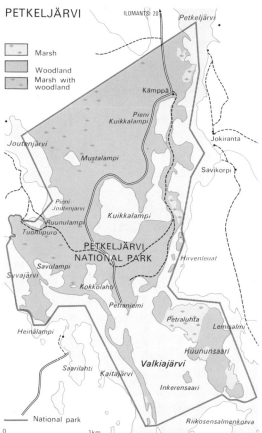

PETKELJÄRVI

- Marsh
- Woodland
- Marsh with woodland

— National park

0 — 1km

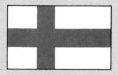

1 ROKUA
Information: Office for National Parks, National Board of Forestry, Box 233, 00121 Helsinki 12
Access: 30km W of VAALA or 25km S of UTAJÄRVI
Open: Unrestricted
Facilities: Marked trails to the park from holiday centre N of the boundary. Camp sites within the park

2 PYHÄHÄKKI
Information: Office for National Parks, National Board of Forestry, Box 233, 00121 Helsinki 12
Access: 30km NE of SAARIJÄRVI
Open: Unrestricted
Facilities: Marked trails within the park. Camp sites

3 LINNANSAARI
Information: Office for National Parks, National Board of Forestry, Box 233, 00121 Helsinki 12
Access: by boat from Oravi, 40km NW of SAVONLINNA or by boat from RANTASALMI
Open: Unrestricted but the park can only be reached by water. There is no regular boat service
Facilities: Marked trails

4 PETKELJÄRVI
Information: Office for National Parks, National Board of Forestry, Box 233, 00121 Helsinki 12
Access: 20km SE of ILOMANTSI
Open: Unrestricted
Facilities: Marked trails within the park. Hiking route to Putkela. Camp site.

5 LIESJÄRVI
Information: Office for National Parks, National Board of Forestry, Box 233, 00121 Helsinki 12
Access: 25km NW of KARKKILA
Open: Unrestricted
Facilities: Marked trails within the park

The National Park is noted for the presence of a rare endemic subspecies of the ringed or Saimaa seal, which in this freshwater area has long been regarded as a post-glacial faunal relict. The seal breeds in the park, but its future is insecure because of the threat of water pollution.

The forest mammal fauna is typical of southern Finland and includes the elk. Among the forest birds are the tree pipit, garden warbler, willow warbler, greenish warbler, spotted flycatcher, willow tit, golden oriole and chaffinch. On the lake there are mallard, goosanders, black-throated divers, herring and common gulls, and about four pairs of ospreys, which breed here most years.

Petkeljärvi National Park
Part of the region of Carelia, a complex area of eskers and lakes close to the Russian border in southern Finland, now lies within the Petkeljärvi National Park. Its landscape is one of wild scenic beauty, with open pine heathland, small bogs, marshy meadows and lakes, which cover about half its total area. The eskers, typically long winding ridges of coarse sand and gravel, here form small hills. They were laid down by meltwater streams within glaciers during the last Ice Age and are common throughout Scandinavia. The park was the scene of military activities during the Second World War, when some damage was done to the landscape by trench digging.

The vegetation ranges from barren pine forests with juniper, heather, bilberry, cowberry, crowberry, wavy hair-grass and lichens to peatlands with ledum, dwarf birch, *Vaccinium microcarpum* and cotton-grass.

The fauna is very similar to that found elsewhere in wilderness areas, with the mountain hare, fox and various small mammals on the alpine heathland. Pine marten and lynx are found in the forests. The bird fauna includes the common redstart, Siberian tit, siskin, crested tit, willow tit, three-toed woodpecker and the parrot crossbill.

Liesjärvi National Park
The wooded National Park of Liesjärvi, in the sparsely populated region of the Tammela uplands, takes its name from a lake, part of whose shores are within the park. Although most of this area of Finland is settled, the region in which the National Park is situated has never had many permanent inhabitants because its soils are rather infertile.

The park has extensive forests of pine and spruce as well as peat bogs, lake shoreline and offshore islands. In forests the ground cover is provided by such plants as bilberry, crowberry, common cow-wheat, chickweed wintergreen and the small reed *Calamagrostis arundinacea*.

The mammal fauna is similar to that found elsewhere in southern Finland, but also includes the elk, badger, mountain hare and pine marten. Among the breeding birds are goldcrests, pied and spotted flycatchers, redwings, siskins and great spotted woodpeckers. A beautiful old farm, now abandoned, is incorporated in the National Park and is managed by the warden.

DENMARK

*Denmark is entirely low-lying, gently undulating
rather than flat, with Ejer Bavnehog (173 metres) in
mid-Jutland the highest point. The countryside is
mostly intensively farmed – as much as 70 per cent
of the land is agricultural – with the emphasis on
dairy and bacon production. The west coast of
Jutland is fringed by an almost continuous series of
sand dunes, often planted with conifers and in
many places enclosing lagoons.*

After many centuries of settlement by man none
of the land surface, in contrast with that of Norway,
Sweden and Finland, can be described as wild and
many of the Nature Parks and nature reserves consist of landscapes which are the result of man's
activities. The exception to this is, of course,
Greenland, which as well as the Faroe Islands is
part of Danish territory.

Danish forests cover 10 per cent of the land
surface and are controlled by the Ministry of the
Environment's Forest Service, which gives special
consideration to conservation and public access.

Nature conservation in Denmark is the responsibility of the Nature Conservation Board of the
Ministry of the Environment, and is based on a
broad philosophy of long-term planning for environmental protection, including cultural, historical
and aesthetic considerations as well as the preservation of the fauna and flora.

As a part of national planning, Danish county
administrations were required in recent years to
survey the landscapes in their region and identify
those which deserved preservation. This has been
done for the whole country, including Bornholm,
and all land has been divided into three categories
according to its natural value.

In addition to the protected landscapes, there are
Nature Parks – picturesque areas open to the public
where nature is also protected – and nature reserves.
However, levels of protection within each of the
reserves and parks differ.

Protected sites are selected by the county
administrations either on their own initiative or else
on the recommendation of a responsible person or
body such as the Danish Nature Conservation
Society. Where the proposed nature reserve is not
purchased, a conservation order may be made by a
special court presided over by a judge. The area
remains private property and compensation, if any,
is decided by the court.

Hunting is generally allowed in protected areas,
game animals – mainly wild boar and deer – being
carefully managed for sport. Danish law gives total
protection to all birds of prey and to many waterfowl, but protection for wild birds in general is not
as comprehsive as in other countries.

HØJE MØN The steep cliffs of Møns Klint were created by
westward-moving glaciers during the last Ice Age.

DENMARK

Though based on a platform of relatively young rocks, Denmark owes its landforms and character to an even more recent event – the Pleistocene Ice Age. Jutting out into the Skagerrak from its narrow junction with the North German Plain, the Jutland Peninsula has a ragged leaf-like appearance. Its west coast is made up of sand-bars and dunes backed by lagoons and fenland, giving way to sandy soils in the interior. The eastern part is thickly covered with glacial deposits, forming a rolling landscape of low hills greatly modified by the action of its rivers and even more so by man, for most of the country is under intensive agriculture. Consequently very little "original" vegetation remains excepting for the west-coast salt marshes and scattered patches of inland heath.

Two distinct landscape regions exist in Jutland. South of Nissum Fjord (just northwest of Ulfborg) on the west coast, and west of a line running down the backbone of the peninsula, glacial outwash material has been deposited around a number of older low-lying plateaux to form a series of "hill-islands". To the north and east of the line, glacially deposited boulder clay has produced a region of low hills with generally much more fertile soils.

The island archipelago of eastern Denmark is likewise largely a product of the retreating ice-sheets. Low hills and moraines provide the only relief, although here man's influence is even more obvious: more than 1.3 million of Denmark's 5 million people live in the capital Copenhagen on the main island of Zealand.

PARK/RESERVE	SIZE (km²)	DESCRIPTION	MAP REF.	PAGE NO.
SKAGEN	43.0	Nature Reserve. Area of fine dune formations at the tip of Jutland.	B1/C1	66
HANSTED	38.0	Nature Reserve. Heathland and dune overlying ancient raised sea-bed. Rich flora of diatoms in nearby lakes.	A2	67
FLYNDERSØ & STUBBERGÅRD SØ	167	Landscape Protection Area. Steep-sided glaciated valley. Extensive heathlands. Oak forest on outwash plains.	A3	67
GUDENÅENS ETC.	6.5	Nature Park. Attractive landscape of meadows, woodland, heaths and lakes. Unique aquatic insect fauna.	B4	67
TIPPERNE VAERNENGENE-NYMINDESTRØM	352	Nature Reserve. Peninsulas formed by sand deposition. Freshwater marsh vegetation predominates. Large population of pink-footed geese. Large numbers of birds breed in the marshes and meadows.	A4	68
SKALLINGEN	23.0	Nature Reserve. Sandy beach with marsh on inland side. Mostly covered with dune vegetation.	A4	68
RØMØ	121	Nature Park. Enormous sandbanks with dunes to the west and tidal flats and meadows on the east.	A4	68
VADEHAVET	1055	Bird Sanctuary. Open marsh, considered to be a most important resting and feeding area for water birds.	A5	69
MOLS BJERGE	27.5	Nature Park. Charming landscape of hills, wide valleys and woodlands. Interesting flora and invertebrate fauna.	C3	70
RANDS FJORD	10.7	Nature Park. Freshwater-lake system. Varied habitats attracting diverse range of birds.	B4	71
FYNS HOVED		Nature Reserve. Narrow promontory with sea birds nesting on steep cliffs. Southern European steppe plants.	C4	71
HINDSHOLM		Nature Park. Triangular peninsula having attractive cultivated landscape. Old deciduous woodland.	C4	71
DRAVED SKOV	2.5	Nature Reserve. Ancient woodland of great biological interest, lying between two drained bogs. Rare flora.	A5	71
NORDSAMSØ & STAVNSFJORD		Nature Reserve and Bird Sanctuary. Area of undulating sand and gravel moraines.	C3/C4	72
NEKSELØ	2.16	Nature Reserve. Narrow island with landscape of meadows and ponds. Uncommon flora and fauna.	C4	72
SELSØ-LINDHOLM-BOGNAES	19.9	Landscape Protection Area. Hilly region of bays, islands and peninsulas. Breeding locality for water birds.	D4	72
FARUM	50.0	Nature Park. Group of scattered protected areas lying in broad valley of marsh and meadowland.	D4	73
ESRUM SØ & GRIBSKOV	72.8	Nature Reserve. Lake with rich aquatic life.	D3	73
TYSTRUP-BAVELSE SØERNE	37.5	Nature Park. Picturesque landscape of forests, fens and springs set in glaciated valley. Bird breeding locality.	C4/D4	74
ULVSHALE & NYORD	11.3	Nature Park. Peninsula formed of flint stones. Hilly landscape in Nyord, now mainly cultivated.	D4/D5	74
HØJE MØN	20.9	Nature Park. Series of parallel crests created by action of glaciers. Beech forest and dry meadow.	D5	74
NORDBORNHOLM	25.0	Nature Park. Area of gneiss and granite bedrocks with series of rift valleys. Interesting rock plants.	D1	74

SKAGEN A beautiful duneland reserve at the northern tip of Jutland. It is a superb place for observing bird migration.

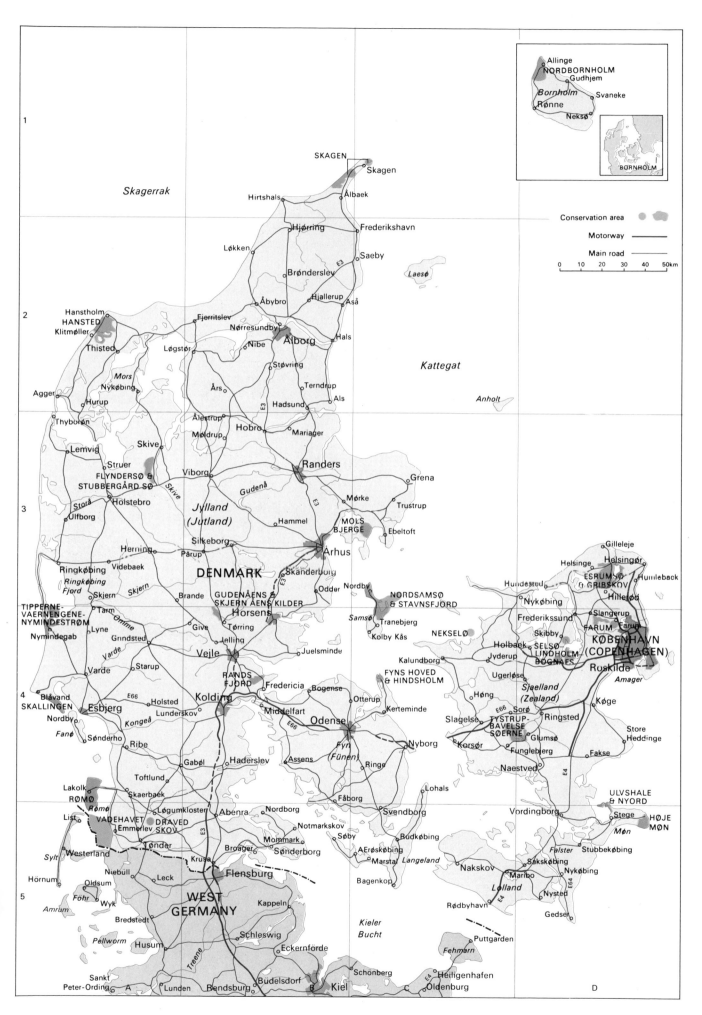

HANSTED

Heath
Marsh
Agricultural land
Woodland
Sand dunes
Nature reserve

0 2 4km

Roshage
Hansted
Hamborg
Hanstholm
Nytorp
Gråbjerg
Ræhr
Gammelsande
Risbjerge
Savbjerg
Sårup
HANSTED
NATURE · RESERVE
Blegsø
Tormål
Bøjebakke
Tved Plantage
Højrimmer
Tved
Klitmøller
Isbjerg
Nors
Vilsbøl Plantage
Hinding
Nors Sø
Nors
Savværk
Agerholm
Vandet Sø
NØRRE VORUPØR 9
THISTED 8
THISTED 5

Skagen Nature Reserve

At the extreme northern tip of Jutland – a slender peninsula formed of sand deposits pointing to the northeast – lies Skagen Nature Reserve. The area has a great variety of dune formations, which geologically are divided into three types – transverse dunes, occurring along the west coast; crescent-shaped dunes, formed from blow-outs, with concave sides facing the wind; and barchans, which are also crescent-shaped and migrate with their convex sides in the direction of the prevailing wind. One of these dunes, Rabjerg Mile, is the largest in Denmark and is still moving. Another interesting feature of Skagen is a type of stone field in which all the stones have been polished and rounded by wind-blown sand. In addition to the usual dune vegetation, there are heathland plants and in some areas conifers have been planted to stabilize the sand.

Skagen's greatest interest is biological; it is an excellent vantage point for watching bird migration. The best time of the year is from early April to early June. Thrushes and crows, which are particularly numerous, are the first to arrive, followed by the birds of prey from the end of April up until early June. Migratory movements vary considerably and the most interesting species are probably seen when the wind is from the east.

GREYLAG GOOSE *below* Its pale forewings are revealed in flight.

SKAGEN *below* The sands of Skagen present a fascinating miscellany of dune structures, which are second only in interest to the reserve's bird life.

Early morning coastal migration is best observed from the north coast, and a small sandy hill called Flagbakken on the west side of Skagen town is the place for watching the migration of birds of prey.

A small wood at the tip of this point is a favourite resting spot for small birds. A great variety of rare species has been recorded. The long list of birds of prey includes common, rough-legged and honey buzzards, red kite, marsh harrier, hen-harrier, sparrowhawk, hobby and merlin.

Hansted Nature Reserve
A large area of old dune and heathland in western Jutland, between Hanstholm in the north and Klitmøller in the south, forms the Hansted Nature Reserve. It was first established as a game reserve in 1930 and was greatly enlarged to its present size in 1937.

Together with other protected areas close by, Hansted is particularly well known for its interesting birdlife. The reserve consists mainly of an area of raised sea bed, which is now covered with dunes. Fossil sea cliffs of chalk can be clearly seen in the northern part of the area and also by the lakes of Sokland, Blegsø and Tormål. The lakes are particularly interesting because they are still natural and unpolluted. They are mostly poor in nutrients with clear water and comparatively little

aquatic vegetation, except for an extraordinarily rich flora of diatoms – small single-celled plants with silica skeletons. The species of diatom found here is rare elsewhere in Denmark and, as it is normally found either in arctic regions or in the Alps, it may be an ice-age relict. Possibly, however, it is here simply because lakes of this nature are themselves rare in Denmark.

Many water birds visit the lakes during migration, numbers sometimes reaching to over 1000. They include the greylag, bean and pink-footed geese, teal, tufted duck, red-breasted merganser, goosander, smew and whooper and Bewick swans. The breeding birds are equally interesting and the nature reserve is famous for its population of golden plovers and wood sandpipers. But perhaps the most remarkable bird is the crane: it first nested here in 1957 and a pair has arrived each year since. In autumn several cranes may be seen on the reserve as small flocks of young gather before migrating.

Flyndersø og Stubbergård Sø Landscape Protection Area
In northern Jutland, about 10 kilometres southwest of the town of Skive, a beautiful glaciated valley with two lakes, Flynder and Stubbergård, has been made a Landscape Protection Area. A good example of the steep-sided glaciated valleys sometimes described as "tunnel" valleys, it has many kettle holes – depressions formed by isolated blocks of ice which melted after the ice-sheets retreated. It is thought that each of these lakes is really a series of linked kettle holes.

On either side of the valley are extensive heathlands, some covered with oak forest, which have developed on outwash plains, made up of fine material, mostly sand and gravel, brought down by glacial meltwater.

Gudenåens og Skjern Åens Kilder Nature Park
In the centre of Jutland, in the Gudenåens and Skjern Åens Kilder Nature Park, Denmark's two largest rivers have their sources only 200 metres apart in the same valley. The Gudenå rises at the foot of a small hill and runs southeast to its outfall at Randers. The Skjern, rising in a swamp, at first flows northwestwards, then westward through a series of lakes, some of which are protected. Because there are many springs in this steep-sided glacial valley, the rivers build up a large quantity of water in a short distance and the valley is known for its numerous water mills. The springs themselves have a rich aquatic insect fauna, unique in Denmark and thought to be an ice-age relict.

Although not natural, the landscape is nevertheless a most attractive mosaic of meadows, woodlands, fields, heath and lakes. The plant life is complex, and its most outstanding feature is an extensive oak scrub – the largest of its kind in Denmark.

1 SKAGEN
Information: Skagen Turistkontor, Sct. Laurentiivej 18, 9990 Skagen
Access: from SKAGEN
Open: Unrestricted
Facilities: Hotels and camp sites within the reserve. Bird observatory

2 HANSTED
Information: Hanstholm Turistkontor, Centervej 31, 7730 Hanstholm
Access: from HANSTHOLM or KLITMØLLER
Open: Closed to the public between April 15 and 16 to protect breeding birds. Unrestricted access during the remaining part of the year except to areas of rushes and reeds
Facilities: Coastal track runs from Hansted Nature Reserve past Hanstholm-reservatet

3 FLYNDERSØ OG STUBBERGÅRD SØ
Information: Skive Turistkontor Østerbro 7, 7800 Skive
Access: from Sevel, 15km SW of SKIVE
Open: Unrestricted but visitors must keep to footpaths
Facilities: Footpaths within the protected area

4 GUDENÅENS OG SKJERN ÅENS KILDER
Information: Vejle Turistkontor, Havnegade 1, 7100 Vejle
Access: from TØRRING
Open: Unrestricted
Facilities: Barge path along the W bank of the Gudenå

Tipperne-Vaernengene-Nymindestrøm Nature Reserve

About 300 years ago, Ringkøbing Fjord, on the west coast of Jutland, was wide open to the sea, but since then a coastal sand-bar has formed cutting off the entrance. Sand, continuing to drift over the bar into the fjord, has now formed the peninsulas of Tippersande and Vaernsande, which are today vegetated and are valuable grazing areas.

Cut-off from the sea, Ringkøbing Fjord became a freshwater lake. However, an inlet cut through the sand-bar to allow fishing boats to move in and out also allows small amounts of salt water to flow back into the fjord, creating brackish conditions. When still open to the sea the dominant vegetation on Tipperne was saltmarsh with glasswort, mud rush, sea aster and sea milkwort. Today the vegetation is nearer that of a freshwater marsh than a saltmarsh.

In places where until 1950 hay was still cut annually, much of the nutrient salts have been washed out and the soil has become acid, so that cross-leaved heath, crowberry, common cotton-grass as well as many sedges grow.

Apart from the northern part of Tipperne Vaerne, which is now a bird sanctuary and fully protected, hunting is still actively pursued on the marshes to the south. After haymaking had been abandoned on the reserve, the grass grew longer and some of the colonial nesting birds such as black-headed gulls, sandwich terns and avocets disappeared. Haymaking was reintroduced in 1972 and the shorter grass is encouraging some of the birds to return, particularly pink-footed geese, which may be seen in flocks of up to 10,000 – most of the Spitzbergen breeding population.

With the change to almost fresh water there has been a considerable increase in the number of mallard, shoveler, teal, garganey, mute swan, common snipe, red-breasted merganser and coot. The breeding bird population is also considerable, and includes sandpipers, gulls, and waders such as the black-tailed godwit, ruff, avocet and Sandwich tern. Meadow-nesting birds such as the lapwing, avocet, oystercatcher and redshank are all present.

Skallingen Nature Reserve

The Vesterhavet, extending along the south-west coast of Jutland from just north of Esbjerg, south to the German border, is in fact a continuation of the German Wadden Sea and has many of the same characteristics. It is a very important wildlife area and contains several protected areas, among them Skallingen Nature Reserve.

Occupying a peninsula northwest of Esbjerg, the reserve consists of a wide sandy beach with a marsh on the inland side, in all about 3 to 4 kilometres broad. The whole area is morphologically very young and has probably developed during the last 350 years; it is still continuing to grow on the inland side, in

TEAL – a dabbling duck which feeds by sifting waterweeds and seeds from the water's surface, occasionally "upending" in deeper water.

Ho Bay. A vast area is covered with typical dune vegetation, and on the wetter east side valuable summer grazing meadows have developed for large herds of cattle. In the north, old scrubby oak trees, which originally grew on moraine soils have during the centuries become buried in the dunes, and now have only the tops of their trunks and main branches projecting above the sand.

Skallingen's main interest as part of the vast Vesterhavet marshland is as a feeding and resting place for migratory birds – pink-footed geese, Kentish plovers, curlews, bar-tailed godwits, greenshanks, spotted redshanks, dunlins, curlew-sandpipers and eiders, which in autumn sometimes number as many as 10,000.

Rømø Nature Park

In the great offshore wetland of Vesterhavet, which stretches from Esbjerg on the west coast of Jutland south to the German border, lies a series of islands running from Fanø in the north, south to the German island of Sylt. In the middle of this chain lies the island Nature Park of Rømø, an enormous sand-bank which is continuing to grow in size and may eventually link up with the sand islands to the north and south.

On the west is an area of vast sand dunes with a forebeach running from north to south offshore and reaching a breadth of from 2 to 4 kilometres. On the east side, tidal flats merge into coastal meadows, which are flooded in stormy weather providing a most

**1 TIPPERNE-
VAERNENGENE-
NYMINDESTRØM**
Information: Skjern
Turistkontor, Banegårdspladsen,
6900 Skjern
Access: from NYMINDEGAB
Open: Tipperne – open Sundays,
from April 1 to July 30 between
0500–1000 and from August 1
to March 31 between 1000–
1200
Facilities: Museum at
Nordladen. Marked footpaths.
Observation tower on Tipperne

2 SKALLINGEN
Information: Oksbøl
Turistkontor, Kirkegade 3, 6840
Oksbøl
Access: from Ho, 8km E of
BLÅVAND
Open: Unrestricted
Facilities: Camp sites within
the reserve

3 RØMØ
Information: Rømø-Skaebaek
Turistkontor, Havnebyvej 30,
Tvismark, 6791 Kongsmark
Access: from SKAERBAEK
Open: Unrestricted

4 VADEHAVET
Information: Rømø, Skaebaek
Turistkontor, Havnebyvej 30,
Tvismark, 6791 Kongsmark
Access: from EMMERLEV
Open: Jordsand is closed to the
public. Access to the remaining
area is unrestricted but
dangerous because of tidal
movements

interesting and valuable habitat for wild birds.

Extensive reed beds grow in the shallower waters, mostly on the west coast, as on the lake of Lakolk, and extend on to marshy land, where birds such as the marsh and Montagu's harrier breed. As the grasslands are grazed by cattle and sheep, the grass is always fairly short and provides an ideal breeding habitat for black-tailed godwit, avocet, and ruff.

The new causeway which crosses the saltings and marshes from the mainland is an excellent place from which to see birds. Built between 1939 and 1948 it replaces the ferry connection between Rømø and the mainland. On either side of the causeway there are many dykes built both to divert the salt water and to encourage the growth of plants which trap silt so that eventually the land can be reclaimed for agriculture.

At low tide when extensive areas of marsh are exposed, and particularly during migration periods, many thousands of birds come down to feed on mussels, marine worms and other creatures. It is possible to see velvet scoters, teal, pintail, wigeon, shoveler, golden plover, grey plover, curlew, whimbrel, redshank, greenshank, bar-tailed godwit, purple sand-piper, curlew-sandpiper and avocet.

Vadehavet Bird Sanctuary
The Vadehavet, extending from the German border north to the large offshore island of Rømø, is a continuation of the German Wadden Sea. It consists of open marsh protected, south of Emmerlev Klev, by a new

MONTAGU'S HARRIER This bird of prey has a characteristic hunting technique, flying low in a leisurely glide before seizing its prey. The male passes food to the female while both are in the air.

dyke built along the landward edge. To the north, between Emmerlev Klev and Hjerp-stad, marsh is absent and the coastline is bordered by a low cliff. The area forms the largest bird sanctuary in Denmark and is now regarded as one of the most important resting and feeding areas for duck, geese and wading birds throughout the whole of Scandinavia.

The marshes are an important moulting area for shelduck. Mallard, wigeon, teal and shoveler congregate to roost in large numbers, sometimes reaching 150,000, and eiders and scoters are very common. Immense numbers of wading birds appear, particularly during the migration periods, and both dark- and pale-bellied brent, as well as pink-footed, geese roost in the area.

South of Rømø the small sandy island of Jordsand is a favourite place for male eiders, which, having left their incubating females, fly to Jordsand to moult their summer plumage. The island and the marshes around it form a nature reserve of 10,600 hectares, consisting mostly of shallow water areas which dry out at low tide. Even though the greatest tide is no more than 2 metres above mean sea level, in stormy weather the whole island is flooded.

The principal breeding bird on Jordsand is the herring gull. Its predatory habits keep down the numbers of other species, such as oystercatchers which attempt to nest here.

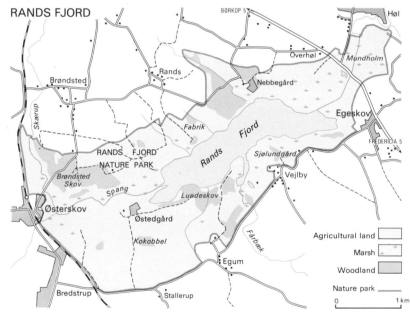

RANDS FJORD

(Map labels: BØRKOP 5, Høl, Overhøl, Mundholm, Rands, Nebbegård, Brøndsted, Egeskov, Skærup, FREDERICIA 5, Fabrik, Fjord, RANDS FJORD NATURE PARK, Rands, Sjølundgård, Brøndsted Skov, Vejlby, Spang, Østerskov, Lundeskov, Østedgård, Kokobbel, Fårbæk, Egum, Bredstrup, Stallerup)

Agricultural land

Marsh

Woodland

Nature park

0 ——— 1 km

Mols Bjerge Nature Park

In the eastern part of Jutland on the Djursland Peninsula, which juts out into the Kattegat, lies a charming landscape of hills, wide valleys and woodlands, mostly of coniferous plantations. A portion of this area, between the two broad embayments of Kalø and Ebeltoft, on the southern coast, is now protected and constitutes the Mols Bjerge Nature Park.

The land was formed during the last part of the Ice Age. After the glaciers had retreated northwards, leaving Jutland ice-free, there followed a period with higher temperatures, after which the climate worsened and ice returned. This time the ice pushed into Jutland from the southeast. The two bays were formed by parallel glaciers, which, as they retreated, deposited material between them that today forms the Mols Bjerge.

Much evidence remains of ancient man throughout the area and there are several Bronze Age burial mounds. With sheltered access from the two bays, occupation by man has probably been more or less continuous over the last 5000 years, and it was only quite recently, during the post-war period, that farming on the area's rather poor soil was abandoned. The former cultivated land is now reverting to heathland, and in order to maintain its open character the managers of the Nature Park have experimented with Greenland sheep and Galloway cattle, which are hardy enough to live on the relatively poor vegetation and remain out on the hillsides throughout the winter.

The sandy heathlands have a number of plants characteristic of this arid habitat, and a total of about 600 species of flowering plants has been recorded. Some of the hills are rocky and have never been cultivated or grazed effectively, so that deciduous trees have been able to grow. Forest also occurs on the slopes of the old shoreline in the north, merging into wetter grasslands which are still being farmed.

One of the most interesting invertebrates is the rare spider *Eresus niger*, which is found in only two localities in Denmark. It excavates a burrow in the sand and in the spring the male – a spectacular animal, bright red with black spots – emerges in search of a female.

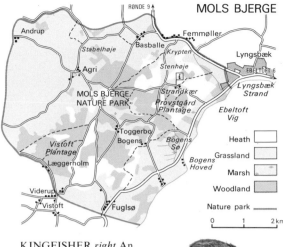

1 MOLS BJERGE
Information: Ebeltoft
Turistkontor, Torvet 9, 8400
Ebeltoft
Access: from Femmøller, 9km
NW of EBELTOFT
Open: Unrestricted
Facilities: Information centre
near the inn "Molskroen" and
at the Øvre Strandkaer farm.
Nature trail

2 RANDS FJORD
Information: Fredericia
Turistkentor, Axeltorv, 7000
Fredericia
Access: from Vejlby, 8km
NW of FREDERICIA
Open: Unrestricted except for
the outermost part of the
original fjord which is closed to
visitors
Facilities: Nature trail

**3 FYNS HOVED &
HINDSHOLM**
Information: Odense
Turistkontor, Rådhuset, 500
Odense C.
Access: 21km NW of
KERTEMINDE
Open: Unrestricted
Facilities: Footpaths within the
reserve

4 DRAVED SKOV
Information: Tønder
Turistkontor, Østergade 2 A,
6270 Tønder
Access: 5km S of
LØGUMKLOSTER
Open: Unrestricted except for
several protected areas where
research is continuing
Facilities: Footpaths within the
reserve

KINGFISHER *right* An
unmistakeable but elusive
bird, it is usually seen as a
flash of colour along the
river bank.

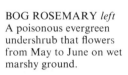

BOG ROSEMARY *left*
A poisonous evergreen
undershrub that flowers
from May to June on wet
marshy ground.

Rands Fjord Nature Park

In southeast Jutland, not far from the town of
Vejle lies the small Rands Fjord, which became land-locked during the last century and
has since gradually changed to a freshwater
lake. The fjord is connected to the sea by a
canal, on either side of which meadows and
marshes with reed beds occupy areas of the
original floor of the old fjord.

One of the interesting birds breeding in this
part of the Nature Park is the bearded tit.
This species is confined to reed beds and, with
its long black "moustaches" down either side
of its throat, its long tail, and ringing call,
like the sound of two pebbles being knocked
together, it is unmistakable.

The lake itself is an important resting place
for wild duck, particularly mallard and teal;
there are greylag geese, Canada geese and
mute swans, and along the lake shore the
heron and the common sandpiper can be seen.

The fjord is situated in the broad elbow-
valley of the River Spang, which extends with
its wooded and scrub-covered slopes right
across the peninsula southward between the
Vejle and Kolding fjords. The variety of
habitats enables many interesting birds to live
in the valley – nightingales in scrubby areas,
snipe in the marshes and the kingfisher and
grey wagtail, which are attracted by fast-
running water, along the River Spang. The
raven also breeds in the park. This species has
increased in recent years all over southern
Jutland, perhaps, as has been suggested,
because the destruction of foxes to control the
spread of rabies in the area has increased their
food supply.

Fyns Hoved Nature Reserve and Hindsholm Nature Park

Situated on the north side of the large island
of Fyn, between Jutland and Zealand, the
Nature Park of Hindsholm covers most of a
triangular peninsula, with hills running in
parallel from north to south.

The peninsula, which was once itself an
island, has an attractive cultivated landscape,
with small fields enclosed by stone walls and
hedges. It has charming villages, particularly
that of Viby with its thatched half-timbered
houses, and several manor houses, such as
Scheelenborg in the north and Hverringe in
the south, which is attractively surrounded by
woodland. At Bjornens Krat there is an
interesting shrubland of hawthorn, hazel and
blackthorn, and on the small island of Romsø,
which has not been cultivated since 1960, lies
a fine old deciduous woodland. Excellent
views can be had from Måle Bakka, the highest
point, no more than 36 metres above sea level,
and also from Baesbanke. The hills are probably lateral moraines deposited by glaciers
during the last Ice Age.

In the north, Fyns Hoved Nature Reserve,
at the end of such a moraine, is an interesting
place for seabirds, particularly black guillemots, which here nest on steep cliffs formed
by coastal erosion. Being a narrow promontory, it is a good viewing point for migratory
birds, both land and water.

Draved Skov Nature Reserve

Ancient woodlands are rare in Denmark and
the Draved wood, in the southern part of
Jutland, is therefore an area of great biological importance. The region has a remarkable history. It is claimed that the woodland
has been relatively undisturbed for thousands
of years, having never been exploited for
forestry, with very little grazing and only
occasional felling. The trees are mainly small-
leaved lime, although in places there is a rich
mixture of ash, oak, elm and aspen.

The history of the wood has been investigated by scientists for a number of years to
trace the development and natural changes
which have taken place since man first
occupied this area of Denmark. The woodland
is situated on a flat, rather wet area between
two former bogs, the Kongsmose in the west
and the Grabjergmose in the east. Both were
once part of the old Forest of Flor and have
now largely been drained and cultivated.

A colony of black terns nests in the
unreclaimed part of Kongsmose, which still
has typical bog plants such as bog rosemary
and a number of interesting plants rather rare
elsewhere in Denmark. The presence of these
bogs is vital to the study of the history of the
wood; tree pollen has been preserved for
thousands of years in the accumulated peat,
and it is possible by taking core samples and
examining the pollen grains contained within
them to trace the changes in vegetation and
climate since post-glacial times.

DENMARK

Nordsamsø og Stavnsfjord Nature Reserve and Bird Sanctuary

The northern part of the large island of Samsø, together with Stavnsfjord and many small islands lying about 25 kilometres south of Mols Bjerge Nature Park, make up the Nordsamsø and Stavnsfjord Nature Reserve. Samsø, formed at the end of the last Ice Age, when the glaciers moved in from the southeast, was originally two islands. When the islands became joined together a flat sandy area, Nordby Heath, was formed between them and is now planted with conifers.

The old northern part of the island is very undulating, and consists of sand and gravel moraines which were laid down by glaciers and end in steep slopes with water-eroded valleys on the Jutland side. Although much of the land is cultivated there are also large areas of grassland with a distinctive flora, similar to that found to the east and south and found here possibly because the area lies in a region with one of the lowest rainfalls in the country.

The Stavnsfjord, with its many islands, formed from the top of a drowned moraine, is a bird sanctuary. Although there is no access to the islands, many of which are uninhabited, a good view of the birdlife can be obtained from the Langør Peninsula to the north and from Besser Rev – a narrow sandbar which protects the fjord on its eastern side. The reserve's principal breeding birds are the eider, which are here more numerous than anywhere else in Denmark – 2000 pairs, breeding mainly on the small islands – and the lesser and greater black-back gulls.

COOT Males fight frequently in defence of their territory and will chase off other species in the breeding season.

Nekselø Nature Reserve

Off the northwest coast of Zealand, in Sejero Bay, is found a small, narrow island, Nekselø, which is a relic of a marginal glacial moraine, with a north–south ridge. The west coast of the island is hilly with a heathy vegetation, while on the east the land is flat and is protected by the westerly hills against the prevailing wind. The landscape consists of meadows and small ponds, with a few deciduous woods. Although islands often have a poorer flora and fauna than the mainland, Nekselø has many uncommon plants and a rich insect fauna and birdlife.

Selsø-Lindholm-Bognaes Landscape Protection Area

About 30 kilometres west of Copenhagen, near the southern end of the 40-kilometre-long Roskilde Fjord, lies a hilly, morainic country with many bays, small islands and peninsulas projecting into the fjord. The portion of this region covered by the Landscape Protection Area lies in three parts; an

BLACK WOODPECKER The largest and most distinctive of European woodpeckers.

NORDSAMSØ *left* The northern part of the island of Samsø consists of sand and gravel hills of glacial origin.

1 NORDSAMSØ OG STAVNSFJORD
Information: Samsø Turistkontor, Langgade 32, 8791 Tranebjerg
Access: from NORDBY or TRANEBJERG
Open: Unrestricted except for Stavnsfjord which is closed to the public
Facilities: Footpaths within the reserve

2 NEKSELØ
Information: Kalundborg Turistkontor, Volden 12, 4400 Kalundborg
Access: by boat from Havnsø, 14 km NW of JYDERUP
Open: Unrestricted

3 SELSØ-LINDHOLM-BOGNAES
Information: Roskilde Turistkontor, Fondens Bro 3, 4000 Roskilde
Access: from ROSKILDE or SKIBBY
Open: Lindholm is closed to the public. Access to the remaining areas is unrestricted but visitors must keep to the footpaths

4 FARUM
Information: Hillerød Turistkontor, Torvet 1, 3400 Hillerød
Access: from FARUM or SLANGERUP
Open: Unrestricted
Facilities: Footpaths within the reserve

5 ESRUM SØ OG GRIBSKOV
Information: Hillerød Turistkontor, Torvet 1, 3400
Access: from HELSINGØR, HILLERØD or HELSINGE
Open: Unrestricted
Facilities: Footpaths within the reserve

area around Selsø Lake, the countryside around the manor of Lindholm to the west, and a larger area in the southern part of the fjord, centred on Bognaes.

Along the fjord shore are numerous meadows, several forests, mostly of beech, and many excellent habitats for water birds. Selsø Lake itself is a good breeding locality for greylag geese, mallard, mute swans and great crested grebes; in winter there are many duck, geese and swans. Birds of prey are frequently seen, particularly the buzzard and marsh harrier, and in most years sea eagles arrive in late summer to stay through the winter until late spring.

North of Selsø Lake, the remarkable Skuldlev ridge consists of layers of sand and gravel deposited by meltwater which was channelled into a steep-sided valley.

Farum Nature Park
Lying in a broad valley of marsh and meadowland, the Bure, Bastrup and Farum lakes are frequently visited, and are within easy reach of Copenhagen, about 20 kilometres to the southeast. The lakes are linked by the Mølle River, which rises between the Bure and Bastrup lakes, in a glacial valley that was originally one of the channels through which water from the melting ice of the last Ice Age reached Roskilde Fjord. The ice stopped just west of Bure Lake and Stenesknold, which, at an altitude of 57 metres, form part of the old marginal moraine.

The Nature Park is made up of a series of scattered protected areas from Farum in the east to as far as Jørlunde in the west, and many parts are inaccessible being covered by dense thickets and swamps.

Esrum Sø og Gribskov Nature Reserve
In the northern part of Zealand, Esrum, one of the largest lakes in Denmark situated between the towns of Helsingfør and Hillerød, is an important wintering area for duck and geese. Mallard, tufted duck, pochard, goldeneye, coot, goosander and great crested grebes are regularly observed, and Canada geese have also been seen. The lake is the richest in aquatic life in the whole of Denmark and has been studied in great detail by the freshwater biological laboratory at Hillerød. Reaching a depth of between 15 and 20 metres very close to its banks, there is only a narrow band of vegetation at the lake margin. It has very little water flowing in or out, and consequently there is hardly any water exchange. In such conditions pollution from sewage is always a problem and attempts are being made to divert waste away from the lake.

On the western side of the lake, Gribskov, the largest forest on the island of Zealand, is situated in a hilly morainic country dotted with small lakes and fens. The wood, mainly beech and conifers, is well worth a visit not only for its beauty but also because of the six pairs of black woodpeckers that live there. Although not numerous – this is the largest European woodpecker species and each pair needs a lot of space – they are easy to locate because of their loud drumming call.

73

TYSTRUP-BAVELSE SØERNE

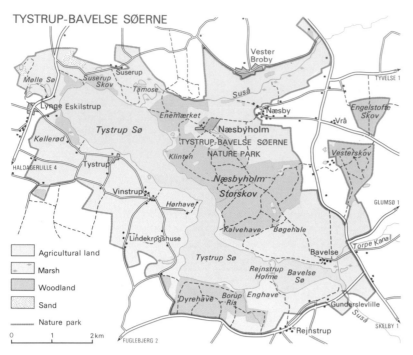

Key:
- Agricultural land
- Marsh
- Woodland
- Sand
- Nature park

0   1   2km

Tystrup-Bavelse Søerne Nature Park

In southwest Zealand the River Suså flows through a glaciated valley surrounded by hilly moraines in a picturesque landscape of forests, fields, fens and springs. Two lakes in this area, Tystrup and Bavelse, together with a portion of the surrounding countryside, form the Nature Park.

Birds breeding around the lakes include mute swans, greylag geese, great crested grebes and a number of duck species: thousands of mallard and tufted duck rest on the water during the winter. It is also a good locality for migrant birds, particularly for bean geese, teal and goldeneye. Birds of prey seen on passage include the sparrow-hawk, hen-harrier, buzzard and osprey. Sea eagles always spend some time in the area during the winter, feeding on the lake.

HØJE MØN

Key:
- Agricultural land
- Marsh
- Woodland
- Nature park

0   1   2km

Ulvshale og Nyord Nature Park

At the northwestern tip of the island of Møn, situated off the southern point of Zealand almost due south of Copenhagen, lies the Ulvshale Peninsula, formed of flintstones carried by the sea from Møn cliff and deposited as a series of parallel beach ridges. Apart from a variety of beach vegetation, Ulvshale contains oakwood heathland, and in the southwest, meadows and shallow ponds surrounded by reeds.

Most of Nyord is an old sea bed raised above sea level, with long beaches in the east and an old moraine, up to 15 metres high, in the west. It forms a hilly landscape that is now mainly cultivated. The low-lying part of the island on the old sea bed is covered with extensive meadow land and is a most interesting place for nesting birds.

Høje Møn Nature Park

The chalk bedrock of the eastern part of the island of Møn, off the southeast corner of Zealand, has been pushed up by glacier ice into more than twenty layers, seen today as a series of parallel crests 7 kilometres long on the steep cliffs of Møns Klint. This structure forms a most unusual feature in Denmark's generally flat countryside. The action of glacial ice has also left a large number of sink holes, some dry and others containing fens.

Nordbornholm Nature Park

The northern part of the island of Bornholm in the Baltic Sea, off the southeast coast of Sweden, is the only part of Denmark with a bedrock of gneiss and granite. These rocks are of several different types. The best known are the almost black Rønne granite and the reddish Hammer granite, a good example of which is exposed along the coast. The Jons Kapel is one of the most impressive formations, its cliff face bright with many different-coloured lichens. It can be reached from a steep path running along the cliff side down to the beach.

The whole of the granite area has a series of straight rift valleys that can be followed for several kilometres. One, Finnedalen, in which lies the Hammer Lake, is 2 to 3 kilometres long and has completely parallel sides. Farther inland the rock is covered by a thin layer of morainic material, with woods and heathland. In grassy areas a number of orchids grow, and other interesting plants are found in the rock crevices. The rare wild service tree is found on Hammeren, the largest roche moutonée in Denmark.

The Nature Park also contains rock engravings dating from the Bronze Age, and the ruin of Hammerhus, which was built between 1250 and 1350 and is the largest medieval castle in northern Europe.

HØJE MØN *right* The high chalk cliffs of Møns Klint form a prominent landmark on Denmark's largely featureless Baltic coast.

1 TYSTRUP-BAVELSE SØERNE

Information: Slagelse Turistkontor, Bredegade 8, 4200 Slagelse
Access: from SORØ or GLUMSØ
Open: Unrestricted
Facilities: Information chart at Hørhavenaesset car park

2 ULVSHALE OG NYORD

Information: Møns Turistkontor, Storegade 5, 4780 Stege
Access: 5km N of STEGE
Open: Unrestricted except for the northern part of Ulvshale and the Nyord meadows which are closed to visitors between March 15 and July 15
Facilities: Camp site in Ulvshale. Observation tower

3 HØJE MØN

Information: Møns Turistkontor, Storegade 5, 4780 Stege
Access: from Magleby, 14km E of STEGE
Open: Unrestricted
Facilities: Small museum at Store Klint

4 NORDBORNHOLM

Information: Bornholms Skovdistrikt, Almindingen, Åkirkeby 3720, Bornholm
Access: from ALLINGE
Open: Unrestricted
Facilities: Information charts throughout the park. Footpaths within the park

WEST GERMANY

The German Federal Republic, although somehat larger than the United Kingdom, is with 62 million inhabitants one of the most densely populated countries in Europe. Great demands are therefore made on the environment by industry, agriculture and forestry and consequently little countryside remains in a natural state. Nevertheless Germany has a long history of concern for the landscape and was the pioneer of the Nature Park concept.

Each of the German states, or Länder, has a large degree of autonomy, particularly with regard to conservation, game hunting and other environmental matters. The federal law, administered by the Federal Establishment for Vegetation Science, Nature and Landscape Protection, lays down the framework within which the Länder legislate to suit their own needs.

Conservation administration in the Länder is at three levels – state, region and district – and is backed by advice from specialist institutes and from representatives of conservation societies. Much of the research is orientated to landscape protection rather than nature conservation as such.

Because of the many pressures on the environment, no sharp line is drawn between nature conservation and other land uses such as recreation, and it is quite usual for agriculture, forestry, fishing and hunting to be permitted in the Landscape Protection Areas, Nature Parks and nature reserves.

Perhaps the most important category of protected land is the Nature Park – an area of attractive countryside, often of considerable scientific interest, which is intensively developed for outdoor recreation such as hiking, camping and boating, but is large enough to provide habitats in which a varied and rich wildlife can survive. Nature Parks are carefully sited in relation to population centres because their main function is to provide rural facilities for people rather than protection for wildlife. At the present time fifty-nine parks cover 18 per cent of the country's land surface.

Although the federal law includes provision for National Parks, only two have so far been created – the Bayerischer Wald and Berchtesgaden – both in the Bavarian Alps, with fine areas of natural forest and alpine scenery. They are well regulated and staffed, acting as large nature reserves as well as giving pleasure to many thousands of people.

Probably the best known and most widespread protected area for wildlife is the nature reserve. There are 1262 of these areas, established by special act in the state in which they are situated. The degree of protection is not as strong as German conservationists would like, because hunting is permitted and some other incompatible activities may also be allowed. Another weakness is their small average size – only 5 per cent exceed 100 hectares – which limits their capacity as effective protection areas. Nevertheless they fulfil an important function in the conservation of wildlife. A related category of protected land is the Nature Protection Park, an area which combines features of both nature reserve and Nature Park.

Nature monuments, of which the Federal Republic has about 35,000, are not described in this chapter because they are small and are not primarily concerned with wildlife. About 27,000 consist of individual trees and another 4000 are geological phenomena such as rocks and cliffs.

Another important category of protected land is the Natural Forest Reserve, selected by the Forest Service on the basis of their "naturalness" or antiquity. The aim is to preserve a representative series of forest areas which contain all types of natural forest vegetation and also examples of ancient forest management.

The only other category of protected site which should be mentioned is the wetland. These number seventeen and have been graded by international authorities, such as the International Council for Bird Protection, as of international importance and are listed by the Federal Republic.

As Germany shares a common frontier with eight other countries, international co-operation over the protection of wildlife is important. Several agreements have been reached over areas extending across frontiers, such as the German-Luxembourg Nature Park, and the proposed alpine National Park in the Berchtesgaden area, planned jointly by Bavaria and the Austrian province of Salzburg. The Wadden Sea, an internationally important wetland extending along the German, Dutch and Danish coasts is still without a conservation agreement, although its protection has been much discussed.

Most endangered plants and animal species are protected by law, but the increasing loss of wildlife habitats by agricultural, industrial and other activities is a cause for real concern. According to the "Red List" of endangered birds, sixty-four out of 242 species need effective protection on nature reserves to ensure their survival.

Voluntary conservation organizations play a significant part in advising and stimulating action to protect German wildlife; some of them, such as the Frankfurt Zoological Society of 1858, the WWF German Appeal, the German League for Bird Protection and the Bavarian League for Nature Protection, are active in raising funds for the purchase of nature reserves.

Most nature reserves are open to the public, although there may be certain restrictions, for instance in bird sanctuaries during nesting periods, and in many areas access is restricted to public footpaths. Increased pressure from tourism is causing problems, particularly in coastal areas.

BERCHTESGADEN A view across the Hintersee in West Germany's extravagantly beautiful National Park on the Austrian border.

Except where the low hills of northern Germany give rise to sea cliffs and a series of offshore islands, much of the northern coast is fringed by extensive mudflats and dune complexes, especially around the mouth of the Elbe. The North German Plain, lying to the south, is largely cultivated, and is criss-crossed by old river channels and glacial margin features that have left wet, marshy areas in their vicinity, interspersed with superficial sandy deposits in places. The geologically older Rhine uplands, dissected by the north-flowing Rhine and its tributaries, have been affected comparatively recently by volcanic activity giving rise to some spectacular gorge features. Between these hills and the Thüringer Wald and Harz Mountains to the east lies a lower region of Triassic limestones and sandstones – a rolling landscape of woodland and farmland. The city of Frankfurt-am-Main sits at the southern end of this region, in the gap between the Spessart and Taunus Mountains, an important historical link between the Rhineland and Hessen.

In the south and west the complicated, predominantly limestone geology of the pre-Alps and high Alps has been moulded by glacial erosion to produce areas of outstanding scenic splendour, with lakes, river gorges and meadows. The middle alpine slopes, in common with the Central German Mountains, carry vast, largely unmodified deciduous and coniferous forests. There is considerable seasonal variation in climate, with warm or even hot summers and very cold winters, except in areas close to the sea. Much of central and northern Germany has been modified by cultivation and industry based on minerals, but the highlands remain relatively unspoilt.

PARK/RESERVE	SIZE (km²)	DESCRIPTION	MAP REF.	PAGE NO.
NORDFRIESISCHES WATTENMEER	14.0	National Park (Proposed). Large area of mud and sand flats, islands and dunes on the Atlantic coast of Schleswig-Holstein, containing ten nature reserves. Vast numbers of waterfowl at all seasons.	B1	80
NORDEROOG	0.08	Bird sanctuary. Small island of low sand dunes surrounded by saltmarsh. Important bird-breeding site.	B1	80
NORDTEIL DES SELENTER SEES	7.05	Nature Reserve. Part of large lake, fringed by alder bog and reedbeds. Important waterfowl locality.	C1	81
AUSSENDEICH NORDKEHDINGEN	9.0	Nature Reserve. Zone of marsh and wet pasture on the River Elbe. Many feeding and breeding wildfowl species.	B1	81
OSTFRIESISCHES WATTENMEER	965	Nature Reserves. Twelve separate reserves lying in region of islands and intertidal flats on northern coast.	A1	82
DOLLART	965	Nature Reserve. Island in estuary of River Ems. Rich bird-feeding ground.	A2	82
JADEBUSEN	455.6	Nature Reserve. Large, silted marine bay with broad, grassy foreshore.	B1	83
WESTLICHE WESERMÜNDUNG	455.6	Nature Reserve. Island of Mellum and areas of sandflats and bars between the Weser and Elbe estuaries.	B1	83
LÜNEBURGER HEIDE	197.4	Nature Reserve. Region of heathland with scattered woodland and marshy areas.	C2	85
HEILIGES MEER	0.55	Nature Reserve. Forest and moorland containing several small lakes formed through collapse of land surface.	B2	84
DÜMMER	36.0	Nature Reserve. Large lake with surrounding swamp, marsh and dunes. Important site for aquatic birds.	B2	84
DIEPHOLZER MOORNIEDERUNG	178.5	Nature and Landscape Reserves. Large area of moor and peat bog.	B2	84
STEINHUDER MEER	57.8	Nature Reserve and Landscape Protection Area. Largest lake in northern Germany. Many bird breeding species.	B2	84
RIDDAGSHAUSEN-WEDDELER TEICHGEBIET	6.5	Europa-Reserve. Series of old fish ponds. Open water, deciduous woodland, marsh and farmland. Many marsh and aquatic birds.	C2	86
WARMBERG-OSTERBERG	0.63	Nature Reserve. Area of low limestone hills with attractive flora, particularly orchids.	B3	87
MEISSNER	6.2	Nature Reserve. Mountain area encompassing scree slopes, grass and heathland plateau with trees and shrubs. Varied fauna and flora containing relict species.	C3	87
GRABURG	1.8	Nature Reserve. Limestone-mountain area with rich flora. Extensive forest.	C3	87
NORDEIFEL	1743	Nature Park. Region of old sedimentary and metamorphic rocks, dissected by deep valleys. Widespread forest. Limestone grassland with rare plants. Interesting mammal fauna.	A3	88
SIEBENGEBIRGE	42.0	Nature Park. Wooded hilly landscape. Flora with many south-European species. Diverse bird life.	A3	88
HEIDENHÄUSCHEN	1.14	Nature Reserve. Basalt peak with cliffs, scree and boulder fields. Extensive deciduous woodland.	B3	89
RHEINAUEN BINGEN-ERBACH	4.75	Nature Reserve. Series of islands in the Rhine with shallow-water areas attractive to wildfowl. Riverine woodland on south bank of river. Rare marsh plants in gravel areas.	B4	90
BAYERISCHER SPESSART	1307	Nature Park. Beautiful part of the Spessart mountains, largely woodland. Stone- and Bronze-Age remains.	B4	90
FRÄNKISCHE SCHWEIZ-VELDENSTEINER FORST	1747	Nature Park. Low mountain region with rocky peaks, steep-sided valleys and water-eroded caves. Forests of conifers and beech. Rich flora on limestone areas.	C4	91
MOHRHOF	6.8	Landscape Reserve. Large number of ponds set in a landscape of meadows, marshes and pine woodland.	C4	92
ALTMÜHLTAL	2908	Nature Park. Portion of Danube tributary-river valley, of both cultural and natural interest.	C4	92
WELTENBURGER ENGE	2.51	Nature Reserve. Impressive river-gorge with cliffs and wooded slopes.	D4	93
UNTERER INN RESERVOIRS	19.6	Nature Reserve. Two reservoirs on the River Inn together with neighbouring riverine woodland, attracting large numbers of duck and waders. Fauna includes beavers and muskrats.	D5	93
DANUBE RESERVOIRS	c.175	Nature Reserve and Landscape Protection Areas. Region of meadows, woodlands, marshes and ponds on the banks of the Danube. Several reservoirs, attracting large numbers of water birds.	C5	95
FEDERSEE	14.0	Nature Reserve. Natural wetland comprising open water and surrounding peatlands and reedbeds.	B5	95
WURZACHER RIED	13.2	Nature Reserve. Large area of peatland with forests meadows and pools. Rich flora. Interesting bird life.	C5	95
BODENSEE	7769	Nature Reserves. Several separate wetland areas on the shores of Lake Constance.	B5	95
BAYERISCHER WALD	130.8	National Park. Undulating forest-covered plateau of granite and gneiss. Large number of tree species and forest plants of interest. Remarkable fauna including many game animals.	D4	96
ISMANINGER TEICHGEBIET	9.0	Nature Reserve. Nutrient-rich reservoir and ponds with rich aquatic flora and fauna.	C5	98
TIROLER ACHEN	5.7	Bird Sanctuary. Estuarine area with sand bars, mud flats and marsh vegetation. Important resting and wintering site for many species of birds.	D5	98
BERCHTESGADEN	208	National Park. Beautiful alpine region. Flat-topped mountains of complex geology. Large area of coniferous and deciduous forest. Diverse flora and fauna.	D5	99

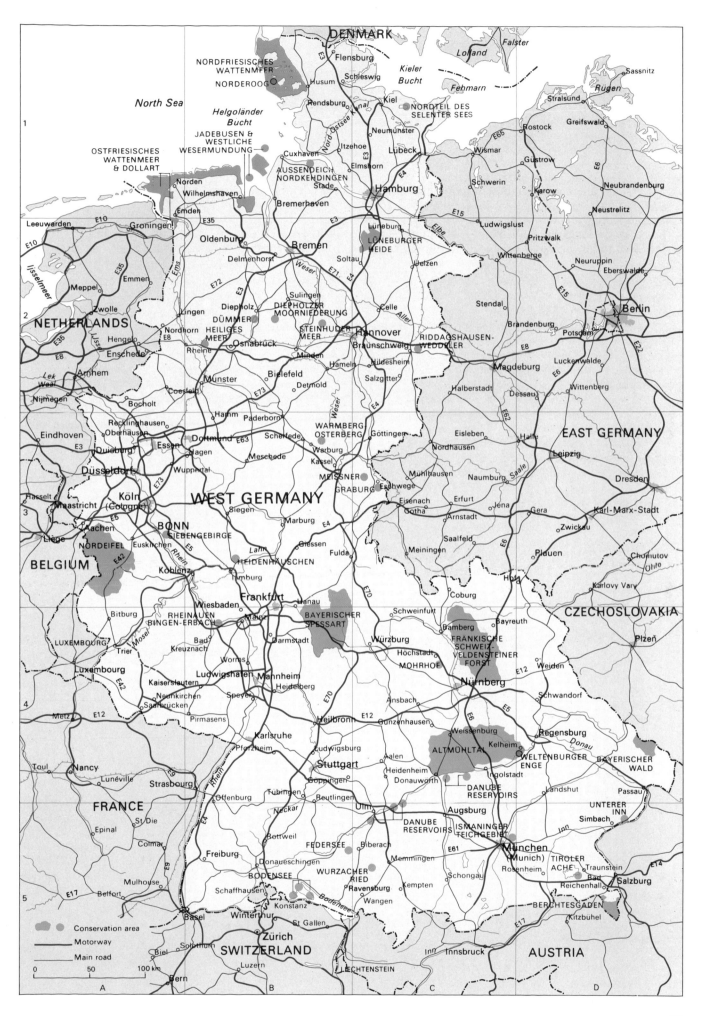

North Sea

NORDFRIESISCHES
WATTENMEER
NORDEROOG

Helgoländer
Bucht

JADEBUSEN &
WESTLICHE
WESERMÜNDUNG

OSTFRIESISCHES
WATTENMEER
& DOLLART

AUSSENDEICH
NORDKEHDINGEN

NORDTEIL DES
SELENTER SEES

DENMARK

Flensburg
Schleswig
Husum
Rendsburg
Itzehoe
Elmshorn
Stade
Cuxhaven

Kieler
Bucht

Kiel
Neumünster

Lübeck

Lofland
Falster

Sassnitz
Rügen
Stralsund

Greifswald
Rostock

Wismar
Güstrow
Schwerin
Karow

Neubrandenburg

Neustrelitz

NETHERLANDS

Leeuwarden
Groningen
Oldenburg
Delmenhorst
Bremen

Wilhelmshaven
Bremerhaven
Norden
Emden

IJsselmeer
Meppel
Emmen
Zwolle
Lingen
Nordhorn
Hengelo
Enschede
Arnhem

Diepholz
DÜMMER
HEILIGES
MEER
Osnabrück
Rheine

Hamburg

Lüneburg
LÜNEBURGER
HEIDE
Soltau
Uelzen
Celle
Aller

DIEPHOLZER
MOORNIEDERUNG
Sulingen

STEINHUDER
MEER
Hannover
Braunschweig
Minden

Ludwigslust
Pritzwalk
Wittenberge
Neuruppin
Eberswalde

Stendal
Brandenburg

Berlin
Potsdam

RIDDAGSHAUSEN-
WEDDELER

Lek
Waal
Nijmegen
Eindhoven
Duisburg
Düsseldorf

Münster
Coesfeld
Bocholt
Recklinghausen
Oberhausen
Essen
Hagen
Wuppertal

Bielefeld
Detmold
Hameln
Hildesheim
Salzgitter

Hamm
Paderborn
WARMBERG
OSTERBERG
Warburg
Kassel
Scherfede

Göttingen

Magdeburg
Halberstadt
Dessau
Wittenberg

Eisleben
Nordhausen
Halle

EAST GERMANY

Leipzig
Dresden

WEST GERMANY

MEISSNER
GRABURG

Eschwege
Eisenach
Gotha

Mühlhausen
Naumburg
Saale
Erfurt
Jena
Arnstadt
Gera

Karl-Marx-Stadt
Zwickau
Chomutov
Ohře

Hasselt
Maastricht
Aachen
Liège
BELGIUM

Köln
(Cologne)
BONN
SIEBENGEBIRGE
NORDEIFEL
Euskirchen
Koblenz

Siegen
Marburg
Giessen
Fulda
HEIDENHÄUSCHEN
Limburg

Saalfeld
Meiningen
Coburg

Plauen
Hof

Karlovy Vary

Bitburg
LUXEMBOURG
Trier
Luxembourg

RHEINAUEN
BINGEN-ERBACH
Bad
Kreuznach

Frankfurt
Wiesbaden
Mainz

Hanau
Darmstadt
BAYERISCHER
SPESSART

Würzburg
Schweinfurt
Höchstadt

Bamberg
FRÄNKISCHE
SCHWEIZ-
VELDENSTEINER
FORST

Bayreuth

CZECHOSLOVAKIA

Plzeň

Worms
Kaiserslautern
Neunkirchen
Saarbrücken
Pirmasens
Metz

Ludwigshafen
Mannheim
Heidelberg
Speyer

MOHRHOF
Ansbach
Nürnberg

Weiden
Schwandorf

Heilbronn
Gunzenhausen
Weissenburg
Regensburg
Donau
BAYERISCHER
WALD

Nancy
Toul
Lunéville
Strasbourg

Karlsruhe
Pforzheim
Ludwigsburg
Stuttgart
Göppingen
Tübingen
Reutlingen

Aalen
Heidenheim
Donauwörth
ALTMÜHLTAL
Kelheim
WELTENBURGER
ENGE

Ingolstadt
DANUBE
RESERVOIRS
Landshut
Passau

UNTERER
INN
Simbach

FRANCE

St Dié
Epinal
Colmar
Freiburg

Rottweil
Donaueschingen
BODENSEE

FEDERSEE
WURZACHER
RIED
Biberach
Memmingen
Ravensburg
Wangen

Ulm
DANUBE
RESERVOIRS
ISMANINGER
TEICHGEBIET
Augsburg
Schongau
Kempten

München
(Munich)
Rosenheim

TIROLER
ACHE
Traunstein
Bad
Reichenhall
Salzburg

Mulhouse
Belfort
Basel
Schaffhausen
Konstanz
Winterthur
St Gallen
Bodensee

Zürich
Biel
Solothurn
SWITZERLAND
Luzern
Bern

LIECHTENSTEIN

Inn
Innsbruck

BERCHTESGADEN
Kitzbühel

AUSTRIA

Conservation area
Motorway
Main road

0   50   100 km

79

REDSHANK Perhaps the most widespread wading bird in western Europe. It nests in meadows, saltmarshes and damp heathlands.

Nordfriesisches Wattenmeer National Park (Proposed)

The Wattenmeer – the German Wadden Sea – is part of an enormous area of sandflats, islands, shallow water and dunes which extends on one side into the Netherlands and on the other into Denmark. It is probably the most important single wildlife area along the coasts of Europe and as the governments of all three countries which it borders have plans for the area which conflict with wildlife conservation it has been the subject of a great deal of discussion and controversy as well as of scientific study.

It is a North Friesian section of the Wattenmeer is a proposed National Park and consists of a group of islands and marshes on the west side of Schleswig-Holstein. With its northern boundary adjacent to the Danish border it contains ten of the finest coastal reserves in Germany, and has a rich variety of unspoilt and nearly untouched ecosystems – large dune areas, sand cliffs of geomorphological interest and important colonies of sea birds.

It is a refuge for nearly a million Eurasian waterfowl, particularly huge flocks of barnacle geese, brent geese, bar-tailed godwits and knots. Some of the most outstanding breeding birds of the area are the gull-billed tern, Sandwich tern, avocet and common

eider. Flocks of shelducks collect here in their thousands for their annual moult, and the intertidal flats form excellent feeding grounds for hundreds of thousands of waders and waterfowl during their seasonal migratory movements. Of the marine mammals, the common seal is present in the largest numbers and is found throughout the entire Wattenmeer region. A few grey seals also occur.

The islands are largely undisturbed. The difficulty of access restricts the number of people travelling to the area and only a few of the islands are visited during the summer. Military firing ranges in the vicinity are interfering with the wildlife.

Norderoog Bird Sanctuary

Lying within the Nordfriesisches Wattenmeer Proposed National Park, the small island of Norderoog is a bird sanctuary, owned by a private organization, for the conservation of sea birds. It is made up of low sand dunes surrounded by saltmarsh vegetation and is important as one of the six breeding sites of the Sandwich tern in Germany. The colony, 1200 to 1500 birds, is large for a small island.

Other ground-nesting sea birds are arctic terns (1200 pairs), common terns (180–200 pairs), common gulls (10–15 pairs), herring gulls (100 pairs), black-headed gulls (1000 pairs), oystercatchers (150-200 pairs), red-

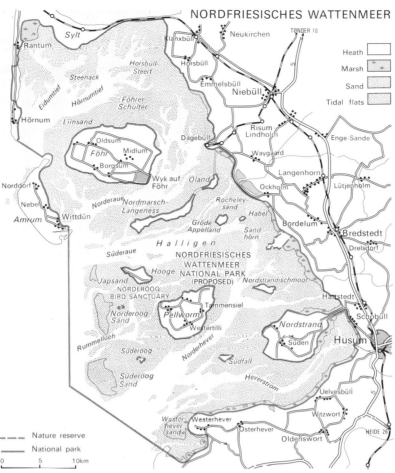

Heath
Marsh
Sand
Tidal flats

- - - Nature reserve
———— National park

0   5   10km

NORDFRIESISCHES WATTEN-
MEER *left* The island of Sylt, seen
here from the south, lies at the

northern end of the proposed
National Park – a large area on the
coast of Schleswig Holstein.

shanks (30 pairs) and ringed plovers (2–4 pairs). The Kentish plover breeds occasionally in the area and the gull-billed tern also formerly nested. The only regularly breeding ducks are the mallard and shelduck, although from time to time the eider nests on the island.

Nordteil des Selenter Sees Nature Reserve
In the hill and lake country of East Holstein is an area with three large lakes lying in a basin of glacial origin. The northern part of one of these, the Selenter See, has been a nature reserve since 1978 and has a natural shoreline varying from flat to steep, fringed in places with vast reed beds and alder bog. In some areas the nutrient content of the water is increasing due to the influx of sewage, and aquatic plants such as water-lilies and water-milfoil cover the surface. Organic matter tends to accumulate because there is little water exchange.

The lake and nearby fish ponds, together with the neighbouring lakes, are of international importance as a breeding, moulting and feeding area for waterfowl. The Selenter See is one of the most important moulting areas in Central Europe for tufted ducks, great crested grebes and gadwall. The last of these sometimes numbers 2000, a very high figure for this species of duck.

Aussendeich Nordkehdingen Nature Reserve
A narrow section of the left bank of the Elbe, 8.5 kilometres long, Aussendeich Nordkehdingen Nature Reserve lies upstream of the estuary, where the river is still tidal but where there is no longer any brackish water influence. It is an undyked marsh zone with wet pastures, remnants of a saltmarsh plant community, and river mudflats between 400 and 1000 metres broad. Extensive sedge and reed beds are found in the transition area from marsh and meadow to mudflats.

In winter large numbers of white-fronted and brent geese visit the saltings and meadows to feed. Golden plovers, Bewick's swans and several wild duck can also be numerous.

As well as the common tern and ruff, which are the commonest breeding birds, many other species breed in relatively small numbers, among them the Kentish plover, black-tailed godwit, redshank, arctic tern, gull-billed tern and dunlin.

The nearby Hullen Nature Reserve (489 hectares), with a similar bird fauna, is a breeding area for avocets and oystercatchers. In the summer the reserve is wardened and can be visited only by permission of the nature protection authorities. Both Hullen and Aussendeich Nordkehdingen suffer some disturbance from the heavy boat traffic on the Elbe and there is a good deal of pollution.

81

OSTFRIESISCHES WATTENMEER & DOLLART

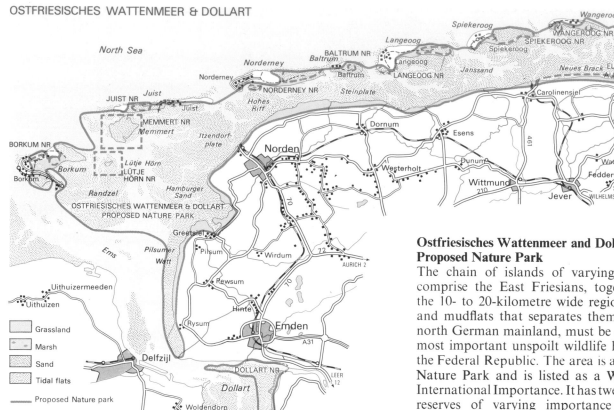

Ostfriesisches Wattenmeer and Dollart Proposed Nature Park

The chain of islands of varying size that comprise the East Friesians, together with the 10- to 20-kilometre wide region of sand and mudflats that separates them from the north German mainland, must be one of the most important unspoilt wildlife habitats in the Federal Republic. The area is a proposed Nature Park and is listed as a Wetland of International Importance. It has twelve nature reserves of varying importance for wild birds, the smallest being only 3.3 hectares.

The Dollart Nature Reserve is separate from the offshore islands and is situated in

LÜNEBURGER HEIDE

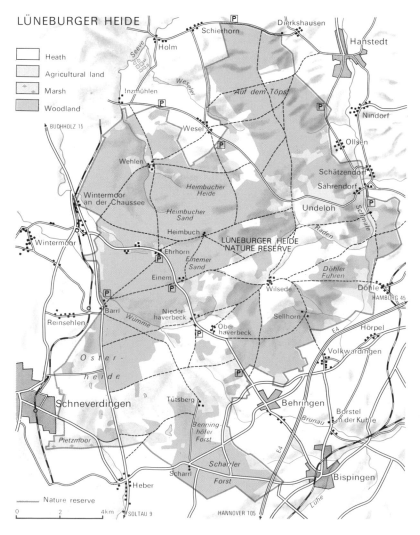

LÜNEBURGER HEIDE Heather and juniper bushes are characteristic of the heath which covers much of this North German reserve.

the estuary of the River Ems at a point where the flow of river water is reduced and extensive banks of very fine mud have formed. Not only are these mudflats very rich feeding grounds – as many as 80,000 to 100,000 birds are sometimes recorded – but being separated from the mainland by a broad band of reeds and other plants they provide shelter for many birds.

Of the East Friesian nature reserves five are of outstanding importance – three are islands, one is a sand bank and the other a strip of coastline north of Wilhelmshaven.

Lütje Hörn (1450 hectares) – an uninhabited flat, sandy island with large breeding colonies of herring and black-headed gulls. These birds are probably responsible for the poor breeding success of the oystercatcher, Kentish plover and ringed plover which have been recorded on the island.

Memmert (2200 hectares) – a rapidly growing island of dunes and sandflats. About 10,000 pairs of herring gulls breed on the reserve. Common gulls, oystercatchers, redshanks and shelduck also breed, but the terns have been driven away by the larger gulls.

Langeoog (600 hectares) – an uninhabited island with a well-formed series of dunes. This area has one of the largest herring gull breeding colonies in Germany. Among the other nesting species are shelduck, curlew, lapwing, oystercatcher, black-tailed godwit, redshank, common tern and common gull.

Spiekeroog-Ostplate (885 hectares) – a raised sand bank on the island of Spiekeroog. The reserve, which became colonized by plants in 1950, has attracted little terns, oyster-catchers, redshanks, Kentish plovers and ringed plovers as breeding species; eider ducks are also seen during the summer.

Elisabeth-Aussengroden (774.7 hectares) – a 13.8-kilometre-long strip of mainland bank south of Wangeroog with mudflats and extensive saltmarshes of salt-marsh-grass grassland and glasswort. Situated on a migration "flightway", it is visited by enormous numbers of birds of a large variety of species. Although there are relatively few breeding species a few avocets nest and the population density of redshanks is said to be the highest in Europe.

Jadebusen and Westliche Wesermündung Nature Reserves

On the southeast side of Wilhelmshaven is situated the broad bay that now forms the Jadebusen Nature Reserve. The rest of this protected area lies a little to the north, on the south side of the Weser estuary, and consists of the Mellum Reserve and two others, situated on the mudflats and sand-bars between the Weser and Elbe estuaries.

The Jadesbusen is a very large marine bay; there is little water movement and a great deal of silt is therefore deposited, causing a gradual reduction in the area of open water but an increase in the area of sand and mud-flats. In front of the dykes along the coast lies a broad margin of grassy foreshore, the Aussengroden, which provides food for pink-footed geese in the winter and a nesting habitat for 1500 pairs of redshanks in summer.

The green island of Mellum, a natural formation dating from 1875, is only 35 hectares in area and is surrounded by 3500 hectares of sand and mudflats. The island has three zones. In the north, near an area where sand is rapidly accreting by a sea wall, is a dune complex which developed in the 1960s and on which grows sand couch and lyme-grass. The central part of the island has areas of seablite, and in the south salt-marsh-grass grassland with sea sandwort and prickly saltwort is found, as well as an increasing area of Townsend's cord-grass.

The birdlife on this small island is extra-ordinarily abundant. Sometimes more than 100,000 redshanks congregate in late summer, together with curlews, grey plovers, bar-tailed godwits and many duck. In July, enormous numbers of shelduck rest on the island *en route* to their moulting grounds. Many brent geese overwinter and on the shoreline there are rock pipits, snow buntings, shore larks and twites.

Lüneburger Heide Nature Reserve

The central region of the North German Plain is a low-lying area, with extensive morainic deposits of sands and gravels. The original vegetation consisted of oak and birch. However, clearance, which began with the first settlements, has left only a very small remnant of this forest type today and in its place has developed a dwarf shrub heathland, mainly of heather, of which the Lüneburger Heide is the best remaining example in northern Germany. The area has been a nature reserve since 1910 and is owned partly by the State and partly by the private organization Verein Naturschutzpark.

Scattered throughout the reserve there are many boggy areas, where a number of interesting herbaceous plants and mosses can be found. Bilberry, bearberry, cowberry are all widespread, with cross-leaved heaths in the damper areas and grey hair-grass on the deeper sands. The heath is well known for its many junipers, which grow as erect columnar bushes and give the landscape its characteristic appearance. Many species of mammals, birds and insects have been recorded, including red and roe deer, wild boar, badgers, foxes and black grouse.

All heathlands will become tree-covered in time, but as the present pattern of heath and scattered trees provides a most varied habitat for plants and animals, the spread of trees is being prevented by the grazing of an ancient breed of sheep, which is said to be related to the mouflon and was probably brought to Germany during the Bronze Age. There are some twelve flocks on the reserve totalling approximately 5000 animals.

1 OSTFRIESISCHES WATTENMEER & DOLLART
Information: for visits to Dollart, Elisabeth-Aussengroden, Lütje Hörn, Langeoog and Spiekeroog-Ostplate: Bezirksregierung Weser-Ems, Höhere Naturschutzbehörde, Postfach 2447, 2800 Oldenburg; for guided tours to Memmert: Inselvogt Reinhard Schopf, Bauamt für Küstenschutz, Jahnstrasse 1, 2980 Norden
Access: to Dollart from EMDEN, to the islands by boat from NORDEN and points along coastal road
Open: Permission required to visit most areas. Particular regulations in force for each island

2 JADEBUSEN & WESTLICHE WESERMÜNDUNG
Information: for Jadebusen: Landkreis Wesermarsch, Untere Naturschutzbehörde, 2880 Brake/Unterweser; for Mellum: Institut fur Vogelforschung An der Vogelwarte 21, 2940 Wilhelmshaven
Access: from WILHELM-HAVEN
Open: Jadebusen is unrestricted, Mellum may only be visited between April 1 and September 30 by prior arrangement
Facilities: Information centre and nature trail on Jadebusen. Wardens on Mellum during the breeding season

3 LÜNEBURGER HEIDE
Information: Verein Naturschutzpark e.V. Stuttgart-Hamburg, Ballindamm 2–3, 2000 Hamburg 1
Access: from LÜNEBURG or SOLTAU
Open: Unrestricted. The information centre at Döhle is open all public holidays; Tuesday to Sunday, May to September, between 1000–1200 and 1400–1800
Facilities: Information centres also at Niederhaverbeck and Undeloh. Hotels and camp sites within the park. Marked trails and footpaths

Heiliges Meer Nature Reserve

About 50 kilometres due north of Münster, near Hopsten in Nordrhein-Westfalen, is a region of forest and moorland with ponds and small lakes. The ponds were formed over a long period by the collapse of the surface sands when the underlying strata of gypsum, salt and anhydrite gradually dissolved away. Funnel-shaped depressions, "Erdfälle", were produced, which became filled with water.

The water bodies vary both in age and in size; the water depth in the Erdfällsee and Grosses Heiliges Meer can be as much as 13 metres, but elsewhere the lakes and ponds do not exceed 1 metre. Originally they were poor in nutrients and the water was clear with little vegetation, but drainage from nearby agricultural land has brought down fertilizers, which have enabled a luxuriant vegetation of aquatic plants to grow in the shallow areas, particularly in parts of the Grosses Heiliges Meer.

The woodlands are varied in composition – pure birch, mixed oak and birch, and pine and alder. The original forest cover, however, is much reduced because centuries of grazing have prevented tree regeneration.

Dümmer Nature Reserve

A large shallow lake, 1.5 metres deep, lying in a valley of glacial origin, Dümmer Nature Reserve consists of open water, raised bog, reedswamp and marsh, inland sand dunes and moraines. It is situated within the

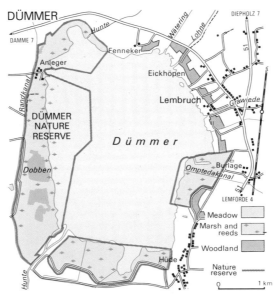

DÜMMER

Dümmer Nature Park and is an important wetland area for water birds and plants.

Not much remains of the original plant life, but thick belts of water-lilies as well as reed and reedmace have formed around the lake shore – the beds are about 800 metres wide in places. Elsewhere there are relict patches of alder bogs and sedge meadows.

Although in the course of time man has greatly altered this habitat, Dümmer is still an important area for aquatic birds; many endangered and rare species breed here, or shelter on migration and in the winter. The list of breeding birds is quite remarkable; 138 species have been recorded nesting in or around Dümmer. The principal species are common stork (8–23 pairs), bittern (up to 20 pairs), the little bittern (1–3 pairs), marsh harrier (11 pairs in 1974), black tern (about 75 pairs), spotted crake and bearded tit as well as several duck species. It is also a popular place for overwintering and as a resting place for migrants. Ospreys visit the lake daily in April and September and as many as 200 buzzards pass through the area in September or October. The hen-harrier is a common winter visitor, and the common crane still occurs, although its numbers have fallen from 2000 in 1963 to about fifty in 1981.

Diepholzer Moorniederung Nature and Landscape Reserves

Situated about 37 kilometres northeast of Osnabrück, the Deipholzer Moorniederung is a vast region of moor and peat bog lying on the glacial sands of the North German plain. Over the centuries the peat deposits have been exploited by man, bringing about considerable changes to the vegetation. Today birch woodland and a heathland of heather, cross-leaved heath and purple moor-grass are the most widespread vegetation types. The original bog flora survives in some areas and includes *Sphagnum* mosses, bog myrtle and several species of cotton-grass.

The reserve is of special interest to the ornithologist because the peaty moors are the breeding site of the southern race of the golden plover. The area has a population of between forty-five and fifty pairs and is one of the last sites in Lower Saxony.

Many other species are recorded from time to time during migration periods or in winter, for example marsh, Montagu's and hen-harriers, short-eared owls and several species of duck. The goshawk and nightjar breed in wooded areas and the common gull, which is rarely found away from the coast, builds its nest in wet areas.

There are three nature reserves in the region – Neustädter Moor, Oppenweher Moor and Grosses Renzeler Moor – and five landscape reserves in which both state and private owners control substantial shares of the land. Peat exploitation is still permitted on the reserves, but attempts are being made to save the best areas and to restore their natural raised bog conditions. Neustädter Moor is more effectively protected than the others because small parts are owned by the German National Appeal of the World Wildlife Fund. Careful management has restored the wet bogs and open moorland.

Steinhuder Meer Nature Reserve and Landscape Protection Area

The largest inland lake in northern Germany, Steinhuder Meer has a surface area of 3000 hectares and lies in a glacial meltwater channel with no inflow of any importance. Even so, the water remains at a fairly constant level and it is believed that the lake is fed by strong-flowing springs in the lake bottom. This may be the reason why its waters are not as rich in nutrients as, for instance, those of Dümmer, and also why the lake has a more varied fish population.

The east bank, where the nature reserve is situated, is the only part of the lake bordered by a broad belt of reedswamp and marsh vegetation. Also on the east bank, and to a lesser extent on the west, remnants of moorland and raised bog survive from a formerly much more extensive area, which has now been largely reclaimed and converted to grassland.

In the winter great flocks of migrating and overwintering duck, particularly mallard and pochard, but also many smew and goosanders, seek shelter and food and the list of breeding birds must be the envy of many other wetland nature reserves.

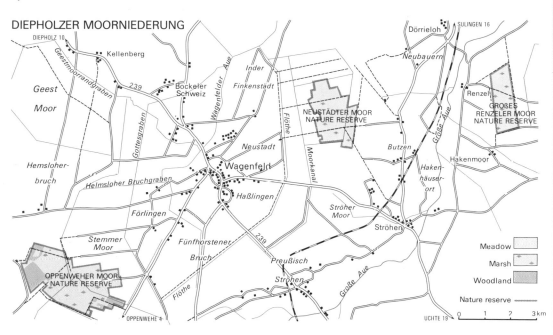

DIEPHOLZER MOORNIEDERUNG

Meadow
Marsh
Woodland
Nature reserve

CORNCRAKE *above* A timid bird, the corncrake or landrail rarely takes refuge in flight, preferring to run for cover in dense undergrowth.

STEINHUDER MEER *left* The lake, which lies in an old glacial-meltwater channel, is thought to be fed from below by springs.

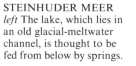

1 HEILIGES MEER
Information: Westfälisches Landesmuseum für Naturkunde, Biologische Station Heiliges Meer, 4534 Recke-Steinbeck
Access: from Ibbenbüren, 40km N of MÜNSTER
Open: Unrestricted except for some protected areas
Facilities: Display and audio-visual exhibition at the biological station

2 DUMMER
Information: Verein Naturpark Dümmer e.V., Niedersachsenstrasse 2, 2840 Diepholz
Access: from Lembruch, 11km S of DIEPHOLZ
Open: Unrestricted

3 DIEPHOLZER MOORNIEDERUNG
Information: Bezirksregierung Hannover, Höhere Naturschutzbehörde, Postfach 203, 3000 Hannover 1
Access: from DIEPHOLZ or SULINGEN
Open: Unrestricted but visitors must keep to tracks and footpaths
Facilities: Marked footpaths within the reserves

4 STEINHUDER MEER
Information: Verein Naturschutzpark e.V., Pfizerstrasse 5–7, Postfach 640, 7000 Stuttgart 1
Access: from Neustadt, 23km NW of HANNOVER or Wunstorf, 23km W of HANNOVER
Open: Unrestricted in the landscape protection area but visitors must keep to marked paths in the reserve
Facilities: Marked footpaths within the reserve

85

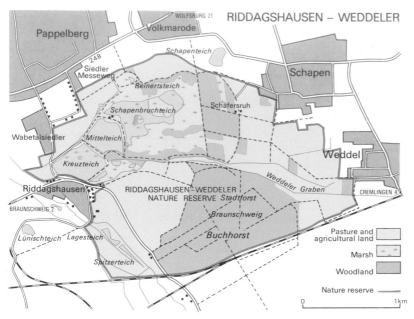

RIDDAGSHAUSEN – WEDDELER

Pasture and agricultural land
Marsh
Woodland
Nature reserve

0   1km

EDIBLE FROG *left* It occurs in a wide variety of watery environments and can be distinguished from other frogs by its green colour and pale dorsal stripe.

RIDDAGSHAUSEN-WEDDELER TEICHGEBIET *below* Constructed as fish ponds to serve a religious house in the Middle Ages, all but fourteen of the original ponds have disappeared.

Riddagshausen-Weddeler Teichgebiet Europa-Reserve

In the year 1200 the Cistercian monks of the Riddagshausen monastery dug a series of ponds in which to rear carp and tench for their table. Over the centuries the ponds have gradually become overgrown and only fourteen have survived to the present day. They are now part of a varied landscape of deciduous woodlands, alder swamps, marshes and arable fields.

The nature reserve was established in 1936 and now extends from the Kreuz pond to the Buchhorst. The largest pond is the Schapenbruch, of which only a quarter of its 63 hectares is open water, the rest being primary reedswamp. The Buchhorst, a woodland area within the nature reserve, was formerly meadow land, but trees invaded the area to form a deciduous forest when grazing ceased at the end of the nineteenth century.

Over 250 bird species have been recorded in the protected area, including fifty-four which either breed now or have bred in the past. Twelve amphibian species have also been found, suggesting that there is a considerable habitat diversity for this group of animals in the reserve. There are, for instance, five frogs of the genus *Rana* – the agile, moor, marsh, edible and common frog.

Warmberg-Osterberg Nature Reserve

Overlooking the valley of the River Warme are several low hills which average about 200 metres, and consist of shell limestone or, in some areas, "wave" limestone – a rock formation in which ripple marks, produced when sediments were laid down, have been preserved. The nature reserve of Warmberg-Osterberg occupies part of this area and consists of three parts – Im Wiegenfuss, Warmberg and Osterberg – each occupying a section of a hilltop and of the slopes forming the east bank of the Warme. All are famous for the abundance of orchids which grow on the semi-dry limestone grassland and in open places among the trees.

Im Wiegenfuss is partly covered with scrub, which is spreading in the absence of cutting or grazing, and some black pines have been planted; both of these developments are detrimental to the orchid habitat.

In grassy areas the military orchid forms large colonies, together with the toothed orchid. In addition there are many fragrant, greater butterfly, bee and fly orchids. The attractive yellow-flowered horseshoe vetch, the food plant of the chalk-hill blue butterfly, is abundant, and large self-heal, here near its northern European limit, also occurs.

The Warmberg section of the reserve lies at a higher altitude and has beech wood on its western slopes. A grassland of mountain melick forms the forest floor vegetation, and the orchids here include the large white helleborine and the lady's slipper as well as rare hybrids of the military and lady orchids.

Much of the third section of the reserve, Osterberg, is covered with scrub and planted black pine, and only isolated grassy strips remain open. Nevertheless, several rare plants of great interest grow there and in addition to those recorded for Im Wiegenfuss there are dark red helleborines, the rare musk orchid and the large field gentian.

Meissner Nature Reserve

Between Kassel and Eschwege lies the Meissner Nature Reserve on the slopes of the so-called "King of the Hessen mountains". The mountain rises gently at first, becoming steeper towards the top, until it reaches a broad plateau with an average height of 720 metres. From Kasseler Kuppe (754 metres), the highest point, can be seen the Harz mountains, the Thuringer Forest, the Röhn Mountains and Hochsauer region.

The reserve, whose boundaries enclose almost the whole of the mountain slopes as well as a few small areas on the plateau, is one of the most important in Hessen; it is the second largest in the area, and has marvellous scenery and a fauna and flora of great interest.

On some of the steep slopes basalt boulders form a type of scree – probably the most natural habitat in the reserve – and on the west side there is a shell limestone, which, when cut, has a surface like marble. The plateau was formerly wooded, but is now covered with grassland or heath which has been grazed for a long time.

The basalt weathers to a rich soil and some of the forest that covers the greater part of the reserve is in a near-natural state – "wildly beautiful", according to an early visitor to the reserve – with magnificent trees, a luxuriant shrub layer and herbaceous flora.

The mountain grassland lying between 660 and 720 metres is very varied: in the drier places mat-grass and arnica occur and elsewhere there is an attractive grass heath with mat-grass, heather, clustered bellflower, Nottingham catchfly, field gentian and the wonderfully scented superb pink. Where the soil is damper the lovely yellow globe flower, common lousewort, red-rattle and the common sundew are found. On the calcareous soils of the shell limestone grow the lady's slipper orchid and the martagon lily, two of the reserve's most beautiful plants.

Of the mammals that can be seen in the area, the red deer is fairly common, the mouflon was introduced in 1953 and the wild cat still survives but is rare. The raccoon, originating from a few animals released in the 1930s, has become well established. In the forests the black woodpecker and Tengmalm's owl breed, and the nutcracker is a regular visitor.

Graburg Nature Reserve

In the central region of the Federal Republic, not far from the border with East Germany, the rocky cliffs and steep slopes of the Ringgau mountain stand out from afar like a gigantic fortress. The Graburg Nature Reserve, on the northern side of the mountain, is composed of a shell limestone with a remarkably rich flora, and is probably one of the best nature reserves in Hessen. Three main plant associations exist within the flora: pre-alpine, submediterranean and submediterranean-continental. On rocky terraces there is a blue moor-grass grassland, which in places is mixed with upright brome. The exposed rock faces are fringed on the upper slopes by a scrubby woodland of oak and whitebeam and on the limestone debris at the foot of the north slopes the woodland is dominated by lime and rowan.

Beech forest is extensive and has one of the most interesting herbaceous floras of the reserve. There are scattered groups of spring snowflakes, martagon lilies and many orchids, including the lady's slipper, which in spite of persecution is still present in fairly large numbers. In some parts of the forest, yew forms an interesting shrub layer, and the Schaferburg ridge is famous for the many hybrids of *Sorbus* species found there.

The fauna is less well known. The peregrine falcon and wild cat still survived at the beginning of the century, but have not been seen for many years.

1 RIDDAGSHAUSEN-WEDDELER TEICHGEBIET
Information: Deutscher Bund für Vogelschutz, Bezirksgruppe Braunschweig (Haus am Europa-Reservat in Weddel), Bauernstrasse 13, 3302 Cremlingen
Access: from BRAUNSCHWEIG
Open: Unrestricted but visitors must keep to footpaths
Facilities: Marked footpaths within the reserve. Guided tours

2 WARMBERG-OSTERBERG
Information: Hessische Landeszentrale für Fremdenverkehr, Abraham-Lincoln-Strasse 38–42 6200 Wiesbaden 1
Access: from Liebenau, 15km E of WARBURG
Open: Unrestricted

3 MEISSNER
Information: Hessische Landeszentrale für Fremdenverkehr, Abraham-Lincoln-Strasse 38–42 6200 Wiesbaden 1
Access: from Meissner, 7km W of ESCHWEGE
Open: Unrestricted

4 GRABURG
Information: Hessische Landeszentrale für Fremdenverkehr Abraham-Lincoln-Strasse 38–42 6200 Wiesbaden 1
Access: from Wiessenborn, 8km SE of ESCHWEGE
Open: Unrestricted

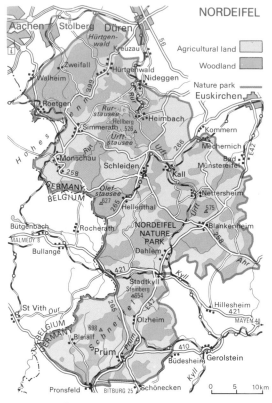

NORDEIFEL

Agricultural land
Woodland
Nature park
Euskirchen

HEATH SPOTTED
ORCHID *left* A common
orchid found throughout
Europe, it thrives on
damp heaths and marshes.
Both the flowers and the
leaves of this plant are
very variable in form.

Nordeifel Nature Park

The northwestern part of the Rhine Schiefer-gebirge was selected as a Nature Park in 1960. Dominated by the Hohes Venn in the north-west and the Schneifel in the southwest, its long western boundary is contiguous with the Belgian frontier and in 1971 the park was united with the Hautes Fagnes-Eifel (Hohes Venn-Eifel) Nature Park of Belgium to form the second Inter-European Nature Park.

The Park is situated on an area of very old rocks – schists, graywackes and sandstones, mainly of Cambrian, Silurian and Devonian origin. Limestone occurs in the northwest and southeast and bunter sandstone, which forms an infertile soil, is found in the north-east. The rainfall is higher in the west, adjacent to the Hohes Venn, and here moors have developed in the mountain woodlands. The landscape is dissected by numerous deep valleys, many of which have been converted into reservoirs by the construction of dams. The public are not allowed on those which provide drinking water, but in other places boating, camping and walking are permitted.

Half of the Nature Park is wooded. About 60 per cent of the trees are coniferous and 40 per cent deciduous – beech, oak, ash, sycamore, alder and birch. A good deal of spruce has been, and is still being, planted.

The park's interesting flora and fauna has many rarities, particularly in the flower-rich dry grasslands and on the limestone hills. Where the soils are sandy the yellow flowers of broom are so conspicuous that the shrub is known locally as "Eifel Gold".

Red and roe deer, wild boar and the introduced mouflon are abundant. The wild cat and black grouse occur on the Belgian side of the Inter-European Park.

Siebengebirge Nature Park

In the Rhine Valley, between the town of Beuel in the north and the deeply cut gorge of the Rheinbreitbacher Graben in the south, lies the Siebengebirge Nature Park, a remark-able landscape of wooded hills and valleys. The region's extraordinarily varied geology and numerous isolated peaks are the result of extensive volcanic activity. It is possible to count forty hilltops in the Siebengebirge, of which Ölberg at 460 metres is the highest.

The region, enjoying a warm climate typical of the Rhine Valley, has a rich fauna and flora. The volcanic rocks have formed fertile soils and over 80 per cent of the area is tree-covered.

There is a marked southern European character about the forest, particularly with regard to its oak and beech trees. In some parts there is a fine development of oak, hornbeam and wild service tree. On the hill

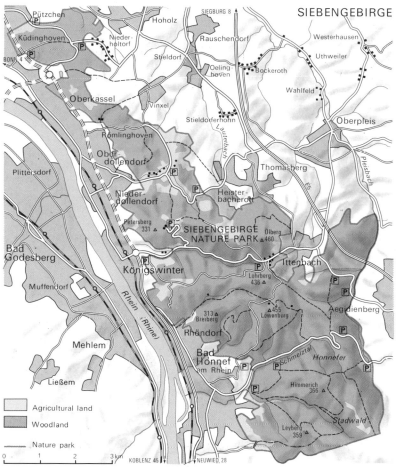

Map labels: Pützchen, Küdinghoven, Niederholtorf, BONN 4, Hoholz, SIEGBURG 8, Rauschendorf, Westerhausen, Stieldorf, Oelinghoven, Bockeroth, Uthweiler, Oberkassel, Vinxel, Wahlfeld, Stieldorferhohn, Oberpleis, Römlinghoven, Oberdollendorf, Plittersdorf, Niederdollendorf, Heisterbacherott, Thomasberg, Bad Godesberg, Petersberg 331, SIEBENGEBIRGE NATURE PARK, Ölberg 460, Ittenbach, Königswinter, Lohrberg 436, Muffendorf, Aegidienberg, 313 Breiberg, 455 Löwenburg, Mehlem, Rhöndorf, Bad Honnef am Rhein, Schmelztal, Honnefer, Rhein (Rhine), Himmerich 366, Ließem, Stadwald, Leyberg 359, KOBLENZ 45, NEUWIED 28

Agricultural land

Woodland

Nature park

0 1 2 3km

WILD BOAR *left* This animal grows a
protective coat in winter when it must
often cover long distances to find food.
The boar's flexible snout enables it to
dig out worms and roots from the soil,
even if the ground is frozen.

of Rabenley is found a submediterranean
plant community with blue gromwell, alpine
squill and the field southernwood.

Along the valleys of the numerous small
streams which flow through the Siebengebirge
lie attractive woodlands of alder and ash,
where the large elegant drooping sedge and
the rare loose-flowered sedge are often found.

The fauna includes roe deer, fallow deer
and wild boar, although none is very common.
Some captive red deer, fallow deer and wild
boar are kept in an enclosure so that the
visitors can see them at close quarters.

The extensive woodland of the Siebengebirge supports a rich bird fauna, with, for
instance, eight species of woodpecker – green,
grey-headed, great spotted, middle spotted,
lesser spotted and black. It is claimed that
one can see all of them, as well as their
near-relative, the wryneck, in the course of
a day's birdwatching. Birds of prey are rather
few, but there are common and honey
buzzards, and the red kite also breeds on the
southern edge of the region. One of the park's
rarer small birds, the rock bunting, is still
seen regularly but has not been recorded
breeding in recent years.

Heidenhäuschen Nature Reserve
On the northern side of the Limburg Basin,
4 kilometres northeast of the town of
Hadamar, lies a forest covered ridge broken
by several peaks – the highest, Heidenhäuschen, which is just short of 400 metres,
was made a nature reserve in 1927. The reserve's predominantly basaltic rock has been
eroded on the main peak to form impressive
cliffs and a small boulder field, or area of
breccia, on the steep southwest slope. On the
cliff peak bushy hornbeam, field maple, large-
leaved lime, hazel and hawthorn fringe the
stony areas.

The reserve's deciduous woodland consists
mostly of beech, but large areas have been
felled and replanted with conifers. The lower
slopes of the main hill are covered with hazel
coppice and a woodland of pedunculate oak
and sessile oak, together with some beech,
service tree, common buckthorn and mezereon. Here the herbaceous flora has several
attractive plants; lily-of-the-valley is abundant in the more open areas and the orchids
include lesser butterfly, bird's-nest, heath
spotted and the long-leaved helleborine. The
last species is so abundant that in some places
it is practically the dominant plant. Although
in the coniferous plantation and dense beech
woodland deep shade suppresses the ground
and shrub vegetation even here there are local
areas with a rich flora of, for example, such
plants as columbine, coral-wort and several
orchid species.

1 NORDEIFEL
Information: Verein
Naturpark Nordeifel e.V.,
Theaterplatz 14, 5100 Aachen
Access: from AACHEN,
EUSKIRCHEN or BITBURG
Open: Unrestricted
Facilities: Information centre.
Hotels, pensions and camp sites
within the park. Marked
footpaths. Observation points

2 SIEBENGEBIRGE
Information: Verschönungs-
Verein für das Siebengebirge,
Breite Strasse 29, 5300 Bonn 1
Access: from BONN
Open: Unrestricted
Facilities: Refuges within the
park. Marked footpaths

3 HEIDENHÄUSCHEN
Information: Hessische
Landeszentrale für
Fremdenverkehr, Abraham-
Lincoln-Strasse 38–42, 6200
Wiesbaden 1
Access: from Hadamar, 9km NE
of LIMBURG
Open: Unrestricted

Rheinauen Bingen-Erbach Nature Reserve

Near Mainz, where the upper Rhine turns to flow in a westerly direction, lie the so-called Rhine islands, which vary in length from 1 to 3 kilometres. In order to deepen the navigable channel at this point and to direct the flow of water along a particular route, artificial banks were formed by depositing stone and rubble along the edge of the river, creating still water areas between the river margins and the channel banks. These shallow water areas are situated mainly around the islands of Rüdesheimer Aue, Ilmenaue, Fulderaue and Mariannenaue, all of which are nature reserves and have now developed a rich vegetation, providing food and shelter for large numbers of waterfowl.

On the south bank of the river, near the Mariannenaue Nature Reserve, lies a broad zone of riverine woodland. In its less disturbed areas, remnants of the old riverine forest of oak, smooth-leaved elm and the rare fluttering elm have survived along with some splendid specimens of white poplar, Norway maple and small-leaved lime. On marshy ground, where gravel has accumulated, there are several interesting plants, such as rare flowering rush, poisonous thorn-apple and lesser and common meadow rue.

The importance of this wetland for migratory birds is heightened by the fact that the nearest wetland to the north is 300 kilometres away, and to the south, 200 kilometres distant. It is not surprising therefore that as many as 10,000 water birds have been counted in the area in winter; the highest number so far recorded is 16,500 in 1973. In recent years the most numerous winter visitors have been pochard, with populations reaching 7500.

Almost all species of European water birds have been seen at some some time or other and the less common ducks – garganey, goldeneye, gadwall, pintail, shoveler and wigeon – occur regularly. Sea ducks such as the common scoter, velvet scoter and long-tailed duck are, however, much less frequent. Scaup, ferruginous duck and the red-crested pochard, are also seen but in small numbers.

The shallow-water areas are important for migrating waders, particularly lapwings, godwits, redshanks, greenshanks, ruffs, common and green sandpipers. Among the breeding birds, which are few in number, are nightingales, icterine warblers and golden orioles; little owls and black kites also breed, but are scarce. Isolated breeding records of the woodchat shrike and the penduline tit exist.

Bayerischer Spessart Nature Park

East of Frankfurt-am-Main, in the hilly wooded country of the Spessart Mountains, lie two Nature Parks, the Bayerischer Spessart and, lying along its northern side, the Hessischer Spessart, which together have been described as the "Jewel of the German Countryside".

The Bayerischer Spessart has long been famous for its 700-year-old "veneer" oak trees, and today the 70,000 hectares of forest form the basis of a very important local industry. The Upper Spessart has retained its deciduous woodland for many centuries and the quality of the timber from its 500- to 700-year-old oaks is such that a price of DM 5000 per cubic metre is not rare. In other parts much deciduous forest has disappeared and been replaced by pine, spruce and larch. However, beech and oak are also being planted so that its deciduous character will eventually return after the conifers have been harvested. In North Spessart, where soils are suitable, Douglas fir, spruce, larch and Weymouth pine have been planted, producing 400,000 cubic metres annually.

In the west the Nature Park consists of gneiss and mica schist, which were exposed when the overlying bunter sandstone was eroded away and deposited in the neighbouring plains. Today this region is an area of hills with peaks generally 100 to 200 metres lower than the eastern Spessart, where the bunter sandstone still remains.

The Spessart has been occupied by man for thousands of years and traces of Stone Age and Bronze Age occupation still remain. In the Middle Ages an important route, the Eselweg, was established to transport salt on donkey-back from Schlüchtern to Engelsberg and other towns. From the fourteenth to seventeenth centuries a glass-making industry was important and many trees were cut down to provide fuel for the furnaces.

Game animals and birds are important and

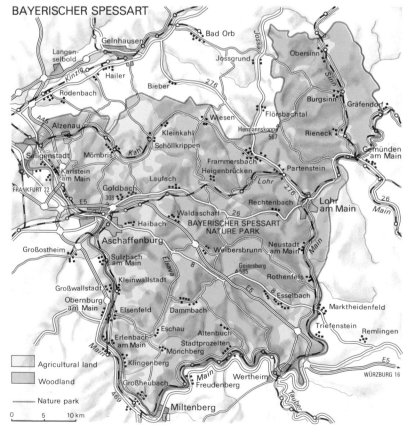

BAYERISCHER SPESSART

Agricultural land

Woodland

Nature park

0   5   10 km

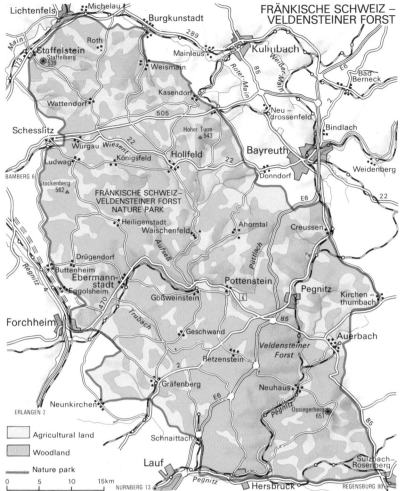

FRÄNKISCHE SCHWEIZ –
VELDENSTEINER FORST

Agricultural land

Woodland

Nature park

0 5 10 15km

FOX *above* Originally found in moor and woodland, the fox may now be seen near urban areas and even in gardens.

1 RHEINAUEN BINGEN-ERBACH
Information: FVV Rheinland-Pfalz, Hochhaus, 5400 Koblenz
Access: from Bingen, 28km W of MAINZ
Open: Unrestricted except for Rüdesheimer Aue and Mariannenaue which are closed to the public
Facilities: Observation points

2 BAYERISCHER SPESSART
Information: Verein Naturpark Spessart e.V., Landratsamt, 8760 Miltenberg
Access: from FRANKFURT or WÜRZBURG
Open: Unrestricted
Facilities: Hotels within the park. Marked paths and nature trails

3 FRÄNKISCHE SCHWEIZ-VELDENSTEINER FORST
Information: Verein Naturpark Fränkische Schweiz-Veldensteiner Forst e.V., 8573 Pottenstein
Access: from NÜRNBERG, BAMBERG or BAYREUTH
Open: Unrestricted
Facilities: Marked footpaths within the park. Nature trails

hunting is a major activity in the region; the red deer is common, but the roe deer occurs only in marginal areas. Hares, rabbits, pheasants, partridges, ring and turtle doves, foxes, badgers and pine martens are frequently seen in low regions; the black grouse and capercaillie are, however, both scarce. The flora and insect fauna are of great interest, as one would expect in a forest with ancient trees.

In boggy areas the marsh fern, giant horsetail, sundew and Cambridge milk-parsley are characteristic species. In the Hessen Spessart, where there are calcareous basaltic rocks, many other plants are found, including the rare lady's slipper orchid.

The Bayerischer Spessart has 400 nature monuments and several nature reserves, protecting places with rare plants and insects, and also some outstanding oak trees, for example the "Steinknuck" oak, which is 50 metres high and 350 years old.

Fränkische Schweiz-Veldensteiner Forst Nature Park

Consisting originally of the 13,314-hectare Veldensteiner forest, this Nature Park was enlarged in 1973 to its present size, and plans have now been prepared to extend it to 240,000 hectares. It is a spacious landscape of Jurassic rocks with a northwest–southeast fault separating the dolomites of the "white" Jura from the "black" Jura to the north.

Although the mountains are low the highest points, Ossinger Berg and Kleine Kulm, are only just over 600 metres – its rocky peaks, steep-sided valleys and sparkling streams are sufficiently striking for the region to deserve fully the title of Frankish Switzerland. In the dolomitic regions there are gigantic rock cliffs and pinnacles, and over 1000 dolines – hollows created by the collapse of underground water courses. Numerous caves have been created by the action of underground water, particularly in the area of Pottenstein. In one of the best known, the 1.2-kilometre long Devil's Cave, which has well-formed stalactites, the skull and bones of an enormous ice-age cave bear have been found. It also has the largest entrance to any cave in Germany.

Forest covers 25 per cent of the park area, with many conifer plantations and beech trees on the dolomitic peaks which emerge from the less fertile sandstones. During the last 100 years spruce and pine have been planted extensively and now account for about 75 per cent of all forest in the park. Away from the large forests, many small woodlands lie scattered throughout the mainly agricultural landscape. The herbaceous flora is richest on the limestone, particularly on the dry and warm upper slopes of the dolomitic cliffs, where there are gentians, aquilegias, lilies, centauries and orchids.

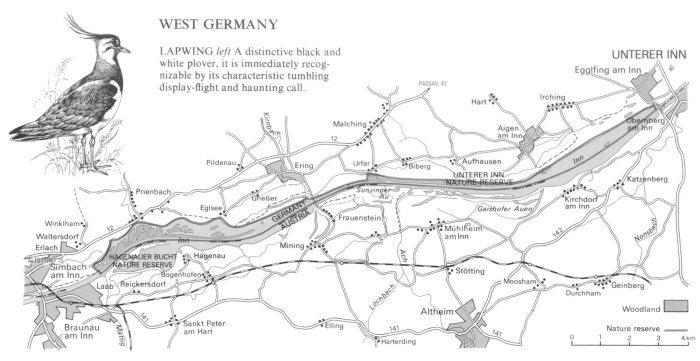

LAPWING *left* A distinctive black and white plover, it is immediately recognizable by its characteristic tumbling display-flight and haunting call.

UNTERER INN

BEAVER The largest rodent in northern regions, the Eurasian beaver lives in burrows with underwater entrances, usually on the banks of large rivers.

ALTMÜHLTAL The meandering course of the Altmühl River has become incised in the uplifted limestones of the Fränkische Alb plateau.

Mohrhof Landscape Reserve

The Mohrhof ponds, which number about 2000, cover an extensive area between Erlangen and Hochstadt, lying 30 kilometres northwest of Nürnburg. The Landscape Reserve occupies, however, only a small part of the total area.

The ponds, of which the largest is as much as 20 hectares, are set in a most attractive countryside of damp meadows and marshes with areas of pine woodland on higher and drier ground. Most of the ponds, which were formed by damming small streams with a succession of barriers, are artificial and are managed for fish culture, mainly for carp. For some time they have developed naturally and several are entirely overgrown by marsh vegetation, while on others there are reed beds, sedge fens and small alder bogs.

Several species of bird, which are either rare or threatened elsewhere in the Federal Republic, breed in the area, notably, 50 to 100 pairs of the black-necked grebe, 50 to 65 pairs of garganey and several pairs of black-tailed godwit.

Altmühltal Nature Park

Situated at the confluence of the Danube with its tributary the Altmühl, the Nature Park occupies 90 kilometres of the river valley from Gunzenhausen to Kelheim. The whole region is of particular interest for its historical and cultural monuments, as well as for its several nature reserves. The main tourist attractions are the castle of Harburg, the Spielberg fort, the Römerkastall Abusina and the remarkable Weltenburg gorge.

Careful study of the Altmühl Valley has revealed that it was originally the course of the Danube, and only after later earth movements had caused the Danube to change its course was the valley taken over by the River

Altmühl. The Park is dominated by the 600-metre-high top of Hahnenkamm, but equally striking are the marble limestone deposits at Treuchtlinger Bucht, which have been used for many important buildings and cathedrals. This stone is rich in fossils of the Jurassic period, particularly fish, and is world famous for one of the most remarkable fossils ever found, that of Archaeopterix. This fossil of the first flying bird shows that these creatures evolved from reptiles.

In addition to the beautiful landscape of rocky valleys, streams and woods, and the many castles, medieval buildings and charming villages, there is much of interest in the fauna and flora. In the west, on sandstone and Keuper (Upper Triassic) deposits, pine dominates with a ground vegetation of heather, bilberry and arnica. On the Jurassic limestone are found beechwoods and hornbeam, and in wet places there are many orchids, butterworts and globe flowers. Fallow deer and mouflon which have been introduced to the park can be seen at Kösching-Kipfenberg.

Weltenburger Enge Nature Reserve
Close to the town of Weltenburg, near the confluence of the Danube and the Altmühl in the Swabian Jura, the Danube passes through a narrow gorge, which is the most impressive in Germany and is now a nature reserve. In many places the cliffs fall vertically down to the river and on the gentler slopes there are scattered areas of woodland where a number of plants, more typical of the Mediterranean region, are found. For many years it has been known as a breeding locality for the eagle owl and the peregrine falcon.

Unterer Inn Reservoirs Nature Reserves
Along the lower reaches of the River Inn, where it forms the frontier between West Germany and Upper Austria, are four shallow reservoirs that were constructed to serve hydroelectric power stations. The two middle reservoirs, one upstream of Ering-Frauenstein and the other upstream of Egglfing-Obernberg, together with parts of the riverine woodland, have been designated the Unterer Inn Nature Reserve.

The River Inn brings down immense quantities of silt from the central alpine area and the deposition of this material in the reservoirs has formed extensive mudflats, backwaters, shallows and islands, which have become vegetated with willows and herbaceous plants such as reeds to form jungle-like woodlands.

There is an abundance of food, and this artificially created habitat provides excellent breeding sites for many waterfowl. Because so many other wetlands in the region have been reclaimed, the Unterer Inn reservoirs attract one of the largest inland concentrations of duck and waders in the Federal Republic.

A total of 280 species has been recorded in the course of the last twenty years, of which 120 breed regularly. Of particular interest are the night heron, purple heron, red-crested pochard, penduline tit, hobby, bluethroat and river warbler. The sea eagle overwinters here every year, and many Mediterranean and southeastern European species occur regularly.

The reserve's aquatic mammals are also interesting; the beaver was reintroduced from Swedish stock and is now established with a population of about 55 along the River Inn and in the lower reaches of the River Salzach. The otter used to be a typical species of the riverine woodlands, but became extinct a decade ago through human persecution. A vigorous population of muskrats, is indicated by heaps of mussel shells beside the river – the remains of its favourite food.

1 MOHRHOF
Information: FVV Franken, Am Plärrer 14, 8500 Nürnberg
Access: from NÜRNBERG or HÖCHSTADT
Open: Unrestricted
Facilities: Footpaths within the reserve

2 ALTMÜHLTAL
Information: Verein Naturpark Altmühltal e.V., Landratsamt, 8832 Weissenberg
Access: from KELHEIM, INGOLSTADT or GUNZENHAUSEN
Open: Unrestricted
Facilities: Camp sites. Marked footpaths, forest and nature trails

3 WELTENBURGER ENGE
Information: Kreisverwaltung Kelheim, Untere Naturschutzbehörde, 8420 Kelheim
Access: from Weltenburg, 5km SW of KELHEIM
Open: Unrestricted
Facilities: Marked footpaths within the reserve

4 UNTERER INN RESERVOIRS
Information: FVV München-Oberbayern, Sonnenstrasse 10, 8000 München 2
Access: from SIMBACH
Open: Unrestricted except for the island areas which are closed to visitors

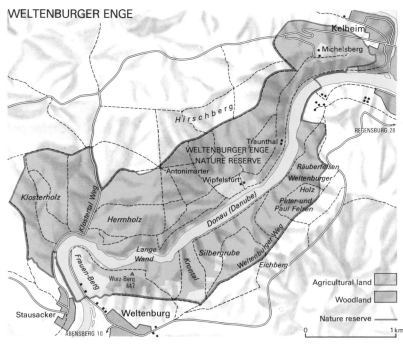

WELTENBURGER ENGE

Agricultural land
Woodland
Nature reserve

0   1km

NIGHT HERON *above*
A squat compact species,
the night heron is more
commonly found in
southern Europe.

RED-CRESTED
POCHARD *below* A
diving duck usually found
on large freshwater lakes
and coastal lagoons.

Meadow

Marsh

Woodland

Nature reserve

0   1   2   3 km

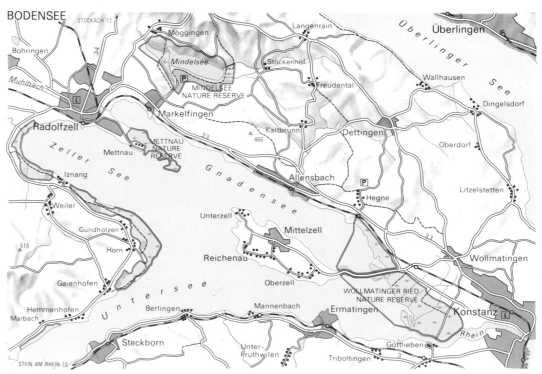

BODENSEE

94

Danube Reservoirs Nature Reserve and Landscape Protection Areas

The 2- to 3-kilometre broad valley lying below the confluence of the Danube and the Ille is regularly flooded in midsummer, when alpine meltwater raises the river's water level. As a result the meadowland on either side of the river cannot be cultivated and is maintained as fields, woodlands, marshes and ponds. Together with other similar parts of the Upper Rhine this region contains the last surviving areas of open meadow woodland in Germany, and provides habitats for many plants and animals which have either disappeared or are threatened elsewhere.

One nature reserve and several landscape reserves, which are either owned by the state, a local authority or are in private hands, make up this area. The whole region is divided into several impoundment levels: the Opfingerstausee southwest of Ulm; the riverine forest area, floodplains and reservoirs of Donauauen and Donaumoos downstream and east of Ulm; Lechstausee bei Feldheim at the mouth of the Lech, near its confluence with the Danube, and the extensive peatlands and reed beds on the right bank of the Danube between Donauwörth and Ingoldstadt.

The greatest conservation interest lies in the series of reservoirs which, built primarily to serve hydroelectric power stations, act as feeding areas for large numbers of waterbirds. On the shores of the Lechstau there is sufficient vegetation to allow a greater number of duck to breed than do so at present.

Downstream of Donauwörth is a region of extensive peatland and reed beds which is of considerable botanical interest and is also an important breeding area for both aquatic and moorland birds.

Federsee Nature Reserve

A natural wetland in Upper Swabia between Lake Constance and the Danube, Federsee Nature Reserve consists of an area of open water surrounded by nearly 1400 hectares of reed beds and peatland vegetation. It is situated in a basin formed during the Riss glacial period and subsequently blocked off by the deposition of sands and gravels. In the eighteenth and nineteenth centuries drainage work lowered the water level and reduced the area of open water by 870 hectares. Since then the accumulation of silt and the growth of marginal vegetation has made the lake ecosystem more varied, although reclamation has caused the decline or disappearance of some animals, birds and plants.

The lake, however, is still noted for several species, including the bittern, little bittern, purple and night herons, black grouse, marsh harrier, short-eared owl and common tern.

Wurzacher Ried Nature Reserve and Landscape Protection Area

In Baden-Württemberg, about 35 kilometres northeast of Ravensburg, lies the Wurzacher Ried Nature Reserve and Landscape Protection area, a vast area of peatland, with birch forest, damp meadows, pools and a wide range of wildlife.

The protected area falls naturally into three distinct parts: the Haidgauer Quellseen, where water collects from the surrounding morainic hills to form springs which feed calcareous marshes, and where orchid species are particularly well represented; the raised bogs of Haidgauer Ried and the Alberser Ried, both of which have stands of dwarf mountain pine on peatlands, with a rich flora of about 500 flowering plants and 150 moss species, including many relics of the last glaciation. The dwarf mountain pine zone also contains areas of marsh and raised bogs, where there are breeding birds such as teal, garganey, spotted crake, common snipe and curlew. The black grouse formerly nested here, but has not been seen in recent years.

Bodensee Nature Reserves

On the frontiers of Germany, Switzerland and Austria lies the large inland lake of Bodensee, which is connected to the Obersee and Untersee and is crossed by the River Rhine as it leaves Switzerland and enters Germany. This important meeting place of cultures and languages has also a series of valuable nature reserves, of which Wollmatinger Ried, Mindelsee and Eriskircher are most important.

The lake complex was once a typical subalpine water body poor in nutrients, but, with the growth of towns around its shores, the flow of sewage and industrial waste has greatly increased and consequently changes have taken place in its fauna and flora.

Around the lake are zones of peat bogs and damp meadows, which have many interesting plants, among them Siberian iris, bird's-eye primrose, marsh gladiolus, bug orchid and sweet-smelling garlic. In some of the drier meadows, the pasque-flower, the sedge *Carex ericetorum* and the spring and large field gentians occur.

The Bodensee is an important moulting area for common and red-crested pochards, and eight species of duck are known to nest, although in small numbers. Around 200,000 duck and geese winter on the lake, which never freezes over completely.

Traditional management is needed to maintain the most attractive conditions for plants and animals and private nature conservation organizations have taken the initiative, particularly in Mettnau and Mindelsee, by erecting gravel-covered floating platforms on which terns can build their nests, and by mowing wet meadows to make them more suitable as breeding sites for wading birds. In the winter Mindelsee is favoured by tufted ducks and pochards, and the reserves are a haven for many thousands of these as well as for large numbers of sholver, gadwall and teal.

1 DANUBE RESERVOIRS
Information: LFVV Baden-Württemberg, Bussenstrasse 23, 7000 Stuttgart
Access: from ULM, DONA&WÖRTH or INGOLSTADT
Open: Unrestricted

2 FEDERSEE
Information: LFVV Baden-Württemberg, Bussenstrasse 23, 7000 Stuttgart
Access: from BIBERACH
Open: Unrestricted
Facilities: Field museum. Footbridge through area of reeds

3 WURZACHER RIED
Information: LFVV Baden-Württemberg, Bussenstrasse 23, 700 Stuttgart
Access: 35km NE of RAVENSBURG
Open: Unrestricted

4 BODENSEE
Information: for Wöllmatinger Ried, DBV-Naturschutzzentrum, Wöllmatinger Ried, Fritz-Arnold-Strasse 2e, 7750 Konstanz and for the Mindelsee, BUND-Naturschutzzentrum, Muulbachstrasse 2, 7760 Radolfzell-Möggingen
Access: from KONSTANZ
Open: Unrestricted.
Information centre for the Mindelsee is open on weekdays 0900–1200 and 1400–1700 and on Saturday and Sunday between 1000–1200 and 1400–1700.
Facilities: Exhibition on nature conservation at the information centre. Guided tours of Wollmatinger Ried between April and September

BAYERISCHER WALD

With the largest forest in central Europe, the border region between Bavaria and Czechoslovakia is an ideal situation for a National Park. On the Bohemian side lies an undulating plateau, which climbs gently to the peaks that form the frontier with Germany. The highest mountains, the Grosser and Kleiner Rachel (1453 metres and 1399 metres), are second only in the Bavarian Forest to the Grosser Arber (1456 metres).

The park is unusual in that it is almost completely wooded – over 98 per cent is tree-covered. The effects of man's past interference are now gradually disappearing; little timber is now felled and the artificial drainage channels are becoming blocked, enabling the boggy areas to regain their moisture. Streams which were altered for transporting wood are returning to their natural courses, and the impoundments constructed in the last century are becoming moulded into the region's landscape.

Geologically the park consists mainly of granite and gneiss, which generate acid soils and support a predominantly coniferous forest. At the higher levels spruce is the main species and, although not many plants can grow under its dark canopy, the shaggy smallreed and bilberry are common. Two attractive flowering plants, mountain tassel flower and chickweed wintergreen, are also

widespread. On the steep slopes remnants of a natural mixed ravine woodland, of spruce, silver fir, maple, elm, ash, common alder, aspen, willows, bird cherry and the occasional yew, have survived. This mixed woodland, but with spruce, silver fir and beech dominant, is also found at lower levels and here the ground flora is characterized by May lily, herb Paris and purple lettuce. The extremely rare Hungarian gentian also occurs and is completely protected, as this is the only place it is found outside the Alps. Arnica grows in the meadow clearings.

In wetter valleys, which are influenced by cold air coming down the steep slopes, and where frosts can occur in any month of the year, spruce is again dominant, with birch, horsetail, the common twayblade and carpets of mosses where the ground is wettest. In many areas raised bogs, forming deep cushions of mosses and accumulated plant remains, and, known in the Bavarian Forest as Filze, rise as much as 5 metres above the surrounding land. In the lower parts of the park the bogs have mountain pine, crowberry, bilberry and cranberry. Insectivorous sundews can sometimes be found, and in summer the marshes are dotted with the white heads of the cotton-grass.

The many crystal-clear streams running through the area are bordered by a lush vegetation of such tall plants as the violet-flowered alpine sow-thistle, which grows as high as a man, the yellow Austrian leopards-bane the spiraea-like goat's-beard, and the

HERB PARIS
A poisonous plant with a single blue-black berry.

RACHELSEE This lovely lakeside reserve lies in the park's northwest corner.

white mountain buttercup. Where springs emerge, the wet patches are the home of the monkshood *Aconitum paniculatum* and the thornless dog rose. Immediately the snow has melted, the fist-sized white-flowering stalk of the butterbur pushes its way through the wet ground, before its leaves begin to show.

Formerly there were many game species in the forest, including bison, lynx, bear, beaver and wolf. Although none of these is now found in the wild state most can still be seen in a 200-hectare enclosure at Neuschönau, where thirty native species of animals and birds are kept.

The birdlife is rich in forest species such as honey buzzards, goshawks, black grouse, hazelhen, Tengalm's and pygmy owls, ring ouzels, red-breasted flycatchers, great spotted, white-backed, three-toed and black woodpeckers. The pygmy owl is the smallest native owl and about fifty pairs nest in the park. The eagle owl, raven and Ural owl, all former residents, are gradually being reintroduced. The red, and particularly the roe, deer have increased considerably under protection and have caused much damage to young trees.

Several areas throughout the park have been set aside to cater for specific interests and to help concentrate the large number of visitors in certain places, leaving the greater part relatively undisturbed. There is a 37-hectare woodland playground for children of all ages; a woodland history zone with a series of nature trails, and a rocky area, to the east of the information centre.

BAYERISCHER WALD The National Park is almost completely forested. The steep slopes are covered with mixed woodland with a rich ground vegetation.

BAYERISCHER WALD
Information: Nationalpark-verwaltung Bayerischer Wald, Freyunger Strasse 2, 8352 Grafenau
Access: from Grafenau, 50km N of PASSAU
Open: Unrestricted
Facilities: Information centre. Refuges within the park. Marked footpaths and nature trails. Guided walks daily and specialist excursions between mid-June and September, Christmas and February, and at Easter

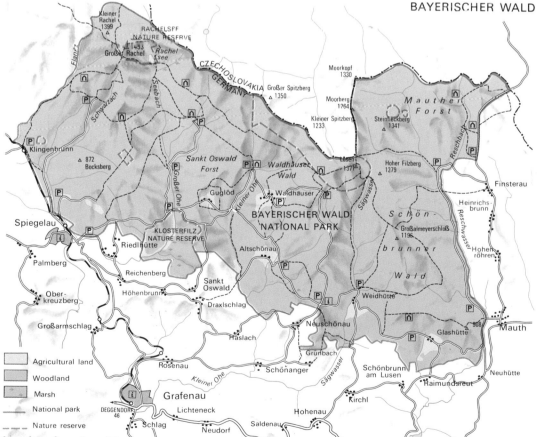

Agricultural land

Woodland

Marsh

National park

Nature reserve

0 1 2 3 4km

BERCHTESGADEN

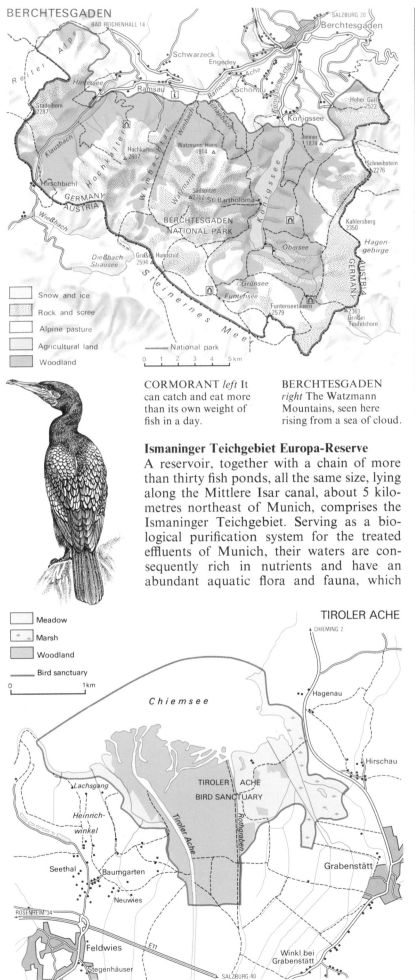

Snow and ice
Rock and scree
Alpine pasture
Agricultural land
Woodland

National park

0 1 2 3 4 5 km

CORMORANT *left* It can catch and eat more than its own weight of fish in a day.

BERCHTESGADEN *right* The Watzmann Mountains, seen here rising from a sea of cloud.

Ismaninger Teichgebiet Europa-Reserve

A reservoir, together with a chain of more than thirty fish ponds, all the same size, lying along the Mittlere Isar canal, about 5 kilometres northeast of Munich, comprises the Ismaninger Teichgebiet. Serving as a biological purification system for the treated effluents of Munich, their waters are consequently rich in nutrients and have an abundant aquatic flora and fauna, which attracts large numbers of water birds throughout the year.

The reservoir and ponds are owned by an industrial firm and although the area does not have the formal status of a nature reserve, it is recognized by the International Council of Bird Protection as a "Europa-Reserve" of international importance for birdlife.

The reed beds and riverine forest at the southern end provide a feeding habitat for many birds – cormorants, night heron, tufted duck, pochard and gadwall. Elsewhere common terns and common gulls nest and after the breeding season red-crested pochard and other species gather on the reservoir and ponds for their annual moult. Huge numbers of wintering waterfowl, as many as 85,000, are recorded each January, partly due to the fact that the water does not freeze over.

Because of the destruction of suitable habitats elsewhere in the region, numbers of waterfowl have increased rapidly in recent years, and it is believed that the present populations now exceed the area's carrying capacity. Industrial development around its margins, and a proposal to build a motorway across the reservoir and ponds, could greatly harm its scientific interest.

Tiroler Ache Bird Sanctuary

In southeast Bavaria, where the great lake of Chiemsee is fed by water from the Alps by the River Ache, lies the Tiroler Ache Bird Sanctuary. The river, falling 5290 metres in 73 kilometres, brings large quantities of gravel, silt and mud down from the mountains and in the course of time has built up

Meadow
Marsh
Woodland
Bird sanctuary

0 1 km

TIROLER ACHE

extensive banks and shoals extending far into the southeast corner of the lake. The estuary, with 200 hectares of water surface as well as sand-bars, mudflats and marsh vegetation, forms the nature reserve. The whole of the lake is a Landscape Protection Area.

The river margins within the delta, wooded with oak, ash and willow, are often flooded, and this is perhaps the reason why the spring snowflake grows in the habitat. Vast reed beds thrive in other areas, and in the lush wet meadows close by, the well-known Siberian iris is found.

The main function of the nature reserve is to provide a sanctuary for wild birds. It is an important resting place for migrants and overwintering species, particularly coot, tufted ducks and pochard. There is an exciting list of breeding species: little ringed plover and common tern on the sand banks; curlew and black grouse on the heathlands; and in the woodland and scrub, river warbler, Savi's warbler, white-spotted bluethroat and hoopoe. It is thought that the number of rare breeding birds in the Ache delta would increase still further if the region's gravel banks, swampy areas, reed beds, riverine woodland, thickets, meadows and moors were more effectively protected.

Berchtesgaden National Park
In the extreme southeast of the Federal Republic, the Berchtesgaden National Park forms a stunningly beautiful enclave of alpine scenery bordered on three sides by Austrian territory. Although the National Park was established as recently as 1978, the area has been a nature reserve since the early 1930s and the property of the state ever since the early nineteenth century, when it became a royal hunting reserve for the Bavarian kings. This area and a landscape protection zone of 25,000 hectares on the north side together form the Berchtesgaden Alpine Park.

Already by the nineteenth century artists and writers had discovered the natural beauty of the region and it soon became popular as a summer resort – in 1975 over 3 million visitors were recorded.

During its period as a royal hunting forest, all the park's predatory animals were destroyed and by the early 1900s the bear, wolf, lynx, otter, lammergeier and golden eagle had disappeared. The main game animals, the chamois and the red deer, are now protected, and the latter is provided with additional food in winter. The red deer population is now ten times its original size, with the result that excessive browsing is causing damage to the forest trees.

The flat-topped mountain structure of the park, with extensive high plateaux falling steeply down to the valleys, differs from the peaks and ridges of other Bavarian mountainous areas. A mosaic of geologically older and harder surface rocks lies over younger and softer deposits, principally of Jurassic limestones, resulting in a variety of soil types and habitats for plants and animals.

There are four mountain massifs in the park – from west to east, the Reiteralpe, Hochkalter, Watzmann and Hagengebirge – separated by three main valleys, of which the Königssee, with its fine glacial lake, 8 kilometres long and reaching a depth of 188 metres, is the best known.

With wide differences in altitude within the region, climatic variation is very great; annual precipitation ranges from 1400 millimetres in the valleys to 2500 millimetres in the mountains. Between these two extremes lies an array of transitional vegetation stages ranging from deciduous woodlands of beech, maple, ash and lime in the valleys, through a broad zone of spruce-beech-fir on the lower slopes, to a subalpine coniferous forest of spruce only, or spruce, larch and arolla pine. Higher still lies a zone of mountain-pine scrub with areas of green alder and, at the highest levels, alpine grassland and bare rock, with a few plants growing in the crevices. About 80 per cent of the area is now forest-covered.

The fauna and flora of the park are fascinating: the tree junipers of the Klausbach valley; the fine arolla pine forest of Reiteralm; the deep blue trumpet flowers of the dragonmouth of the Funtensee; the magnificent apollo butterflies of the alpine meadows in late summer and the marmots on the rocky mountain slopes. The golden eagle has returned to the Berchtesgaden mountains and it is proposed to reintroduce the lammergeier and the lynx. Intensive studies are being made of both the fauna and flora.

1 ISMANINGER TEICHGEBIET
Information: FVV München-Oberbayern, Sonnenstrasse 10, 8000 München 2
Access: from Ismaning, 10km NE of MÜNCHEN
Open: Unrestricted

2 TIROLER ACHE
Information: FVV München-Oberbayern, Sonnenstrasse 10, 8000 München 2
Access: from Chieming, 10km W of TRAUNSTEIN
Open: Unrestricted except for the sanctuary where landing by boat is only permitted at certain times

3 BERCHTESGADEN
Information: Nationalpark-verwaltung Berchtesgaden, Im Tal 34, 8243 Raumsau
Access: from Berchtesgaden, 18km SE of BAD REICHENHALL
Open: Unrestricted
Facilities: Information centre. Refuges within the park. Marked footpaths and nature trails

AUSTRIA

Austria, lying at the gateway to eastern Europe is one of the continent's smaller countries. It is entirely landlocked and is positioned where the high, folded mountains of the Alps meet the lowlands of the Danube Plain. Nearly 40 per cent of Austria's 7.5 million inhabitants live in four major cities, Vienna, Graz, Linz and Salzburg; Vienna, the national capital with a population of 1.6 million, is by far the largest. The remainder live largely in the eastern plains and only 8 per cent inhabit the alpine region, 60 per cent of which has no permanent settlements at all. Many thousands of visitors annually explore Austria's beautiful countryside merely for the glory of its mountain scenery, but most biologists would assert that it had much else to offer besides.

There are fine forests – 39.1 per cent of the land is tree covered – and permanent pasture, including alpine grasslands and meadows, covers 26.7 per cent of the area. The latter include the Pannonian Steppes close to the Hungarian border. Among its marshes and wetlands, Austria contains several areas of international importance, in particular the Neusiedler See and Seewinkel, which is a unique area for wildlife.

The number of official nature reserves and other protected areas in the country totals nearly 400, and in addition there are many privately protected sites. An inventory has recently been prepared and the areas described here include some of the most important, selected to illustrate the ecological diversity of the country.

As Austria is a republic consisting of nine Federal Provinces (Bundesländer), each with its own autonomous legislation for many activities, including nature conservation, wildlife protection lacks cohesion. The absence of a federal law for the protection of the fauna and flora and their habitats has led to considerable differences between the provinces both in terms of effectiveness of the legislation and in the creation of protected areas.

Every year officials responsible for nature protection in each of the provincial governments meet to discuss mutual interests – but decision-making on national problems is slow. This explains why Austria finds it difficult to contribute to international agreements on nature protection. It has for example, not yet signed the Ramsar Convention on Wetlands of International Importance.

The categories of protected areas are the same as those in West Germany – National Parks, Nature Reserves (in the strict sense), Natural Monuments, Protected Landscapes and Nature Parks. However, the definitions of these terms vary from one province to another. Some provinces distinguish between Strict Nature Reserves, where all interference is prohibited, and Partial Nature Reserves, where some interference is permitted for sound economic

interests such as agriculture, or fishing and forestry.

The regulations for species protection also vary from province to province, but this is often because the species themselves vary – for example the Tirol has a mainly alpine flora and fauna, while that of the flat landscape of Burgenland is determined by continental and sub-Mediterranean influences.

Among plant species, those having "complete" protection may not be dug up or picked, while those with "partial" protection may be picked but not dug up. The first category includes many orchids, lilies and edelweiss. Other plants, such as the snowdrop, lily-of-the-valley and narcissus, are only protected from picking for commercial purposes.

Animals are protected either by the federal hunting laws, for instance birds of prey, which are classified as game (but are now protected all the year), or by nature protection laws, which apply to many insects, amphibia, reptiles, birds, bats and other small mammals. A bird species of special interest is the great bustard, a few pairs of which survive in Niederösterreich and in the eastern part of Burgenland, where a reserve has been created for their preservation.

HOHE TAUERN   The Grossglockner, Austria's highest peak, towers above this National Park in the heart of the Austrian Alps.

At present Austria is one of the very few western European countries which has no National Park; although proposals were first made many years ago, none has yet been accepted. Four areas have been listed as suitable – Hohe Tauern, Niedere Tauern, Neusiedler See and Donau-Marchauen. The Hohe Tauern will probably soon become the Austrian's first National Park.

Four areas have been proposed for inclusion in the List of Wetlands of International Importance published by the Ramsar Convention. These are Neusiedler See and Seewinkel in Burgenland, Marchauen, near Marchegg in Niederösterreich, the reservoirs on the Lower Inn River in Oberösterreich and the Delta of the Rhine in Lake Constance in Vorarlberg. In 1969 the European Diploma for Nature Conservation was awarded to the Krimml Waterfalls, which lie within the proposed Hohe Tauern National Park.

The most important private organization for nature conservation is the Austrian League for Nature Protection, founded in 1914. It has an office in each province and works very closely with the official nature protection agencies in publicity and educational work. It owns or leases many nature reserves and has a membership of 60,000. It publishes an excellent journal, *Natur und Land*. Other organizations which work for nature conservation are the Austrian WWF, the Austrian Alpine Society and the Austrian Friends of Nature, as well as several bodies of local or regional importance. The activities of the private organisations are co-ordinated in Vienna by the Austrian Association for Nature and Environment Protection.

Research on nature conservation problems is not well advanced in Austria, but in nearly all the provinces university institutes and museums are able to provide scientific assistance and expert advice. In Burgenland, the Burgenland Landesmuseum and the Biological Research Station at Neusiedlersee are of particular note, and the famous Haus der Natur, in Salzburg, has played a considerable role in furthering an awareness of nature conservation, particularly through its educational work with the young.

Nearly three-quarters mountainous, Austria lies at the extreme eastern end of the Alpine chain on the edge of the Hungarian Plain. The entire western and much of the southern part of the country consists of folded alpine sediments and crystalline rocks, which reach their highest elevations in the Ötzal Alps and the Hohe Tauern – where towers the Grossglockner (3797 metres), Austria's highest peak. The Austrian Alps can be divided into three distinct zones of contrasting structure and geology. North of a line running along the Inn, Salzach and Enns rivers, the rocks are largely limestone and of Mesozoic Age. Between this line and the Drava Valley to the south, the mountains are composed of granites, gneiss and schist. Farther south there is a narrow zone of limestones and graywacke.

To the north of the Danube lies the Bohemian Massif, a much older and lower plateau area composed largely of granite. The Alpine Foreland stretches between this highland region and the Alps to the south. It forms an upland area rising to no more than 760 metres and is composed mainly of glacial morainic and outwash material overlying an impervious marl.

The eastern lowlands around Vienna form a down-faulted sedimentary basin covered superficially by sands and gravel. This region contains Austria's oil and natural gas reserves. Farther south lies the Austrian hill country, a region of dissected uplands with a history of vulcanism and known today for its warm mineral springs.

Austria's climate is continental, modified particularly in the north and west, by Atlantic influences which both increase precipitation and modify temperature. Rainfall varies greatly with altitude and aspect and is least in the south and east. In the Alps the daily range of temperature is very great and incidence of frost is high. Spectacular temperature inversions are common in winter, when at night temperatures on the mountain slopes are many degrees higher than in the valley bottoms.

Much of the country is wooded, although not nearly as extensively as in the past, when forest, excepting for the highest altitudes, formed a blanket across the entire country. The eastern lowland is the part of the country which has been modified by man to the greatest extent, but even here large areas of woodland still occur.

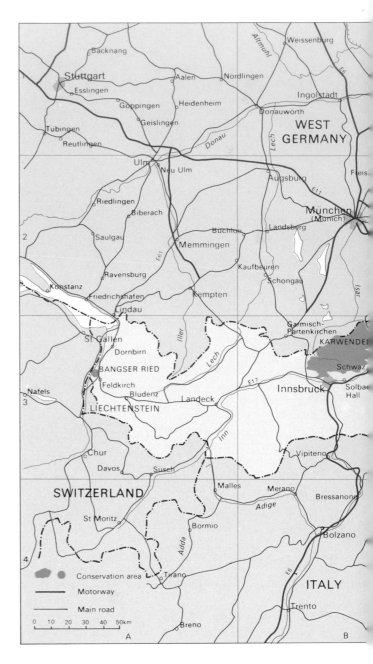

PARK/RESERVE	SIZE (km²)	DESCRIPTION	MAP REF.	PAGE NO.
BANGSER RIED	0.63	Nature Protection Area. Flat moorland area near Swiss frontier. Wet meadows with irises, gentians and orchids.	A3	104
KARWENDEL	720	Nature Protection Area. Magnificent mountain scenery. Alpine pastures and ancient sycamore woodland.	B3	104
HOHE TAUERN	2500	National Park (Proposed). Impressive mountain region containing the highest peak in Austria and the Krimml Waterfalls. Characteristic fauna and flora of both alpine and subalpine regions. Interesting bird species.	C3	105
MUSSEN	3.87	Nature Protection Area. Alpine pasture region of particular botanical interest. Many rare flowering plants.	C4	105
HAGENAUER BUCHT	1.0	Nature Protection Area. Area of shallow banks, sandflats and meadow woodlands on the banks of the River Inn. Large and varied waterfowl fauna.	C2	106
PÜRGSHACHEN MOOR	0.46	Nature Reserve. Floristically interesting peat bog. One of the best-preserved areas of high moorland in Austria.	D3	106
NIEDERE TAUERN	750	National Park (Proposed). Crystalline mountain region with lakes and waterfalls between rivers Enns and Mur.	C3	106
TRÖGENER KLAMM	2.5	Nature Protection Area. Superb 3-kilometre-long gorge with alpine and subalpine plants and relict pine woodland.	D4	106
BLOCKHEIDE EIBENSTEIN	1.2	Nature Protection Area and Nature Park. Harsh barren landscape north of Gmund with granitic erratics.	D1	108
ROTHWALD	6	Nature Reserve. Largest virgin forest in central Europe.	D2	108
NEUSIEDLER SEE & SEEWINKEL	500	Landscape Protection Area and Nature Reserve. One of the three finest wetlands in Europe. Salt-tolerant vegetation, damp meadows with rare plants. Large, diverse bird fauna.	E2	109
SCHACHBLUMENWIESEN	1.0	Partial Nature Protection Area. Seasonally flooded damp meadow land, important for the fritillary.	E3	109
LAINZER TIERGARTEN	25	Nature Protection Area. Austria's largest game park. Meadows, ancient forests, with variety of large mammals: Wild boar, deer, oxen, horses and mouflons.	E2	110
LOBAU	20	Landscape and Nature Protection Area. Wilderness area near Vienna with herons, birds of prey and deer.	E2	110
MARCHAUEN	11.18	Nature Protection Area. Largest area of near-natural alluvial forest and meadowland in Austria.	E2	110

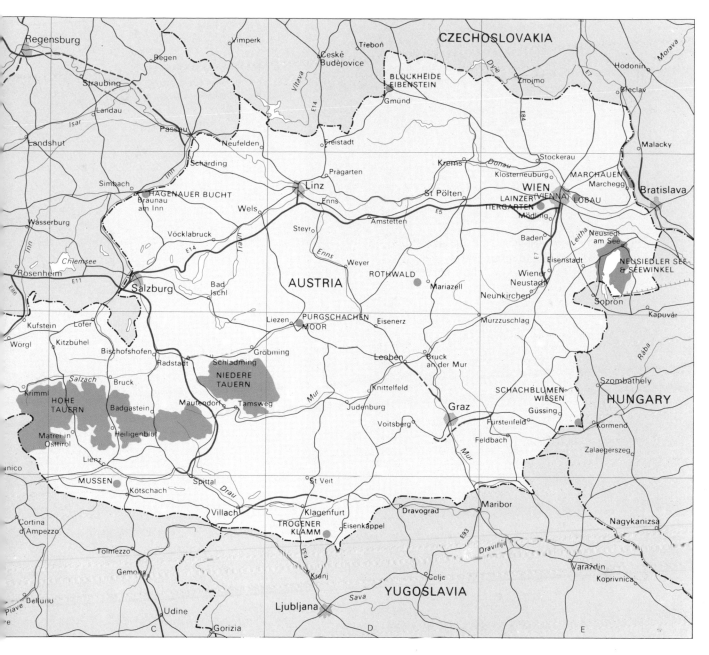

KARWENDEL
Although the limestone peaks of the Karwendel are not the highest in Austria, the region's mountains are said to be among the most beautiful.

HOHE TAUERN *above* The Krimml Falls, the eighth highest in the world, cascade down from the 1470-metre-high Krimml Ache Valley in the north-west corner of the National Park.

FALSE RINGLET *left* Smaller than the more common ringlet butterfly, this rare species is usually seen in wet meadows and lowland marshy areas.

Bangser Ried Nature Protection Area

For about 800 years, this flat moorland on the Swiss frontier, between the rivers Rhine and Ill, has been used by man as "litter" meadows. Although the vegetation of sedges, rushes, purple moor-grass and reeds found in the heart of the Ried was too poor for hay-making, it has been used over the centuries as animal bedding material and also as food for horses. The landscape which has developed as a consequence of this usage has resulted in the formation of a variety of plant and animal microhabitats.

Ground water from the two rivers keeps the meadows wet, ideal conditions for marsh gladiolus, Siberian iris, marsh gentian and many orchid species. The area is rich in invertebrate species and the stimulus for placing it under protection was the appearance of the false ringlet, one of Europe's rarest butterflies.

Karwendel Nature Protection Area

The largest Nature Protection Area in Austria, the Karwendel, north of Innsbruck in the northern calcareous Alps, is renowned for its magnificent mountain scenery and has been described as a picture-book landscape of enchanting beauty. It contains splendid mountain forests, peaks, alpine pastures, lakes and streams. Golden eagles, chamois and alpine marmots are found here as are such distinctive alpine flowers as the edelweiss, gentian and alpine rose. In one of its most beautiful pastures, in the Ahornboden region, there are about 2500 sycamore trees, some more than 600 years old. Intensive grazing has prevented the trees from regenerating, however, and a replanting scheme was carried out from 1962 to 1966 in an attempt to restore the original balance.

Several research institutes use the Nature Protection Area to study the relationships between man and wildlife in order to find ways of enabling them to live together harmoniously in a natural environment.

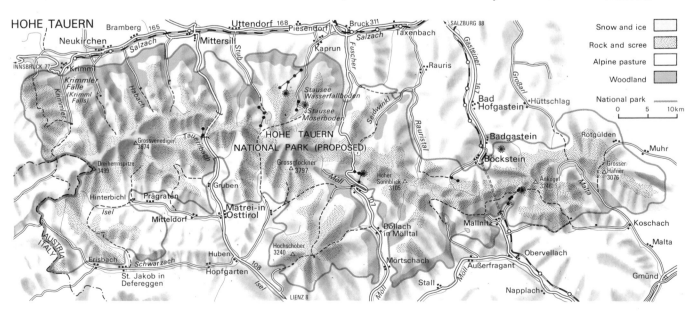

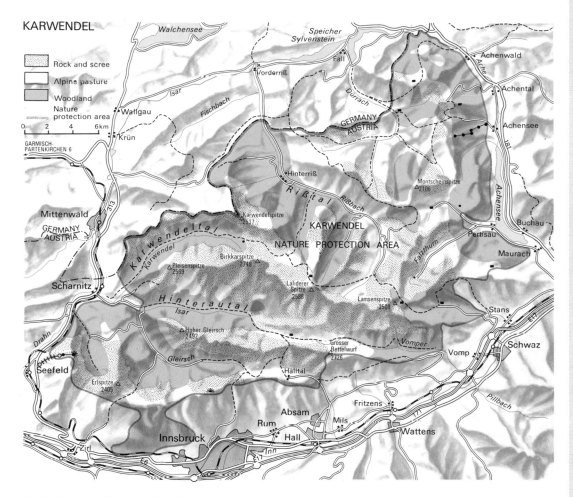

KARWENDEL

Rock and scree
Alpine pasture
Woodland
Nature
protection area

0 2 4 6km

GARMISCH-
PARTENKIRCHEN 6

1 BANGSER RIED
Information: Landesfremden-
verkehrsamt Vorarlberg,
Römerstrasse 7/1, 6901
Bregenz
Access: from Bangs, 3km NW
of FELDKIRCH
Open: Unrestricted

2 KARWENDEL
Information: Tiroler Fremden-
verkehrswerbung, Bozner Platz 6,
6010 Innsbruck
Access: from INNSBRUCK or
Pertisau, 17km N of SCHWAZ
Open: Unrestricted

3 HOHE TAUERN
Information: Nationalpark-
kommission Hohe Tauern,
Johann-Panzl-Strasse 5, 9971
Matrei in Osttirol
Access: from HEILIGENBLUT,
MATREI IN OSTTIROL, BRUCK
or BADGASTEIN
Open: Unrestricted

4 MUSSEN
Information: Landesfremden-
verkehrsamt Kärnten,
Kaufmanngasse 13, 9010
Klagenfurt
Access: from KÖTSCHACH
Open: Unrestricted

Hohe Tauern National Park (Proposed)

At present this impressive alpine region is only partially protected by designated Landscape and Nature Protection Areas. The first proposal to establish Hohe Tauern as a National Park was made in 1913, but it was not until 1971 that the three provincial governments of Kärnten, Salzburg and Tirol reached agreement on its creation. However, despite its undeniable scientific importance and superb natural beauty, the park has yet to be formally established.

Within the proposed park are an extensive crystalline massif in the heart of the eastern Alps, the highest mountain in Austria, the Grossglockner (3797 metres) and one of the largest glaciers in this part of the Alps. Numerous waterfalls add to the splendour of the scenery, the most famous of which are the Krimml falls, awarded the Council of Europe, Europa Diploma for Nature Conservation in 1967. Cascading 400 metres down into the valley in three great stages and discharging 7 cubic metres of water per second, the falls rank eighth in importance among the great waterfalls of the world.

The wildlife habitats are high montane with flora and fauna characteristic of alpine and subalpine regions. As many as fifty immature griffon vultures from Yugoslavia annually spend part of the summer in the Rauristal, south of Taxenbach and a special World Wildlife Fund feeding programme has been arranged to cater for them. Formerly widespread in the Alps, this species is now rare. In addition, pygmy owls, snow finches and golden eagles are frequent visitors to the Rauris area, and it is claimed that the lammergeier, a bird more typical of southern Europe, can occasionally be seen.

Mussen Nature Protection Area

Of special botanical interest is the Mussen Nature Protection Area, an alpine pasture region in the Lienz Dolomites, between the rivers Drau and Gail, close to the Italian frontier. Grazing has artificially depressed the tree limit to about 1800 metres in many places, thus extending the area of grassland. Several rare plants, such as St Bruno's lily, the orange lily, martagon lily and many orchids, including the lady's slipper, and the red helleborine, thrive in the lower levels. During the summer, the rocky areas have a display of primulas, gentians, aquilegias and campanulas, which grow in patchy areas of grass and form a natural rock garden. The yellow globe flower together with vast numbers of alpine anemones carpet the damp, low-lying hollows.

Plants characteristic of moorland areas occur on lime-free deposits of Werfener schist or quartz sandstone. Near the peak ridge on the sheltered side of the slope is a scrub woodland of green alder, with a rich field layer containing several species of sow-thistles, monkshoods, leopardsbanes, cranesbills and gladioli.

AUSTRIA

GREAT WHITE EGRET A rare and endangered species in Europe, it grows plumes or "egrets" during the breeding season.

Hagenauer Bucht Nature Protection Area

In 1942, a power station was built on the River Inn, where it forms the border with West Germany, north of Salzburg. A large artificial lake was created when the river was dammed, producing a much richer fauna and flora than existed before. Its shallow bays, sand and mud banks, and new meadow woodlands soon proved attractive breeding sites for more than fifty species of water birds, including the grey heron, great white egret, and many ducks and waders. The reservoir has also become an important refuge for resting and over-wintering birds. All species are protected.

Pürgschachen Moor Nature Reserve

A peat bog of great floristic interest, Pürgschachen Moor is located in the Steiermark Ennstal. It was formed during the post ice-age period on the site of an extensive valley-lake created from melt-water as the glaciers retreated. Today, the water table in the bog is maintained by the relatively high rainfall of the region. The peat layer, mainly of *Sphagnum* mosses, is 7 to 9 metres thick and vegetated with mountain pine, heather and a rich flora of herbaceous plants, which combine to make Pürgschachen one of the best-preserved high moors in Austria. Plants such as sundew, bog rosemary, cranberry and Rannoch rush reflect its ancient origin. In the damp marshes, which surround the moor, masses of Siberian iris and rare narrow-leaved daffodil *Narcissus stellaris* bloom in their thousands each spring – a truly magnificent and enchanting site.

Among the insects found in the reserve are species regarded as ice-age relics, such as the moth *Anarta cordigera* and the long-legged fly *Dolichopus annulipes*.

The reserve is managed by the Austrian World Wildlife Fund and is leased from the Benedictine Foundation of Admont.

Niedere Tauern National Park (Proposed)

In 1977, the Steiermark provincial government agreed to create a National Park in the area between the Enns and Mur valleys. Plans were also made to extend it into the Province of Salzburg. Unfortunately the differences between the many competing interests have yet to be resolved, and so the area has only "Protected Landscape" status. In 1980, however, a strict nature reserve was created in the Klaffer-kessel region.

The mountains within the future park are composed of crystalline rocks and have acid soils, the highest peak, Hochgolling, reaching 2863 metres. Stands of arolla pine often dominate the tree limit, which varies between 1700 and 2050 metres. The rare form of purple saxifrage, *Saxifraga oppositifolia blepharophylla*, is found among the alpine and sub-alpine plant life which is typical of this part of Austria. Both the golden eagle and eagle owl nest in the region.

The beauty of the landscape is enhanced by 300 lakes and 150 waterfalls, as well as numerous peat bogs, most of which are concentrated in the planned southwest (Salzburg) extension.

Trögener Klamm Nature Protection Area

Cut into Mesozoic and Palaeozoic limestones and situated close to the Yugoslav frontier is a beautiful 3-kilometre-long gorge, the Trögener Klamm. A trout stream, the Trögener Bach, flows through the site. The vegetation is of considerable geobotanical interest, for at 700 metres above sea level alpine and sub-alpine species grow alongside plants characteristic of illyrian karst woodland.

On the steep walls of the gorge red pine and black pine form relic stands. Interspersed among them are whitebeam, alpine laburnum, hairy alpenrose and dwarf alpenrose. In the warmer areas there are fragments of deciduous woodland, consisting of ash, beech and hop-hornbeam. This is the only place in Austria where the Thore's buttercup can be found – a slender alpine species with a distinctive kidney-shaped lower leaf.

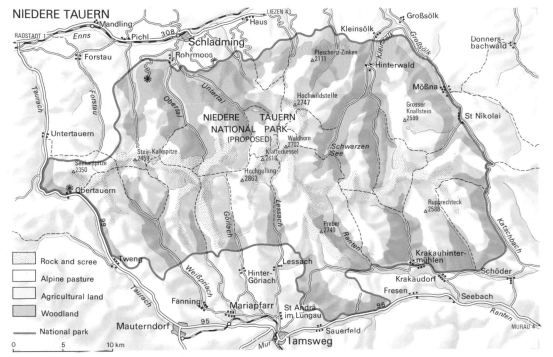

NIEDERE TAUERN

Rock and scree
Alpine pasture
Agricultural land
Woodland
National park

0   5   10 km

NIEDERE TAUERN *below* Steep scree slopes skirting high frost-cracked peaks slope down to the floor of a hanging valley lying above an area of alpine pasture and coniferous forest.

1 HAGENAUER BUCHT
Information: Oberösterreichisches Landesfremdenverkehrsamt, Schillerstrasse 50, 4010 Linz
Access: from BRAUNAU AM INN
Open: Unrestricted
This area appears on the Unterer Inn map on page 92

2 PÜRGSCHACHEN MOOR
Information: WWF Österreich, Postfach 1, Ottakringerstrasse 120, 1162 Wien (Vienna)
Access: from LIEZEN
Open: Unrestricted

3 NIEDERE TAUERN
Information: Amt der steiermärkischen Landesregierung, Landesfremdenverkehrsabteilung, Herrengasse 16, Landhaus, 8010 Graz
Access: from SCHLADMING or TAMSWEG
Open: Unrestricted

4 TRÖGENER KLAMM
Information: Landesfremdenverkehrsamt Kärnten, Kaufmanngasse 13, 9010 Klagenfurt
Access: from EISENKAPPEL
Open: Unrestricted

**NEUSIEDLER SEE &
SEEWINKEL** *right*
Spoonbills are one of 300
species that can be seen
on this, Austria's finest
wetland area.

PURPLE HERON
A retiring bird found near
marshes and reed beds.

NEUSIEDLER SEE & SEEWINKEL

Agricultural land
and pasture

Reeds

Woodland

Landscape
protection area

Nature reserve

0   5km

Parndorf

304

Breitenbrunn   Winden   Jois   Neusiedl
am See

304   Weiden

51

Purbach

Donnerskirchen   Gols

Wulka   Mönchhof

Neusiedler

Schützen   *See*

EISENSTADT 6   NEUSIEDLER   SEE   Podersdorf
am See   Frauenkirchen

Oggau   LANDSCAPE   PROTECTION   AREA

St. Margarethen   *Oberer
Stinkersee*

Rust

*Unterer
Stinkersee*   St. Andrä

Zicksee

Seewinkel

*Zick
Lacke*

Mörbisch   *Lange
Lacke*

Illmitz

Kirchsee   Apetlon   52

AUSTRIA
HUNGARY

Kroisbach   Wallern

Pamhagen

ÖDENBURG ½   AUSTRIA
HUNGARY

*Einser-
kanal*

Blockheide Eibenstein Nature Protection Area and Nature Park

In the region north of Gmünd, close to the Czechoslovak frontier, is an area of peculiarly shaped granitic boulders. These are not erratics, deposited by ice movement in the past, but remnants of a preglacial weathering period. The landscape has a harsh, barren appearance, with Scots pine woodlands, extensive heather moor and relic species of plants which owe their origin to the Ice Age. Unusual insects such as the Hungarian glider butterfly and the scarce copper butterfly have been sighted here.

Rothwald Nature Reserve

Scientific evidence from pollen analysis of the soils indicates that Rothwald, the largest virgin forest in central Europe, has probably never been cut for timber. Lying in a fairly remote area of the northeastern calcareous Alps, on the eastern side of the Dürrenstein between 950 and 1500 metres, it has been strictly preserved since 1873 for nature conservation and as a game reserve by its private owners.

The tree cover of mixed spruce, fir and beech is similar to the composition of the managed woodlands in the area, although the absence of larch is remarkable. This undisturbed forest is distinguished by trees of all ages, including some of immense size. Clusius' primrose, which is confined to the eastern Alps, and the attractive grass *Festuca versicolor* are among the many alpine species that brighten the landscape.

The reserve makes an excellent refuge for the capercaillie, eagle owl, golden eagle, black grouse and hazelhen. Among the mammals found here are red and roe deer, pine martens, otters, badgers and mountain hares. A substantial amount of dead wood, a feature of primeval forests, attracts a rich fauna of insects, particularly beetles.

Neusiedler See Landscape Protection Area and Seewinkel Nature Reserve

Located on the steppe plains of eastern Austria, the Neusiedler See, a UNESCO Biosphere Reserve, has because of the richness of its wildlife been designated one of the three best wetland areas in Europe. The lake is 30 kilometres long and 7.5 kilometres wide at its broadest point. Adjacent to it are several smaller lakes in an area known as Seewinkel. A characteristic common to all these lakes is the high salt content of the water, which is mainly due to carbonates and sulphates originating from underground water that reaches the surface through fissures in the ground. The smaller lakes frequently dry out in the summer, and even the great lake itself dried out completely in 1865. When this occurs, the salts give the lake floors a brilliantly white coating. The water table still fluctuates widely, but today the levels are regulated by means of sluices in the Einserkanal.

The salts have enabled a salt-tolerant vegetation to develop, with many rare species such as annual seablite, the glasswort *Salicornia prostrata*, saltmarsh-grass *Puccinellia* spp., sea aster and the pepperwort *Lepidium*

crassifolium. The shallowness of the water, averaging about 1 metre in depth, has also resulted in the growth of an extensive reed belt of about 5 to 6 kilometres wide around the lake. This has become a haven for numerous marsh and aquatic birds, including the great white and little egrets, spoonbill, purple heron, bittern, little bittern, greylag goose, bearded and penduline tits and aquatic and moustached warblers. About 300 bird species have been observed on the Neusiedler See and approximately half this total breed on the lake.

In the damp meadows to the north of the lake, a number of rare plants and animals have been recorded, such as the wormwood, *Artemisia lacinata*, Orsini's viper and the beautiful large moth *Chondrosoma fiduciaria*, which is an eastern steppe species. In the spring, the bright yellow flowers of yellow pheasant's eye and the lovely violet pasque-flowers *Pulsatilla grandis* and *P. nigricans* enliven the dry grasslands of the so-called "puszta", which are thought to have evolved from an original forest cover subsequently destroyed by grazing. *Iris pumila* and common feather-grass are also widespread, and in the late summer large areas are coloured blue with spiked speedwell.

In the absence of National Park status, protection for the various wildlife habitats is difficult to provide. Nearly all the land is privately owned, and many areas have been reclaimed for agriculture, vine growing, or have been developed for tourism. Further progress cannot be made until the conflict of interests between the many different forms of land-use and nature conservation has been effectively resolved.

Schachblumenwiesen Partial Nature Protection Area

In early spring, thousands of flowering heads of the fritillary carpet these damp meadows, situated in the southeast corner of Burgenland, near Luising, in the confluence area of the rivers Strembach and Pinka on the Hungarian border. Agricultural reclamation, particularly reseeding with grass and the use of artificial fertilizers, has caused this plant, a member of the lily family, to disappear from many sites, but it has survived in meadows where traditional hay-cutting and seasonal flooding have continued. The only other place in Austria where the fritillary grows is in a narrowly defined area in East Steiermark. It flowers very well in the remnants of alluvial woodlands, which may have been its original habitat. The large pendulant blooms appear in early spring, and when they are present in their thousands, as they are at Schachblumenwiesen, they produce a most beautiful and colourful effect. It often appears in association with the chickweed *Moenchia mantica*. Belgian gagea, the alpine squill and the snowdrop also grow in the woods of this Nature Protection Area.

1 BLOCKHEIDE EIBENSTEIN
Information: Naturparkverein Blockheide, 3950 Eibenstein bei Gmünd
Access: from GMÜND
Open: Unrestricted
Facilities: Information centre. Nature trail and circular footpath. Observation tower open from mid-March to November

2 ROTHWALD
Information: Rothschild'sche Forstverwaltung, 3294 Langau bei Gaming
Access: from Rothwald, 26km W of MARIAZELL
Open: Permission required; the reserve is privately owned

3 NEUSIEDLER SEE & SEEWINKEL
Information: Landesfremden-verkehrsverband für das Burgenland, Schloss Esterhazy, 7000 Eisenstadt
Access: from EISENSTADT or NEUSIEDL AM SEE
Open: Unrestricted except for the strict nature reserves which may not be entered
Facilities: Lake Museum. Marked footpaths. Observation platforms

4 SCHACHBLUMEN-WIESEN
Information: Fremdenverkehrs-verband "Region Güssing", 7540 Güssing
Access: from Luising, 18km SE of GÜSSING
Open: Unrestricted
Facilities: Footpaths within the protected area

AUSTRIA

Lainzer Tiergarten Nature Protection Area

Because its population of larger animals is artificially maintained, the Lainzer Tiergarten cannot be called a nature reserve in the strict sense of the word. The Tiergarten is the original site of the famous Vienna Woods and became a protected hunting ground in the fifteenth century. Kaiser Karl VI took possession of a large part of it and Maria Theresa added further woodlands and meadows. She also had a wall, 22.6 kilometres long and 2.5 metres high, constructed around its outer limits. In 1923 the Tiergarten was opened to the public and, in 1941, it became a Nature Protection Area. This, Austria's largest game park, is probably best known for its wild boar, which number about 360 and are easily seen, its red, roe and fallow deer, its semi-wild oxen and horses and its mouflon, which were introduced by Prince Eugen.

As a conservation area, the Tiergarten is important because of the diversity of habitats it contains – ancient forest, meadows and streams – and also for the long period during which it has been protected from all disturbance apart from hunting. The black stork, honey buzzard, common buzzard, sparrow-hawk, little owl, nightjar, golden oriole and several species of woodpecker are among the most important of the many birds recorded in this area.

WILD BOAR *above*
Found throughout most of Europe, the wild boar is still hunted for sport.

Lobau Nature Protection Area

Only 16 kilometres from the famous Cathedral of St. Stephen lies Lobau, "a green wilderness on the great river". It is situated on the banks of the Danube adjacent to the new UNO-city in Vienna and consists of a stretch of alluvial woodland, which, together with the adjoining Donauauen to the east, is the largest surviving area of this type in central Europe. It consists of a wide range of habitats, including original woodland, thorn-scrub formations, reed-swamp, pools, oxbows, gravel deposits and dry grassland areas. Although it has been a UNESCO Biosphere Reserve since 1978, its future is threatened by pollution, river regulation and tourism.

Its character was altered dramatically when the Danube was regulated in the latter part of the last century, with the result that high water was no longer able to reach many of the side-arms of the river. These have gradually become silted up, enabling a swampy jungle-like woodland to become established, particularly in the eastern part of the reserve. Fish, frogs and toads abound in the waterways, and provide food for birds such as kingfishers and colonies of herons, storks and several species of birds of prey, which use the old, dying trees as breeding sites. Lobau is a traditional overwintering place for the sea eagle, a bird which previously bred in the area. The "Heisslands", warm, dry gravel banks, are favourite haunts of reptiles and insects.

Lobau was at one time a protected hunting area for the Austrian Imperial family and the red deer found here are said to be larger and have more powerful antlers.

Marchauen Nature Protection Area

In the estuary area of the River March, on the Austrian–Czechoslovak border, there is an extensive area of near-natural alluvial forest and meadowland which forms the largest complex of its type in Austria. Half of it is owned by the Austrian World Wildlife Fund, the remainder is in private hands.

The seasonal variation in water level has resulted in a complex zoning of habitats, encompassing ponds, oxbows, bogs, meadows, alder carr and original woodland. In the ponds, yellow and white water-lilies grow alongside the rare water chestnut, while the wild vine can be found climbing among the lowland trees. A type of alkaline steppe woodland, dotted with halophytes such as *Aster sedifolius canus*, sea wormwood and hog's fennel, occurs in localized areas.

Notable among its rich and varied birdlife are grey herons and cormorants. The reserve also possesses the largest tree-nesting colonies of the white stork in Austria. An occasional autumnal visitor is the rare black stork. More than 600 species of butterflies and moths have been observed, including two which are rarely seen in Austria, the southern festoon and the lesser purple emperor.

MARCHAUEN

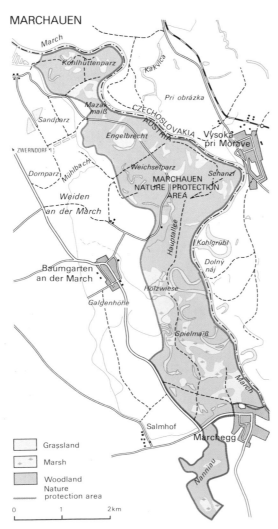

Grassland

Marsh

Woodland
Nature
protection area

0   1   2km

LOBAU

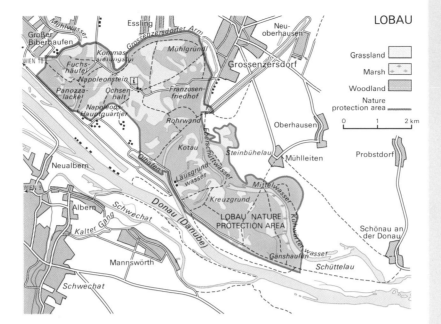

Grassland
Marsh
Woodland
Nature
protection area

0 1 2 km

LOBAU *below* Poplars emerging from water suggest a primeval atmosphere. This attractive landscape of meadows and trees, flooded annually by the Danube, lies just outside Vienna.

1 LAINZER TIERGARTEN
Information: Fremdenverkehrs-verband für Wien, Kinderspital-gasse 5, 1095 Wien 9
Access: from WIEN
Open: All public holidays and Wednesday to Sunday, April to October between 0800 and 1800. The Hermesvilla-Park (within the Lainzer Tiergarten) is open all year, Wednesday to Sunday between 0900 and 1600
Facilities: Information centre within the nature protection area. Marked paths and tracks. Observation points.

2 LOBAU
Information: Fremdenverkehrs-verband für Wien, Kinderspital-gasse 5, 1095 Wien 9
Access: from WIEN
Open: All public holidays and Sunday between 1300 and sunset
Facilities: Museum. Marked footpaths within protected area

3 MARCHAUEN
Information: WWF Österreich, Postfach 1, Ottakringerstrasse 120, 1162 Wien
Access: from MARCHEGG or Raumgarten an der March, 42km E of WIEN
Open: Unrestricted
Facilities: Marked footpaths Observation points.

SWITZERLAND

Although Switzerland, with an area of 41,107 square kilometres, is one of the smallest countries in Europe, it has a great variety of landscape types, ranging from the high mountains of the Alps to the rolling hills of the Jura and the plains of the northeast. There are more than 1400 natural lakes and 140 glaciers comprising 1560 square kilometres of ice. This great store of water feeds many of Europe's major rivers and gives rise to two of the most important – the Rhine, which flows into the North Sea, and the Rhône, which flows through Lake Geneva south into the Mediterranean.

Urban spread and industrialization have created pollution problems in many of the larger Swiss lakes, particularly Lugano, Lucerne and Geneva, where undesirable changes are taking place in the fish fauna and vegetation. Efforts, however, are now being made to prevent further deterioration.

Lowland Switzerland is fertile farmland and intensively cultivated. With a high population density of 199 per square kilometre, nature reserves in this region tend to be small and dependent on forms of land use which are compatible with wildlife conservation. In the mountains, however, where mechanized farming is difficult, traditional methods of agriculture and forestry have survived in many areas, and with them the diversity of habitat needed by many plants and animals. Nevertheless, even these changes are taking place as more local people become dependent on the tourist industry for their income and second homes spread higher up the mountain valleys.

Because Switzerland is a federal country, the creation and management of nature reserves is complex. There are twenty-six member states or cantons and each has a large measure of autonomy in matters of regional planning, including nature conservation. The Federation generally confines itself to providing financial support, but it has power to take direct action in protecting areas of national

importance and also endangered plants and animals if this is necessary.

The Swiss National Park in the Grisons was originally established by Federal Act in 1914 and is managed by the State and the Swiss League for the Protection of Nature. Because of the strict management regime employed to protect its fauna and flora, it is perhaps one of the best known in Europe. The park was established too late to save the lynx, lammergeier and ibex, which were exterminated in the nineteenth century, and just missed saving the brown bear: the last specimen was killed in its valleys in 1904. The ibex has been successfully reintroduced and is now well established in the park and elsewhere. Attempts are now being made to reintroduce the lynx and the beaver, which had also disappeared; there is at least one thriving colony of the latter not far from Geneva.

The Swiss League for the Protection of Nature is a voluntary organization and probably the most important conservation body in the country. Founded in 1909, it now has a membership of about 100,000 and owns or leases approximately three hundred nature reserves.

At the request of the government, it has prepared an inventory of over four thousand sites of national, regional or local importance for nature conservation in an effort to assist cantons in avoiding damaging important areas when making regional planning decisions. The Swiss League works in close collaboration with the cantonal administrations and the communes in matters of nature reserve establishment and wildlife protection.

In 1976 the League opened Switzerland's first Ecology Centre on the Riederfurka in Upper Valais. It is situated above 2000 metres and overlooks the incomparable scenery of the Aletsch glacier with its subalpine forests of larch, mountain and arolla pines. It is accessible only from Mörel in the Rhône Valley. In summer the centre offers many courses in alpine ecology and conservation.

THE ENGADINE If Switzerland is the roof of Europe, its National Park, south of the Engadine Valley, must be the apex.

113

SWITZERLAND

Switzerland is a region of unusually complex geology; a region in which wind and frost, rushing torrents and slow-moving glaciers have attacked and contorted the uplifted rocks of a young mountain range to carve a spectacular landscape of pyramidal peaks, knife-edge ridges, glistening snow-fields and deep fertile valleys.

Across the northern part of the country stretches a rolling plateau – enclosed to the northwest by the gently curving barrier of the Jura Mountains. To the south of the plain rise the ramparts of the Alps. Their northern range, dominated by the Jungfrau and the Eiger, is separated, by the headwaters of two great rivers, from the southern range, which culminates in the peaks of Monte Rosa and the Matterhorn. These headwaters mark a major watershed; the Rhine flowing east and then north to the North Sea while the Rhône flows west and south to the Mediterranean.

Switzerland's central European climate is modified by Atlantic influences and by altitude. The southern valleys such as those of Como and Lugano have mild winters, but elsewhere the winters are cold with widespread heavy snow. Frequent stable high-pressure cells bring the bright, crystal-clear, mist-free weather that has helped make Switzerland the winter playground of Europe. Summer is generally hot and dry, punctuated by the short, sharp thunderstorms which are typical of mountain country everywhere.

Lowland Switzerland is totally dominated by man, its plains providing lush pasture and rich arable land, and space for the country's larger cities. Most of the natural forest has long since been cleared, but the natural zoning of montane vegetation can be seen everywhere. Oak, beech and chestnut flourish in sheltered valleys and spruce and fir clothe the lower and middle slopes, but above about 1700 metres even the hardy shrubs give way to the dense, compact, ground-hugging forms so typical of alpine plant communities.

VALLEE DE JOUX A nature reserve in the limestone mountains of the Jura. It is an exceptionally fine area for alpine flowers.

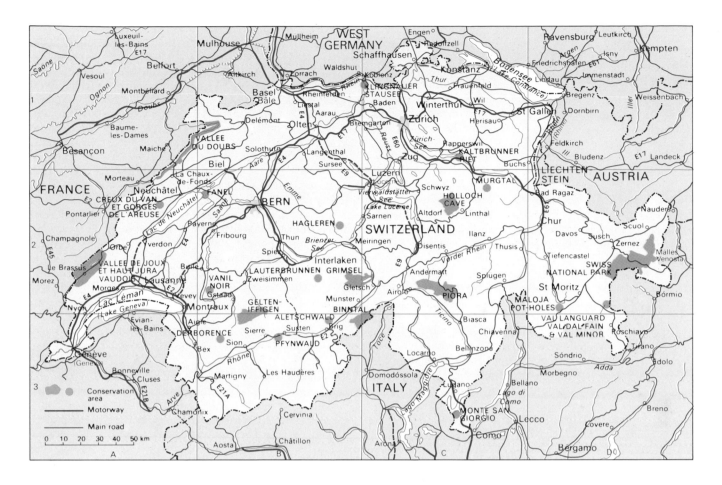

PARK/RESERVE	SIZE (km²)	DESCRIPTION	MAP REF	PAGE NO.
VALLEE DU DOUBS	34.0	Nature Reserve. Incised river valley in Jura mountains with forest, marsh and pasture land. Areas of limestone vegetation. Many orchid species. Rich birdlife.	A1/B1	116
FANEL	4.00	Nature Reserve. Important ornithological site. Lake with marginal reed beds and artificial islands.	B2	116
CREUX DU VAN ET GORGES DE L'AREUSE	11.0	Nature Reserve. Glacial cirque and large river gorge. Contrasting coniferous and deciduous forest, alpine pasture. Interesting dry-tolerant vegetation. Rare plants. Large number of bat species.	A2	116
VALLEE DE JOUX ET HAUT JURA VAUDOIS	220.0	Nature Reserve. Large limestone-mountain area. Forests and alpine pasture. Interesting flora. Reed swamp and lagoons with wading birds in breeding season.	A2	116
KLINGNAUER STAUSEE	1.96	Nature Reserve. Man-made lake, important for overwintering waterfowl. Observation point for migratory waders: reedswamp and wooded meadows at southern end of lake.	C1	118
HAGLEREN	0.60	Nature Reserve. Low-lying area of heather moor, forest and bog on sandstones and slates.	B2	119
HÖLLOCH CAVE	92.4	Nature Reserve. Immense cave lying in karst landscape east of Schwyz. Rare cave fauna.	C2	119
KALTBRUNNER RIET	0.25	Nature Reserve. Small wetland area with reed-fringed lake and wet pastures.	C1	119
MURGTAL	0.50	Landscape Protection Area. Typical northern alpine landscape with outstanding flora.	C2	119
VANIL NOIR	6.76	Nature Reserve. Calcareous pre-alpine region north of Chateau d'Oex. Rich flora. Diverse fauna.	B2	120
GELTEN-IFFIGEN	43.0	Nature Reserve and Landscape Protection Area. Alpine area with waterfalls and mountain lakes. Fine example of vegetation zonation. Oldest site of human habitation in Switzerland.	B2/B3	120
DERBORENCE	c 10.0	Landscape Protection Area. Virgin-pine forest lying on old landslip. Mountain pastures at high altitude.	B3	120
PFYNWALD	10.0	Nature Reserve. Large Scots-pine forest in sparsely populated area. Rich insect fauna.	B3	121
LAUTERBRUNNEN	26.3	Nature Reserve. Alpine river valley bordered by high cliffs. Many waterfalls, including famous Trümmelbach Falls. Pine forests and interesting alpine plants.	B2	122
ALETSCHWALD	3.06	Nature Reserve. Coniferous forest at edge of large glacier. Interesting herbaceous vegetation.	B3	122
BINNTAL	46.5	Nature Reserve. Beautiful alpine valley of geological significance. Large number of heath and bog plant species	B3/C3	122
GRIMSEL	100	Nature Reserve. High alpine landscape with lakes, snow fields and glaciers.	B2/C2	122
SWISS NATIONAL PARK	168.7	Superb mountain area in the Engadine with extensive forests. Flora influenced by calcareous soils. Several East-European plant species. Typical alpine fauna. Reintroduced ibex.	D2	124
PIORA	37.0	Landscape Protection Area. Alpine river valley of outstanding scenic value. Mountains, lakes, woods and marshes. Moorland of floristic interest.	C2	126
VAL LANGUARD/DALFAIN/ MINOR	17.5	Nature Reserve. High mountain area in the Graubünden. Largest ibex colony in Switzerland at Piz Albris. Fine forests and rich alpine flora.	D2	126
MALOJA POT-HOLES	0.31	Nature Reserve. Series of deep depressions in metamorphic rock formed by glacial melt water.	D2	127
MONTE SAN GIORGIO	25.0	Nature Reserve. Forest-clad mountain bordering Lake Lugano. Flora modified by Mediterranean influences.	C3	127

Vallée du Doubs Nature Reserve

A deeply cut river bed in the Jura forming a striking landscape of steeply wooded slopes and lakes, Vallée du Doubs is a popular place with visitors. Two of the most notable features are the Cirque de Moron and the waterfall of Saut de Doubs. Apart from areas of forest, which have suffered little disturbance and are probably in a near-natural state, there are, in the valley bottoms, several areas of marsh and poor pasture, in which grow many orchid species. In addition patches of stone and scree, with a vegetation characteristic of limestone soils are found at higher levels. Where there are grasslands kept moist by winter floods, the lovely bell-shaped flowers of the snakeshead lily, or fritillary appear in April and May. This is the only locality in Switzerland in which this increasingly scarce plant is known to occur.

The birdlife, rich in species, includes the red kite, peregrine falcon, raven, heron and kingfisher. The otter and wild cat occur and the reserve is one of the few localities in the Jura inhabited by the fire salamander.

PEREGRINE This large falcon usually kills its prey by one blow from its talons after a "stoop" or steep dive.

FANEL

Zihlkanal · Rothus · Neue Zeit · Räckholteren · FANEL NATURE RESERVE · Seebodenkanal · Islerenkanal · Gampelen · Seeboden · Tannenhof · Seewald · Lac de Neuchâtel · Tannenhüsli · Lindenhof · INS 4 · Reservat Witzwil · Canal de la Broye · Ulmenhüsli · La Sauge · CUDREFIN 3

Agricultural land
Marsh
Woodland
Nature reserve

0   1 km

Fanel Nature Reserve

Lake Neuchâtel is one of the most important ornithological sites in Switzerland and the only one included in the Ramsar list of those having international status. On the northeast side, between the Broye and the Zihl canals, a nature reserve has been established. The canals were constructed during the last century and connect the smaller lakes of Morat and Bieler See with Lake Neuchâtel.

The nature reserve, with its extensive marginal reed beds fringed by deciduous woodland, is of considerable biological interest. Artificial islands, constructed close to the northeast shore, are the breeding grounds of large populations of black-headed gulls and terns. On the lake some 10,000 duck feed and roost in winter. The marsh vegetation, consisting of bog-rushes, moor grasses, helleborines and the marsh gentian, is very attractive and supports an interesting and varied insect population.

Creux du Van et Gorges de l'Areuse Nature Reserve

Situated between the Val de Travers and Lake Neuchâtel is a reserve formed by the cirque of Creux du Van and the Gorges de l'Areuse, the largest in the Jura. Ecologically the area is of great interest; the north-facing slopes are entirely wooded, mostly with conifers, whereas the south-facing aspects have areas of broad-leaved trees, alpine meadows and small villages. The cirque, consisting of Jurassic and Cretaceous rocks, has a rich flora, including several species tolerant of dry conditions growing on rock faces exposed to the south, and many arctic-alpine plants at the base of scree slopes, where the soils are subject to freezing. The Creux du Van is the only place in the eastern part of the country where the narrow-leaved valerian is found. The woolly hawkweed, found in dry, grassy and rocky areas and known from very few other places in Switzerland, also occurs in the reserve.

The chamois and ibex are both found here as well as the lynx, which has recently been reintroduced, and for which Creux du Van is its only locality in Switzerland. In addition, the fauna includes the marmot, raven, wallcreeper and several smaller birds of prey. The reserve is the only place in Switzerland where more than ten species of bat have been recorded.

Vallée de Joux et Haut Jura Vaudois, Nature Reserve

A large mountainous area of limestone cliffs and crags, this reserve is one of the most interesting parts of the Swiss Jura for wild plants. Mixed forests of sycamore, beech and *Sorbus* species cover much of the slopes; the higher parts are mainly alpine meadow. In the early summer the rocks and alpine meadows are blue with gentians and pink with garland flowers. The areas around the Col de Marchairuz and the Dent du Vaulion are particularly good sites for plant life and the latter gives superb views of the limestone cliffs.

At the southern end of Lac de Joux on a marshy area of reedswamp and shallow lagoons many wading birds may be seen during the breeding season. Although June is the best month for visiting this areas from the point of view of its flora, many interesting plants can be seen throughout the summer.

CREUX DU VAN ET GORGES DE L'AREUSE

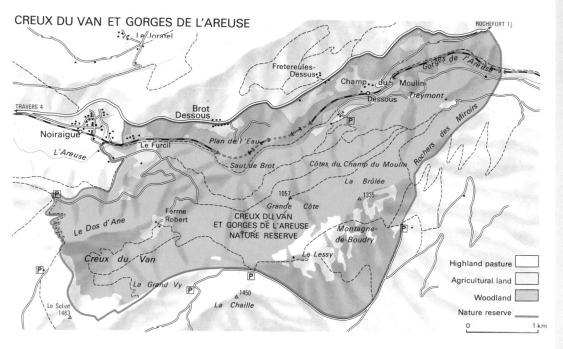

1 VALLEE DU DOUBS
Information: Office neuchâtelois du tourisme, 9 rue du Trésor, Case postale 812, 2001 Neuchâtel
Access: from LA CHAUX-DE-FONDS
Open: Unrestricted
Facilities: Valley walk by waterfalls

2 FANEL
Information: Verkehrsverband Berner Mittelland, c/o Offizielles Verkehrsbüro der Stadt Bern, Bahnhofplatz 10, Postfach 2700, 3001 Bern
Access: From NEUCHATEL or BERN
Open: Unrestricted but best between April and October
Facilities: Camp site. Observation hill

3 CREUX DU VAN ET GORGES DE L'AREUSE
Information: Office neuchâtelois du tourisme, 9 rue du Trésor, Case postale 812, 2001 Neuchâtel
Access: from Noiraigue, 17km SW of NEUCHATEL
Open: Unrestricted but best between April and October
Facilities: Marked footpaths within the reserve

4 VALLEE DE JOUX ET HAUT JURA VAUDOIS
Information: Swiss League for Nature Protection, P.O. Box 73, 4020 Basel
Access: from Vallorbe, 40km NW of LAUSANNE
Open: Unrestricted
Facilities: Hotels and camp sites within the park

CREUX DU VAN ET GORGES DE L'AREUSE
below The cliffs reveal an almost perfect S-shaped fold, picked out by freshly fallen snow in the massively bedded limestones of the Jura Mountains.

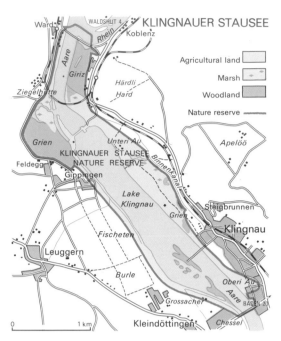

KLINGNAUER STAUSEE

Agricultural land
Marsh
Woodland
Nature reserve

Klingnauer Stausee Nature Reserve
In the lower reaches of the River Aare, just before it joins the Rhine at Koblenz, lies the nature reserve of Lake Klingnau. Despite its situation, close to industrial and urban centres, the lake is of international importance as a wintering area for waterfowl, particularly gadwall, teal, mallard and pintail. Over 250 species of birds have been recorded. Black-headed gulls and terns breed and in recent years about ten pairs of red-crested pochards have established themselves on the reserve. The lake is also well known as an observation point for migratory waders. The first sightings in Switzerland of killdeer, terek sandpiper and pectoral sandpiper were made here. The lake, embanked along its length for a distance of 3 kilometres and dammed at its northern end, must really be regarded as an artificial waterway. Water is supplied to the Klingnau power station, which sits on the dam at the northern end of the lake. At the southern end there are silt and mud areas with reedswamp, and by the outfall, on the alluvial plain, meadows with ash, oak, alder and willow.

KILLDEER *below* A North American plover, seen occasionally in Europe during migration, this ground-nesting bird may be identified by its noisy call and conspicuous double breast-band.

Hagleren Nature Reserve

To the southwest of Lucerne and west of Sarner Lake is an area of low-altitude heather moor, mountain-pine forest and bog lying across the boundary between two cantons. Although it is not a particularly striking landscape, it is of considerable ecological interest and the Swiss League for the Protection of Nature has set aside part as a nature reserve. The extensive wet moors have an annual rainfall of at least 1800 millimetres, most of which falls during the summer, resulting in the formation of numerous bogs.

Mountain pines, festooned with lichens, grow in many boggy areas and a fine example of the forest type can be seen between 1700 and 1800 metres. Numerous species of sedges characteristic of bogs have been recorded, including *Carex vaginata*, which grows around 1700 metres and is a great rarity in Switzerland. Other plants of interest known from the area are marsh clubmoss, marsh arrow-grass, few-flowered sedge, the rush *Juncus stygius* and the bent-grass, *Agrostis schleicheri*. Above 1800 metres the pine forest disappears and only isolated groups of small trees survive. As the soils are derived from easily weathered sandstones and slates and are therefore acid and impermeable, the flora is not rich in species. However, in addition to bog plants there is a well-developed dwarf-shrub zone of alpenrose and juniper with lichens, and around the peak of Hagleren extensive cushions of creeping azalea.

Hölloch Cave and Karst Landscape Nature Reserve

Below an extensive and, in part, easily accessible karst landscape of Cretaceous limestone, between the towns of Schwyz and Glarus, lies a famous series of shafts and caves. Hölloch cave, the best known, having a length of 133 kilometres, is the second largest measured cave in the world. It has a rich stalactite and stalagmite formation and many other unusual, deeply coloured concretions.

Unknown at the beginning of the century, the cave has been studied comprehensively since 1949, leading to the discovery of a rare cave fauna. Only about 5 kilometres are open to the public. In the low-lying areas, the karst has a well-developed grassland of moor-grass, but elsewhere there is an extensive coniferous forest in which the capercaillie is well established. The higher parts of the karst formation are largely devoid of vegetation, although many plants survive in rock crevices. One of the most attractive is yellow coris, a subshrub with bright yellow flowers.

Kaltbrunner Riet Nature Reserve

Southeast of Zurich, in intensively cultivated land, lies a small area of wetland that has survived the reclamation of a once-extensive bog. Apart from the Linth Canal, which lies along the reserve boundary, there is a reed-fringed lake with surrounding wet pastures.

For some time Kaltbrunner Riet was the only breeding site in Switzerland for both the black-headed gull and the redshank. The black-headed gull now breeds more commonly and seven colonies exist throughout the country. The redshank, on the other hand, has not been recorded nesting since 1916. Many species of duck have bred here, including shoveler, garganey, teal and pochard, as well as the black-necked grebe and several species of rail.

The level of the water table is controlled to maintain the best conditions for waterfowl and to achieve a balance between reedswamp and meadow. By this means it is hoped to attract more wading birds, in particular the black-tailed godwit, as breeding species.

Murgtal Landscape Protection Area

The valley of the River Murg is typical of the landscape of the northern Alps. Rising from several small lakes at the head of the valley, the river flows north to meet the Walensee at the village of Murg. At high altitudes, mountain and arolla pines with alpenrose and green alder characterize the vegetation, while at

CAPERCAILLIE The largest European grouse, the male is known for his spectacular courtship display.

lower levels, nearer the Walensee, the forest is of chestnut and lime and has a rich herb flora. Plants of particular interest in the Murg valley are the alpine woodsia, Pyrenean violet, slender gentian and the musk milfoil. Near Murg is a wood consisting of *Tilieto-Asperuletum taurinae*, which is regarded as a relict from warmer postglacial times. Typical of the species found here are the small-leaved lime, broad-leaved lime, Norway maple, black bryony, broad-leaved spindle-tree, bladder-nut, *Asperula taurina* and the sowbread. There is little information available about the area's birdlife and mammal fauna.

1 KLINGNAUER STAUSEE
Information: Swiss League for Nature Protection, P.O. Box 73, 4020 Basel
Access: from KOBLENZ
Open: Unrestricted

2 HAGLEREN
Information: Swiss League for Nature Protection, P.O. Box 73, 4020 Basel
Access: from Flühli, 45km SW of LUZERN
Open: Unrestricted
Facilities: Marked footpaths within the reserve

3 HÖLLOCH CAVE
Information: Verkehrsverband Zentralschweiz, Pilatusstrasse 14, Postfach 191, 6002 Luzern
Access: from Hinterthal, 15km SE of SCHWYZ
Open: Unrestricted except for Hölloch cave, open between 0800 and 1800, which may be visited with a guide

4 KALTBRUNNER RIET
Information: M. Markus Feusi. Hinterstadt 3, 8730 Uznach
Access: from Uznach, 45km SE of ZÜRICH
Open: Unrestricted
Facilities: Exhibition open on Saturday and Sunday, April to June. Observation tower

5 MURGTAL
Information: Verkehrsverband Ostschweiz, Bahnhofplatz 1a, Postfach 475, 9001 St Gallen
Access: from Murg, 50km NW of CHUR
Open: Unrestricted

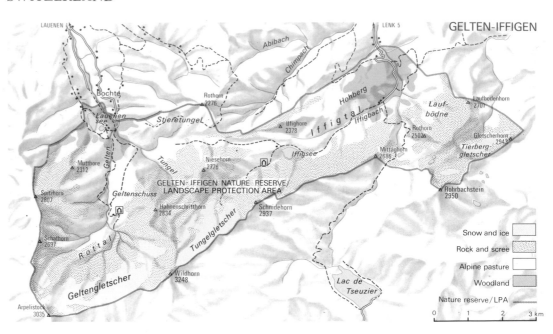

GELTEN-IFFIGEN

CHAMOIS A graceful
goat-antelope it has small
erect horns, recurved at
the tips. The females and
kids live in herds, the
males joining them during
the rutting season.

MARSH WARBLER
A small brown bird,
distinguishable from the
reed warbler only by its
song, which often mimics
that of other birds.

Vanil Noir Nature Reserve

Centred on two peaks, Vanil Noir (2389 metres) and Dent de Ruth (2236 metres), the reserve lies in the mountains, north of Chateaux-d'Oex. The region, broadly typical of calcareous pre-alpine terrain, is characterized by rocky cliffs, alpine and subalpine meadows and marshy areas. The flora is exceptionally rich and a long list of plants has been recorded, *Gagea minima*, variegated monkshood, alpine clematis, Monte Baldo anemone, Thore's buttercup, Parnassus-leaved buttercup, alpine poppy, Mount Cenis pansy and the mountain pansy *Viola lutea* var. *helvetica*, to name but a few. The mammal fauna, less well known, includes the chamois and ibex. The golden eagle, ptarmigan, rock partridge, crag martin, water pipit, alpine accentor, rock thrush, wallcreeper, alpine chough and snow finch are among the many birds occurring within the reserve.

Gelten-Iffigen Nature Reserve and Landscape Protection Area

An alpine landscape of calcareous rocks, Gelten-Iffigen differs from the other nature reserves in the Bernese Oberland in its possession of splendid waterfalls and mountain lakes. The highest falls are the Geltenschuss, where the waters tumble down a 200-metre cliff. In the 1950s a proposal to use the falls for generating electricity was successfully opposed by the local people who waged a vigorous campaign in their defence.

South of Laufbodenhorn, at 2701 metres, evidence of occupation by man during the Palaeolithic era has been found. This is the oldest known site of human habitation in Switzerland.

Gelten-Iffigen is part nature reserve and part Landscape Protection Area. The nature reserve occupies the western Gelten area and the landscape protection zone, the eastern Iffigen portion. On the gently sloping rocky ridge of Hohberg there is a fine example of vegetation zonation from larch and arolla pine to dwarf-shrub heath and alpine grassland. In the Gelten Reserve picking wild flowers is forbidden. However, the rarest species, black sedge, arctic rush and trifoliate bitter-cress, are rather insignificant plants and of interest only to the specialist. The Lauhen See, lying at 1381 metres, is one of the highest known breeding sites in the whole of Switzerland for several species of interesting marsh and water birds such as coot, water rail and marsh warbler.

Derborence Landscape Protection Area

In the Rhône valley a little west of Sion, a small steep-sided tributary valley runs due north to the small settlement of Derborence, from which it takes its name. At its highest point lies a small lake surrounded by a virgin pine-forest, which forms part of a nature reserve managed by the Swiss League for the Protection of Nature.

The forest originated in a curious way. In 1714 and again in 1749 about 50 cubic metres of rock became detached from the wall beneath the summit of the Les Diablerets Mountains and fell into the alpine meadows below, destroying one hundred chalets and killing several people. The rock avalanche, 5 kilometres in extent, spread out over the area on which the forest stands today. Since that time it has developed naturally and is claimed to be the only undisturbed virgin forest in Switzerland. The rock fall barred the course of the Derborence River, creating a lake which is gradually infilling with silt and consequently dries out during periods of low rainfall in summer.

Because the steep slopes of the lower part of the valley have prevented exploitation over a long period, some of the trees reach a height of 45 metres and are said to be between 300 and 350 years old. A fine zonation of vegetation exists between the valley bottom and the tree limit above Derborence. Higher still are extensive mountain pastures, rock walls and scree slopes lying along the sides of an impressive amphitheatre, with the rocky peaks of the Diablerets on the skyline. A carpet of mountain avens, *Vaccinium* species, saxifrages, wintergreens, helleborines and gentians forms the alpine heath, which in this reserve is especially fine. In the valley alpine larkspur, alpine leek, the eyebright *Euphrasia viscosa* and the ghost orchid are among the most interesting plants. The wildlife includes the chamois, marmot, ibex, black woodpecker, crested tit, nutcracker, black grouse and golden eagle among many other species.

Pfynwald Nature Reserve (Proposed)

Comprising the largest Scots pine wood in Switzerland, 7 kilometres long, Pfynwald is situated in the Rhône valley between Sion and Susten. For a long time it formed one of the boundaries between the French- and German-speaking areas of Switzerland and because, until the last century, it was sparsely populated it has therefore escaped exploitation. The River Rhône meanders through the more open parts of the forest, leaving behind areas of sand and stones. The climate, characterized by long, dry summers and low rainfall has a strong influence on the flora. Species of particular note are the restharrow, *Ononis pusilla*, large yellow restharrow, *O. natrix*, bladder senna, the silky milk-vetch, *Oxytropis halleri* var. *velutina*, Teesdale violet, spring heath, *Lappula echinata*, *Onosma vaudensis*, spiked bellflower and *Aster linosyris*.

Pfynwald is especially rich in insects and has a number of interesting bird species such as scops owl, rock bunting, red kite and Bonelli's warbler. The reserve is the only place in Switzerland where the tawny pipit is known to have bred – a bird often found in open heathland and grassland.

1 VANIL NOIR
Information: Swiss League for Nature Protection, P.O. Box 73, 4020 Basel
Access: from Grandvillard, 40km S of FRIBOURG
Open: Unrestricted

2 GELTEN-IFFIGEN
Information: Kur- und Verkehrsverein Gstaad, Hauptstrasse, 3780 Gstaad
Access: from Lauenen, 7km SE of GSTAAD
Open: Unrestricted
Facilities: Mountain refuges within the reserve

3 DERBORENCE
Information: Swiss League for Nature Protection, P.O. Box 73, 4020 Basel
Access: from Aven, 8km W of SION
Open: Unrestricted but best between June and October

4 PFYNWALD
Information: Office du Tourisme, Avenue Max-Huber 2, 3960 Sierre
Access: from SUSTEN or SIERRE
Open: Unrestricted

PFYNWALD

Agricultural land
Woodland
Sand and gravel
Nature reserve

0 ____ 1km

DERBORENCE *below* Claimed to be the only virgin forest in Switzerland, the nature reserve lies on an area of rock and scree, north of the Rhône, formed by two major land slides in the eighteenth century.

121

Lauterbrunnen Nature Reserve

The 18-kilometre-long Lauterbrunnen Valley, bordered on each side by 300- to 500-metre-high walls of calcareous rocks, is one of the most famous in Europe. Supplied by water from thirteen glaciers, seventy-two streams flow down its precipitous sides, giving the valley more waterfalls than any other in the Alps. The best known is the Trümmelbach Falls, which forces its way into the open through a series of large eroded pot-holes.

The first of the alpine meadows that make up the reserve was bought by the Swiss League for the Protection of Nature in 1947. Originally they were greatly overgrazed, but, by agreement with local farmers, stocking has been reduced to preserve the pasture's rich alpine flora. In some areas the league has carried out reafforestation with arolla pine. Among the more interesting plants found in the valley are Scottish asphodel, entire-leaved primrose and, at its westerly limit in the Bernese Oberland, the leafless saxifrage.

Aletschwald Nature Reserve

High in the centre of the Swiss Alps and close to the longest of the alpine glaciers is the famous forest of Aletsch, which became a nature reserve in 1933. The forest, lying between 1600 and 2400 metres on the north and northwest slopes of the Riederhorn, is unusual. Few forests have developed quite so impressively on the edge of a glacier, above the normal tree limit. Since 1933, measures taken to prevent overgrazing have allowed the herbaceous ground cover to develop and the trees, arolla pine and larch, to regenerate.

The pioneer vegetation along the moraines at the glacier's edge is also of great interest. At first the young forest contains mainly deciduous species, such as willow and birch, eventually becoming more varied with the addition of larch, spruce and some arolla pine. Above 2100 metres, where only the arolla pine persists, the herbaceous vegetation consists largely of moisture-loving plants, such as floating bur-reed, the sedges *Carex paupercula* and *Carex fusca*, thread rush, bog violet, nodding willowherb, and common cotton-grass.

The forest, lying in the middle of a 250-square-kilometre no-hunting area, has a typically alpine fauna of great interest.

Binntal Nature Reserve

On the south side of the Rhône valley, close to the Italian frontier, lies the Binntal Nature Reserve, a beautiful alpine valley, partly cut off by glaciated mountains and with several attractive small lakes along its south side. This area, in the upper Binn valley, is of great geological interest and is famous for its variety of minerals; over 60 different kinds have been found of which fifteen are known only from this area.

The profusion of interesting plants found on the alpine heathlands and boggy areas is a delight to the botanist. Some species such as the rupture-wort, glacier wormwood and red alpine catchfly are small and relatively inconspicuous, while others, particularly Monte Baldo anemone, *Astragalus halleri,* silky milk-vetch, roseroot, *Gentiana schleicheri* and the lovely long-flowered primrose have beautiful, colourful flowers. In addition the reserve is a breeding locality for the water pipit, a bird usually associated with open rocky places.

Grimsel Nature Reserve

To the east of the Aletsch glacier and separated from it by the 4274-metre-high Finsteraarhorn lies the Grimsel Nature Reserve, a high alpine landscape of great beauty and scientific interest. The reserve, occupying the source area of the River Aare, contains lakes, snow-fields and, between 1900 metres and 4160 metres, several glaciers. The vegetation and fauna, typically alpine and subalpine in character, are without rare species of special note. The most interesting plants are found on calcareous and silicate rocks. In the region of Aarboden an arolla-pine forest has recently developed.

ROSEROOT
A succulent plant, growing on scree or rocks at altitudes of up to 3000 metres

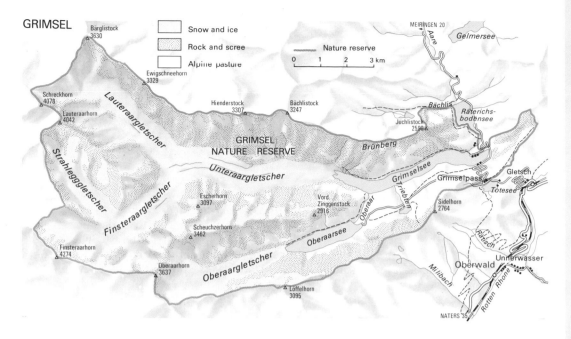

GRIMSEL

Snow and ice
Rock and scree
Alpine pasture

Nature reserve
0   1   2   3 km

Bärglistock 3630
Ewigschneehorn 3329
Schreckhorn 4078
Lauteraarhorn 4042
Lauteraargletscher
Strahleggletscher
Finsteraargletscher
Hienderstock 3307
Bächlistock 3247
GRIMSEL NATURE RESERVE
Brünberg
Escherhorn 3097
Unteraargletscher
Vord. Zinggenstock 2916
Scheuchzerhorn 3462
Oberaar
Oberaarsee
Finsteraarhorn 4274
Oberaarhorn 3637
Oberaargletscher
Löffelhorn 3095
MEIRINGEN 20
Aare
Gelmersee
Bächlis
Räterichs- bodensee
Juchlistock 2590
Grimselsee
Triebten
Grimselpass
Gletsch
Totesee
Sidelhorn 2764
Rätsch
Unnerwasser
Oberwald
Millibach
Rotten Rhone
NATERS 35

1 LAUTERBRUNNEN
Information: Swiss League for Nature Protection, P.O. Box 73, 4020 Basel
Access: from Stechelberg, 21km S of INTERLAKEN
Open: Unrestricted
Facilities: Mountain paths for hikers within the reserve

2 ALETSCHWALD
Information: Centre écologique d'Aletsch, Villa Cassel, 3981 Riederalp VS. (Address between November and March: Swiss League for Nature Protection, P.O. Box 73, 4020 Basel)
Access: cable-car to the Riederalp from Mörel, 7km NE of BRIG
Open: The centre is open from mid-June to mid-October
Facilities: Exhibition and botanic garden at the centre

3 BINNTAL
Information: Verkehrsbüro, Marktplatz, 3900 Brig
Access: from Binn, 27km NE of BRIG
Open: Unrestricted

4 GRIMSEL
Information: Verkehrsverein Meiringen/Haslital, 3860 Meiringen
Access: from the Grimsel Pass, 38km SE of MEIRINGEN or 48km NE of BRIG
Open: The public road into the Grimsel valley is only open during the summer

ALETSCHWALD *below* The Aletsch glacier lying to the north of the Rhône Valley, near the town of Brig, is the largest in the Alps. In this view, looking up the glacier towards the Jungfrau massif the medial moraines, formed of debris scraped up by the glacier, stand out as dark parallel bands.

①④
②③

SWISS NATIONAL PARK

In 1914, when the Swiss National Park was established, there were very few protected areas in Europe. It became a model for other countries to follow and today it is probably the best managed and studied conservation area in Europe. It combines superb scenic beauty with great wildlife interest and, with the splendid National Park House at Zernez, provides a highly convincing demonstration of the educational value of nature conservation. It is estimated that around 300,000 people visit the park each year.

With its southern boundary running along the frontier with Italy, the park occupies a high mountain region in the Engadine, adjacent to the Italian National Park of Stelvio. It has several magnificent peaks – the highest, Piz Quattervals, rising to 3165 metres – separated by deep, narrow valleys with many streams and extensive winter snow fields but no permanent glaciers. About half its 5000 hectares of forest consists of scrubby dwarf mountain pine, giving the park the greatest concentration of this species in Switzerland. Although the tree limit, between 2300 and 2400 metres, is relatively high for the Alps, because the park itself lies at high altitude, large areas of countryside lie above the tree-line and the park contains as much as 10,000 hectares of alpine grassland.

The forests have been allowed to develop without disturbance since the second half of the nineteenth century. For many centuries previously, exploitation had been intense, mainly for charcoal to smelt the local iron-ore deposits. The dry climate and strong sunlight prevent a number of trees from establishing themselves in the area, notably firs, elm, beech, oak and lime, and only a few species – the Scots pine, spruce, larch and arolla pine – are widespread.

The continental climate and calcareous soils, derived from the predominantly dolomitic rocks, have had a strong influence on the park's flowering plants, which number over 640 species. The plant communities, which have developed since the last Ice Age, 16,000 to 18,000 years ago, have penetrated the park area along its numerous valleys. One of the most important of these is the Engadine, on the park's northern border. It is the only valley in Switzerland which drains into the Danube, consequently giving access to the plains of Hungary. Several species probably spread into the area by this route, for example the melick *Melica transilvania*, *Sisymbrium strictissimum* and alpine bells, which here are at the western limit of their distribution on the European Continent.

For the visitor, one of the most delightful experiences is to climb up into the alpine zone in the early summer, where the thin soils over the limestone rocks support a profusion of colourful plants that flower at this time of the year, and produce a display which is most probably unrivalled elsewhere in the central Alps – gentians, orchids, saxifrages, rockroses as well as many others.

The mammal fauna is similar to that generally found in other parts of the Alps. As elsewhere the larger carnivores – the brown bear, wolf, lynx and wild cat – were exterminated by hunting in the nineteenth or early twentieth centuries. The red deer disappeared about 70 years ago, but returned by natural immigration from Austria and, under protection, has increased to such an extent that overgrazing is now a problem in some areas. The ibex also became extinct in the last century, but was reintroduced between 1920 and 1924 and now has a vigorous population. The chamois is common and is easily seen. Roe deer, however, are far less numerous. The most typical animal is the marmot; its chattering call rings out over the open mountainsides, and is particularly noticeable in rocky places and on scree slopes. It has become accustomed to people and can often be seen at close quarters.

The birdlife has many interesting species but no particular rarities and there are few birds of prey. The golden eagle, however, nests in several places and the magnificent eagle owl and several smaller owl species are found in the forests. Other impressive forest birds such as the capercaillie, nutcracker and black woodpecker can also be seen. The ptarmigan and rock partridge nest above the tree line. The smaller mountain birds include the alpine accentor, ring ouzel, wallcreeper, snow finch, alpine chough and raven.

APOLLO A large number of local variations of this delicately marked butterfly are found throughout the mountain regions of Europe.

SWISS NATIONAL PARK Lying to the South of the Engadine Valley at Zernez, most of the National Park lies above 2000m. Its inaccessibility in the past preserved the area's rich flora and fauna from human interference.

VAL TANTERMOZZA
This forest-clad valley in
the western part of the
park typifies the wooded
nature of the region.

SWISS NATIONAL PARK
Information: Nationalparkhaus,
7530 Zernez, GR
Access: from ZERNEZ or
SCUOL
Open: Unrestricted but visitors
must keep to marked footpaths.
The park is inaccessible by foot
during winter
Facilities: Parkhouse open
from June 2 to October 30
between 0900–1200 and
1400–1830. Sundays from July
5 to August 9. Block house and
hotel within the park

SWISS NATIONAL PARK

Snow and ice
Rock and scree
Alpine vegetation
Woodland
National park

0 1 2 3 4 km

PIORA

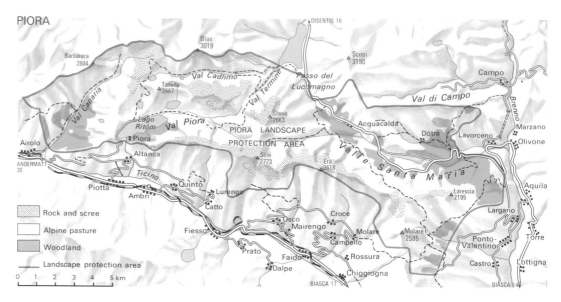

Rock and scree

Alpine pasture

Woodland

Landscape protection area

0 1 2 3 4 5 km

Piora Landscape Protection Area
The beautiful Piora Valley, lying between the St Gotthard and Lucomagno passes, and the Lucomagno Valley, situated farther to the east, are both listed by the Swiss League for the Protection of Nature as landscapes of special merit. The scenery, comprising mountains, lakes, woods and marshes overlying dolomitic and ancient crystalline rocks, is incomparable throughout the central alpine area. The largest lake, Lake Ritóm, is situated at 1800 metres.

A small forest of arolla pine, fine examples of alpine moor-vegetation, both in the Piora Valley, and two plants of special interest – the eyebright *Euphrasia christii*, known from only

four valleys in Switzerland, and the Arctic mugwort *Artemisia borealis* var. *nana*, are among the area's outstanding features.

Val Languard–Val dal Fain–Val Minor Nature Reserve
The Bernina region, southwest of the Swiss National Park, is one of the most beautiful parts of the Graubünden Canton. It has numerous glaciers and several high valley lakes of ecological interest and an extensive forest of near-natural larch and arolla pine which reaches to the unusually high altitude of 2300 metres. The flora is very rich and includes such species as the sedge *Carex norvegica*, glacier dianthus, alpine aquilegia,

TREE FROG *above*
A small smooth-skinned amphibian, the tree frog has adhesive pads on its fingers and toes which help it climb trees.

FIRE SALAMANDER
right A nocturnal amphibian found in mountainous regions of up to 1000 metres, the fire salamander is protected by a poisonous skin secretion.

Wulfen's houseleek, king of the Alps and flesh-red lousewort. At Piz Albris (3166 metres) is found the largest ibex colony in Switzerland. The animals are relatively easy to see, particularly in the spring before they return to the high pastures. The colony was started from two pregnant females brought from the Swiss National Park during the summer of 1921.

Maloja Pot-Holes Nature Reserve
Although first discovered in 1884 and described in detail ten years later, the Maloja Pot-Holes were forgotten until over fifty years later. In 1953 the land containing the pot-holes was purchased and presented to the Swiss League for the Protection of Nature to save the pot-holes from speculators and make them accessible to the public.

The holes, mainly conical in shape but some with narrow "waists", are thought to have been formed after the last Ice Age by glacial meltwater, laden with sand and stones, cascading down on to the rocks below and creating whirlpools, which cut deep spiral grooves in the rock. The size of the largest holes, 6 to 11 metres deep and 10 to 22 metres in circumference, is astonishing because, unlike the famous Lucerne pot-holes, which are cut into sandstone, these holes are carved out of gneiss, a hard metamorphic rock.

On the reserve, which lies at 1800 metres, the vegetation is mainly mountain pine with alpenrose and *Vaccinium* species. In some places there are stretches of alpine pasture.

Monte San Giorgio Nature Reserve
In the most southerly part of Switzerland, close to the Italian border, lie the cool, open-forested slopes of Monte San Giorgio, rising to about 1100 metres above Lake Lugano. The warm Mediterranean influence shows itself in the vegetation, which is very different from that found farther north in the Alps. The forest, primarily of oak, sweet chestnut, beech and ash with a good deal of *Robinia* has a long history of coppicing, but is now left largely undisturbed. May, June and July are the best months for plants, although later, in the autumn, the forest floor is carpeted with cyclamen and common cow-wheat. The soils, derived from a variety of Permian and Triassic sedimentary rocks, vary in fertility; those with a high chalk content are the richest. This variability is displayed in the variety and wealth of the vegetation.

The herbaceous flora varies with soil and aspect and includes such plants as heathers and bilberry, together with herb Paris, dyers' greenweed, lily-of-the-valley and the green hellebore. On the warmer, drier slopes on the south side of the mountain, where there are areas of grazed meadow land, hairy inula, European Michaelmas daisy, mountain hartwort and yellow ox-eye are found growing.

The edible dormouse, polecat, pine marten, badger, red squirrel and fox are all found within the reserve and among the many species of birds are the black kite, buzzard, hoopoe, fieldfare, Orphean warbler and little owl. There are two species of lizard plus the fire salamander and the tree frog *Hyla arborea*.

1 PIORA
Information: Fondàzione Rosbaud, Casella postale 10, 6777 Quinto
Access: from ANDERMATT or BIASCA
Open: Unrestricted
Facilities: Cable car to Lake Ritom from Piotta

2 VAL LANGUARD–VAL DAL FAIN–VAL MINOR
Information: Kur- und Verkehrsverein Pontresina, 7504 Pontresina
Access: from Pontresina, 10km E of ST MORITZ
Open: Unrestricted
Facilities: Marked footpaths. Chair-lift to Alp Languard from Pontresina

3 MALOJA POT-HOLES
Information: Swiss League for Nature Protection, P.O. Box 73, 4020 Basel
Access: from Maloja, 17km SW of ST MORITZ
Facilities: Observation tower close to reserve

4 MONTE SAN GIORGIO
Information: Ente turistico Mendrisiotto e Basso Ceresio, 6850 Mendrisio
Access: from Mendrisio, 20km S of LUGANO
Open: Unrestricted
Facilities: Fossil museum at Meride. Nature trail

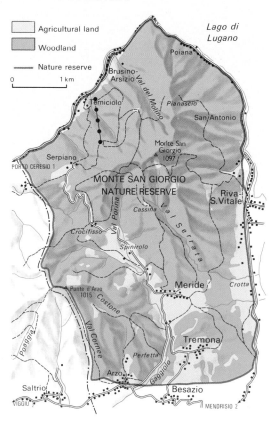

MONTE SAN GIORGIO

Agricultural land

Woodland

Nature reserve

0   1 km

Lago di Lugano

Poiana

Brusino-Arsizio

Val del Molino

Pianascio

San Antonio

Terniciolo

Monte San Giorgio 1097

Serpiano

PORTO CERESIO 1

MONTE SAN GIORGIO NATURE RESERVE

Riva-S.Vitale

Cassina

Val Serrata

Crocifisso

Va Porina

Spinirolo

Punte d'Arzo 1015

Meride

Crotta

Costone

Tremona

Val Cornée

Poaggia

Perfetta

Arzo

Gaggiolo

Saltrio

Besazio

VIGGIÙ

MENDRISIO 2

NETHERLANDS

In spite of its small size, 37,186 square kilometres, and a population density of nearly 413 persons per square kilometre which, except for city states such as Hong Kong and Monaco, is the highest in the world, the Netherlands has many fine nature reserves and an international reputation for the quality of its ecological research, much of which is concerned with the protection and management of wildlife. Many biologists, both amateur and professional, have contributed to the success of its conservation movement and there are many well-known Dutch names in the field of international conservation.

This level of activity seems surprising in view of the fact that nearly all of the Netherlands has been greatly modified by man's activities and most semi-natural habitats are now found in only a few areas – on the sandy coasts, in the Wadden Sea and as relict heathlands on glacial sands in the centre of the country. Nevertheless there are 1215 protected areas covering 180,000 hectares – 4.9 per cent of the surface area of the country. Of these the State owns 715: the Ministry of Cultural Affairs, Recreation and Social Welfare (CRM) owns 560, the State Forest Service owns 112 and the Ministry of Finance 53.

The need to farm intensively and use all available land in a productive way, whether to grow food, trees or for urban development, means that nature reserves tend to be small and are often isolated from other semi-natural areas. This is inevitable in a small country with a high population density and it is, perhaps, an indication of what might happen elsewhere in Europe in the future.

The difficulty of preserving wildlife on farmland in the Netherlands is shown by the disappearance of forty-eight plant species since the beginning of the century and the possible disappearance of thirty others. In addition, over 700 species are now thought to be endangered and a study of fifty rare plants has shown that 93 per cent of the localities where they occurred in 1900 have now been lost. On the other hand the Netherlands is known for the many interesting birds that have adapted very successfully to man-made habitats – black-tailed godwits, in the wet meadows; marsh harriers, in the sown reedbeds on new polders; little ringed plovers, on sand and gravel excavations and the many wild duck found on newly formed water bodies.

National Parks and nature reserves are not established by law, but either by purchase or agreement; that is, the protection status of a wildlife area is derived from its ownership rather than from state legislation. The principal owners are the Ministry of CRM and other public departments, and the larger private nature conservation organizations. For example, of the three areas known as National Parks, the Kennemerduinen is managed by the Provincial Waterworks of North Holland, whereas the Hoge Veluwe and Velewezoom are controlled by private bodies.

The Nature Conservation Council advises the Ministry about suitable management regimes for state controlled reserves; the draft plans must first be approved by both the Research Institute for Nature Management and the State Forest Service.

The largest and oldest nature protection society, Vereniging tot behoud van Natuurmonumenten, was founded in 1905 and in the following year purchased the famous Naardermeer, which at that time was threatened with reclamation. This reserve has one of the few breeding colonies of spoonbills in the Netherlands and is closed to the public. It is therefore not described on the following pages.

The importance of the voluntary movement in the Netherlands cannot be overemphasized. Natuurmonumenten has a membership of more than 265,000, taken from a total Dutch population of 14 million. In Britain the membership of all the County Naturalists' Trusts is just 130,000 out of 56 million. Comparison is difficult, however, because the National Trust, which owns many important wildlife areas, has a membership of over one million and there is no similar Dutch organization.

Natuurmonumenten manages 40,000 hectares of nature reserves and receives substantial government support in carrying out this work. In 1980 its grant from the government and provincial authorities was D.fl.11.5 million and it also received a share of the D.fl.14.8 million set aside by the government to help voluntary organizations purchase land for nature reserves. There are also three other important private nature conservation societies as well as several smaller provincial organizations.

The Netherlands is also one of the few countries which is backed by a research institute for nature management, the "Rijksinstituut voor Natuurbeheer", which advises on the selection and management of nature reserves. The institute has taken part in a nationwide survey of surviving semi-natural land of conservation interest and other areas of wildlife importance, which should be protected in the future. This information has not been published, but a map exists showing the selected areas.

The Dutch approach to nature conservation seems rather complicated, with separate ministries in the government as well as local authorities and private organizations all contributing in different ways. In fact the system has a peculiar strength, because if one part fails through lack of funds or for others reasons, other organizations can fill the gap – rather like the ecological concept that "diversity creates stability".

There are notable examples elsewhere in Europe, where nature conservation work appears to be vulnerable. This usually coincides with a weak government organization or a weak private sector. The best administrations are found where both are active and well supported.

The legislation for nature conservation and wild-life protection in the Netherlands is effective and comprehensive and is based on the 1967 Nature Conservancy Act. This Act gives total protection to many plants and animals, but only to two insects, the stag beetle and the large copper butterfly. Legislation also protects all protected areas irrespective of whether they are state or privately owned, an advantage not shared by private reserves in other countries. The regulations endeavour to ensure that no activities are permitted which conflict with the conservation objectives. For example, farming is not allowed unless it is necessary for management purposes and commercial forestry is forbidden, although this does not include the removal of exotic trees. Hunting is generally not permitted except where it is necessary for the removal of pest animals such as the rabbit. Fishing is allowed and in some reserves the fish are sold to the general public to raise funds to help finance nature conservation activities. The proceeds from the sales are said to bring in over D.fl. 1 million per year nationally.

The selection of reserves in the following account illustrates the diversity of wildlife habitats in the Netherlands, but it is, nevertheless, a small part of the whole.

TERSCHELLING The Boschplaat, with a variety of dune and marshland environments, is one of three nature reserves on the island of Terschelling. The Boschplaat is the largest and best known and was awarded the Council of Europe Diploma for Nature Conservation in 1970.

The Dutch landscape is quite unlike any other in Europe for, in the west at least, it is almost entirely man-made – the result of a 1000-year-long battle with the North Sea. Roughly 40 per cent of the land area lies below sea level, most of it reclaimed from the sea and now protected by a vast complex of retaining dykes and sluices.

The geology of the country is very simple. Thick sand and gravel deposits clothe the eastern part; the centre and northern regions are mainly river and glacial deposits, generally flat but locally forming high ridges – the "push-moraines" of the Riss glaciation, while in the south, terraces of the Rhine and Maas give way to rising ground culminating in the highest point in the country – the 322-metre Vaalserberg near Maastricht. In the far west a long chain of sand dunes impounds thick deposits of peat and clay. To the north, these dunes form the Friesian Islands, but in the south, aided by engineering projects, the dune belt is now an integral part of the mainland.

So intensive is Dutch land utilization that very little of the natural marsh, fen and forest land remains. The reclaimed areas furnish the richest farmland in northwest Europe and sites for the country's densely populated urban developments, while the inland marsh and fen areas, now mainly drained, provide more lush pasture and arable land. The higher ground of the south, largely cleared of natural forest is now used as pasture or left as heathland. The few remaining woodlands provide cover for the much reduced mammal fauna. The greatest concentrations of wildlife are found in the vast tracts of open water, where resident and migrant seabirds, waders and waterfowl congregate.

DE WEERRIBBEN Ancient peat cuttings, now flooded, have made the nature reserves of De Wieden and De Weerribben the beautiful mosaics of land and water they are today.

PARK/RESERVE	SIZE (km²)	DESCRIPTION	MAP REF.	PAGE NO.
SCHIERMONNIKOOG	25.0	Nature Reserves. 14-kilometre-long sandy island with dunes and salt marshes. Two separate protected areas.	C2	132
TERSCHELLING	53.0	Nature Reserves. Island largely covered with salt marsh, meadowland, scrub and dunes.	B2/C2	133
TEXEL	23.8	Nature Reserves. Large island with areas of scrub, woodland, mudflats and dunes. Two separate protected areas.	B2	133
ZWANENWATER	5.92	Nature Reserve. Dune system with large wet valley and fresh water lakes. Over 100 breeding bird species.	B3	134
BOSWACHTERIJ SCHOORL	20.0	Nature Reserve. Area of inland dunes extensively planted with Corsican pine. Heathlands with ericaceous shrubs.	B3	134
NOORDHOLLANDS DUINRESERVAAT	47.6	Dune Reserve. Two separate areas of wet slacks and inland dunes, largely planted with trees. Large number of bird breeding species. Interesting butterfly fauna.	B3	134
DE KENNEMERDUINEN	12.4	National Park. Inland dunes with sea buckthorn scrub, creeping willow and pines.	B3	136
AMSTERDAMSE WATER-LEIDINGDUINEN	33.7	Nature Reserve. Large scrub-covered calcareous dune area. Buckthorn, creeping willow, hawthorn and spindle trees. Interesting herbaceous flora with many orchid species.	B3	137
MEIJENDEL	12.8	Nature Reserve. Dune area with grassland scrub and deciduous woodland. Interesting flora and birdlife.	B3/B4	137
DUINEN VAN VOORNE	9.1	Nature Reserve. Fine calcareous-dune system. Wide range of vegetation types. Over 700 plant species, many of which are rare. Large number of breeding-bird species. Ecologically interesting dune lake.	A4	137
LEUVENUMSE BOS & LEUVENHORST	18.6	Nature Reserves. Two former country estates with wide variety of woodland types. Fine riverside flora. Interesting amphibian and insect fauna.	C3	138
HULSHORSTER ZAND	2.7	Nature Reserve. Mobile dunes covered largely by lichens and woodland.	C3	138
KOOTWIJKERZAND	5.9	Nature Reserve. Area of mobile sands with lichen mats and heath.	C3	138
DE HOGE VELUWE	54.5	National Park. Largely stabilized region of drifting sand in attractive landscape. Wide variety of vegetation types. Coniferous and deciduous woodland, wet and dry heath, wooded fens.	C4	138
DEELERWOUD	11.5	Nature Reserve. Large and attractive heathland with scrub and woodland.	C4	139
VELUWEZOOM	47.2	National Park. Part of glacial bank with melt-water slopes and dry valleys. Pine and deciduous woodland.	C4	139
DORDTSCHE, SLIEDRECHTSE & BRABANTSE BIESBOSCH	19.8	Nature Reserves. Three protected areas in region of creeks, polders, marsh and swampy woodland, east of the Hollands Diep. Important bird-breeding area.	B4	140
LOONSE EN DRUNENSE DUINEN	15.2	Nature Reserve. Sandy heathland of glacial origin. Areas of drifting sand and blow-outs.	B4	140
OISTERWIJKSE VENNEN	3.19	Nature Reserve. Pine woodland and heath in fenland. Bog plantlife in wet areas.	B4/C4	140
KAMPINA	11.1	Nature Reserve. Relict semi-natural heathland with ericaceous plant species. Acid fenland.	B4/C4	140
DE GROOTE PEEL & MARIAPEEL	20.4	Nature Reserves. Two remnant areas of peat moorland. Wide range of habitats. Woodland, heath and marsh.	C5	140
DRENTSCHE AA	11.7	Nature Reserve. Bogs, wet alder-sallow woodland and pine forest in rolling heathland landscape.	D2	142
DE WIEDEN & DE WEERRIBBEN	72.1	Nature Reserves. Variety of bog and marsh habitats in area of old peat cuttings. Many rare plants.	C3	142
OOSTVAARDERSPLASSEN	60.0	Nature Reserves. Lakes and marshland with large population of greylag geese.	C3	143
SAVELS BOS	1.76	Nature Reserve. Deciduous woodland and grassland on calcareous soils. Widely varied fauna.	C5	143

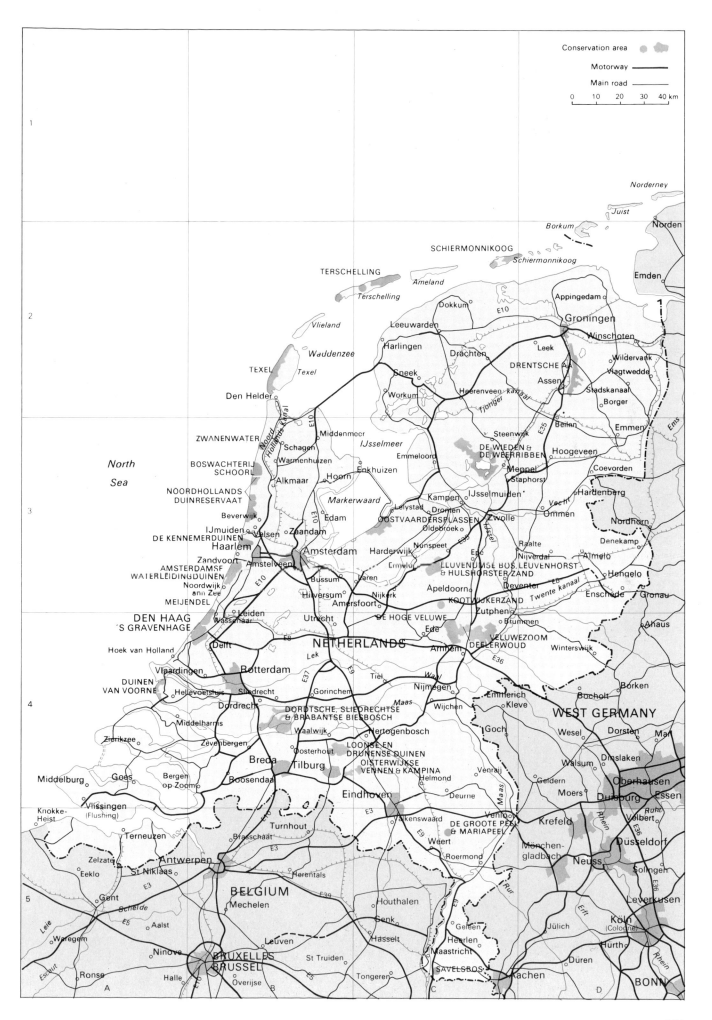

Conservation area

Motorway

Main road

0   10   20   30   40 km

North

Sea

Norderney

Juist

Borkum   Norden

SCHIERMONNIKOOG

Schiermonnikoog

Emden

TERSCHELLING

Ameland

Vlieland

Terschelling

Dokkum   Appingedam

Leeuwarden   E10   Groningen

Waddenzee   Harlingen   Leek   Winschoten

Drachten   Wildervank

TEXEL   *Texel*   Sneek   DRENTSCHE AA   Wagtwedde

Workum   Hoerenveen   *kanaal*   Assen   Stadskanaal

Den Helder   *Tjonger*   Borger

ZWANENWATER   Middenmeer   Steenwijk   Beilen   Emmen

Noord   Schagen   *IJsselmeer*   E35

BOSWACHTERIJ   Warmenhuizen   Emmeloord   DE WIEDEN &   Hoogeveen

SCHOORL   Alkmaar   DE WEERRIBBEN

Hoorn   Enkhuizen   Meppel   Coevorden

NOORDHOLLANDS   Staphorst

DUINRESERVAAT   *Markerwaard*   Kampen   IJsselmuiden   Hardenberg

Beverwijk   Lelystad   Dronten   *Vecht*   Ommen

Edam   OOSTVAARDERSPLASSEN   Zwolle   Nordhorn

IJmuiden   Oldebroek

DE KENNEMERDUINEN   Velsen   Zaandam   Harderwijk   Nunspeet   Epe   Denekamp

Haarlem   LLUVENUMSE BOS, LEUVENHORST   Nijverdal   Almelo

Zandvoort   Amsterdam   Ermelo   & HULSHORSTER ZAND   *IJssel*   Raalte

AMSTERDAMSE   Amstelveen   *Twente kanaal*   Hengelo

WATERLEIDINGDUINEN   Bussum   Laren   Apeldoorn   Deventer   Enschede   Gronau

Noordwijk   Hilversum   Nijkerk   KOOTWIJKERZAND   Zutphen   Ahaus

ann Zee   Amersfoort

MEIJENDEL   Leiden   Utrecht   DE HOGE VELUWE   Brummen

DEN HAAG   Wassenaar   Ede   VELUWEZOOM   Winterswijk

'S GRAVENHAGE   NETHERLANDS   Arnhem   DEELERWOUD

Delft   *Lek*   E36

Hoek van Holland   Börken

Vlaardingen   Rotterdam   Tiel   *Waal*   Nijmegen   Bocholt

DUINEN   Hellevoetsluis   Slidrecht   Gorinchem   Emmerich

VAN VOORNE   Dordrecht   *Maas*   Wijchen   Kleve   WEST GERMANY

Middelharnis   DORDTSCHE, SLIEDRECHTSE   Goch   Wesel   Dorsten   Ma

& BRABANTSE BIESBOSCH

Zierikzee   Waalwijk   's Hertogenbosch   Dinslaken

Zevenbergen   LOONSE EN

Oosterhout   DRUNENSE DUINEN   Walsum

Breda   OISTERWIJKSE   Venrai   Geldern

Middelburg   Goes   Bergen   Tilburg   VENNEN & KAMPINA   Helmond   Moers   Oberhausen

op Zoom   Roosendaal   Eindhoven   Deurne   *Maas*   Duisburg   Essen

Knokke-   Vlissingen   Venlo   *Ruhr*

Heist   (Flushing)   Valkenswaard   DE GROOTE PEEL   Krefeld   Velbert

Turnhout   E3   & MARIAPEEL   Mönchen-   Düsseldorf

Terneuzen   Brasschaat   Weert   gladbach   Neuss

Zelzate   E3   Herentals   Roermond   *Rhein*   Solingen

Eeklo   St Niklaas   Antwerpen   Geleen   Jülich   Köln

Gent   *Schelde*   BELGIUM   E39   Houthalen   (Cologne)

Leie   Mechelen   Hürth

Lys   Aalst   Genk   Heerlen   Köln

Waregem   E5   Hasselt   Maastricht   Düren

Ninove   BRUXELLES   St Truiden   SAVELSBOS   Aachen   BONN

Ronse   BRUSSEL

Halle   Overijse   Tongeren

Escaut

TERSCHELLING

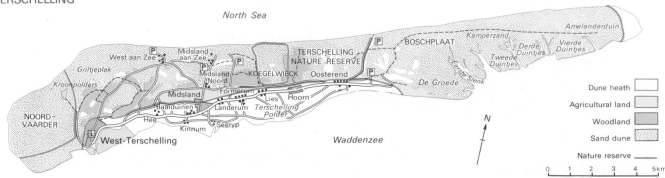

COMMON SEAL *below left* This species of seal is usually found in shallow coastal areas and sheltered bays along the shores of northern Europe. The pups are typically born on rocks or sandbanks.

TEXEL *below right* Drifting sand has overwhelmed man-made defences and vegetation alike on this the largest and most westerly of the Friesian Islands. The island contains two nature reserves.

The island reserves of Schiermonnikoog, Terschelling and Texel form part of a system of sand dunes running parallel to the Dutch coast and enclosing an extensive shallow-water area known in the Netherlands as the Waddenzee. To the east, the islands stretch into the Federal Republic of Germany and along the lower part of the west Jutland coast as far as Esbjerg in Denmark. The whole ecosystem is one of the most important single wetland areas in western Europe and functions both as a nursery ground for many fish and crustaceans of commercial value and as a resting and feeding place for vast flocks of wildfowl. It also serves as a summer recreation area for several hundreds of thousands of people.

Many parts of the Waddenzee, which has an average water depth of between 2 and 3 metres, dry out at low tide, forming expanses of sand or mud intersected by creeks. At the margins of the islands there are extensive areas saltmarsh which, although of great botanical interest, do not attract as much attention as the birdlife. Nesting species

include avocet, spoonbill, sandwich tern and little tern. A small population of common seals still lives in the area, but numbers are declining.

The Waddenzee, which in recent years has had to combat such adverse factors as increased recreational use and water pollution, is also threatened by a series of plans for its future development and exploitation; military-training areas are being sought; gas and oil exploration is taking place and the construction of dykes to create freshwater reservoirs and prevent tidal movements has been suggested. These proposals have met with strong opposition and an intense campaign is being waged in the area's defence which has stimulated much new research. Although these activities have met with some success some major government decisions affecting the Waddenzee's future have only been deferred for a few years.

Schiermonnikoog Nature Reserves
The island of Schiermonnikoog, over 14 kilometres long, is essentially a sand-bar with dunes, saltmarshes and sand plains. Although

SCHIERMONNIKOOG

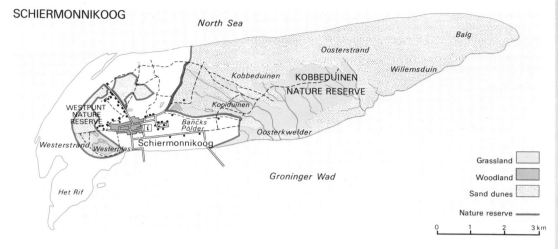

1 SCHIERMONNIKOOG
Information: VVV
Schiermonnikoog Reeweg 5,
9166 PW Schiermonnikoog
Access: by ferry from
Lauwersoog, 42km NW of
GRONINGEN
Open: Unrestricted except for
Kobbeduinen which is closed
between April 15 and July 15.
Guided walks available
throughout this period
Facilities: Visitor centre

2 TERSCHELLING
Information: Natuurmuseum en
Zeeaquarium, Burg.
Reedekerstraat 11/Postbus 5,
8880 AA, West-Terschelling
Access: by ferry from
HARLINGEN
Open: Unrestricted except for
the military range at
Noordvaarder and the
Boschplaat, most of which is
closed between March 15 and
September 1
Facilities: Visitor centre.
Natural history museum and
sea-aquarium. Guided walks and
bicycle trails

3 TEXEL
Information: Natuurrecreatie
Centrum, Ruyslaan 92, 1796 AZ
de Koog, Texel
Access: by ferry from DEN
HELDER
Open: May and most of
Slufter are closed between
March 1 and August 30 and
parts of De Geul on Wester-
duinen are closed between
March 1 and August 30
although guided tours are
available throughout these
periods. It is advisable to book
in advance. The Natuurrecreatie
Centrum is open Monday to
Saturday between 0900 and
1700. Between August 30 and
March 1 visitors to the reserves
must keep to the marked
footpaths
Facilities: Visitor centre
within the reserve. Nature trail.
Marked footpaths

the whole area is rather like a huge nature reserve, there are in fact only two nature reserves proper, Westpunt (100 hectares) and Kobbeduinen (2400 hectares). Westpunt is a wet dune valley with a rich flora, including many orchids. There is also a freshwater lake which attracts many birds.

As well as for the benefit of its birdlife and vegetation, Kobbeduinen was also established to protect the common seals which breed on the shore and which are now very scarce. It consists of brackish and freshwater dune valleys, marshes, mudflats and sandy plains.

Terschelling Nature Reserves
The second largest island in the Dutch Waddenzee. Terschelling has three nature reserves – Koegelwieck (250 hectares), Noordvaarder (650 hectares) and Boschplaat (4400 hectares). The island itself covers 12,000 hectares, of which about 8000 hectares are in a semi-natural state; there is a human population of about 4300.

The Boschplaat reserve, the largest and best known, was awarded the Council of Europe Diploma for Nature Conservation in 1970. It is uninhabited and occupies the eastern end of the island. Farmers are allowed to graze young cattle on the 300 hectares of dune meadow on the reserve.

Because of its rich and varied nature the plantlife has been well studied. It ranges from pioneer species such as glasswort, on the saltmarsh, to mud rush, creeping fescue, thrift and distant sedge at the highest levels of the sandflats. Behind the dunes lies a thick scrub of sea buckthorn and crowberry. In some areas there are beautiful dune valleys with orchids, dyer's greenweed, marsh gentian and impressive areas of dune heath. The flora of the reserve also includes some interesting immigrant species from the north, notably the bearberry and the chickweed wintergreen, both normally montaine plants.

The birdlife is extraordinarily rich for a habitat of this type and illustrates again the scientific importance of the Waddenzee. Among the less common and more unusual birds breeding on the island are the Kentish plover, avocet, black-tailed godwit, hen-harrier, Montagu's harrier and several species of duck, for example the eider and pintail, and also occasionally the sandwich tern. Among the many smaller birds also found nesting are the red-backed shrike, stonechat, marsh warbler, golden oriole and lesser redpoll. Perhaps the most exciting and rarest species is the spoonbill.

The Noordvaarder and Koegelwieck reserves are both extensive dune valleys with sand containing a low lime content on which a rich flora has developed. They are also interesting as resting places for several species of wading birds.

Texel Nature Reserves
The largest and probably best known of the Waddenzee islands, Texel attracts birdwatchers from all over Europe. It has two nature reserves, De Geul en Westerduinen (1681 hectares) and De Muy en De Slufter (700 hectares). The Slufter area consists of a coastal plain with mudflats and a shallow lagoon connected to the North Sea by several creeks. Its chief interest lies in its breeding-bird fauna, which includes shelduck, eider duck, oystercatcher, avocet, Kentish plover, black-tailed godwit and several other common species.

At De Muy, which is largely an area of dune lakes with scrub and woodland, the breeding birds include a small colony of spoonbills, yellow wagtails, wheatears, red-backed shrikes and water rails. De Geul, at the south end of the island, contains open dunes, wet valleys and areas of scrub and mudflats. The flora has many interesting species, notably orchids, grass of Parnassus, wintergreens, moonwort, adder's tongue and royal fern. Pintail, terns, marsh harriers and the rare spoonbill breed on the reserve. Westerduinen, lying a little to the north, is a sand dune area with heathland consisting mainly of crowberry.

On Texel there are several other protected areas; the Dutch conservation organization, Natuurmonumenten is responsible for eighteen of these sites and there are also ten state reserves. Most are closed to the public, but some can be seen on guided tours.

The sand dunes that run almost without interruption along the entire Dutch mainland coast, together with the Waddenzee, consitute one of the most valuable semi-natural habitats in the country. The dunes, which began accumulating some 7000 years ago, were, until about the fourth century AD, *covered with vegetation, including extensive forests. Around* AD *1000 severe weather conditions, combined with tree-felling by man, which weakened the dunes as a line of defence against the sea, caused extensive flooding and brought about a fresh cycle of sand deposition. Yet more dunes developed at the beginning of the sixteenth century.*

Since about 1800 man has attempted to fix and stabilize the dunes and today most of the sand-dune systems have been artifically modified in order to strengthen them. Where the dunes extend inland they are often cultivated and have long been grazed by domestic stock, mainly sheep. Since the last war they have become of great importance as recreation areas and nature reserves, roles they have acquired in addition to their vital functions of sea defence and water purification.

The great Dutch cities close to the Rhine have relied for many years on the river for their domestic water supply. However, by the time the Rhine reaches the Netherlands it has become highly polluted by effluent picked up en route. To make the waters fit to drink the Dutch use the country's extensive coastal-dune system as cleansing filters, ridding the water of harmful contaminants as it percolates down to lower levels from where it is pumped out.

Zwanenwater Nature Reserve

Owned by Natuurmonumenten, and established in 1972, Zwanenwater Nature Reserve is a dune system containing a large wet valley with two freshwater lakes. As the sand in the reserve is deficient in lime, a heathland vegetation has developed on the dunes. Several interesting plants such as bogbean, tufted loosestrife, *Cladium*, orchids, sundews, grass of Parnassus, marsh cinquefoil and lousewort are found in the valleys. More than 100 breeding bird species, including a large colony of spoonbills, are found in the reserve and the butterfly fauna is of considerable interest.

Boswachterij Schoorl Nature Reserve

An extensive dune area of 2000 hectares, Boswachterij Schoorl has been protected by the State Forest Service since 1894. Nearly half the total area – 850 hectares of inland dunes – has been planted with Corsican pines, which bind the sand and shelter the surface from wind-blow. The whole dune system is poor in nutrients and over a long period of time natural leaching by rainfall has gradually removed all trace of calcareous material. The vegetation that has developed on the sands of Boswachterij Schoorl, as is usual on an area of this type, is a heathland

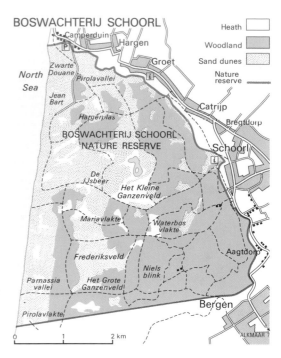

GRASS OF PARNASSUS *right* With heart-shaped leaves and a flower which smells of honey, the grass of Parnassus is one of the most appealing wetland plants.

COMMON SUNDEW *left* A small herbaceous plant found on wet heaths and peat bogs it has reddish leaves with sticky hairs which attract and trap insects.

of ericaceous shrubs with, in this case, crowberry as the dominant plant. In other areas there are old meadows which, like the heathland, are kept open by grazing.

Noordhollands Duinreservaat

This reserve consists of two parts – a large area between the villages of Wijk aan Zee and Egmond, and a smaller one around Bergen, a little to the north. South of Egmond the dunes, reaching a height of 45 metres above mean sea level, are among the highest in the Netherlands. The flora is rich and has representative species from several different plant communities. The reserve is managed by the Provincial Water Works Company of North Holland and unfortunately the wet slacks that existed previously have virtually disappeared because of water abstraction.

The inland dunes, which have been planted with trees, are a breeding ground for many interesting birds such as the tufted duck, shelduck, curlew and many song birds. Young plantations, such as are found here, often provide the cover needed by such species.

1 ZWANENWATER

Information: Vereniging tot
behoud van Natuurmonumenten,
Schaep en Burgh,
Noordereinde 60, 1243 JJ
's-Graveland or VVV Callantsoog,
Postbus 10 1759 HA,
Callantsoog
Access: from Callantsoog, 9km
NW of SCHAGEN
Open: Unrestricted but visitors
must keep to marked footpaths
Facilities: Guided walks in
May and June by appointment
with the warden

2 BOSWACHTERIJ SCHOORL

Information: Bezoekerscentrum
''Het Zandspoor'',
Boswachterij Schoorl,
Oorsprongweg 1A, 1871 HA
Schoorl
Access: from Schoorl, 11km
NW of ALKMAAR
Open: Unrestricted except for a
small area which is closed from
March to September 15
Facilities: Visitor centre
within the reserve. Guided
walks

3 NOORDHOLLANDS DUINRESERVAAT

Information: Bezoekerscentrum
''De Hoep'', Noordhollands
Duinreservaat Zeeweg,
Castricum
Access: from Castricum, 8km
N of BEVERWIJK or Bergen,
9km NW of ALKMAAR
Open: Daily, sunrise to sunset.
A permit is required to visit the
area. This may be obtained at
any of the entrances to the
Duinreservaat
Facilities: Visitor centre
within the reserve. Guided
walks, Nature trail. Wardens
on site

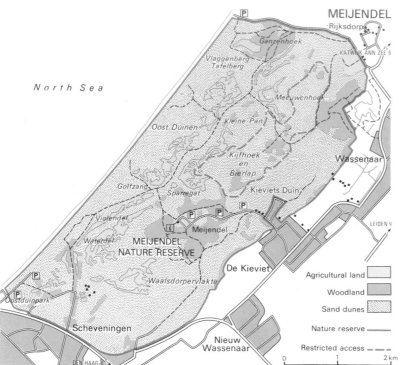

MEIJENDEL

De Kennemerduinen National Park

The National Park was created in 1950 "to protect the landscape and its typical fauna and flora and to allow the Dutch people to enjoy them".

Although the land is managed by the Provincial Waterworks Company of North Holland, the government, the province of North Holland and the nearby towns of Amsterdam and Haarlem all participated in its foundation. A total of 600,000 people visit Kennemerduinen each year and the park is particularly heavily used during the summer. Nevertheless it is claimed that most of the visitors use only about 16 per cent of the area, so that even at the height of the tourist season many areas have few people.

POLECAT *right* A little larger than a stoat, the polecat is easily recognized by its facial markings. Although it is widely distributed throughout wooded lowland areas of Europe, it has declined where it is not protected.

Throughout the park there are areas of open dune, sea buckthorn scrub, creeping willow and privet, Corsican pine and Scots pine plantations and several dune lakes which have been formed by excavating below the now sinking water table. On some of the sand dunes, spindle-tree has unusually replaced sea buckthorn as the dominant plant.

As in other mainland dune areas, the wet slacks have disappeared because the water has been abstracted for drinking purposes. Plants, typical of this habitat, have however reappeared around the margins of the shallow excavated lakes. The black-headed gulls which have colonized the area have increased so rapidly that it has been decided to control their population by restricting the number of their nests to between 400 and 500. Black-necked grebes also breed in the park.

In the winter of 1956–57 two female fallow deer, which probably escaped from the nearby Haarlem deer park, were seen in the dune woodland. Later a buck was liberated in the area and since then several young deer have been born.

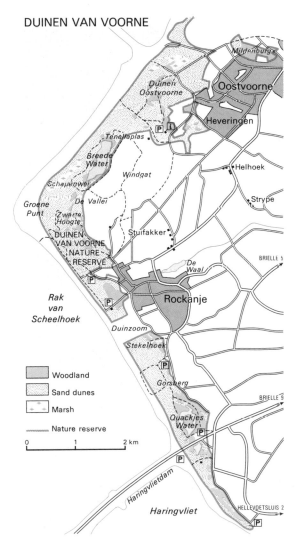

DUINEN VAN VOORNE

Woodland
Sand dunes
Marsh
Nature reserve

0   1   2 km

BOG PIMPERNEL *left* A delicate creeping plant which thrives in peaty areas and damp grassland. The bog pimpernel has small pink flowers that open in sunny weather and close when it is dull. This species is becoming increasingly uncommon.

Amsterdamse Waterleidingduinen Nature Reserve

On the Dutch coast close to Haarlem lies another large dune area used primarily for drinking-water extraction. In this area, managed by the Amsterdam Waterworks Company, the dunes are somewhat calcareous in composition and large areas are covered with sea buckthorn, creeping willow, hawthorn and spindle-tree. The interesting herbaceous flora, similar to that of Kennemerduinen National Park, which lies a little to the north, contains many orchid species, grass of Parnassus and the round-leaved wintergreen. The fauna includes the roe deer, fox and polecat, and many birds of prey can be seen on passage.

Meijendel Nature Reserve

A great favourite with the Dutch public, Meijendel is very crowded during the tourist season. Although it is owned by the Dune Waterworks Company of the Hague and is used as a water abstraction area, its nature conservation role is also important.

The vegetation is varied and the reserve contains areas of dune grassland, scrub and mixed deciduous woodland as well as lakes and marshes. There are many plants and birds of interest and much research has been carried out by the University of Leyden. Within the reserve is a protected area, Kijfhoek en Bierlap, which is open only to permit holders.

Duinen van Voorne Nature Reserve

A nature reserve ever since 1927, Duinen van Voorne, owned by the private organizations of Natuurmonumenten and Stichting Zuid-hollands Landschap, is regarded as one of the most interesting calcareous dune areas in the Netherlands. A complete range of vegetation from foreshore to wooded inland dunes is found on the reserve and more than 700 species of plants have been recorded, of which 240 are rare. For ten of these Duinen van Voorne is the best or only locality in the Netherlands. The reserve's birdlife contains 111 breeding species – 66 per cent of the Dutch total. The birds breeding in the area include the bearded tit, reed warbler, water rail, bittern, little bittern, marsh harrier and hobby as well as several species of duck.

There are two large dune lakes, one of which, Breede Water, is surrounded by scrub and woodland. The other, Quackjeswater, is of great ecological interest and contains a beautiful stretch of alder marsh having many fen plants such as moonwort and the lovely bog pimpernel.

The reserve is threatened in many ways by the extension of the nearby Europort harbour; part of the area will no longer be subjected to tides, and new roads, pipelines and industrial development will encroach on the reserve. There has already been a fall in the ground-water level of about 1 metre.

1 DE KENNEMERDUINEN
Information: Het Nationale Park de Kennemerduinen, Militairenweg 4, 2051 Ev Overveen
Access: from HAARLEM
Open: Sunrise to sunset
Facilities: Visitor centre within the park. Camp site. Guided walks

2 AMSTERDAMSE WATERLEIDINGDUINEN
Information: Bezoekerscentrum ''De Oase'', Amsterdamse Waterleidingduinen, Vogelenzangseweg 21a, Vogelenzang
Access: from HAARLEM or ZANDVOORT
Open: Unrestricted except for central area
Facilities: Visitor centre within the reserve. Nature trails

3 MEIJENDEL
Information: Duinswaterleiding Van 's-Gravenhage, Postbus 710, 2501 CS 's-Gravenhage
Access: from 'S-GRAVENHAGE or WASSENAAR
Open: Unrestricted except for the water catchment area which is closed to visitors
Facilities: Visitor centre. Nature trails, which are changed according to the season

4 DUINEN VAN VOORNE
Information: Bezoekerscentrum ''Tenellaplas'', Duinstraat 12, Rockanje, Gemeente Westvoorne
Access: from Rockanje, 8km NW of HELLEVOETSLUIS or Oostvoorne, 14km N of HELLEVOETSLUIS
Open: Only members of the managing societies have free access to major parts of the reserve although membership cards can be acquired at the visitor centre. Some areas are accessible on day tickets
Facilities: Visitor centre within the reserve. Guided walks. Nature trails

137

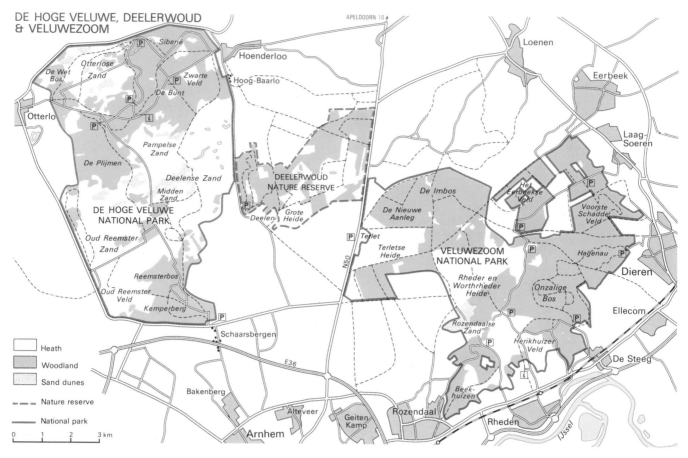

DE HOGE VELUWE, DEELERWOUD & VELUWEZOOM

Heath

Woodland

Sand dunes

- - - Nature reserve

National park

0   1   2   3 km

PINE MARTEN
A beautiful and agile predator, the pine marten lives mainly in coniferous forests. It preys on squirrels and small rodents and sometimes robs nests.

The region known as the Veluwe covers about 1200 square kilometres in the centre of the Netherlands and consists of sands and gravels deposited during the Saalien and Weichselien glacial periods. The soils are predominantly sandy and tend to be rather acid. Human occupation, ever since 4500 years ago, when farming and forest clearance began, has greatly modified the natural vegetation. Removal of the tree cover, cultivation and grazing has caused sand movement and now much of the Veluwe has been converted to heathland.

In the nineteenth century, the area was extensively replanted with conifers, mainly with Scots pine, and today there are areas re-afforested with birch, beech and oak as well. The main heathland plants are heather, Erica *species,* Vaccinium, *moor-grass, wavy hair-grass, bracken, bird cherry, lichens and* Sphagnum *mosses. Among the rare plants are the sedge* Carex ericetorum, *dwarf vipergrass, arnica, twinflower and chickweed wintergreen.*

Leuvenumse Bos, Leuvenhorst and Hulshorster Zand Nature Reserves
Both formerly private country estates, Leuvenumse Bos and Leuvenhorst are known for their variety of woodland types and their sand hills, known as "fortresses", which were formed by material carried by the wind from the surrounding plains. The wooded banks of the Hierdense Beek, a small brook which flows through the reserves, are interesting floristically. In the brook itself there are lampreys, trout, several species of amphibians and there is also an interesting insect fauna. Red deer, roe deer, wild boar, fox, badger and pine marten are found in the area, together with goshawk, honey buzzard and short-toed treecreeper.

Hulshorster Zand, which lies a little to the northeast, consists mainly of mobile dunes, together with large expanses of lichens and stands of pines and junipers. Although the reserve, like other areas of this type, is poor floristically it is of great interest to the invertebrate zoologist and is known particularly for its digger wasps, bees, beetles and spiders.

Kootwijkerzand Nature Reserve
Most of the inland sand deposits in the Netherlands are stabilized by natural vegetation or else have plantations of coniferous trees established on them. At Kootwijkerzand, however, the sand is still in a mobile state, perhaps because it has been disturbed by grazing animals, so that the vegetation has no opportunity to spread over the sand, binding it with its roots.

In addition to the extensive mobile dunes, there are frequent lichen "mats", where the leached sand is acid and poor in nutrients. Where the ground is damp, cross-leaved heath grows together with the attractive yellow-flowered arnica and vipergrass, both very local species in the Netherlands.

De Hoge Veluwe National Park
A popular area combining an attractive landscape with nature conservation and cultural interest, De Hoge Veluwe consists

1 LEUVENUMSE BOS, LEUVENHORST & HULSHORSTER ZAND
Information: VVV Harderwijk, Postbus 68, 3040 AB Harderwijk
Access: from HARDERWIJK, ERMELO or NUNSPEET
Open: Unrestricted except for several protected areas
Facilities: Guided walks

2 KOOTWIJKERZAND
Information: VVV Apeldoorn, Stationsplein 6, 7311 NX Apeldoorn
Access: from Kootwijk, 15km E of APELDOORN
Open: Unrestricted
Facilities: Guided walks

3 DE HOGE VELUWE
Information: Het Nationale Park De Hoge Veluwe, Apeldoornseweg 250, Hoenderloo
Access: from APELDOORN, EDE or ARNHEM
Open: Unrestricted except during the rutting season (mid-September to mid-October)
Facilities: Visitor centre. Camp site within the park. Marked footpaths. Observation park

4 DEELERWOUD
Information: VVV Arnhem, Verkeershuis, Stationsplein 45, Arnhem
Access: from ARNHEM
Open: Unrestricted except during the rutting season (mid-September to mid-October)
Facilities: Marked footpaths within the park. Guided walks

5 VELUWEZOOM
Information: Bezoekerscentrum "De Heurne", Nationale Park Veluwezoom, Heuvenseweg 5A, 6991 JE Rheden
Access: from ARNHEM
Open: Unrestricted except for several enclosed areas
Facilities: Visitor centre. Marked footpaths within the park. Guided walks between June and August

of three parts: a so-called game reserve, to which red deer and mouflon have been introduced, and two smaller areas where both wild boar and roe deer are found.

Formerly three-quarters of the park area was covered by drifting sand and was virtually desert. However, about 100 years ago attempts were made to stabilize the area by tree-planting and today mixed plantations cover 1562 hectares. Another 1250 hectares of heath is being invaded by Scots pine seedlings and is fast becoming woodland. The remaining 2812 hectares consist of heathland, inland dunes and grassland. Throughout these areas there is a wide variety of vegetation types, many of which are of botanical interest: oak-birch forests, juniper woodlands, woodland fens, dry and wet heathland as well as areas of drifting sand.

Fox, badger, polecat and pine marten all live in the park; birds of prey are not as numerous as they were at one time, but the buzzard, hobby, honey buzzard, merlin and sparrowhawk can still be seen.

Deelerwoud Nature Reserve
Between the National Parks of De Hoge Veluwe and Veluwezoom lies a large and attractive area of heathland owned by the Dutch conservation organization, Natuurmonumenten. Essentially a continuation of the heathland habitats of the two parks, much of the area is grazed by sheep and about 400 hectares consist of pine woodland. Some old stands of oak scrub still survive in western parts.

GOLDEN ORIOLE Brightly coloured and secretive the oriole is found throughout the Veluwe.

The red, roe and fallow deer, fox, polecat, stoat and weasel live on the reserve. In all, about seventy species of birds, including several birds of prey, curlew and nightjar, have been recorded, and the raven, which has been reintroduced, now breeds on the reserve.

Veluwezoom National Park
Lying in an area where Natuurmonumenten has owned land since 1911, Veluwezoom has a long tradition of nature conservation. It is situated in the southeast area of the Veluwe on what is part of a glacial moraine bank. Melt-water slopes and steep-sided dry valleys formed by ice action are also present and on the south side several streams run off the heathland to the Rhine.

The vegetation consists of pine and deciduous woodland and extensive areas of heathland. On the north side, where the dunes are planted with pines, there is a ground flora of *Vaccinium* spp. and on the open heathlands heather and *Erica* spp. dominate. Large areas of bracken are found in the beech and oak woodland in the southeast part of the park.

The fauna, which includes red and roe deer, wild boar, badger and fox, is similar to that of both the nearby Deelerwoud Nature Reserve and De Hoge Veluwe National Park. Among the larger and more interesting birds found in the park are the buzzard, goshawk, sparrowhawk and great grey shrike.

Dordtsche, Sliedrechtse and Brabantse Biesbosch Nature Reserves

At the point where the Rhine crosses into the Netherlands it divides into the several branches that form its famous delta. Near where two of these branches, the Waal and the Bergse Maas, flow into the Hollands Diep there is a large and complex area of creeks, polders, reservoirs, marshland and swampy woodland known as the Biesbosch, within which lie the Dordtsche, Sliedrechtse and Brabantse Biesbosch reserves.

Although it has always been a largely freshwater area, the Biesbosch was tidal until 1970, when the Haringvliet dam across the mouth of the Rhine was completed. Today tidal movement has virtually ceased and the average daily rise and fall is no more than about 15 centimetres. As a result the plant and animal life of the area is changing

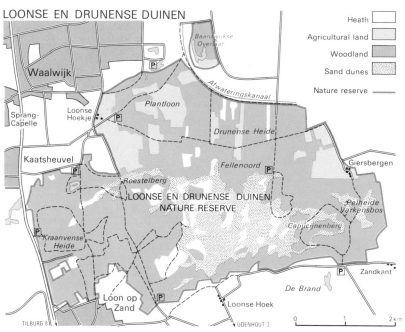

and, although weed species such as nettles and thistles have increased considerably and have in places changed the appearance of the landscape, it is not yet certain whether the gains balance the losses.

The Biesbosch is still a most interesting place for birds. Breeding species include the night heron, grey heron, greylag goose, shelduck, gadwall, marsh harrier, corncrake, kingfisher and bearded tit.

Loonse en Drunense Duinen Nature Reserve

On the south side of the town of Waalwijk, in an area of extensive sandy heathland of glacial origin, lies the Loonse en Drunense Duinen Nature Reserve, owned by Natuurmonumenten since 1922.

Its original vegetation cover of forest was cleared when man settled in the area and has been replaced by heathland. Where the vegetation was destroyed or damaged locally, wind erosion has resulted in areas of drifting sand and large depressions known as blow-

outs. In the nineteenth century Austrian and Corsican pines were planted to stabilize the mobile sands and today the vegetation consists of plantations of these species as well as small stands of oak and an area of heathland containing moor-grass *Molinia*, the distinctive grey hair-grass, marram grass, sand sedge, creeping willow and birch trees.

Oisterwijkse Vennen and Kampina Nature Reserves

Although almost adjacent, these two reserves, which are both the property of Natuurmonumenten, have quite different landscapes.

In Oisterwijkse Vennen there are old stands of pine trees and wet areas which have developed into fens. These features are probably old wind-eroded blow-outs which have later filled with water. In other areas the blow-outs have filled naturally with drifting sand and have become overgrown with trees and heathland vegetation.

Because in most of the wet areas the water is rather acid, the plant life is similar to that found in bogs. Species characteristic of these areas are moor-grass, *Erica* species, *Sphagnum* mosses, sundews, cotton-grasses, the rare water lobelia, shore-weed, alternate water-milfoil, bladderworts, pillwort, lesser skull-cap, bog pimpernel and common quillwort. The birdlife is similar to that of many other Dutch heathland reserves and includes the kingfisher and black tern.

Kampine Nature Reserve, much larger than Oisterwijkse Vennen, is a relict of a semi-natural heathland landscape in which heather and *Erica* species dominated. Here also there are some acid fen areas with alder marsh, sundew, marsh gentian, cranberry, bog asphodel and the bog rosemary.

De Groote Peel and Mariapeel Nature Reserves

Separated by about 5 kilometres, these two reserves, situated on the boundary between the North Brabant and Limburg provinces and managed by the State Forest Service, are both surviving remnants of a vast peat moor which once extended over 30,000 hectares. Most of the peat has been exploited and the land reclaimed for agriculture. As the arable farming conducted in the area requires that the water table is maintained at a low level, both reserves are dependent on control measures to ensure that an adequate supply of water is provided to keep them in their original marshy state.

Groote Peel, which is partly open water, has a range of habitats with dry, moist and wet areas. The vegetation consists of woodland, heath and marsh.

The fauna includes the badger, fox, otter, roe deer and polecat, as well as several species of rodents, reptiles and amphibians. There is a breeding colony of black-headed gulls and several other species are seen regularly, such as the marsh harrier, hen-harrier, hobby, black grouse and little grebe.

DORDTSCHE, SLIEDRECHTSE & BRABANTSE BIESBOSCH

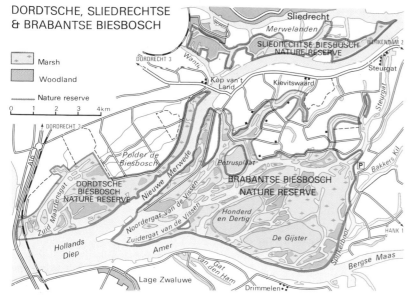

Marsh

Woodland

Nature reserve

0 1 2 3 4km

NIGHT HERON *above*
A small heron with long,
white head plumes. It is
usually seen flying at dusk.

OISTERWIJKSE
VENNEN *below* Many
of the reserve's lakes and
ponds such as the one
seen here lie in old
blow-outs.

1 DORDTSCHE, SLIEDRECHTSE & BRABANTSE BIESBOSCH
Information: for Dordtsche &
Sliedrechtse Biesbosch: Het
Staatsbosbeheer, Van
Speykstraat 13, 2518 EV
's-Gravenhage. For Brabantse
Biesbosch: Het Staatsbosbe-
heer, Prof. Cobbenhagenlaan
225, P.O. Box 1180, 5004 BD
Tilburg
Access: (Dordtsche &
Sliedrechtse Biesbosch) from
DORDRECHT or SLIEDRECHT
(Brabantse Biesbosch) from
Lage Zwaluwe, 15km NW of
OOSTERHOUT
Open: Best visited by boat.
These may be hired in nearby
villages
Facilities: Guided walk in the
Sliedrechtse Biesbosch

2 LOONSE EN DRUNENSE DUINEN
Information: VVV Tilburg,
Spoorlaan 416A, 5038 CG
Tilburg
Access: from WAALWIJK
Open: Unrestricted except for
several signposted areas which
are closed to the public
Facilities: Guided walks

3 OISTERWIJKSE VENNEN & KAMPINA
Information: VVV Tilburg,
Spoorlaan 416A, 5038 CG
Tilburg
Access: from TILBURG or
EINDHOVEN
Open: Entry to Oisterwijkse
Vennen may be restricted during
the bird breeding season.
Kampina is open only to
members of Natuurmonumenten
Facilities: Guided walks

4 DE GROOTE PEEL & MARIAPEEL
Information: VVV Limburg,
Postbus 811, 6300 AV
Valkenburg
Access: from Ospel, 10km NE
of WEERT or Meijel, 20km NE
of WEERT
Open: Unrestricted except for
some areas between March 15
and July 15, and October 15 and
November 15. Visitors are
required to keep to marked
footpaths
Facilities: Visitor centre at
Groote Peel. Guided walks

DE WIEDEN & DE WEERRIBBEN

Woodland

Marsh

Nature reserve

0 1 2 3 4 5km

OOSTVAARDERSPLASSEN *right* Avocets and godwits rest on the shores of the Ijsselmeer. The reserve's lakes and marshes attract a rich bird-life.

LARGE COPPER *left* The largest and finest race of this widely distributed but now declining butterfly species is confined to a few Dutch fenland localities.

Drentsche Aa Nature Reserve

Named after a local river, Drentsche Aa Nature Reserve lies on the east side of the town of Assen and consists of the area of the river valley and its tributaries.

Within its rolling landscape of heathland, bogs, wet alder-sallow woodland and pine forests are found a wide variety of plants, including heather, orchids, sundews, marsh gentian, mat-grass and, in areas of sandy soil, many lichens. On the more acid peatlands grow common cotton-grass, cranberry, bog rosemary, reeds, sedges, bogbean and marsh cinquefoil. The pure river water supports an interesting aquatic fauna and flora.

The animal life, including such species as deer, fox, polecat, stoat, otter, adder and many smaller animals, is similar to other heath and woodland reserves. In addition to the many typical meadow birds, such as the corncrake, which nest in the reserve, the garganey and black grouse can also be seen.

De Wieden and De Weerribben
Nature Reserves

In the province of Overijssel which, along with the neighbouring province of Friesland, has long been famous for its extensive peat deposits, laid down several thousands of years ago, lie the nature reserves of De Wieden and De Weerribben. After man had settled in the area and had learned how to control the water level, it became possible to exploit the peat deposits for fuel. The peat was cut out in long trenches at right-angles to the main waterways, a pattern that can be clearly seen on present-day maps. Because the workings were abandoned at various depths of excavation and have in some cases collapsed, a variety of marsh and bog habitats now exists.

Corresponding with the different depths of water found throughout the reserve a whole series of vegetation-recolonization stages can be seen, ranging from aquatic plants, in areas of open water, to alder marsh. Apart from reeds, sedges and *Sphagnum* mosses, the vegetation's most characteristic plants, glorious displays of less common species such as the water soldier can be seen. This most attractive aquatic plant floats at the surface in the summer, produces a white flower and sinks to the bottom, where it remains during the winter. In shallow water, floating mosses, sedges, ferns and other plants have spread across the surface to form what is known as a quaking bog. When it is consolidated, it is quite possible to walk over the surface.

The reserves contain many plants which are seldom found outside the area, par-

142

ticularly orchids. Among these rarities are the fen orchid, the slender cotton-grass, the grass *Calamagrostis neglecta*, grass of Parnassus and the very rare sedge *Carex buxbaumii*, which is known to occur in very few places throughout Europe.

The birdlife is equally interesting. There are breeding colonies of purple herons, grey herons, bitterns, marsh and hen-harriers and curlews, as well as colonies of many ducks, terns and gulls. Savi's warbler and the golden oriole are also known to breed in the area. The reserves are of special interest to the entomologist because they preserve the habitat of the rare large copper butterfly, one of the most beautiful of European insects.

Oostvaardersplassen Nature Reserve

On the west side of the new polder of Zuidelijk Flevoland, a large area has been set aside as a nature reserve by the State Department for the Ijsselmeerpolders. The reserve consists of marshes and lakes, and although vegetation is developing on the newly created land, plant succession is being retarded by a large population of greylag geese, which find the reserve a favourable feeding area. The area is an excellent site for observing many species of birds, particularly ducks, geese, terns, gulls, harriers, buzzards, sea eagles, ospreys, bitterns, herons, spoonbills and grebes.

Savelsbos Nature Reserve

In the extreme south of the Netherlands, on the banks of the River Meuse close to the Belgian frontier, lie the only calcareous soils in the country, some of which are now protected by the state reserve of Savelsbos.

Although the reserve lies mainly on the slopes of the Meuse Valley, it also contains several dry-erosion side valleys. The attractive valley woodland is made up of several species of deciduous trees, particularly oak, hornbeam and birch. In other places chalk grasslands are found with several typical calcicole herb species such as yellow archangel, common lungwort, rust-back fern, narrow-leaved bellflower and several orchids.

Among the birds that can be seen in the reserve are the lesser spotted woodpecker, firecrest, hawfinch, golden oriole, buzzard, little owl, goshawk and sparrowhawk. There is a varied fauna of reptiles, amphibians and small mammals, together with badgers, foxes, polecats, weasels, stoats and martens.

The reserve is famous for its Neolithic flint mines, which consist of holes dug in the chalk down to a flint layer. The stones were mined from radiating galleries.

143

BELGIUM AND LUXEMBOURG

With a population of 9.6 million and a surface area of only 30,153 square kilometres it is perhaps not surprising that large areas of Belgium, particularly in the north and northeast, seem to consist of only towns and farmland. However, this is a misleading impression. Belgium has a remarkable variety of countryside, from the sandy heathlands of the Campine to the limestone hills and caves of the Lesse et Lomme region and the forests of the Ardennes in the extreme south. The coastline is short and the dune systems and coastal marshes are much modified by man. But in the east of the country, close to the German border, extensive bogs and moors in the vicinity of the Hautes Fagnes National Park form one of the most interesting ecosystems for the naturalist and scientist.

Unlike their immediate neighbours in the Netherlands, who are active and progressive in the field of nature conservation, there was until recently a general impression that the Belgian public did not take a great interest in the subject.

After 1945 however influential private natural history organizations began to take a close interest in the creation of nature reserves and the promotion of wildlife protection, and in 1952 decided to combine their resources to form the National Union for the Protection of Nature. In 1958 the association "Ardenne et Gaume" published a monograph on the Belgian nature reserves under its own management and a similar volume followed in 1962. The Association of Nature and Bird Reserves of Belgium and the Wielewaal Association are also active in setting up nature reserves, in press campaigns, in preparing publications and using their influence in official circles to support the cause of nature protection.

The government has been slower to accept responsibility for nature conservation and it was not until 1957 that the Council for Nature Conservation was founded as part of the Ministry of Agriculture with responsibility for creating nature reserves and formulating a national policy for nature conservation. The first two state reserves were established in the same year.

The strategy developed by the council became the Nature Conservation Law of 1973. This act distinguishes three categories of nature reserve: State Reserves, protected for their fauna and flora; State Forest Reserves, where, in some instances, silvicultural exploitation and hunting may be permitted; and Private Reserves, which were established independently but may be assisted by public authorities both financially and in a supervisory capacity, if need be.

By the end of 1980 there were eighteen State Reserves, three State Forest Reserves and about fifty private reserves, including so-called "free" reserves, sponsored by private groups but managed by the landowner as he thinks fit. The private sector and the state hold about the same area in nature reserves, in all totalling over 13,000 hectares.

The purpose of State Nature Reserves is defined rather more broadly than in some other countries in northwest Europe. The fauna and flora are assured of protection, scientific research may be carried out and the managers encourage tourist use and educational activities, providing they are compatible with nature protection.

The private nature conservation organizations in Belgium receive financial support from the state in the same way as similar bodies in the Netherlands. In 1977 this was B.Frs. 2 million and in 1980 it totalled B.Frs. 3 million.

Two ministers are charged with the responsibility of implementing the guidlines laid down by the 1973 Act, one in Flanders and the other in the Walloon

region, to meet the needs of the Dutch- and French-speaking communities respectively. In addition to the support for private reserves, a sum of B.Frs 10 million was made available in 1980 for the management of the eighteen state reserves. A separate fund is provided to cover the cost of their supervision and administration.

THE GRAND DUCHY OF LUXEMBOURG is a very small country and is usually considered together with Belgium in relation to tourism and nature conservation matters. Its population of 338,000 gives it a density of 130 persons per square kilometre, considerably less than that of either Belgium or Holland. The Grand Duchy has no National Parks or State Nature Reserves, although it shares a Nature Park – the German-Luxembourg Nature Park – with Germany. This area is mainly recreational, but also contains the Eenz Noire sandstone cliffs, which is a protected area.

Legislation protects all birds of prey throughout the country and some wild plants and game animals are preserved within hunting reserves. One of these, the Grunewald hunting reserve, covers 1050 hectares and also protects other wildlife.

The Law for Nature Conservation (1965) gives certain powers to the Service for Nature Conservation in regulating building in rural areas, forestation and deforestation programmes as well as drainage works, hedgerow maintenance and the siting of camp sites. But it is not empowered to establish nature reserves.

There are about twenty voluntary groups concerned with nature conservation in the Grand Duchy, all affiliated to one association, The Luxembourg League for the Conservation of Nature and the Environment, which has a total membership of about 100,000. The league is subsidized by the government – B.Frs. 5 million in 1980 – and owns or manages several small reserves, most about 10 hectares in area.

ARDENNES In this gentle wooded countryside lie Belgium and Luxembourg's largest and most popular protected areas.

Like the Netherlands, the landscape of Belgium is one of recent geology on which man has superimposed considerable change. A belt of sand dunes along the coast forms a natural boundary to a broad area of low-lying land, artificially reclaimed and drained for agriculture in precisely the same way as the neighbouring Dutch polders. Inland, beyond the flat plain of Flanders, the land forms an undulating fertile plateau, seldom rising more than 300 metres above sea level and consisting in the main of rich wind-blown deposits. The land is largely cleared for agricultural use, but here and there are small remnants of formerly widespread forests of oak and beech.

This central plateau area, overlain by deposits of sand and fertile clay, has a dense population and is an important region for horticulture and market gardening. It also contains Belgium's principal textile and metal-based industries and the capital city of Brussels, which as well as being of national importance is also a European political and administrative centre.

The Sambre-Meuse Valley on the plateau's southern edge contains the country's major centres of heavy industry and its largest concentration of population. Along the axis of the valley lies one of the continent's most important coal fields, a fuel resource which has played a fundamental role in Belgium's economic development. The attractive city of Namur with its ancient citadel is situated at the confluence of the two rivers and is surprisingly free of heavy industrial development.

Southern Belgium and the northernmost part of the Grand Duchy of Luxembourg contain one of Europe's most ancient forests – the oak, beech and hornbeam woodlands of the Ardennes – now much reduced in area but still a beautiful region, in which boar and wild cat are still to be found. Geologically the region consists of sandstones, slates and limestone, and its poor infertile soils and high rainfall have made it unsuitable for arable farming. The small area that is devoted to agriculture is mostly permanent pasture on which beef and dairy cattle are grazed.

Maritime influences play an important part in the climate of the area, particularly in the lowland regions of the west. But away from the coast the climate takes on progressively more continental characteristics. Rainfall increases from about 760 millimetres in the west to more then 1270 millimetres in the Ardennes, and while the Belgian winter is generally mild, that of Luxembourg is markedly colder, with heavier and more persistent snow.

HAUTES FAGNES At one time forest covered large parts of what is now a nature reserve within the Hautes Fagnes-Eifel Natural Park.

PARK RESERVE **BELGIUM**	SIZE (km²)	DESCRIPTION	MAP REF.	PAGE NO.
WESTHOEK	3.4	Nature Reserve. Dunes and wet slacks, containing rare plants. Fringing woodland of poplar, alder, elm and oak.	A1	148
DE BLANKAART	4.0	Nature Reserve. Large shallow lake with interesting birdlife. Reed beds and alder carr.	A2	148
ZWIN	1.25	Nature Reserve. Region of saltmarsh and mudflats at mouth of River Zwin. Many water-bird breeding species.	A1	148
KALMTHOUTSE HEIDE	8.51	Nature Reserve. Fragment of formerly extensive heathland area. Mobile dunes and small lakes.	B1	148
DE ZEGGE	0.55	Nature Reserve. Relict area of peat cuttings, largely tree-covered. Several rare aquatic plants.	C1	150
DE MECHELSE HEIDE	3.96	Nature Reserve. Heath-covered hills of sand and stones. Marshland and woodland.	C2/D2	150
DE SINT PIETERSBERG	0.52	Nature Reserve. Limestone grassland with interesting flora and fauna. Twenty-four species of orchids.	D2	150
PLATEAU DES TAILLES	2.85	Nature Reserve. Shallow basin containing raised peat bog. Marshes and wet heathland.	D3	150
DE ZWARTE BEEK	0.39	Nature Reserve. Area of peat bog in river valley fringed by coniferous plantations and heathland.	C1	152
DE TEUT	2.11	Nature Reserve. Surviving area of campine heathland. Ponds, copses and marshland. Interesting bog plants.	C2	152
GENK	2.2	Nature Reserve. Thirty-five small lakes surrounded by heath and dune land. Several rare aquatic plants.	C2	153
FURFOOZ	0.50	Nature Reserve. Complex of rocks and caves of archaeological interest in limestone topography.	C3	154
CHAMPALLE & POILVACHE	0.51	Nature Reserve. Two separate areas of limestone cliff and grassland. Rare shrubs and herbaceous plants.	C3	154
LESSE ET LOMME	9.7	Nature Reserve. Large area of deciduous woodland, limestone grassland, scrub and cultivated land.	C3	155
ROUGE PONCE	0.37	Nature Reserve. Part of Saint-Hubert state forest. Bog land covered largely by downy birch woodland.	C3	155
FAGNES DE ROUMONT	0.38	Nature Reserve. Large peat bog surrounded by deciduous woodland and heathland.	C3	155
HAUTES FAGNES-EIFEL	500	Natural Park. Semi-natural beech and oak forest, high spruce and beech forest, pasture and farmland.	D2/D3	156
HAUTES FAGNES	40	Nature Reserve. High peat moorland surrounded by woodland. Typical moorland and woodland birdlife.	D2	156
LUXEMBOURG				
GERMAN-LUXEMBOURG	725	Internationally protected upland area of woods, gorges and meadows.	D3	157

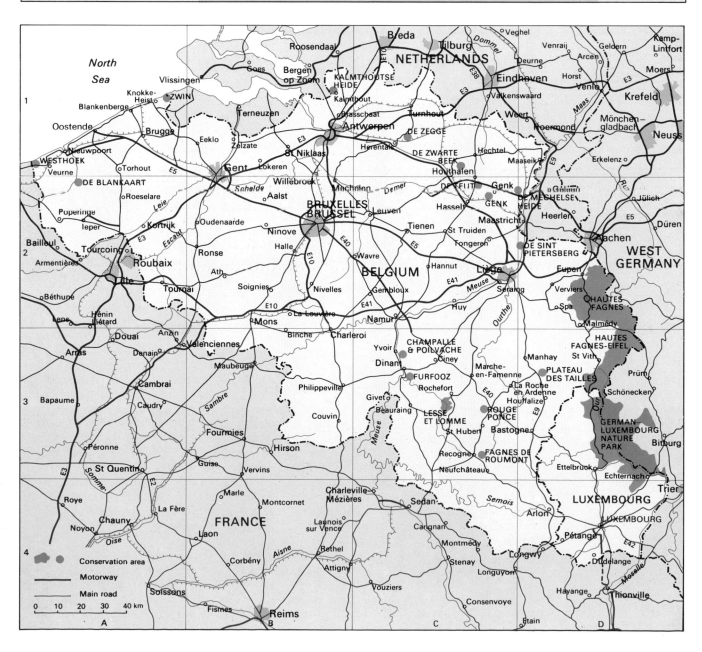

BELGIUM

Westhoek Nature Reserve

Belgium has little coastline – only about 60 kilometres between the French and Dutch borders. As the shoreline is low and mostly sandy it is therefore not surprising that the area is subjected to considerable recreational pressure and urban development, and perhaps the only region which has survived in anything like its natural state is the Westhoek reserve.

The beach at Westhoek is very wide and at ebb tide extends for about 450 metres from the dunes on the landward side to the water's edge. Nearly all the beach, however, is outside the reserve and only a strip 30 to 40 metres wide at the foot of the dunes lies within its boundaries. The dunes vary in width from 150 to 250 metres and, on the east side of the reserve, are low and often penetrated by the highest spring tides, so that slacks are formed behind. The largest is vegetated, mainly with creeping willow, sea buckthorn, the bush-grass *Calamagrostis epigejos*, dewberry and the burnet rose. The slacks contain some plants which are now rare in Belgium, for example musk and fen orchids, marsh helleborine and broad helleborine.

In the centre of the reserve lies an extensive

KENTISH PLOVER – a small wader which nests on sandy beaches and shingle coasts.

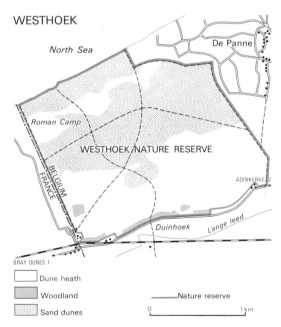

WESTHOEK

North Sea

De Panne

Roman Camp

WESTHOEK NATURE RESERVE

BELGIUM
FRANCE

ADINKERKE 2

Duinhoek   Lange leed

BRAY DUNES 1

Dune heath

Woodland   Nature reserve

Sand dunes   0   1 km

dune ridge with large areas of mobile sand, much of which is encroaching on the vegetation. This part is an area of soft sand and is not easy to walk over. It has an air of wilderness about it, even though in the distance one can see the tower blocks of the town of De Panne. On the south side of the reserve the dunes have a more varied vegetation cover, with marram, sand sedge, the grasses sand cat's-tail and creeping fescue, and such plants as stonecrops and storksbills which are typically found in areas of stabilized sand.

The mammal fauna includes the hare, rabbit, stoat, weasel and polecat. There are many small warblers and other birds in the bushy vegetation, but perhaps the rarest

species is the Kentish plover, which occurs on the sandy margins of the flooded slacks.

De Blankaart Nature Reserve

A few kilometres south of Diksmuide in northwest Belgium is a 70-hectare lake of considerable ornithological importance, listed in the Directory of Western Palaearctic Wetlands. The lake, lying on the edge of a sandy-loam region in the plain of the River Ijzer, probably dates from about 1500, having originated as a large peat-cutting.

As with most water-filled peat cuttings, the water is shallow and gradual silting has resulted in wide expanses of reed beds with fringing alder carr. The lake and its surroundings are an important breeding site for little and great-crested grebes, bittern and little bittern, black-tailed godwit, mallard, shoveler, pintail and garganey. The grey heron has been reintroduced and there is now a fine heronry of 120 nests in the trees around the old duck decoy, which is still used, but only for migration research; the decoy attracts birds which are then caught and banded with numbered rings before being released.

The primary reedswamp in the reserve covers about 20 hectares and provides a nesting habitat for Cetti's warblers, Savi's warblers, grasshopper warblers, great reed warblers, hen and marsh harriers. The lake attracts about 20,000 overwintering ducks of several species and between 20,000 and 30,000 waders.

Zwin Nature Reserve

A private reserve on the Belgian coast adjacent to the Dutch border, the protected area comprises a region of saltmarshes and mudflats in the former mouth of the River Zwin. The vegetation is typically halophytic, with such salt-tolerant plants as glassworts, sea-lavenders, sea purslane, annual seablite, common salt-marsh-grass and thrift. The reserve was created by Count Lippens, a pioneer Belgian conservationist, in conjunction with l'Association des réserves naturelles et ornithologique de Belgique.

For the visitor, the main features of interest are the waders and waterfowl which visit the mudflats, and the aviaries and enclosures where many birds are kept in semi-confinement. In 1960 three large lagoons were created to encourage waterfowl to remain and breed. As a result breeding species have increased in number and now include the common tern, several species of gull, avocet, oystercatcher, shelduck, redshank, ringed plover and Kentish plover. Perhaps the reserve's most spectacular success has been with greylag geese and storks. Starting with wounded birds which could not fly, the wildlife park, within the reserve, has built up populations of both species – neither of which are confined.

Kalmthoutse Heide Nature Reserve

A fine heathland reserve situated close to the

Dutch border, a few kilometres north of the great port of Antwerp, Kalmthoutse Heide forms part of a much larger conservation area, covering about 1750 hectares in total and acting as a peripheral zone of protection to the reserve itself. The reserve, a fragment of a formerly extensive area of heathland in the Campine district, still retains a wide variety of habitats, ranging from mobile dunes to small lakes. In their flora and fauna, the dunes display certain maritime elements such as marram grass and creeping willow, and possess some invertebrate species which are normally found on the coast. The heathland is maintained in an open condition by sheep, a special local breed, which prevents trees from becoming established.

The wet areas, which are sometimes flooded in winter, are dominated by the cross-leaved heath. There are also extensive areas of *Sphagnum* bog with bog asphodel, cottongrass and the rare bog orchid. The lakes attract large numbers of birds, and more than 100 species, including about ten birds of prey, have been recorded breeding in the reserve. The species of special interest are blacknecked grebe, ruff, black tern, great grey shrike as well as several species of duck.

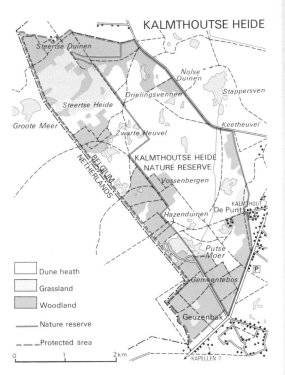

KALMTHOUTSE HEIDE

Dune heath

Grassland

Woodland

Nature reserve

Protected area

0   1   2km

ZWIN *below* Coastal dunes protect the reserve's salt marsh and mudflats from inundation. The area, located on the Dutch border, is an important breeding site for many species of waders and waterfowl.

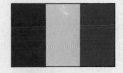

1 WESTHOEK
Information : Bestuur van Waters en Bossen, Houtvesterij Brugge, Twijnstraat 6, 8000 Brugge
Access : from VEURNE
Open : Unrestricted but visitors may only enter on foot and must keep to marked footpaths
Facilities : Guided walks

2 DE BLANKAART
Information : Federatie voor Toerisme in Oost-Vlanderen, Koningen Maria-Hendrikaplein 27, 9000 Gent
Access : from Woumen, 19km N of IEPER
Open : Unrestricted for part of reserve
Facilities : Visitor centre. Guided walks from March to October, on the first and third Sunday of each month between 1030 and 1430

3 ZWIN
Information : Federatie voor Toerisme in Oost-Vlanderen, Kuningen Maria-Hendrikaplein 27, 9000 Gent
Access : from KNOKKE-HEIST
Open : Unrestricted except for some protected areas
Facilities : Guided walks every Sunday at 1000 and Tuesday from March to September at 1000. Aviary within the reserve

4 KALMTHOUTSE HEIDE
Information : Bestuur van Waters en Bossen, Houtvesterij Antwerpen, Weidestraat 60, 2600 Berchem
Access : from KALMTHOUT
Open : Unrestricted except for several protected areas where dunes are unstable
Facilities : Marked footpaths within the reserve. Observation tower

De Zegge Nature Reserve

The Royal Zoological Society of Antwerp, best known for its famous zoo, also takes a keen interest in conserving natural habitats, and since 1953 has owned the small peatland reserve of De Zegge, a relic area of peat cuttings which has survived because it was too difficult to reclaim. As the area is surrounded by intensively cultivated land, all of which has now been drained, the reserve would dry out if special measures were not taken to maintain a flow of water through it.

Apart from some water-filled excavations, much of the peatland is tree-covered with eared sallow, common sallow, alder, birch and aspen. There are a number of aquatic and fen plants of interest, and in addition the royal fern, common sundew, bog arum – now rare in Belgium – and the heath spotted and lesser butterfly orchids are also found.

For such a small area, the birdlife is particularly interesting and many small warblers breed here, including the bluethroat, which is very scarce in Belgium. There are also at least six pairs of golden orioles. The marsh species include the bittern, spotted crake, water rail, snipe and birds of prey such as marsh and Montagu's harriers.

De Mechelse Heide Nature Reserve

Created a State Reserve in 1967, De Mechelse Heide is one of the last surviving examples of high Campine landscape. It is situated in northeast Belgium between Hasselt and the German frontier and consists of stony sand hills, originally deposited by the River Meuse, and now covered with a natural vegetation of heathland plants. Heather is widespread in the dry areas, together with needle furze, hairy greenweed and certain plants rare in Belgium such as bell heather, the clubmoss *Lycopodium tristachyum* and Iceland lichen.

Between the sand hills are areas of marshy ground which are temporarily inundated during periods of heavy rain. Here the cross-leaved heath is common and semi-aquatic species such as shore-weed, cotton-grass, mud sedge, bog asphodel, common sundew, white beak-sedge, brown beak-sedge and *Sphagnum* mosses are found. There are also fragments of the typical Campine oak-birch forest, most of which have now disappeared.

De Sint Pietersberg Nature Reserve

De Sint Pietersberg is one of many reserves which have been established and are maintained by l'Association des réserves naturelles et ornithologique de Belgique. The reserve consists of two parts, Eben-Emael and Visé, both of which are areas of limestone grassland with a flora and fauna of considerable interest. The larger part, Visé, lies on a hill on the west bank of the Meuse and is honeycombed with disused marlstone workings. Some of these excavations, made over the centuries, extend as tunnels into the hillside and are used by bats for roosting.

No less than twenty-four species of orchids have been recorded at Visé, including the military, green-winged, burnt, man, bug and early spider orchids, and the white helleborine. Among the other interesting plants are jagged chickweed, slender-leaved tufted vetch, grass of Parnassus, large field gentian and juniper. The limestone grassland is no longer grazed by sheep as it was in the past and scrub is now beginning to invade.

There is also a rich insect fauna, particularly digger wasps and beetles, and the area is known for smooth snakes and slow-worms.

Plateau des Tailles Nature Reserve

About 50 kilometres south of Liege, near the main road to Houffalize, lies Plateau des Tailles Nature Reserve in a shallow basin or amphitheatre where peat has accumulated to form a raised bog. The reserve, which, together with the surrounding area, was exploited in the past for fuel, consists of several parts – Robièfa and Nazieufa northwest of Baraque de Fraiture, and A Sacrawé, La Grande Fange, Grand Passage and La Petite Champa to the southeast.

The largest area, La Grande Fange, consists of a single raised bog of *Sphagnum* mosses surrounded by marshes and wet heathland lying on old peat cuttings. On the wetter areas grow bog asphodel, willows and rushes. Cross-leaved heath is widespread in areas which are not waterlogged, and on the drier parts there is a dwarf-shrub community

DE SINT
PIETERSBERG *below*
The reserve, lying in the valley of the River Meuse, contains over twenty orchid species.

PLATEAU DES
TAILLES *right*
Situated in a low-lying area south of Liège, the reserve's land was once exploited for peat.

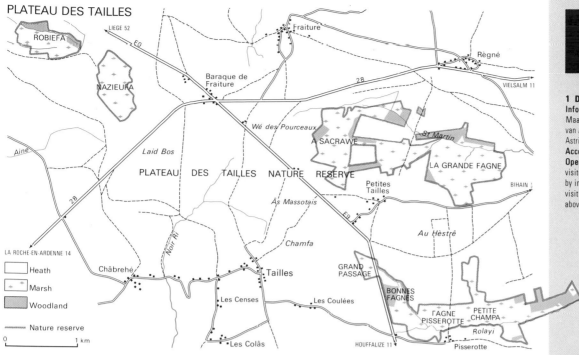

PLATEAU DES TAILLES

ROBIEFA

NAZIEUFA

LIEGE 52

Fraiture

Règné

VIELSALM 11

Baraque de Fraiture

Wé des Pourceaux

Laid Bos

À SACRAWE

St Martin

LA GRANDE FAGNE

BIHAIN

PLATEAU DES TAILLES NATURE RESERVE

Petites Tailles

Aine

Às Massotais

Au Hèstrê

Chamfa

Noir Ri

LA ROCHE-EN-ARDENNE 14

Châbrehé

Tailles

GRAND PASSAGE

Heath

Marsh

Woodland

Les Censes

Les Coulées

BONNES FAGNES

FAGNE PISSEROTTE

PETITE CHAMPA

Nature reserve

0   1 km

Les Colâs

HOUFFALIZE 11

Rolayi

Pisserotte

of bilberry and cowberry. Most of the surrounding area has been reclaimed or planted with spruce, and therefore the reserve, as well as preserving wildlife habitats, also protects the last remnants of an ancient environment where man dug peat, cut heather and grazed his stock. The area is of considerable ornithological interest and has a rich insect fauna, including several boreo-alpine species.

DIGGER WASP *left* A slender insect, the digger wasp is so-called because of its method of nest-building. Most members of the species excavate burrows or holes where eggs are laid on previously paralysed caterpillars or spiders.

1 DE ZEGGE
Information: Koninklijke Maatschappij voor Dierkunde van Antwerpen, Koningin Astridplein 26, 2000 Antwerpen
Access: from HERENTALS
Open: Reserve can only be visited by organized groups, not by individuals. Permission to visit must be obtained from the above address

2 DE MECHELSE HEIDE
Information: Provincial Verbond voor Toerisme in Limburg, Domein Bokrijk, 3600 Genk
Access: from Niel-Bij-As, 22km NE of HASSELT
Open: Unrestricted but visitors must keep to marked footpaths
Facilities: Marked footpaths within the reserve

3 DE SINT PIETERSBERG
Information: Fédération Touristique du Luxembourg belge, Quai de l'Ourthe 9, 6980 Lu-Roche-en-Ardenne
Access: from Visé, 17km NE of LIÈGE
Open: Unrestricted

4 PLATEAU DES TAILLES
Information: Ingénieur des Eaux et Forêts, 6690 Vielsalm
Access: from Baraque de Fraiture, 15km N of HOUFFALIZE or Petites Tailles, 12km N of HOUFFALIZE
Open: Unrestricted

151

De Zwarte Beek Nature Reserve

The reserve is situated in the valley of the Zwarte Beek, a stream flowing between the catchment areas of the great rivers Meuse and Scheldt in the east of the country.

Along the middle course of the stream there is a raised bog on which grow many plants typical of this habitat type, such as sundew, lousewort, bog asphodel, lesser bladderwort, bog rosemary and orchids. The poor sandy soils which fringe the valley are mostly covered with conifer plantations, but heathland with such species as cowberry, juniper, clubmosses and lichens survive in places.

SMOOTH SNAKE *left* A small harmless reptile of variable coloration, the smooth snake has usually a dark lateral stripe running from neck to nostril. It feeds mainly on other reptiles, both lizards and snakes.

NIGHTJAR *below* Agile and nocturnal, the nightjar is often seen at dusk over heaths and forest edges. It nests on the ground and is beautifully camouflaged by its barred and mottled plumage.

Beneath trees along the stream banks grow the May lily and the lily-of-the-valley, together with the wood anemone and bistort. In the alder carr are found two local plants, *Selinum carvifolia* and the lesser skull cap.

The birdlife of the reserve has been carefully studied and 110 breeding species have been recorded, among them the nightingale, sparrowhawk, hobby, great grey shrike, wheatear, red-backed shrike, corncrake, black woodpecker and fieldfare. The presence of eleven species of amphibians, the lamprey and the smooth snake make this reserve of special interest in Belgium.

De Teut Nature Reserve

North of Hasselt the acid sands and peat deposits of the vast Campine plateau at one time supported extensive areas of heathland, much of which has now been cultivated or planted with conifers, particularly spruce. De Teut, one of the surviving areas of original heathland, has been declared a nature reserve and lies under the protection of l'Association

des réserves naturelle et ornithologique de Belgique.

With wet and dry areas, ponds and small copses the heathland displays a wide variety of environments. The most interesting plants are those which grow in wet or marshy areas and include such species as cranberry, bog rosemary, *Comarum palustre*, bog myrtle, marsh gentian, the bog asphodel and the cotton-grass *Eriophorum angustifolium*.

Among De Teut's many interesting birds are the black grouse, curlew, black-tailed godwit, kingfisher, great grey shrike, nightjar, bluethroat, ortolan bunting and nightingale. This site and nearby Genk Nature Reserve are complementary to one another in that both have the same history of exploitation by grazing, peat cutting and forest clearance and share the same fauna and flora.

Genk Nature Reserve
An interesting private reserve established in 1956 by l'Association des réserves naturelle et ornithologique de Belgique, Genk consists of a series of thirty-five small lakes which were constructed many years ago for fish culture. While being used for this purpose the lakes were regularly emptied and cleared of vegetation before refilling, thus maintaining the area of open water. The adjacent land is covered with a heathy vegetation which is burnt from time to time and grazed by sheep.

Between the lakes lie ridges of mobile and fixed dunes on which grow sand sedge, grey hair-grass and heather. Cross-leaved heath grows in damper areas and bog asphodel, eared and common sallow, bog myrtle are found on marshy ground.

In the shallow water of the ponds are several plants, now rare in Belgium, notably shore-weed, lesser water-plantain, *Baldellia repens*, *Scirpus pauciflorus* and delicate quillwort, known only from this locality in Belgium.

A total of 153 bird species has been recorded, of which eighty-five breed on the reserve. The breeding species include black and whiskered terns, long-eared owl, great crested grebe and black-necked grebe.

1 DE ZWARTE BEEK
Information : Provinciaal Verbond voor Toerisme in Limburg, Domein Bokrijk, 3600 Genk
Access : from Koersel, 24km NW of HASSELT
Open : Unrestricted

2 DE TEUT
Information : Bestuur van Waters en Bossen, Housvesterij Hasselt, Torenplein 6, 3500 Hasselt
Access : from Zonhoven, 7km N of HASSELT
Open : Unrestricted
Facilities : Guided visits

3 GENK
Information : Conservateur, Genk Natuurreservaat, Kriekboomstraat 10, 3600 Genk
Access : from GENK or HASSELT
Open : Permission to visit must be obtained from the Conservateur who will arrange conducted tours

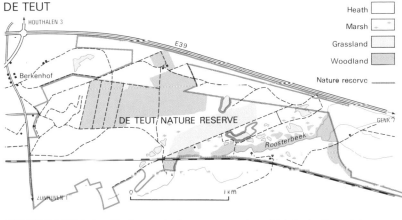

DE TEUT

HOUTHALEN 3

Berkenhof

E39

DE TEUT NATURE RESERVE

Roosterbeek

GENK 7

ZONHOVEN

0   1km

Heath
Marsh
Grassland
Woodland
Nature reserve

CORNCRAKE *below* Modern agricultural methods are highly injurious to the corncrake, which typically nests in hay meadows or fields with cereal crops.

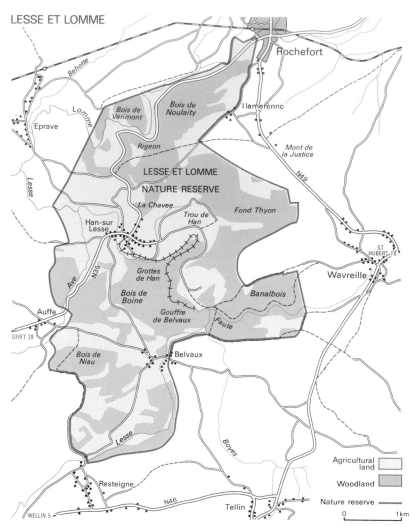

LESSE ET LOMME

Furfooz, Champalle and Poilvache Nature Reserves

Two small nature reserves occupying riverside positions overlying limestone rocks lie in the province of Namur.

The Furfooz Reserve sits in a loop of the Lesse, a river famous for its picturesque deep valley, rocky Carboniferous and Devonian limestone cliffs, numerous caves and underground springs. It consists of a complex of rocks and caves and is of considerable archaeological interest. There have been several finds of bones and other relics of the upper Palaeolithic and it seems that the caves were occupied over a long period by Cro-Magnon man and again in the Neolithic age, when they were used as burial chambers. The flora and fauna is comparable with that of the Lesse et Lomme Nature Reserve, which lies farther up the Lesse valley.

A short distance north of the confluence of the Lesse and the Meuse, and south of Yvoir, is the small reserve of Champalle et Poilvache. The reserve, which protects calcareous rocky cliffs on the east bank of the river, consists of two separate parts, together totalling 51 hectares. On south-facing slopes a fine limestone grassland of *Sesleria* forms the vegetation and species such as bloody cranesbill and rockrose are widespread. Box and hornbeam are also found as well as hybrids of the rare downy oak. It is also the only place in Belgium where the yellow whitlow-grass *Draba aizoides* var. *montana*, a plant of the Alps and Pyrenees, is found.

SCARCE SWALLOW-TAIL *above* A broad-winged butterfly found throughout the Palearctic region, it is usually seen in lowland areas near fruit orchards.

LESSE ET LOMME *right* Grottes de Han – the largest of several caves in the reserve – lies on the River Lesse, south of Han-sur-Lesse.

Lesse et Lomme Nature Reserve

Situated in southern Belgium, in a picturesque landscape of fertile valleys and wooded limestone hills with rocky cliffs, Lesse et Lomme forms one of the largest protected sites in the country. The rocks are limestones and schists of the middle and upper Devonian, which are greatly modified by erosion and are covered by later deposits. Consequently the soils are varied and the flora rich; over 600 species of flowering plants and sixteen pteridophytes (ferns, horsetails and clubmosses) have been found. The area's natural and semi-natural habitats range from rock faces, dry limestone grassland, juniper and cornelian cherry scrub, oak and beech woods to agricultural land.

The reserve is situated near the confluence of the rivers Lesse and Lomme, both of which cut deep valleys into the Devonian rocks. The Lesse flows through the centre of the reserve, disappearing underground at the Gouffre de Belvaux and re-emerging at the Trou de Han about 1 kilometre to the northwest. At the Trou de Han lies the largest of the numerous caves found in the region. The cave lies close to the little town of Han-sur-Lesse and attracts many visitors each year.

The flora has been well studied and is known to include some species of great interest. In the deciduous forests there are oaks, beech, ash, sycamore, maple, wild cherry, lime, elm, wild service, hornbeam and mountain ash. Perhaps the most interesting tree is the downy oak, which is typically a Mediterranean tree and is here at its most northerly station in Europe. The flowers found growing on the calcareous rocks and in the dry grasslands include some most attractive species, such as burnet rose, bloody cranesbill, common cotoneaster, the speedwell *Veronica prostrata*, *Libanotis montana*, pasque-flower, carthusian pink and wild daffodils. Among the many orchids found in the park are the white helleborine, fly orchid, bee orchid, burnt orchid, military orchid and dark red helleborine.

Rouge Poncé Nature Reserve

On the Saint-Hubert Plateau, which varies from 500 to 700 metres in height and forms part of the Belgian Ardennes, soils are poor and peat bogs, much exploited in the past, are widespread. The Rouge Poncé Reserve, lying within the state forest of Saint-Hubert, an area famous for its beautiful beech woodland and many game animals, is probably the most important surviving example of peat bog in the region.

The reserve's bog flora is similar to that at Kalmthout and Hautes Fagnes, with heather, crowberry and *Sphagnum* mosses. Apart from a few open areas, most of the reserve is covered with downy birch, the natural colonizer of these soils; some of the trees are very old despite their small size. The reserve is one of the few sites in the country where the chickweed wintergreen grows. Although this plant is found widespread in pine forests and on peat moors in northern Europe, in Belgium it is confined to the high plateaux of the Ardennes.

Fagnes de Roumont Nature Reserve

Fagnes de Roumont, a large peat bog isolated from the surrounding countryside by birch and oak woodland, has been a State Reserve since 1976. Protruding above the bog surface, which has been greatly modified by peat-cutting for domestic use, are numerous islands of uncut peat on which grow crowberry, while in the cut areas there are extensive stretches of *Molinia* and wild daffodils. Heathland containing bilberry, heather, mat-grass and arnica lies at the margin of the bog. Two plants rarely found in Belgium occur in marshy areas – bog arum and an attractive fern, crested buckler fern.

The reserve is of interest to the historian not only because it preserves an ancient landscape bearing evidence of peat excavations, grazing and heather cutting but also because along the stream which crosses the site there are numerous mounds which have been identified as spoil heaps from gold siftings, probably of Celtic origin. The gold-bearing rocks are of Cambrian and early Devonian age and the site is the most important of its type in the Ardennes.

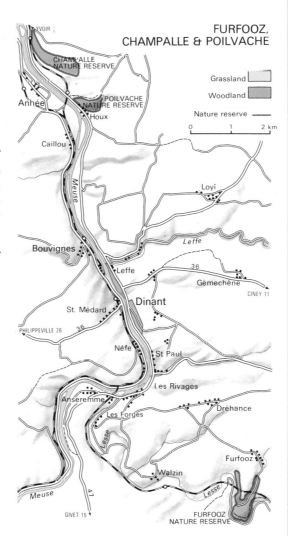

FURFOOZ, CHAMPALLE & POILVACHE

Grassland
Woodland

Nature reserve ———

0   1   2 km

1 FURFOOZ, CHAMPALLE & POILVACHE

Information: for Furfooz: Ardenne et Gaume, rue Marie de Bourgogne 41, 1040 Bruxelles for Champalle & Poilvache: Ingénieur des Eaux et Forêts, rue Daoust 14/3, 5500 Dinant
Access: (Furfooz) from Furfooz, 8km SE of DINANT (Champalle & Poilvache) from YVOIR
Open: (Furfooz) March 15 to November 15 (Champalle & Poilvache) Unrestricted
Facilities: Museum and exhibition at Champalle & Poilvache

2 LESSE ET LOMME

Information: Fédération du Tourisme de la Province de Namur, rue Notre-Dame 3, 5000 Namur
Access from ROCHEFORT
Open: Unrestricted
Facilities: Hotels and camp sites within the park. Marked footpaths. Caves and wild animal reserve at Han-sur-Lesse

3 ROUGE PONCE

Information: Ingénieur des Eaux et Forêts, Centre Administratif, avenue Nestor Martin 10A, 6900 St-Hubert
Access: from ST-HUBERT or LA-ROCHE-EN-ARDENNE
Open: Unrestricted but visitors must keep to marked footpaths
Facilities: Marked footpaths within the reserve

4 FAGNES DE ROUMONT

Information: Ingénieur des Eaux et Forêts, route de Villance 90E, 6910 Libin
Access: from Libramont, 2km NE of RECOGNE
Open: Unrestricted but reserve may only be reached on foot

BELGIUM AND LUXEMBOURG

Hautes Fagnes-Eifel Natural Park

Situated along the frontier with the German Federal Republic, the Hautes Fagnes-Eifel Natural Park lies next to the German Nature Park of Nordeifel, with which it is twinned. The park, which contains the Hautes Fagnes Nature Reserve and the Forest Reserve of Rurbusch near Elsenborn, has vast semi-natural forests of beech and oak on acid soils in the north, as well as plantations of spruce. In the central part there is an attractive landscape of small fields and beech hedges. The higher parts, covered with spruce and beech forests, have hidden within them long valleys of permanent pasture in which grow two plants of great botanical interest – *Meum athamanticum* and *Thesium pyrenaicum*.

The southern part of the park consists mainly of the picturesque valley of the River Our, where perched on promontories over-looking the river are the lovely old villages of Lommersweiler, Ouren and Reuland with its fortified chateau. Two large artificial lakes, one at Bütgenbach, which has water sports facilities, and the other at Robertville, lie at the edge of the park.

Hautes Fagnes Nature Reserve

Situated at the northern end of the Natural Park, the Hautes Fagnes Nature Reserve lies in a landscape that is one of Belgium's most distinctive and interesting, and has for long attracted naturalists, scientists and archaeologists. The reserve is at a relatively high level, between 500 and 700 metres, on a plateau of peat moor and bog ringed by woodland. It has a rigorous climate with rather low mean temperatures and is often snow-covered in the winter. The remarkably high average annual rainfall, 1400 millimetres, helps to maintain the growth of peat. The acid boggy ground has not encouraged human settlement and only a few villages have been established at the edge of the area.

The originally extensive forest of oak, beech, birch and alder has been exploited for timber, fuel and charcoal production and in the course of time most of it has been cleared. Peat-digging for fuel was also extensive in the past and abandoned excavations can be seen in certain parts of the reserve. Modern tree-planting has been mostly of spruce, which is now the most abundant tree.

Today the vegetation is composed of the common grasses, mat-grass and purple moor-grass, and the woody plants bilberry, cowberry, bog wortleberry, cross-leaved heath, crowberry and needle furze. In addition there are many locally occurring plants of great interest such as the marsh gentian, bog asphodel, bog pimpernel, cotton-grasses, chickweed wintergreen, white beak-sedge and common sundew, *Drosera rotundifolia*.

The mammal fauna includes the red deer, roe deer, fox, wild boar and the rare wild cat. The birds are typically moorland and wood-land species and many are of considerable

BOG ROSEMARY An evergreen undershrub with lantern-shaped flowers, bog rosemary, or marsh andromeda, is found on heaths and bogs.

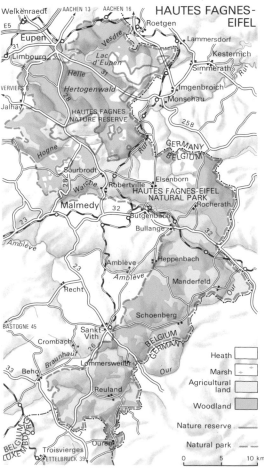

HAUTES FAGNES-EIFEL

Heath
Marsh
Agricultural land
Woodland
Nature reserve
Natural park

0   5   10 km

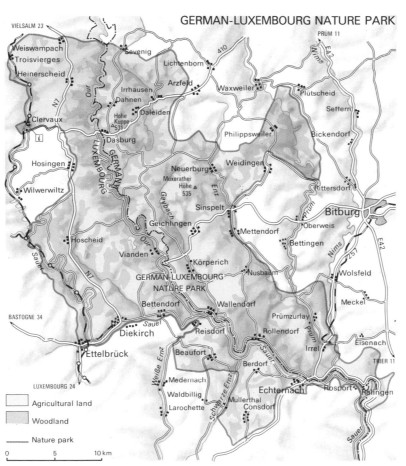

1 HAUTES FAGNES-EIFEL
Information : Fédération du
Tourisme de la Province de
Liège, Bd. de la Sauvenière 77,
4000 Liège
Access : from EUPEN,
MALMEDY or ST VITH
Open : Unrestricted
Facilities : Information centre.
Refuges within the park. Marked
footpaths

2 HAUTES FAGNES
Information : Fédération du
Tourisme de la Province de
Liège, Bd. de La Sauvenière 77,
4000 Liège
Access : from EUPEN,
VERVIERS or MALMEDY
Open : Unrestricted except at
times of fire risk. Visitors must
keep to marked footpaths
Facilities : Hotels and camp
sites within the park. Wardens
on site

Agricultural land

Woodland

Nature park

0   5   10 km

HAUTE FAGNES *left* A crisp covering of early morning frost lies over the reserve.
Haute Fagnes, situated on a high plateau of the Ardennes, is an area of peat bogs
and wet moorlands surrounded by oak, birch and beech woodland.

**3 GERMAN–
LUXEMBOURG NATURE
PARK**
Information : Vereinigung
deutsch-luxemburgischer
Naturpark, 5521 Irrel, W.
Germany
Access : from LUXEMBOURG,
TRIER or BITBURG
Open : Unrestricted
Facilities : Information centre.
Hotels and camp sites within
the park. Marked footpaths

interest, notably the black grouse, great grey
shrike, Tengmalm's owl, long-eared owl,
buzzard, hen-harrier, goshawk, ring ouzel,
redstart, fieldfare, firecrest, black woodpecker and common and short-toed tree-
creepers, all of which breed in the reserve.

Archaeologists have investigated several
early settlements and a Roman road, the Via
Mansuerisca, which runs through the reserve.
Excavation has shown that the road consists
of oak logs laid crosswise with stone rubble
packed between them – a form of construction
unique in Western Europe.

German-Luxembourg Nature Park
International Nature Parks and National
Parks are post-war phenomena and are
an excellent demonstration of friendship
between nations. This combined park ratified
in October 1965, was the first in Europe.

The River Our and part of the Sauer run
through the centre of the area and form the
frontier between the two countries at this
point. In the German section, the Sudeifel
Nature Park, there are four plateaux in the
southern region separated by the rivers Enz,
Prüm, Kranz, Fleisbach and Gaybach and
several gorges. The northern part is less
dissected, but it is here that one can experience
the peculiar charm of the richly varied Eifel
landscape of meadows, woods, hills, valleys
and gorges, dotted with churches and forts.

Only about 31 per cent of the park is
forest-covered, but the trees are so distributed
that the landscape everywhere seems to be
dominated by them. They are mainly deciduous, with beech, oak, sycamore, ash and
alder in the valleys. Here and there are
plantations of pine, spruce, larch and Douglas
fir. The soils are generally not very productive,
nevertheless there is a rich flora, with 36 orchid
species and many rare plants.

Red and roe deer are widespread, and there
are many wild boars, foxes, badgers, hares
and rabbits. Both pine and beech marten and
polecat may be seen; the wild cat, however,
is rare. Several birds of prey breed in the
park – the red kite, sparrowhawk, goshawk,
buzzard and occasionally the peregrine falcon,
which is now very rare.

The Luxembourg part of the park, known
as the Luxembourg Switzerland, has been a
favourite tourist area for 50 years. Impressive
cliffs tower above the roads to Berdorf,
Waldbäling and Beaufort, and the Müllertal,
with its numerous footpaths, is a favourite
recreation area. The picturesque town of
Diekirch, famous for its Roman mosaics, is
close to an area of wild craggy cliffs, and the
hilltops above Vianden, over which towers
an imposing castle, can be reached by taking
the chair lift. Near Vianden grows a 400-year-
old oak tree, the "King's Oak", which is 4·8
metres in circumference and 40 metres high.

UNITED KINGDOM AND EIRE

Nature conservation in Britain dates from the early part of the twentieth century, when dedicated naturalists bought land for preservation as nature reserves. In this way the National Trust, which was established in 1889, acquired Wicken Fen, Cambridgeshire, in 1909, and Charles Rothschild presented Woodwalton Fen in 1919 to the Society for the Promotion of Nature Reserves, which had been established in 1914. However, it was not until the war years of the early 1940s that efforts were made to formulate a national policy for nature conservation in Britain.

At that time great changes were taking place in the landscape because of the need to increase food and timber production. These developments resulted in the loss of many heathlands, fens, ancient grasslands and forests, including several of high scientific interest. Since then many other changes have affected the landscape, for example the widespread use of herbicides and insecticides, the loss of hedgerows, the spread of coniferous forest and increased building development and mineral exploitation. Many forms of wild life, particularly the less common plants, have declined as a result.

But not all landscape changes have been bad. New habitats have been created such as reservoirs and worked-out sand and gravel pits, and quarries. In addition legislation to protect wildlife is now much more comprehensive and effective.

Government support for nature conservation did not come until 1949, when the Nature Conservancy, now the Nature Conservancy Council, was formed. By 1980, 165 National Nature Reserves totalling 127,000 hectares had been established, ranging in size from the magnificent 26,000 hectares of the Cairngorms in the Scottish Highlands to the 2 hectares of Cothill Fen in Oxfordshire.

In addition to the National Nature Reserves for which the Nature Conservancy Council is directly responsible there are also 3500 Sites of Special Scientific Interest. These sites remain in private ownership, but planning developments which affect them are within the powers of the local authorities, whose responsibility it is to avoid damage to conservation interests. Many of these sites are already adequately protected because they are owned by the National Trust, County Naturalists' Trusts or other bodies.

The great strength of nature conservation work in Britain lies in the remarkable progress made by the voluntary County Naturalists' Trusts Movement. The first one was created in Norfolk in 1926 and today the country is covered by forty-one trusts, with a total membership of over 135,000.

Between them the Trusts manage over 1300 reserves, a number which increases year by year. The Royal Society for the Protection of Birds (RSPB), also an important voluntary body, has seventy-eight bird reserves.

Although the National Trust is mainly concerned with the preservation of Britain's historical and cultural heritage, much of its 187,000 hectares of land and 630 kilometres of coastline is of wildlife interest and includes many sites of national importance. The National Parks in Britain were created to provide rural amenities for the public, but because of their large size and situation they are also important wildlife areas. Most have National Nature Reserves, Sites of Special Scientific Interest and County Trust Reserves within their boundaries. There are ten National Parks in England and Wales, but none in Scotland, because much wild upland

still remains relatively untouched and the need for the traditional park is therefore less pressing.

In 1978 the Countryside Commission for Scotland identified forty National Scenic Areas, which include the most magnificent unspoilt landscapes in the country and total one-eighth of the land and water surface area.

In Northern Ireland the Department of the Environment has powers to create nature reserves and Areas of Scientific Interest under the Amenity Lands Act of 1965. There are now thirty National Nature Reserves, thirty-seven Areas of Scientific Interest, fourteen Forest Nature Reserves and several private reserves managed by the RSPB, the National Trust and other bodies.

THE REPUBLIC OF IRELAND has few statutory protected areas. However, a survey, of Areas of Scientific

DARTMOOR Sunlight bursting through the rainclouds lends an air of mystery to the imposing landscape of the National Park.

Interest in Ireland in 1981, has identified 1059 important wildlife localities. In 1977 the Wildlife Act (1976), which is to be implemented by the Department of Fisheries and Forestry, came into force, but so far no nature reserves have been established. Nevertheless, several important areas in state-owned forests have been selected and will be declared in the near future.

National Parks in the Republic of Ireland are the responsibility of the Office of Public Works, and plans are well advanced for the creation of a series of four parks which will contain some of the finest landscapes in Ireland. As in Scotland there are still extensive regions, particularly in the west, where large tracts of unspoilt countryside remain.

UNITED KINGDOM AND EIRE

The series of islands constituting Great Britain and Ireland lies on the broad off-shore shelf of the European continent and, until recently, formed a single landmass connected to the mainland. Ancient rocks make up the low mountains and high hills of Scotland, northern England, Wales, southwestern England and many parts of Ireland, whereas the English Midlands and much of the southern part of the country consist of more recent clays, sands and limestones. The landscape is heavily modified by glacial erosion features such as screes, steep peaks and wide valleys in the uplands of the north and by glacial deposits and periglacial features in the south.

Its range in geology and relief, its many river systems, long coastline and strong association with the Continent have created a complex habitat pattern.

The climate influences are varied. In the west the Atlantic Ocean brings warmth and rain and has in the north and west encouraged extensive peat formation. The east is subject to cold Arctic air in winter, but in summer experiences hot, dry air, normally associated with continental high-pressure areas. The number of days during which plants can grow throughout the year varies markedly – from 180 days in the far north of the country to 230 days in the south.

PARK/RESERVE	SIZE (km²)	DESCRIPTION	MAP REF.	PAGE NO.
UNITED KINGDOM				
INVERPOLLY	108.6	National Nature Reserve. Remote area of mountains and lochs. Outstanding fauna. Important geological site.	B2	162
BEINN EIGHE	47.6	National Nature Reserve. Superb mountainous region with remnant Scots pine forest and alpine vegetation.	B2	162
CAIRNGORMS	259.5	National Nature Reserve. Magnificent wilderness of mountains, cliffs and corries.	C2	162
RHUM	106.8	National Nature Reserve. Island of volcanic origin noted for sea birds. Herds of red deer and feral goats.	B2	162
LOCH LOMOND	274	National Scenic Area. Large inland loch in region of contrasting mountain and lowland scenery.	B3	164
	0.68	Nature Reserve. Islands with semi-natural oak woodland and loch-shore area important for wildfowl.	B3	164
TENTSMUIR POINT	5.05	National Nature Reserve. Fine coastal dune system. Important wildfowl roosting and feeding area.	C3	164
ISLE OF MAY	0.57	National Nature Reserve. Small island in Firth of Forth. Important point on bird-migration routes.	C3	165
CAERLAVEROCK	55.0	National Nature Reserve. Coastal marshland in Solway Firth. Important wintering area for geese.	C3	165
LAKE DISTRICT	2280	National Park. Dome-shaped mountain area, grass covered with relict forest. Rounded rugged peaks. steep-sided valleys, radial drainage pattern with numerous lakes.	C3	166
LINDISFARNE & THE FARNE IS.	33.1	National Nature Reserve/National Trust area. Island group important as wildfowl nesting site.	C3	168
MOOR HOUSE	38.9	National Nature Reserve. Region of peat-covered moorland with blanket bog, grasses and heather.	C3	168
PEAK DISTRICT	1404	National Park. Gritstone uplands with heather and grasses in the north. Limestone hills with woodland and grassland in central and southern part. Considerable agricultural and quarrying activity.	C4	169
WYRE FOREST	2.4	National Nature Reserve. Old oak forest heavily exploited in the past. Rich woodland flora.	C4	169
NEWBOROUGH WARREN	6.33	National Nature Reserve. Coastal area of dunes and dune grassland with interesting flora and birdlife.	C4	170
SNOWDONIA	2171	National Park. High glaciated mountain region reaching above 1000 metres. Relict deciduous forests. Coastal marshlands with important water-bird populations.	C4	170
SKOMER ISLAND	3.07	National Nature Reserve. Flat-topped island with important sea-bird colonies.	B5	171
OXWICH	2.61	National Nature Reserve. Calcareous sand-dune system with fresh- and salt-water marsh and cliff woodlands.	C5	171
BRAUNTON BURROWS	6.04	National Nature Reserve. Large dune system with many flowering plants.	C5	172
EXMOOR	686	National Park. High heather-covered plateau with remnant deciduous forest. Large numbers of red deer. Wide variety of coastal and upland scenery.	C5	172
DARTMOOR	954	National Park. Granite tableland fringed by steep-sided wooded valleys. Large tracts of heath and heather moorland. Boggy areas contain interesting flora.	C5	172
AYMOUTH TO LYME REGIS UNDERCLIFFS	3.21	National Nature Reserve. Stretch of coastal ash woodland. Important undisturbed example of plant recolonization. Rich flora and insect life. Mesozoic fossils.	C5	173
HOLKHAM	17.0	National Nature Reserve. Largest coastal reserve in England. Important resting place for migrant birds.	D4	174
HICKLING BROAD	4.87	National Nature Reserve. One of several ancient peat cuttings. Large numbers of rare migrant-bird species.	D4	174
CASTOR HANGLANDS	0.90	National Nature Reserve. Small area of grass heath, scrub and deciduous woodland.	D4	174
WICKEN FEN	3.05	National Trust Reserve. Classic East Anglian fenland site.	D4	175
MINSMERE	6.3	Wildfowl Reserve. Shallow valley containing marsh and woodland. Large range of migrant bird species.	D4	175
BROWNSEA ISLAND	2.08	Naturalists' Trust Reserve. Part of small sandy island. Large heronry. Lagoon with birdwatching facilities.	C5	176
NEW FOREST	283.3	Large semi-natural area of woodland, heath and bog without formal conservation status. Rich flora and fauna with many rare species. Ancient grazing rights.	C5	176
KINGLEY VALE	1.46	National Nature Reserve. Fine yew woodland with chalk grassland and shrub communities.	D5	177
WYE	1.32	National Nature Reserve. Chalk grassland with rich flora and insect fauna. Ash and hazel coppice.	D5	177
KEBBLE	1.23	National Nature Reserve. Lake, grassland and coastal cliff. Important seabird breeding colony.	B3	178
OXFORD ISLAND	0.53	National Nature Reserve. Meadow, scrub and woodland on lake peninsula. Extensive reed beds. Large numbers of breeding and wintering bird species.	B3	178
QUOILE PONDAGE	1.98	National Nature Reserve. Grassland, alder and willow woodland bordering man-made lake on River Quoile.	B3	178
MURLOUGH	2.82	National Nature Reserve. Irish east-coast system of sand dunes and mud flats.	B3/B4	178
MARBLE ARCH FOREST	0.24	National Nature Reserve. Unique area of ash woodland on limestone with rich ground-cover flora.	A3/B3	179
EIRE				
GLENVEAGH	100.0	National Park (Proposed). Beautiful wilderness-mountain valley overlying granitic rocks.	A3/B3	180
BURREN	259	National Park (Proposed). Terraced limestone pavement. Remarkable botanical region. Many caves.	A4	180
KILLARNEY	85.0	National Park. Region of woodland lakes and bogs with several south European plant species.	A4	180
WEXFORD	1.66	Wildfowl Refuge. Wetland important for migrant birds. Greenland white-fronted geese in winter.	B4	180

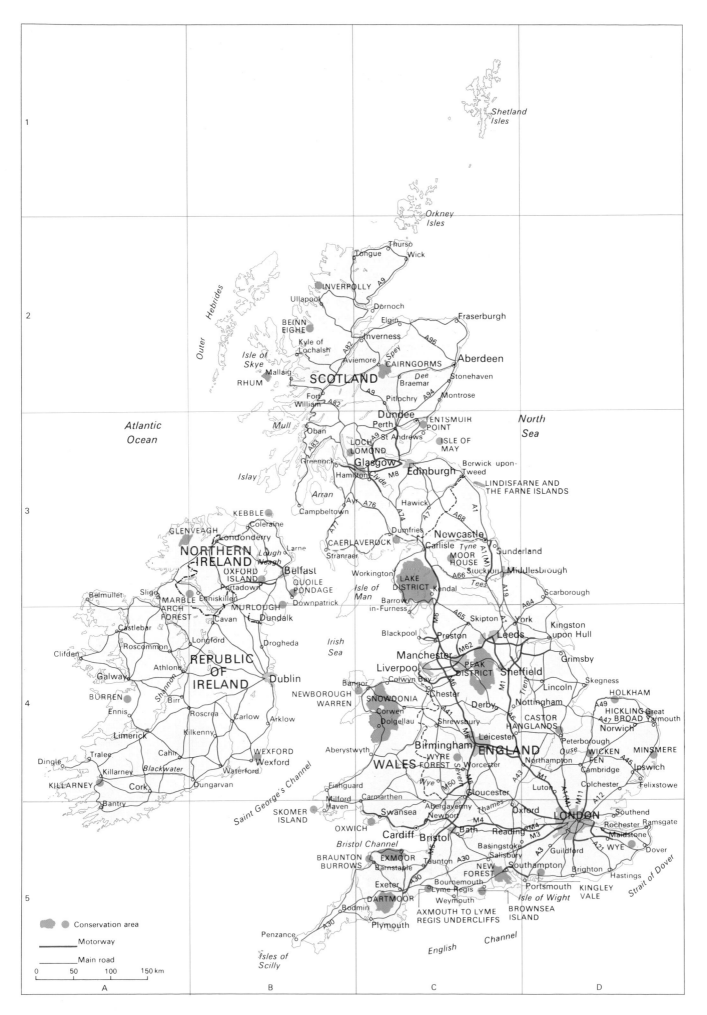

Shetland
Isles

Orkney
Isles

Thurso
Tongue   Wick

INVERPOLLY
Ullapool
Dornoch
BEINN   Elgin   Fraserburgh
EIGHE
Kyle of   Inverness
Lochalsh
Isle of   Aviemore   Spey   CAIRNGORMS   Aberdeen
Skye
Mallaig   Dee   Stonehaven
RHUM   SCOTLAND   Braemar
Fort   Pitlochry   Montrose
William
Dundee   TENTSMUIR
Mull   Perth   POINT
Oban   St Andrews
LOCH   ISLE OF
LOMOND   MAY
Greenock   Glasgow
Islay   Edinburgh   Berwick upon-
Hamilton Clyde M8   Tweed
Arran   Ayr A76   LINDISFARNE AND
Hawick   THE FARNE ISLANDS
KEBBLE   Campbeltown
Coleraine   Newcastle
GLENVEAGH   Dumfries   Carlisle Tyne Sunderland
Londonderry   CAERLAVEROCK   MOOR
NORTHERN   Lough Larne   Stranraer   HOUSE Stockton Middlesbrough
IRELAND   Neagh   Workington   A66   Tees
OXFORD   Belfast   Isle of   LAKE   Scarborough
ISLAND   Man   DISTRICT Kendal
Portadown   QUOILE   Barrow-
Belmullet   Sligo PONDAGE   in-Furness   Kingston
MARBLE   Enniskillen Downpatrick   Blackpool Skipton York   upon Hull
ARCH   Cavan MURLOUGH Dundalk   Preston   Leeds
FOREST   Manchester   Grimsby
Castlebar   Longford Drogheda   Irish   Liverpool Colwyn Bay PEAK Sheffield
Roscommon   Sea   Bangor   DISTRICT   Skegness
Clifden   SNOWDONIA Chester   Lincoln
REPUBLIC   Athlone   Dublin   NEWBOROUGH   Derby   HOLKHAM
Galway   OF   Birr   WARREN   Corwen   Nottingham   HICKLING Great
BURREN   IRELAND Shannon Roscrea   Dolgellau   CASTOR   A49 BROAD Yarmouth
Ennis   Carlow   Aberystwyth   WYRE Leicester HANGLANDS Norwich A47
Limerick   Kilkenny   Arklow   FOREST Birmingham ENGLAND Ouse WICKEN MINSMERE
Tralee Cahir   WEXFORD   Worcester   Northampton FEN Ipswich
Dingle   Blackwater   Wexford   Fishguard Carmarthen Wye ENGLAND Cambridge A45
Killarney Cork Waterford   Milford WALES Abergavenny Severn Gloucester Luton Colchester Felixstowe
KILLARNEY   Dungarvan   Haven Swansea Newport M50 Thames Oxford LONDON Southend
SKOMER   OXWICH   M4   Bath Reading M3   Rochester Ramsgate
ISLAND   Cardiff Bristol   Basingstoke A3 Guildford Maidstone
Bristol Channel   Salisbury   Brighton WYE Dover
BRAUNTON   EXMOOR   Taunton A30   Southampton   Hastings
BURROWS Barnstaple   NEW Bournemouth Portsmouth KINGLEY
Exeter   Lyme Regis FOREST Weymouth Isle of Wight VALE
DARTMOOR   AXMOUTH TO LYME BROWNSEA
Bodmin   REGIS UNDERCLIFFS ISLAND
Plymouth
Penzance
English   Channel
Isles of
Scilly

Atlantic
Ocean

North
Sea

Outer Hebrides

Irish
Sea

Saint George's Channel

Strait of Dover

Conservation area
Motorway
Main road
0   50   100   150 km

A   B   C   D

1

2

3

4

5

Inverpolly National Nature Reserve

The northwest highlands is one of the most picturesque regions of Scotland and the Inverpolly reserve, second only in size in the British Isles to the Cairngorms reserve, is one of its finest examples. It is jointly managed by the Nature Conservancy Council and three private estates, which own most of the land. There is a wide range of habitats from seashore and islands to scree and mountaintops. The area includes many lochs with birch-clad islets, streams and bogs. The three sandstone peaks of Cul Beag, Stac Polly and Cul Mor dominate the wild terrain. The Inverpolly region is a renowned wildlife area, and is the home of the pine marten, wild cat, otter, buzzard and golden eagle, among many other species. From the car park at Knockan a nature trail leads the visitor along the Knockan cliff, a site of international geological importance. Here older metamorphic rocks known as the Moine Schists have been forced over younger limestones and sandstones to produce a reversal of the more normal situation of younger rocks overlying older ones. This classic exposure gave early insight into the power and forces involved in mountain-building. The cliff is botanically fascinating. Plants of lime-poor soils are found on the upper part and lime-loving plants such as moss campion and mountain avens grow on the lower sediments.

Beinn Eighe National Nature Reserve

A spectacular region of mountain and forest in the Northwest Highlands, the reserve is situated on the southern shores of Loch Maree, where a remnant of ancient Scots pine forest still survives. Fine alpine vegetation carpets the mountain tops, which reach to

WILD CAT *above* In Britain the wild cat is found only in Scotland.

nearly 1000 metres. Red and roe deer, wild cat, pine marten, black-throated diver and ptarmigan are all found within the reserve. The red deer are culled between September and February and visitors during these months are recommended to consult the warden before entering the area.

Cairngorms National Nature Reserve

The most magnificent wilderness area surviving in Britain and the largest tract of mountainous country over 1000 metres anywhere in the British Isles, the Cairngorms forms a region of high plateau dominated by broad summits, the highest being Ben Macdui (1309 metres). Vertical rocky cliffs and cauldron-like corries, steep-sided glens deepened by ancient glaciers and vast areas of high moorland blend together to form the spectacular scenery. The plant-life is characteristic of acid igneous soils and consists of bell heather, cross-leaved heath, bearberry, mountain crowberry, creeping azalea, cloudberry, dwarf cornel and alpine lady's mantle. Fragments of ancient pine forest survive on the lower mountain slopes. Most of the carnivorous mammals of Britain are found here except for the pine marten. In addition there are several hundred red deer and an introduced herd of reindeer. The bird life is rich and includes crested tits, crossbills, capercaillies and black grouse. The golden eagle, osprey, peregrine falcon and merlin nest within the reserve and large flocks of snow buntings can be seen in winter. Ptarmigan and dotterel can be found in the higher regions above the tree line.

Rhum National Nature Reserve

The island of Rhum lies in the Inner Hebrides, south of the Isle of Skye, between the small islands of Canna and Eigg. More than 1800 different plants have been recorded here, although there are a few rarities among them. Although the woodland on the island is mostly of recent origin some fine trees now grow at Kinloch and along the shores of Loch Scresort.

Being an island there are few wild mammals, except for herds of deer and feral goats. The red deer have been intensively studied from the point of view of biology, behaviour and their commercial potential. The studies have shown that breeding success is closely related to environmental conditions such as soil fertility, climate and vegetation, and that the quality of the population as a whole is improved by heavy culling.

The island is noted for its sea-birds, particularly the Manx shearwaters, which are found nesting in holes on the mountainside. Golden eagles, peregrine falcons and merlins also nest on the island and in recent years the Nature Conservancy Council has reintroduced the sea eagle, which, it is hoped, will become established on the island and will eventually spread to other parts of mainland Scotland.

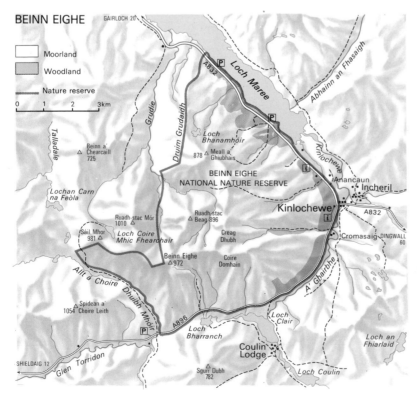

BEINN EIGHE

- Moorland
- Woodland
- Nature reserve

0 1 2 3km

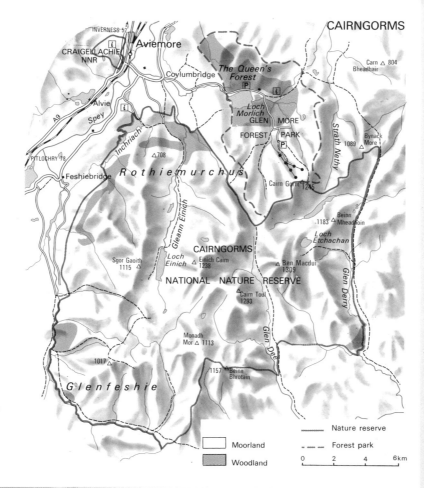

GOLDEN EAGLE *above*
75 to 90 centimetres in
length with a 2-metre
wingspan, the eagle needs
a 12 sq km territory.

RHUM *below* A rainbow
hangs over Beinn Askival,
the highest peak on the
island.

Moorland

Woodland

Nature reserve

Forest park

0   2   4   6km

1 INVERPOLLY
Information: Regional Officer
for the North West, Nature
Conservancy Council, Fraser
Darling House, 9 Culduthel
Road, Inverness IV2 4AG
Access: from Inverpolly, 59km
N of ULLAPOOL
Open: Unrestricted except
during deer-stalking season
(mid-July to mid-October)
Facilities: Information centre.
Nature trail

2 BEINN EIGHE
Information: Regional Officer
for the North West, Nature
Conservancy Council, Fraser
Darling House, 9 Culduthel
Road, Inverness IV2 4AG
Access: from Kinlochewe,
87km NW of INVERNESS
Open: Unrestricted except
during deer-stalking season
(mid-July to mid-October)
Facilities: Information centre.
Mountain and nature trails.
Camp site

3 CAIRNGORMS
Information: Regional Officer
for the North East, Nature
Conservancy Council, Wynne-
Edwards House, 17 Ruhislaw
Terrace, Aberdeen AB1 1XE
Access: from BRAEMAR or
AVIEMORE
Open: Unrestricted except
during deer culling (August to
October)
Facilities: Information centre.
Nature trail. Camp site Ski-lift
to summit of Cairn Gorm

4 RHUM
Information: Regional Officer
for the North West, Nature
Conservancy Council, Fraser
Darling House, 9 Culduthel
Road, Inverness IV2 4AG
Access: by boat from MALLAIG
Open: Permission required to
visit parts of reserve away from
the Loch Scresort area
Facilities: Nature trails

163

LOCH LOMOND

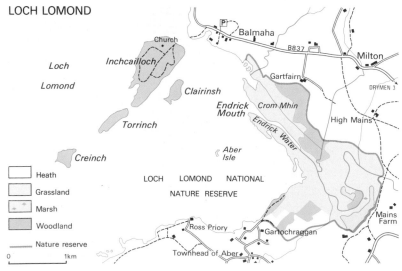

Loch Lomond National Scenic Area and National Nature Reserve

Loch Lomond, the largest water body in Great Britain, forms with Ben Lomond the central part of the Loch Lomond National Scenic Area. As the Highland Boundary Fault – the geological feature that separates Highland from Lowland Scotland – runs across the southern end of the loch, the scenery ranges from hilly along the southern shore to fjord-like at the northern head, near Ardlui. The fault occurs at the junction between Old Red Sandstone and Dolomite Fault Rock, the latter containing the mineral

serpentine, which has a marked influence on the local flora.

The nature reserve lies straddling the boundary fault at the southeast corner of the loch near Balmaha and consists of five islands together with part of the mainland shore. The islands are of special interest because of their semi-natural deciduous woodland and in particular for their stands of sessile oak. The mainland part of the reserve is notable as a wintering place for wildfowl and as a stopping place for birds on migration; common sandpipers nest along the rocky shores and buzzards breed in the forest areas.

Tentsmuir Point National Nature Reserve

There are over one hundred dune systems around the Scottish coasts. Four of the most outstanding, of which Tentsmuir Point is the finest, have been designated National Nature Reserves and many of the others are scheduled as Sites of Special Scientific Interest. A comprehensive study has been made of the flora and fauna of over ninety selected sites in order to protect the best examples of this habitat type from being spoiled when areas are selected for development in connection with the construction of oil terminals.

At Tentsmuir Point, the reserve's foreshore saltings are important roosting and feeding areas for pink-footed and greylag geese. Large numbers of eider and mallard duck, wigeon, scaup, scoter, merganser and shel-

LOCH LOMOND
From Conic Hill, above the nature reserve, the Highland Boundary Fault runs across the southern end of the loch. The islands are part of the shatter belt associated with the fault, one of Britain's principal geological features.

BLUETHROAT *below*
A small robin-like bird, rare in Britain. Breeding males alone have the characteristic blue throat and then only in summer.

duck can be seen, particularly in the autumn, and both grey and common seals are known to haul up on the sand flats. The inland dune formation is remarkable for its rapid growth over the last forty years, presenting today a wide range of habitats from newly formed (embryo) dunes and wet areas to alder, birch and willow scrubland. Over 400 species of flowering plants have been recorded within the reserve which is known to contain the best British population of lyme-grass a handsome species of dune grass, much longer than the more common marram. The reserve has an abundance of purple milk-vetch, coralroot orchid, baltic rush and crowberry. The rich flora, the fine dwarf-shrub heaths with many lichens and the mixture of vegetated and mobile dunes all provide habitats for the area's diverse invertebrate fauna, particularly for such creatures as moths, beetles and spiders.

Isle of May National Nature Reserve
The rocky island of May, situated at the entrance to the Firth of Forth, 8 kilometres southeast of Anstruther, is the site of Scotland's earliest lighthouse and has been famous as a bird observatory for nearly fifty years. It is composed of hard volcanic rock that towers above the sea on the west coast in cliffs 45 metres high. The island has been carved into four separate parts by a series of water-eroded faults that flood at high tide.

Today the island is a nature reserve under the auspices of the Nature Conservancy by agreement with the Commissioners for Northern Lighthouses. There are few unusual plants and, apart from grey seals, few mammals on the island. Its main conservational interest lies in its importance as a resting place for the immense numbers of migrant birds that cross the North Sea in spring and autumn. For many of them the island is the first landfall after leaving the European continent. The regular visitors include some very rare species such as bluethroats, scarlet grosbeaks and red-breasted flycatchers. The fine cliffs, which are found on the west side, have been eroded into a striking series of rock arches, stacks and caves, and many sea birds nest on the rocky ledges. Kittiwakes, guillemots, razorbills, shags and puffins are particularly numerous and there are about 150 pairs of eider ducks and 130 pairs of fulmars. In 1946 four separate species of tern were known to nest on the island's grassy top, but the growth in the population of herring gulls and lesser black-backed gulls, at an annual rate of 13 per cent, has caused a rapid decline in the number of terns and none has nested on the island since 1960. The total gull population, which before 1972 numbered around 17,000 pairs, has been reduced by culling to between 3000 and 4000 pairs.

Caerlaverock National Nature Reserve
The Solway Firth, lying half in England and half in Scotland, has long been famous as a winter haunt of wildfowl. The Caerlaverock National Nature Reserve protects a 10-kilometre stretch of marshes lying along the Scottish shore between the River Nith and Lochar Water. The inner Solway comprises the third largest system of intertidal mud flats in Britain and is designated as a site of international importance. In the winter months the total population of wildfowl may exceed 20,000 and the wading birds may reach a peak of 130,000. The nature reserve is the most important roosting site in Scotland for pink-footed geese and has a seasonal population of up to 10,000 individuals – 10 per cent of the world population. It is also of outstanding importance as the principal wintering ground for the Spitzbergen population of barnacle geese. There is in addition a large winter population of duck, including pintail, mallard, teal, wigeon, shelduck and shoveler among others.

Above the foreshore is one of the largest expanses of saltmarsh in northern Britain. The saltmarsh grasslands, known in Scotland as merse, are grazed by sheep and cattle and are the main breeding haunt of lapwing, redshank, dunlin, oystercatcher, lesser black-backed gull, black-headed gull, common tern and skylark. The rare natterjack toad reaches its northern limit at Caerlaverock and a thriving colony breeds in the shallow pools fringing the merse.

1 LOCH LOMOND
Information: Regional Officer for the South West, Nature Conservancy Council, The Castle, Loch Lomond Park, Balloch, Strathclyde
Access: from Balmaha, 34km NW of GLASGOW
Open: Islands unrestricted. Organized groups intending to visit should notify the Regional Officer in advance. Permission required to visit parts of the mainland. Camping on Inchcailloch by permit only
Facilities: Nature trail. Camp site available to permit-holders only

2 TENTSMUIR POINT
Information: Regional Officer for the South East, Nature Conservancy Council, 12 Hope Terrace, Edinburgh EH9 2AS
Access: from ST ANDREWS
Open: Unrestricted except Abertay Sands, which are closed to the public

3 ISLE OF MAY
Information: Regional Officer for the South East, Nature Conservancy Council, 12 Hope Terrace, Edinburgh EH9 2AS
Access: by boat from Anstruther, 15km SE of ST ANDREWS
Open: Unrestricted

4 CAERLAVEROCK
Information: Regional Officer for the South West, Nature Conservancy Council, The Castle, Loch Lomond Park, Balloch, Strathclyde
Access: from Bankend, 10km SE of DUMFRIES
Open: Permission required to visit part of reserve

LAKE DISTRICT

"Beauty, horror and immensity" were feelings evoked in an eighteenth-century visitor by the splendour of the Lakeland scenery. Beloved of poets and artists – a landscape for the romantic – the Lake District has been admired ever since man stepped back from his hand-to-mouth existence with nature and looked with detachment at the countryside around him.

Situated in northwest England, the Lake District is the largest of the British National Parks and is probably the most popular with tourists and naturalists. It is a dome-shaped mountain area moulded by glaciers, which have created a system of radiating, steep-sided valleys. The underlying rocks formed before the doming took place have broadly speaking an east–west orientation and bear no relation to the radial pattern of the scenery. This phenomenon is known as superimposed drainage and the Lake District is one of the best examples to be seen anywhere throughout Europe.

The region contains seventeen major lakes and numerous smaller ones, at high altitude, known locally as tarns. Glacial erosion is responsible for many of the area's characteristic features – hanging valleys, waterfalls and scree-sided slopes. The old forest cover is now much reduced, but valuable relics of oak, yew, ash and hazel still remain, particularly in Borrowdale. Much forest clearance took place in Viking times and the word "thwait", in which many Lake District place names end, is a Viking term meaning "a clearing in the forest". During the Elizabethan period laws were passed to control the number of trees that were being felled for charcoal, which was, until the beginning of the industrial revolution, widely used instead of coal in the iron-ore smelting process.

The predominant features of the upland landscape are the fells – green, rounded hills with springy turf kept short by grazing sheep. To the south, the pale scarp slopes of the

BUTTERMERE
Scots pines line the lakeside shingle shore.

carboniferous limestone are patterned by the dark shapes of ancient yew trees. The northern area is older and of volcanic origin. The park includes part of the southwest Cumbrian coastline, where the famous Drigg Dunes and Ravenglass gullery form an important Local Nature Reserve.

The importance of the park as a wildlife preserve is indicated by the presence of four National Nature Reserves and 115 Sites of Special Scientific Interest within its boundaries. The park has both native red and roe deer populations and is an important refuge for badgers, otters, pine martens and red squirrels. Upland birds such as the curlew, golden plover and common sandpiper are widespread and buzzards are known to breed throughout the area. Both the peregrine falcon, which is recovering slowly after a population crash caused by the indiscriminate use of pesticides, and the golden eagle, which in 1969 returned to breed in England after an absence of over 100 years, are found within the National park.

LOUGHRIGG TARN *above* Trees, hills and quiet water – the Lake District is seen here in pastoral mood. Loughrigg Tarn lies 3km due west of Ambleside.

LAKE DISTRICT
Information: Information Officer, Lake District National Park, Bank House, Windermere, Cumbria LA23 1AF
Access: from CARLISLE or KENDAL
Open: Unrestricted
Facilities: Information centres at Ambleside, Borrowdale, Bowness, Coniston, Glenridding, Hawkshead, Keswick, Pooley Bridge, Waterhead. Hotels and camp sites within the park. Nature trails. Guided walks by wardens on site

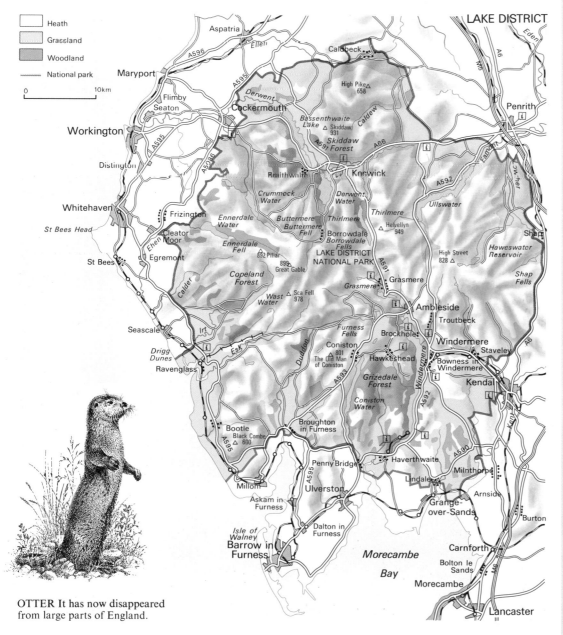

OTTER It has now disappeared from large parts of England.

167

Lindisfarne National Nature Reserve and the Farne Islands

Lindisfarne, or Holy Island as it is better known, lies 15 kilometres southeast of Berwick upon Tweed. To the south are the twenty-eight small islands owned by the National Trust which make up the Farne Islands. The whole complex is well known for its wildfowl, seabird and grey seal populations as well as for its historical association with St. Aidan, who founded the church and monastery on Holy Island in AD 635, and St. Cuthbert, who was Bishop of Lindisfarne from 685 to 686 and is said to have been the first person in Britain to create a wildlife refuge. During his years as a hermit on Inner Farne he forbade visitors to disturb the nesting eider ducks.

The Farne Islands grey seal colony, presently some 8000 strong, has long been famous. The islands provide nesting sites for a total of 13,000 pairs of puffins, 3000 pairs of guillemots, 4000 pairs of kittiwakes and 450 pairs of shags. Herring gulls and lesser black-backed gulls are common breeding species and over 15,000 eiders, perhaps the best known bird of the Farne Islands, nest. Cormorants, around 250 pairs, nest on North Wamses. Large nesting colonies of arctic, common and Sandwich terns are a feature of Inner Farne and Brownsman. The mud and sand flats around Holy Island are the winter resort of over 20,000 wigeon, more than 700 pale-bellied brent geese and herds of whooper swans as well as many thousands of waders, principally bar-tailed godwits, knots, dunlins and oystercatchers. The flats are the only wintering ground of the pale-bellied brent goose in Britain.

Moor House National Nature Reserve

A wide expanse of sheep-grazed moorland, situated around the headwaters of the River Tees, Moor House has been an important centre for ecological research for over twenty-five years. The reserve lies centrally in a long tract of uninhabited country between the east–west Stainmore and Hartside passes across the Pennines. It is largely covered by peat, which forms a boggy terrain, known

WILD CHERRY
Common throughout Britain and Ireland, the wild cherry has white flower clusters and a bitter red fruit.

FARNE ISLANDS
Shags, kittiwakes, puffins and guillemots are among the species of seabird that breed on Staple Island.

LINDISFARNE AND THE FARNE ISLANDS

locally as blanket mire. Cross Fell (882 metres), the highest point in the Pennines, lies just outside the north boundary of the reserve. The birdlife is not rich, but high moorland species such as curlew, dunlin, golden plover, red grouse and meadow pipit are well represented. The vegetation on undisturbed peat surfaces is dominated by heather, cotton-grass, cloudberry, crowberry and cross-leaved heath. In wetter areas there are several species of *Sphagnum* mosses and an abundance of asphodel and sundew.

No roads cross the reserve and access is difficult. The Pennine Way, a long-distance footpath that runs the entire length of the Pennines, crosses the reserve from north to south and is popular with walkers and hikers.

Peak District National Park
Established in 1957, the Peak District was the first of Britain's National Parks. It is visited by over sixteen million people each year and is highly accessible from the major urban centres of Manchester, Sheffield, Derby and Stoke-on-Trent. In the north the "Dark Peak", a gritstone tableland, reaching to over 600 metres on Kinder Scout and Bleaklow, is separated by the Hope Valley from the "White Peak", an area of limestone uplands, dissected by lovely wooded dales and clear, flowing streams, of which the Dove is the most famous. The peat-covered moorlands of the north, dominated by heather, bilberry

and cotton-grass, are managed for grouse shooting and sheep grazing. The impermeable rock of the gritstone region is suitable for water storage and the water authorities own a 200-square-kilometre catchment area which feeds fifty-five reservoirs. The limestone plateau is important for dairy farming, and there is considerable exploitation of the rock for roadstone and cement manufacture. The economic and tourist pressures on the park, when taken into consideration with a resident population of 40,000 people, pose a severe conservation problem. The skill of the park authorities in largely overcoming these difficulties was recognized by the award of the first European Diploma of Conservation by the Council of Europe in 1965.

Although several areas within the park have been designated as of particular conservation importance, only one area, which includes Monk's Dale and Lathkill Dale, has been set aside as a National Nature Reserve. On the carboniferous limestone of the reserve grow some of the finest ashwoods in the country. The absence of grazing within the nature reserve has allowed a rich flora to develop, embracing scarce species such as lily-of-the-valley, mezereon, green hellebore, bird's-nest orchid and yellow star of Bethlehem. Limestone grassland, a fast disappearing habitat in the British Isles and beloved by naturalists for its rich flora of flowering plants, is well represented. The ring ouzel inhabits the high crags of the peaks and golden plovers and curlews are common in moorland areas.

Wyre Forest National Nature Reserve
The nature reserve forms part of the much larger ancient Forest of Wyre, a woodland area that, due to the demand for timber in the nearby industrial towns, has been greatly exploited since the Industrial Revolution. The forest, lying only 32 kilometres from the centre of Birmingham, is situated on the River Severn. Dowles Brook, a tributary of the Severn, crosses the middle of the forest and its attractive steep-sided valley provides one of the main scenic features of the area. Although the oak forest has been coppiced for centuries to provide charcoal for smelting iron, two remarkably large specimens still survive – the Mawley Oak and the Goodmoor Oak. The rich flora includes such rarities as the long-leaved helleborine, the wild columbine and autumn crocus. Ramsons, lily-of-the-valley and common spotted orchids are a delight to the eye in early summer.

Badgers, foxes, dormice, harvest mice and fallow deer are all found within the reserve. The rare insect population includes the splendid Kentish glory moth, now very scarce in Britain, the curious land caddis-fly, the alder kitten moth and the white-barred clear-wing moth. Along Dowles Brook dippers, kingfishers and grey wagtails can be seen. The wooded valley sides provide a home for pied flycatchers and wood warblers.

1 LINDISFARNE
Information: Regional Officer for NE England, Nature Conservancy Council, Archbold House, Archbold Terrace, Newcastle-upon-Tyne NE2 1EG
Access: from Beal, 13km SE of BERWICK-UPON-TWEED
Open: Accessibility of Holy Island determined by state of the tide. Some areas restricted during breeding season (May to July)

2 MOOR HOUSE
Information: Regional Office for NW England, Nature Conservancy Council, Blackwell, Bowness-on-Windermere, Windermere, Cumbria LA23 3JR
Access: by track from Garrigill, 50km SE of CARLISLE
Open: Permit required to visit areas away from public rights of way

3 PEAK DISTRICT
Information: The Peak National Park Office, Aldern House, Baslow Road, Bakewell, Derbyshire DE4 1AE
Access: from MANCHESTER, LEEDS or SHEFFIELD
Open: Unrestricted except during grouse-shooting season (August 12 to December 10), when some moors may be closed
Facilities: Information centres at Bakewell, Castleton, Edale. Hotels and camp sites within the park. Guided walks. Rangers on site

4 WYRE FOREST
Information: Regional Officer for the West Midlands, Nature Conservancy Council, Attingham Park, Shrewsbury, Shropshire SY4 4TW
Access: from Bewdley, 35km SW of BIRMINGHAM
Open: Permission required to visit areas away from footpaths
Facilities: Information centre

CARLINE THISTLE *above* This small yellow-flowered thistle grows on dry grassland and dunes.

SNOWDONIA *above* The peaks of Mount Snowdon and Gribgoch glow in the pale light of an early winter morning. Snowdon has the highest rack-and-pinion railway to be found anywhere in Britain.

SNOWDONIA

Moorland
Agricultural land
Woodland
National park

0   10   20 km

Newborough Warren National Nature Reserve

On the southwest side of Anglesey, close to the Menai Straits, separating the island from mainland Wales, is one of the principal dune and saltmarsh systems in Britain. Prior to the fourteenth century, most of this area was agricultural land, but a series of violent storms moved the dunes inland and buried it.

Apart from the coastal dune system, which suffers erosion by both wind and visitors, there is an extensive inland area of dune grassland, where the sand has been completely stabilized. The flora includes many interesting species such as meadow saxifrage, common wintergreen, carline thistle, birds-foot trefoil, wild thyme and several species of orchid. In low-lying wet areas, known as slacks, the creeping willow is common. The blue flowers of the common butterwort and the beautiful white cups of the grass-of-Parnassus can be seen in July and August.

In the northern part of the reserve, consisting of the Cefni saltmarsh and the Malltraeth Pool, shelduck, curlew and redshank are frequently found, and wild swans, goldeneye ducks and migrant waders, such as black-tailed and bar-tailed godwits, ruff and greenshank, have also been recorded.

Snowdonia National Park

Within this park, the second largest in Britain, lie eight ranges of mountains, five in the north and three in the south, with fourteen summits exceeding 900 metres. At 1085 metres Snowdon is the highest. Two spectacular glaciated valleys, Llanberis and Nant Ffrancon, separate Snowdon and the other two mountains in this group – Glyder Fawr (999 metres) and Carnedd Llewelyn (1062 metres) – from one another. In the southern part of the park the Cader Idris (893 metres) rises above the

Mawddach estuary in a tremendous north-facing escarpment. On the south side is Cwm Cau, one of the finest corries in Britain. Between the northerly and southerly mountain regions are the rocky summits of Rhinog Fawr (720 metres) and Rhinog Fach (711 metres), an area of rugged terrain, boulder-strewn slopes and extensive heather moors, this is probably the park's least known region.

Lying along Snowdonia's 37 kilometres of coastline are two fine nature reserves – the dune and saltmarsh systems of Morfa Dyffryn and Morfa Harlech. Both are notable for marsh and dune plants. Morfa Harlech has several orchid species, maiden pink and sea-side pansy, and both are rich in mosses. Flocks of mallard, teal, pintail, wigeon and shelduck frequent the coastal marshes and a colony of black-headed gulls breeds on stretches of freshwater marsh.

Ten woodland nature reserves, consisting mostly of oak but often with other deciduous trees such as elm, ash, hazel, hawthorn and alder, some growing on inaccessible, steep rocky slopes, lie within the park. Many of the areas are open only to permit-holders because of the fragile nature of their plant communities. The woods have rich floras of ferns, mosses and lichens, which thrive in the high humidity. Of the ten woodland reserves, Coedydd Maentwrog and Coed Ganllwyd deserve particular mention. The south-facing part of Coedydd Maentwrog lies on the northern slopes of the Vale of Ffestiniog, near the village of Maentwrog, and is drier than most other comparable localities. Although the dominant tree is the sessile oak, there are also many rowans, ash, alders and sycamores.

Coed Ganllwyd occupies a gentle slope on the east side of the Rhinog Mountains. On the north side is the famous rocky gorge of the Afon Gamlan and the beautiful waterfall of Rhaiadr-ddu. The atmospheric humidity of the locality is accentuated by the sheltered nature of the site and the spray from the falls. These conditions have encouraged the development of a wide variety of rare ferns, liverworts and mosses, which suggests that the tree cover has been preserved for a very long period, otherwise these sensitive plants would not have survived.

Skomer Island National Nature Reserve

The Pembroke coast has been a favourite haunt of the birdwatcher for many years, principally because of the island sea-bird colonies on Grassholm, Skokholm and Skomer. All three islands are now protected, although Skomer is the only one that is a National Nature Reserve.

Skomer lies at the southern tip of St. Brides Bay, separated from the mainland by Jack Sound, a rocky channel about 1 kilometre wide. The island is flat-topped and has an average height which is no more than about 60 metres above sea level.

Rabbit holes near the cliff edge are occupied in the summer by puffins and Manx shear-waters, which nest in vast numbers. As many as 100,000 shearwaters are said to nest, but being largely nocturnal it is difficult to assess their numbers accurately. Puffins are easily approached, and although about 6,500 pairs are thought to breed, this is a low figure compared with that of thirty years ago. Several species of gulls nest on the island, including the kittiwake, lesser black-backed gull, greater black-backed gull and herring gull.

The few pairs of choughs breeding on the island choose inaccessible cliff crevices for their nests. The birds are only obvious when they begin searching for insect life in the short turf of the cliff tops. The five species of mammal present include the Skomer vole, a larger and paler race of the normal bank vole found on the mainland.

Oxwich National Nature Reserve

Sheltered from the westerly winds, Oxwich Bay is one of the most popular sites on the Gower coast. The National Nature Reserve supports a wide range of habitats, the most important ones being sandy and rocky shore, calcareous sand dunes with a series of dune slacks, saltmarsh, freshwater marsh, and cliff woodlands. The flora, insect and bird life are of particular interest. The saltmarsh is the habitat of a small spider, *Acanthophyma gowerensis*, known from only one other site in Britain and one in Ireland. The freshwater marsh lying on the north side of the coast road consists of extensive reed beds and pools with their own rich aquatic flora. The woods are composed mainly of oak, ash, elm, beech and some lime trees.

1 NEWBOROUGH WARREN
Information: Regional Officer for North Wales, Nature Conservancy Council, Plas Penrhos, Fford Penrhos, Bangor, Gwynedd LL57 2LQ
Access: from Newborough, 25km SW of BANGOR
Open: Permission required to visit areas away from public rights of way

2 SNOWDONIA
Information: Snowdonia National Park Office, Penrhyndeudraeth, Gwynedd LL48 6LF
Access: from ABERYSTWYTH, BANGOR, CORWEN or COLWYN BAY
Open: Unrestricted

3 SKOMER ISLAND
Information: The West Wales Naturalists' Trust, 7 Market Street, Haverfordwest, Dyfed SA61 1NS
Access: from Marloes, 15km W of MILFORD HAVEN
Open: Landing fee. Permission required to visit areas lying outside the nature trail

4 OXWICH
Information: Regional Officer for South Wales, Nature Conservancy Council, 44 The Parade, Roath, Cardiff CF2 3AB
Access: from Oxwich, 20km SW of SWANSEA
Open: Permission required to visit areas off footpaths away from beach

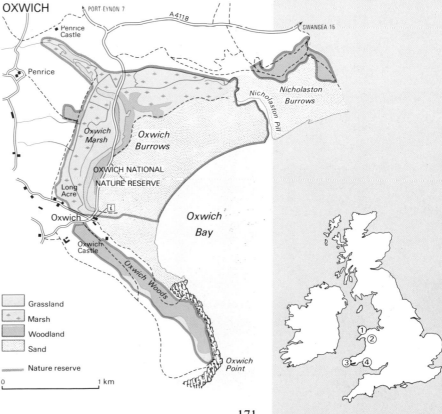

OXWICH

PORT-EYNON 7   A4118   SWANSEA 15

Penrice Castle

Penrice

Nicholaston Pill   Nicholaston Burrows

Oxwich Marsh   Oxwich Burrows

OXWICH NATIONAL NATURE RESERVE

Long Acre

Oxwich

Oxwich Bay

Oxwich Castle

Oxwich Woods

Oxwich Point

Grassland
Marsh
Woodland
Sand
Nature reserve

0   1 km

171

Braunton Burrows National Nature Reserve

Because of the many studies that have been made of Braunton Burrows it is one of the best-documented dune systems in Britain. It is also one of the ten largest. The nature reserve extends northwards from the estuary of the rivers Taw and Torridge on the northern coast of Devon. In places the sand hills exceed 30 metres in height, and between the ridges are numerous moist slacks rich in plant life. Over 375 species of flowering plants have been recorded, including some species which are found only locally such as sea club-rush, water germander, sea knot-grass, sharp rush, shore dock and sand toadflax.

Exmoor National Park

The second smallest of Britain's National Parks, Exmoor has a special charm of its own and contains some of the finest parts of the North Devon and Somerset coastline. The interior of the park is a high heather-covered plateau with swift streams flowing through steep-sided valleys. There are ten hills rising to more than 500 metres and the highest point, Dunkery Beacon (519 metres), stands out as one of the more striking features of the high moorland landscape. The coasts, valleys, woodlands and moors provide a wide range of scenery, and even in the height of summer, when the neighbouring beaches are crowded with holidaymakers, there are many places in the park where there is neither sound nor sight of human presence.

Although there are no National Nature Reserves within the park, there are several areas of comparable scientific interest. Some are owned and protected by the National Trust – for example, the 405 hectares of oak, ash, wych elm and birch woodlands adjoining Dunkery Beacon on the valley sides of Holnicote and Horner Water in Somerset.

This typical area of Exmoor woodland is resplendent in lichens and is an important wintering area for the native red deer, which here form one of the three largest concentrations in England.

The area has its own hardy breed of pony, the Exmoor pony, which is thought by some to be a direct descendant of the native British wild stock rather than a domestic animal that has been allowed to go wild. The birdlife includes most of the typical moorland species, such as buzzard, raven, ring ouzel, dipper and curlew. In the woodlands, redstart, wood warbler and pied flycatcher are found. Of particular interest is the black grouse, which although a native to the area now survives only in small numbers.

Dartmoor National Park

The high plateau of ancient granite rocks known as Dartmoor has been described as the last wilderness area in southern Britain. It is an open rolling landscape of moors and bogs, dotted with curious rocky outcrops known as tors. The plateau is fringed by steep-sided valleys containing craggy woodlands and fast-flowing streams. The highest points, High Willhays and Yes Tor in the north of the park, exceed 600 metres and rise well above the general level of the plateau. Being close to the Atlantic Ocean, and with prevailing south-westerly winds, Dartmoor has a relatively high rainfall and is well known for its mists and fogs.

Although much of the park is covered with heather, there are many boggy areas containing a rich and fascinating plant life. Two large areas of moorland and several smaller areas of heath and woodland have been designated Sites of Special Scientific Interest. There are also three woodland- and two forest-nature reserves. Among the most important is

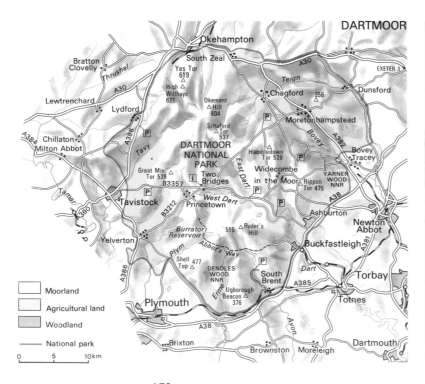

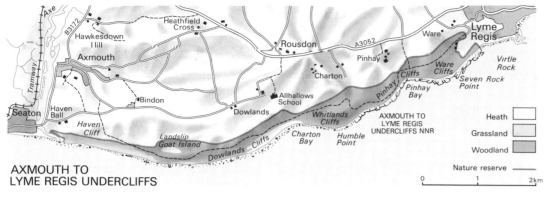

AXMOUTH TO LYME REGIS UNDERCLIFFS

Heath ☐
Grassland ☐
Woodland ▨

Nature reserve ———

0   1   2km

1 BRAUNTON BURROWS
Information: Regional Officer
for SW England, Nature
Conservancy Council,
Roughmoor, Bishops Hull,
Taunton, Somerset TA1 5AA
Access: from BARNSTAPLE
Open: Unrestricted on foot

2 EXMOOR
Information: Exmoor National
Park Centre, Exmoor House,
Dulverton, Somerset TA22 9HL
Access: from BARNSTAPLE or
MINEHEAD
Open: Unrestricted, but visitors
should keep to public rights of
way
Facilities: Information centres
at County Gate, Lynmouth,
Dulverton, Combe Martin.
Hotels and camp sites within
the park. Waymarked walks and
nature trails. Wardens on site

3 DARTMOOR
Information: Dartmoor
National Park Centre, Parke,
Haytor Road, Bovey Tracey, nr.
Newton Abbot TQ13 9JQ
Access: from PLYMOUTH or
EXETER
Open: Unrestricted
Facilities: Information centres
at Newbirdge, Princetown,
Postbridge, Steps Bridge,
Tavistock, Okehampton (Easter
to October). Hotels and camp
sites within the park. Guided
walks

**4 AXMOUTH TO LYME
REGIS UNDERCLIFFS**
Information: Regional Officer
for SW England, Nature
Conservancy Council,
Roughmoor, Bishops Hull,
Taunton, Somerset TA1 5AA
Access: from Seaton, 35km E of
EXETER or LYME REGIS
Open: Permission required to
visit areas away from footpath

AMMONITE *right*
Fossils such as this 100-
million-year-old mollusc
are common in the lime-
stone cliffs of Lyme Regis.

Yarner Wood in the valley of the River Bovey
on the east side of the park. This area, together
with the nearby Bovey Valley woodlands,
provides the finest remaining example of the
once-extensive Dartmoor forests. The variations of slope, aspect and soil type, combined
with a damp maritime climate, encourages a
rich and distinctive fauna and flora. Below
the dense canopy of sessile-oak woodland,
which contains some of the largest specimens
in Western Europe, there is an understorey of
holly and rowan. On the drier slopes the
vegetation consists mainly of bilberry,
bracken, heather and the common cow-
wheat. The rare heath lobelia occurs in some
abandoned fields. In the more fertile valley
soils, the flora includes primrose, sanicle,
royal fern and golden saxifrage. Where the
soils are rich in lime, the pedunculate oak
replaces the sessile oak, and ash, alder, birch
and beech are all more common.

Among the interesting birds found in this
nature reserve are buzzards, ravens, redstarts,
wood warblers, dippers and grey wagtails.
The pied flycatcher, here at the extreme southwest limit of its range in Britain, first bred in
nest boxes erected in Yarner Wood.

Axmouth to Lyme Regis Undercliffs National Nature Reserve

On Christmas Day 1839, after a period of very
wet weather, part of the cliff between Seaton
and Lyme Regis on the coast of Devon and
Dorset became detached and slid slowly sea-
wards, leaving a chasm nearly 70 metres deep
in places. The detached portion, now called
Goat Island, included 5.5 hectares of land,
which is still cultivated. The event is well
documented by contemporary drawings and
by later photographs, which record the vegetation succession in the chasm and on the
detached section of land. Today the results of
140 years of natural development without
interference by man can be viewed over more
than 10 kilometres of coastline.

The most distinctive feature is the extensive
ash woodland that covers most of the reserve
and represents one of the best examples of
"plant succession" to be found in Britain.
The rough terrain in the chasm has prevented
access by all except the most agile and has allowed the vegetation to develop undisturbed.
The flora includes the purple gromwell, a
species found only locally. Climbing plants
such as traveller's joy and ivy are widespread
throughout the woodland reserve. The insect
life is extremely rich, and includes the rare
wood white butterfly; in open chalky areas
an uncommon burrowing spider, *Atypus
affinis*, can be found.

The Lyme Regis area, including the land-
slip, has long been renowned for its abundance
of Triassic, Jurassic and Cretaceous fossils.
The soft rocks of the sea cliffs are continually
being eroded by wave action, exposing new
material, which is eagerly sought by amateur
fossil hunters.

DARTMOOR Outcropping granite rock betrays
Dartmoor's origins; both it and nearby Exmoor are
portions of a vast granitic body which stand out
above the surrounding countryside.

HOLKHAM

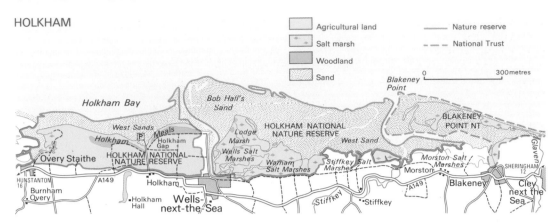

Agricultural land · Nature reserve
Salt marsh · – – National Trust
Woodland
Sand

0   300 metres

BLACK-TAILED
GODWIT A straight
bill, white wingbars and
chestnut plumage in
summer distinguish this
godwit from other waders.

DUKE OF BURGUNDY
FRITILLARY A
lowland species, usually
seen in woodland
clearings.

Holkham National Nature Reserve

The north Norfolk coast is a unique part of
the British coastline. Between Holme and
Salthouse there are 26 kilometres of sand
dunes and saltmarshes, all of which are
protected within ten specific areas, Holkham
National Nature Reserve being the largest.

The first area of coastline to be protected
was the famous Blakeney Point, owned by the
National Trust and a nature reserve since
1912. Scolt Head Island, to the west of Holkham Dunes, consists of more than 6 kilometres of dunes and saltmarsh isolated from
the mainland at high tide. It became a National
Nature Reserve in 1953 and, like Blakeney
Point, is a splendid area for coastal plants,
insects and birds. It is particularly attractive
in autumn, when vast areas of sea-lavender
are in bloom on the saltmarshes.

Holkham National Nature Reserve, established in 1967, is now the largest coastal
nature reserve in England. The sand dunes
were planted with pine trees from 1850 on-
wards to protect the reclaimed farmland
behind from wind-blown sand. To the east of
the town of Wells, the reserve includes one of
the largest saltmarshes in England – of great
importance as a resting place for migrant
birds and as a refuge for wildfowl during the
winter. In the spring and autumn, large
numbers of migratory birds move along the
Norfolk coast and often include many rare
species among their number. In winter, large
numbers of geese, predominantly brent geese,
rest and feed on the marshes, and numerous
birds of the high Arctic may be seen offshore.
In the breeding season the common coastal
birds include the ringed plover, oystercatcher,
common tern, redshank, black-headed gull
and shelduck. Little terns also nest in many
areas and the Sandwich tern nests in a large
breeding colony on Scolt Head Island.

Hickling Broad National Nature Reserve

Hickling Broad, together with Heigham
Sound, Horsey Mere and the adjacent
marshes, is probably the best known of all the
Norfolk Broads – a complex system of water
bodies situated in eastern Norfolk. Altogether
about forty-six broads still survive and form
together the most extensive wetland area in
the British Isles. Until the 1950s the Broad-

land lakes were thought to be natural formations, but careful research has shown that
they originated as peat cuttings which later
became filled with water due to a rise in the
sea level during the Middle Ages.

Hickling is the largest of all the broads,
and being at the head of a river system is both
freer from silting and from many of the
pollution problems suffered by other broads.
The extensive reed beds make ideal nesting
habitats for marsh harriers, bitterns and
bearded tits. Many rare plants and insects are
found on the marshes. The best known is the
swallowtail butterfly, a slightly different race
from that found on the continent of Europe.

A long list of rare migrant birds observed
on the reserve has been compiled. In May, for
example, one might easily see ospreys, spoonbills, black terns, grey plovers, spotted redshanks, black-tailed and bar-tailed godwits,
reeves and ruffs. Until recently Hickling
Broad was one of the best localities for certain
rare aquatic plants, of which the best known
was the holly-leaved naiad. However, despite
Hickling Broad's favourable location, in the
last fifteen to twenty years the increased input
of phosphate-rich guano from a winter gull
roost and the seepage of fertilizers from
agricultural land has stimulated the rapid
growth of freshwater algae, which have
clouded the water to such an extent that
bottom-dwelling freshwater plants are unable
to survive.

Castor Hanglands National Nature Reserve

Within a short distance of the town of
Peterborough and lying on the flat East
Midland Plain are four important National
Nature Reserves: Woodwalton Fen and
Holme Fen, on the peatlands at the edge of the
Fenland Basin; the ancient woodland of
Monks Wood, on the clay upland between
Peterborough and Huntingdon; and the
smallest, Castor Hanglands, lying about 6
kilometres to the west of Peterborough and
consisting of grass heath, scrub and mixed
deciduous woodland. In medieval times
Castor Hanglands was part of the ancient
Forest of Nasborough, a wooded region
which has now largely vanished.

Limestone heath, a habitat preserved by
grazing, was formerly much more extensive

within the reserve than it is now. In 1930 sheep grazing ended and the rabbit, another important grazer, almost disappeared after the introduction of myxomatosis in 1954. As a result hawthorn and blackthorn scrub have invaded the reserve and now cover considerable areas. Oak–ash woodland accounts for about half of the reserve. In the past the area was well known for its fine, large trees; however, during the Second World War most of the commercially valuable timber was felled to serve the national need.

In the northern part of the reserve, close to the point of entry, there are abandoned limestone quarries covered with short, grassy vegetation and lime-loving plants such as yellow-wart, felwort, common rockrose and salad burnet. Some forty-three species of butterfly have been recorded in the reserve and it was, until recently, one of the best localities in Britain for the Duke of Burgundy fritillary, black hairstreak and the chequered skipper; the latter unfortunately has not been seen for some years. Among the fifty-four species of birds that have been recorded nesting within the reserve are the lesser whitethroat, blackcap, grasshopper warbler, spotted flycatcher and nightingale. A herd of fallow deer, probably originating from a nearby estate, lives within the reserve.

Wicken Fen Nature Reserve

The famous fenland nature reserve of Wicken Fen has been studied by botanists and zoologists for over a hundred years, and is particularly well known for its rich insect fauna. In 1955 a mere was excavated in Adventurers Fen, which has over the years added many new species of birds, such as bitterns and bearded tits, to the fauna of the reserve. However, neither of these birds yet breed within the area.

In spite of centuries of peat cutting, a layer over a metre thick survives in most parts, and the local vegetation of reeds and sedges is still cut for thatching. This activity is important conservationally as it controls the spread of common sallow and alder buckthorn, which if unchecked would soon cover the area. The open fen created is favoured by such attractive plants as yellow and purple loosestrife, angelica, milk parsley and the marsh pea, and provides a favourable environment for the reserve's famous insect population.

Exactly why so many different insects, particularly rare moths and beetles, are found in this area is unknown, but it may have something to do with the fact that its vegetation has survived relatively unmodified over a long period of time. Some changes are gradually taking place; parts of the peat surface are becoming progressively more acid, allowing *Sphagnum* mosses to recolonize.

Minsmere Reserve

The Royal Society for the Protection of Birds' reserve at Minsmere and the neighbouring National Nature Reserve at Walberswick are both examples of the ease with which habitats for rare birds can be re-created. They are both shallow valleys containing sandy heathland lying on either side of extensive marshes. In the past the marshland lying in the valleys was drained and, prior to 1940, used as cattle grazing. As a safeguard against invasion during the Second World War the valleys were flooded and allowed to revert to marshland. After the war, representations made by both the RSPB and the Nature Conservancy Council; the high cost of draining the land and the land-owners' willingness to retain the

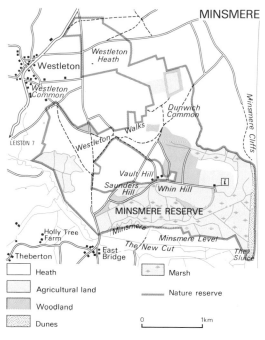

areas in their marshy state were sufficient to ensure that both areas were left unaltered and became nature reserves.

The Westwood marshes, lying between Minsmere and Walberswick, one of the largest uninterrupted freshwater reed beds in Britain, can be seen from the heathlands situated to the north of Minsmere. At the head of the marshes lies a woodland with sallow, alder and birch, and a great deal of *Sphagnum* beneath the canopy. The bittern, bearded tit, reed warbler, marsh harrier and water rail breed regularly in the marshes, as well as large numbers of duck – mallard, teal, shoveler and gadwall.

On the north side of Walberswick reserve, the extensive saltmarshes of the River Blythe estuary attract large numbers of migrant wading birds and wildfowl during the winter months. Short-eared owls, merlins and hen-harriers are regular winter visitors.

The heathland areas are covered with scrub in many places, particularly gorse, and are not rich floristically, although a number of less common clovers do occur. The heathland birdlife contains a number of interesting species; the great grey shrike is a regular winter visitor.

1 HOLKHAM
Information: Regional Officer for East Anglia, Nature Conservancy Council, 60 Bracondale, Norwich, Norfolk NR1 2BE
Access: from Holkham, 55km NE of KINGS LYNN
Open: Unrestricted except for farmland

2 HICKLING BROAD
Information: Regional Officer for East Anglia, Nature Conservancy Council, 60 Bracondale, Norwich, Norfolk NR1 2BE
Access: from NORWICH or GREAT YARMOUTH
Open: Permission to visit from The Norfolk Naturalists' Trust, 72 The Close, Norwich, Norfolk NR1 4DF (boating unrestricted within navigation channel)
Facilities: Water-trail. Observation hides

3 CASTOR HANGLANDS
Information: Regional Officer for the East Midlands, Nature Conservancy Council, Godwin House, George Street, Huntingdon, Cambs PE18 6BG
Access: from PETERBOROUGH
Open: Permission required except for Ailsworth Heath

4 WICKEN FEN
Information: The Warden, The Warden's House, Lode Lane, Wicken, Ely, Cambs CB7 5XP
Access: from Wicken, 18km NE of CAMBRIDGE
Open: Daily by permit only obtainable from William Thorpe Building, Lode Lane
Facilities: Information centre. Nature trail

5 MINSMERE
Information: Minsmere Reserve, Westleton, Saxmundham, Suffolk IP17 3BY
Access: from Westleton, 43km NE of IPSWICH
Open: Admission strictly controlled, and on some occasions only available to members. Entry fee for non-members
Facilities: Information centre. Marked walks between hides. Observation hides, some especially for the disabled

Brownsea Island Reserve

The entrance to the great harbour of Poole is dominated by Brownsea Island, which has been the property of the National Trust since 1960. About one-third of the island has been leased to the Dorset Naturalists' Trust and is managed as a nature reserve. A special hide has been built overlooking a large shallow lagoon lying within the reserve to provide visitors with bird-watching facilities. Brownsea is well known for its peacocks, which have existed in a semi-wild state for many years. Golden pheasant, blue-eared pheasant and Swinhoe's pheasant have been introduced by the Ornamental Pheasant Trust to build up stocks for eventual release in their native habitats. In the south of the island, the old daffodil fields, relics of previous cultivation, are ablaze with colour during April. The reserve contains one of the largest heronries in the British Isles to which guided tours are available at certain times.

The New Forest

Formerly a Royal Forest created by the Norman Kings in the eleventh century, the New Forest, although without formal status, is one of the most important conservation sites in Britain. Located almost on the south coast, it is the largest single tract of semi-natural vegetation in lowland England – a glorious mosaic of woodland, grassland, heath and bog.

Long-established common rights to graze livestock on more than 20,000 hectares of the forest have kept the heathlands relatively open and preserved their character. In addition to the common land, there are about 8300 hectares of enclosed woodland managed for commercial forestry. The Forestry Commission is the responsible authority and works very closely with the Nature Conservancy Council to ensure that the unique wildlife features are maintained. The New Forest's size and the long continuity of semi-natural conditions on the coast close to the European mainland have helped to make it one of the

richest areas in the British Isles for plants and animals; there are more rarities here than in any other comparable place in the country. Easy access from large urban centres results in millions of visitors each year, and the Forestry Commission, with whom the responsibility rests, has the problem of ensuring that the wildlife is preserved without imposing too many restrictions on public access within the forest.

The birdlife is largely made up of heathland species, such as woodlark, stonechat, Dartford warbler and, in open woodland glades, the nightjar. In the forests the honey buzzard, hobby and goshawk, all rare birds of prey in Britain, breed in small numbers. The rare European sand lizard and smooth snake are found on some heaths.

Of the many unusual insects, the most interesting are the silver-studded blue butterfly and the New Forest cicada, found nowhere else in Britain. The large marsh grasshopper is found in wet areas and nearby the handsome raft spider can be seen floating on the water of stagnant pools. The plant life, typical of the acid sands and gravels of heathlands, contains several rare species, mostly in boggy and wooded areas. The commonest trees are beech and oak, often growing through an understorey of holly, yew and hawthorn. Freedom from human interference has allowed a large number of overmature trees to survive, their dead boughs and hollow trunks providing ideal habitats for the area's diverse and interesting population of invertebrate animals.

PYRAMIDAL ORCHID
above Easily recognized by its bright pink pyramidal-shaped flowerhead, this orchid is found throughout lowland Britain.

NEW FOREST *left*
The ponies, which play an important part in the New Forest's ecology, are not wild but in all cases privately owned.

Kingley Vale National Nature Reserve

The yew woodland of Kingley Vale, considered to be one of the finest in Europe, has long been famous. The reserve is situated on the southern part of the South Downs and includes the chalk outcrop known as Bow Hill. With their dark spreading canopy contrasting starkly with the foliage of other trees the yew trees are a magnificent sight. Although some are more than 500 years old, in general the wood is of fairly recent origin and is known to have developed from a few old trees that were growing in Kingley Vale during the first half of the nineteenth century. Earlier still, the greater part of the area was open downland grazed by sheep. As sheep grazing declined, allowing the earlier vegetation to re-establish itself, the yews spread rapidly through the closely cropped turf.

A wide variety of other trees grow among the yews, mainly ash, oak, hawthorn, blackthorn, wild privet, holly and dogwood. The steeper turf-covered slopes are rich in plant life, including bee and early purple orchids, thyme and common rockrose. More than seventy species of birds have been recorded, among them nightingale, chiffchaff, marsh tit, yellowhammer, blackcap, grasshopper warbler and green woodpecker. Fallow deer, roe deer, fox and badger are also found. The chief management problem is in preventing the remaining downland from becoming overgrown by scrub and young trees. Some areas are mown, and on other parts ponies are grazed to help control the growth of woody plants.

Wye National Nature Reserve

Chalk grassland was formerly much more widespread in Britain than it is today and now survives only in isolated places, mainly on the steeper slopes of the English downs.

Wye National Nature Reserve is the most easterly of the chalk grassland reserves and occupies 132 hectares of scarp slope on the Kentish North Downs. The fauna and flora of Kent is perhaps the richest of any county in Britain, probably because it is the part of Britain closest to the European mainland.

The reserve includes a number of dry valleys or coombs which have been protected from past cultivation by their steep sides; the grandest being the Devil's Kneading Trough.

Chalk grassland, with its rich variety of flowers and many fascinating insects, is largely the product of centuries of grazing by sheep and cattle. At Wye the turf contains many typical chalk plants such as wild thyme, marjoram, salad burnet and common rockrose. Of the seventeen species of orchid that have been recorded in the reserve, the fragrant and pyramidal orchids are the most common.

About a third of the area is woodland, mainly ash and hazel coppice with a few whitebeams and yew trees. There is also one small area of beech. A rich scrub provides a valuable habitat for small birds.

1 BROWNSEA ISLAND
Information: The Warden, The Villa, Brownsea Island, Poole
Access: from BOURNEMOUTH
Open: April to September, between 1000 and 2000 Winter visits by arrangement
Facilities: Nature trail

2 NEW FOREST
Information: Southern Tourist Board Information caravan, Lyndhurst Car Park, Lyndhurst SO4 7BN (April to September)
Access: from BOURNEMOUTH, SOUTHAMPTON or SALISBURY
Open: Unrestricted. Camping restricted to the period between April and September
Facilities: Camp sites. Forest walks

3 KINGLEY VALE
Information: Regional Officer for SE England, Nature Conservancy Council, "Zealds", Church Street, Wye, Ashford, Kent TN25 5BW
Access: West Stoke, 6km N of CHICHESTER
Open: Permission required to visit Bow Hill
Facilities: Information centre. Nature trail

4 WYE
Information: Regional Officer for SE England, Nature Conservancy Council, "Zealds" Church Street, Wye, Ashford, Kent TN25 5BW
Access: from Wye, 35km E of MAIDSTONE
Open: Permission required to visit areas away from Broad Downs
Facilities: Information centre. Nature trail

Kebble National Nature Reserve
An extensive area of lake and grassland, Kebble National Nature Reserve is situated on the western tip of Rathlin Island, the whole of which has been designated an area of scientific interest. The reserve's principal feature is its coastal cliff, which contains an important seabird breeding colony. The most abundant species are the guillemot, razorbill, puffin, kittiwake, fulmar and shag. Many other birds of interest breed in the reserve, among them buzzards, peregrine falcons, ravens, choughs, black guillemots and Manx shearwaters. Rathlin Island, 7 kilometres from east to west and 5 kilometres from north to south, is an ideal size for the hiker to explore thoroughly in a few days.

Oxford Island National Nature Reserve
Oxford Island is in fact a peninsula and lies in the southeast corner of Lough Neagh, the largest lake in the British Isles. The reserve contains areas of meadowland, scrub woodland and an extensive region of reed beds along the shoreline. It is important for its large number of breeding and wintering birds and has perhaps the largest breeding colony of great crested grebes in Great Britain. Other birds include the tufted duck, shoveler, gadwall and pochard and, in meadow and scrub, the grasshopper warbler and corncrake.

Quoile Pondage National Nature Reserve
Lying 2.5 kilometres north of Downpatrick on the Quoile River, Quoile Pondage comprises 4 kilometres of river and river bank which, until the building of a flood control barrage in 1957, formed a tidal estuary. The change from saltwater estuary to freshwater lake has been most marked along the foreshore, which, prior to the barrage, was kept free of vegetation by the action of the tide. Today there are areas of reed beds, rushy grasslands, alder and willow carr and, a little farther inland, scrubby woodland. The former mudflats are now a species-rich grassland colonized in places by canary- and sweet-grass. The pondage is well known as a wild-fowl refuge and particularly noted for greylag geese and pochard.

Murlough National Nature Reserve
Part of the sand-dune system which has developed across Dundrum Bay at the foot of the Mourne Mountains near Newcastle in County Down, Murlough Nature Reserve is nearly 5 kilometres in length and lies on a peninsula that is bounded by the sea on all but the southern and southwestern margins. The vegetation of the younger dunes is similar to that of calcareous dune grassland, while the older landward dunes on the other hand have leached, somewhat acid, soils and a form of heathland vegetation. Other parts are dominated by the attractive burnet rose, heather and lichens. The invertebrate fauna has been particularly well studied and includes

SHAG A slender seabird which nests on rocky coasts and cliff ledges, the shag is known for the determined defence of its young it exhibits during the breeding season.

MURLOUGH *above* The reserve, close to the beautiful Mourne Mountains has one of the finest undisturbed sand-dune systems in Northern Ireland.

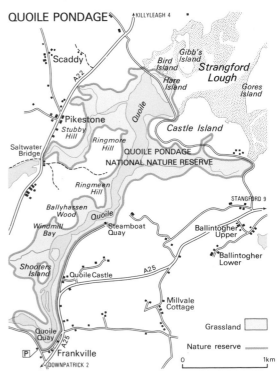

1 KEBBLE
Information: The Warden, Portandoo Countryside Centre, 8 Bath Road, Portrush, Co. Antrim
Access: by boat from Ballycastle, 40km NE of COLERAINE

2 OXFORD ISLAND
Information: Information and Nature Exhibition Centre, Oxford Island, Craigavon, Co. Armagh
Access: from LURGAN

3 QUOILE PONDAGE
Information: The Warden, Marine Biology Station, Portaferry, Co. Down
Access: from DOWNPATRICK
Open: Area on right bank of Quoile River open all year. Visits to other areas only by arrangement with the warden

4 MURLOUGH
Information: The Warden, Murlough, Dundrum, Co. Down
Access: from Slidderyford Bridge, 15km SW of DOWNPATRICK
Open: Permission required to visit part of the reserve

5 MARBLE ARCH
Information: The Warden, Castle Archdale Country Park, Irvinestown, Enniskillen, Co. Fermanagh
Access: 15km W of ENNISKILLEN
Open: Permission required to visit part of reserve
Facilities: Riverside walk to Marble Arch caves

butterflies such as the grayling, dark green fritillary and common blue. Fifty-three species of birds are known to have bred on the reserve, many of them in a small area of woodland at the northeast end. The mudflats on the inner part of Dundrum Bay are visited by thousands of waders and waterfowl.

Marble Arch Forest National Nature Reserve
Situated in a narrow, steep-sided glen on the Cladagh River, Marble Arch Forest is a fine example of ash woodland on limestone, a vegetation type found only in this part of Northern Ireland. A number of other trees, notably beech, larch, fir and spruce, are scattered through the reserve. As there is no grazing the ground-cover flora is well developed and contains many mosses and liverworts that are characteristic of limestone soils. Two rare plants, loose-flowered sedge and an attractive grass, *Melica uniflora*, grow in the reserve. The glen is of considerable interest geologically and contains many karst limestone features, including an extensive cave system. The feature known as "Marble Arch" is the point at which the River Cladgh emerges from the system to form one of the largest springs in the British Isles.

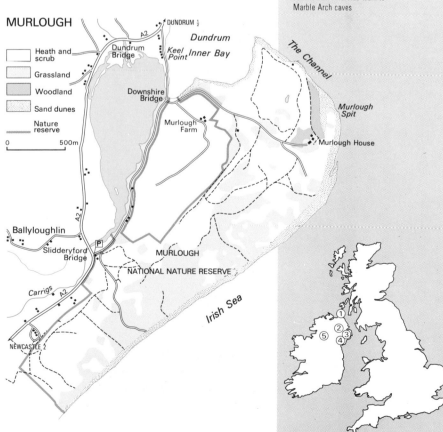

MURLOUGH

Heath and scrub
Grassland
Woodland
Sand dunes
Nature reserve
0   500m

179

Glenveagh National Park (Proposed)

A wild and beautiful area in the Derryveagh Mountains of west Donegal, Glenveagh's remoteness has a wilderness character that is perhaps better preserved here than in almost any other part of Ireland. Glenveagh is only a proposed National Park and arrangements have not yet been made to provide facilities for the public. It lies in a glacial valley running southwest-northeast, on mainly granite rocks with some outcrops of schist and gneiss on the adjacent hills. The high valley slopes are covered with blanket bog consisting mainly of *Sphagnum* moss, grasses and heathers. There are three small woodland areas of oak and birch. Little information is available at present about the area's fauna; a herd of red deer has been introduced to the National Park.

Burren National Park (Proposed)

A region of terraced limestone pavement in north County Clare overlooking Galway Bay, the Burren is one of the most interesting parts of Ireland. The name "Burren" means the great rock and is aptly applied to this wild, sparsely populated area.

The tops of the hills are flat and bare and fall away sharply on the west side to form low sea-cliffs. On the eastern side there are a number of lakes known as turloughs, with water levels that rise and fall in relation to the level of underground water. Not surprisingly the Burren is Ireland's most important area

SIKA DEER Originally a native of Eastern Asia, this small deer is now found in the wild in many parts of Europe.

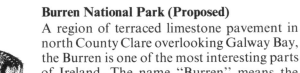

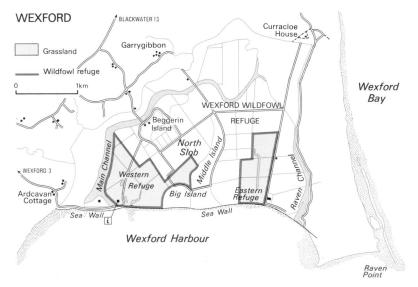

WEXFORD

Grassland

Wildfowl refuge

0   1km

BLACKWATER 13

Garrygibbon

Curracloe House

WEXFORD WILDFOWL

REFUGE

Beggerin Island

North Slob

Middle Island

Western Refuge

Big Island

Eastern Refuge

Main Channel

Raven Channel

WEXFORD 3

Ardcavan Cottage

Sea Wall

Sea Wall

Wexford Harbour

Wexford Bay

Raven Point

for caves and underground streams – only one river flowing through the region reaches the sea by a surface route. The branched-passage caves on the east side of Slieve Elva can be explored for nearly 11 kilometres, but have not been developed to cater for tourist parties and should not be entered by the inexperienced. The region is a proposed National Park and at the present time only 300 hectares in the region of Mullaghmore are protected.

To the botanist the Burren is one of the really remarkable regions of western Europe. Not only is there a rich flora of limestone-loving plants but also a curious mixture of southern, northern and even montaine plants. The mountain avens, a typical mountain plant of Scotland, Scandinavia and the Alps, is found growing together with the shrubby cinquefoil, a rare plant found in very few other places in the British Isles. There is an abundance of ferns which flourish in the moist atmosphere. Other rarities include the red helleborine, the spring gentian and, in one or two places, the rare fen violet.

Although not as spectacular as the plants, the Burren has some interesting insects. The most striking species is a moth known here as the Burren green, which, although not uncommon on the European continent, is not found in any other locality in the British Isles. The Burren is also the only place in Ireland where the pearl-bordered fritillary can be seen.

Killarney National Park

An extensive area southwest of the town of Killarney, the park includes areas of fine natural oak and yew woodland, lakes and upland bog as well as commercial forestry plantations. The region's oceanic climate encourages the luxuriant growth of mosses and ferns and the locality is well known to botanists for the strawberry tree, which, as well as being found along the Mediterranean, is also a native of this area. Other southern species include the Irish spurge, the large-flowered butterwort and the kidney saxifrage. Red deer, the only herd of native Irish stock, and the sika deer are found in the park.

The Bourn Vincent Memorial Park, presented to the Irish nation in 1932, lies within the National Park.

Wexford Wildfowl Refuge

Wexford Wildfowl Refuge is one of forty-six wildfowl sanctuaries in the Republic of Ireland, designated by the Department of Lands as no shooting areas. Situated on the north side of Wexford Harbour on an area known as the North Slob, the area lies on land partly bought and partly leased by the Department of Lands in association with the Irish Wild Bird Conservancy. The marshland of the South Slob, lying on the southern shore of Wexford Harbour, is also an important ornithological site. The refuge is of considerable international renown, largely because, during the winter months, it has the largest concentration of Greenland white-fronted geese in the world. More than 50 per cent of the total world population of 13,000 geese pass the winter in this region and a further 20 per cent winter in other parts of Ireland. Many other birds – breeding, passage migrant and wintering – are found within the reserve, including several other species of geese such as the bean, greylag, barnacle, pink-footed, Canada, brent, snow and lesser white-fronted. Wild swans, both whooper and Bewick's, are annual visitors, and twenty-three species of wild duck have been recorded.

SPRING GENTIAN
above Extremely rare in Britain, the spring gentian is a variable species and may have blue, pink or white flowers.

KILLARNEY *below*
Mountains, lakes and forests are essential ingredients of the Killarney landscape. The National Park occupies one of the best-known and most scenically beautiful parts of the Irish countryside.

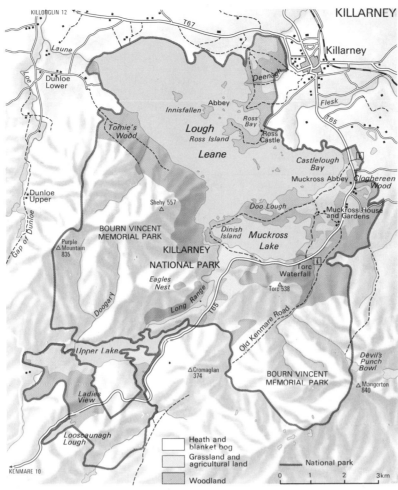

KILLARNEY

KILLONGLIN 12
T67
Killarney

Laune

Dunloe
Lower

Deenagh

Abbey
Innisfallen

Flesk

Lough
Leane

Ross Island

Ross
Bay

Ross
Castle

T65

Tomie's
Wood

Castlelough
Bay

Muckross Abbey

Cloghereen
Wood

Dunloe
Upper

Shehy 557

Doo Lough

Muckross House
and Gardens

BOURN VINCENT
MEMORIAL PARK

Dinish
Island

Muckross
Lake

Gap of Dunloe

Purple
Mountain
835

KILLARNEY

NATIONAL PARK

Eagles
Nest

Torc
Waterfall

Long Range

Torc 538

Doogary

T65

Old Kenmare Road

Upper Lake

Cromaglan
374

BOURN VINCENT
MEMORIAL PARK

Devil's
Punch
Bowl

Mangerton
840

Ladies
View

Looscaunagh
Lough

KENMARE 10

Heath and
blanket bog

Grassland and
agricultural land

National park

Woodland

0   1   2   3km

1 GLENVEAGH
Information: Park Superintendent, Glenveagh National Park, Churchill, Letterkenny, Co. Donegal
Access: from Letterkenny, 35 km W of LONDONDERRY
Open: Unrestricted

2 BURREN
Information: Office of Public Works, 51 St Stephen's Green, Dublin 2
Access: from GALWAY or ENNIS
Open: Unrestricted

3 KILLARNEY
Information: Park Superintendent, Killarney National Park, Muckross, Killarney, Co. Kerry
Access: from KILLARNEY
Open: Unrestricted
Facilities: Information centre. Nature trails

4 WEXFORD
Information: The Warden, Wexford Wildfowl Reserve, Wexford, Co. Wexford
Access: from WEXFORD
Open: Daily, 0930 to sunset
Facilities: Information centre. Observation tower and hide

181

FRANCE

France, lying at the heart of western Europe, can claim to share the natural history of all the countries around it – the Atlantic seabird colonies of the northwest, the wildlife of the great Alpine chain which penetrates into central Europe, the distinctive flora and fauna of the Pyrenees in the southwest and of the Mediterranean coast with its flamingos – a bird more typical of North Africa. It is a country of superlatives: magnificent landscapes, Europe's highest mountain, impressive gorges, superb forests, great rivers, and a vast coastline which stretches from Belgium to the Pyrenees on the Atlantic, and from the Pyrenees to the Italian border on the Mediterranean seaboard.

With a relatively low population density, 49 persons per square kilometre it should perhaps have been easier to establish National Parks and nature reserves than, for example, in the densley populated countries of the Netherlands and Britain. However, conservation legislation came rather late to France and even now there are relatively few protected areas. The first State Reserve was established in 1961 and the first National Park in 1963.

By far the most important category of protected land in France is the National Park. Six parks have now been created, each by a special law. The parks consist of two parts – an inner or central zone, the "park proper", and a surrounding peripheral zone. The inner zone is managed by a director and staff on the advice of a council of administration and a scientific committee, with the protection of wildlife

as its first objective. This means that there is a ban on hunting (although there are exceptions), road construction, building, camping and other activities likely to damage the wildlife interest. The peripheral zone on the other hand is controlled by a Departmental Committee, with the principal objective of maintaining the area's traditional landscape and way of life, while at the same time providing facilities for the tourist.

Five of the six parks are in the mountains, and in each the inner zone is situated largely in the area of the highest altitude, where there is no permanent human settlement. This means that the middle and lower mountain slopes of each park fall within the peripheral zone and many interesting localities in these areas are therefore not completely protected and may in fact be subjected to intense public use at

certain times of the year. The bias towards mountain tops is accentuated by the fact that over half the area protected in France lies in the Alps.

The French zoning system has not been adopted in other countries, except Greece, possibly because in some instances it has created conflict between the objectives of the two areas. In the Vanoise National Park, for example, there is continual pressure from developers to build more chair lifts, ski runs and roads from the peripheral into the central zone in order to extend tourist penetration.

In 1967 legislation was passed for the establishment of Regional Parks, and there are now twenty-three. Although these parks are often situated in attractive countryside and may be of considerable interest to the naturalist, their main aims, like the peripheral zones of the National Parks, are to provide facilities for the tourist, to preserve traditional architecture and landscapes, to stimulate local enterprise and bring more prosperity to the region. Wildlife preservation in these areas is incidental and there is no restriction on hunting except where a a nature reserve has been created within a park.

It is surprising to conservationists in other countries to find that there are few State Nature Reserves in France. Up to 1973 there were only five, but in 1971 the government embarked on a policy of creating a network of wildlife reserves. Three hundred and fifty sites of national importance were identified and 100 selected for preservation. By 1977 fifty-nine reserves had been established, but progress is slow because the government prefers not to purchase but instead to seek agreement with local private landowners.

Fortunately wildlife habitats are protected in various other ways, notably as hunting or game reserves, of which there are many different sorts. In most of them game is shot but the preservation of the habitat enables other wildlife to survive. In others, the Pointe d'Arçay, for example, all wildlife is protected and no shooting is permitted in order to allow game species to multiply.

Important nature reserves have also been created by private nature conservation societies. The most effective of these organizations is the National Society for the Protection of Nature (SNPN) and one of the oldest is the Society for the Study and Protection of Nature in Brittany, where the majority of private reserves are situated.

The protection of individual species of birds and mammals outside nature reserves and National Parks has always been difficult in France, mainly because of the powerful political influence of the hunting associations. On the other hand all birds of prey, including owls and a number of other species, are now completely protected, in so far as it is possible to enforce the law.

ECRINS The snow-capped mountain of La Meije, rising to 3983 metres above the little town of La Grave, lies in the north of the park.

Four distinctive upland areas of resistant crystalline and sedimentary rocks form a containing arc around the vast lowland Paris Basin, floored by a variety of much younger deposits. The low, eroded Armorican massif occupies the northwestern peninsula of Brittany and part of Normandy; two smaller massifs, the Ardennes and the Vosges, form a discontinuous barrier of rounded and extensively wooded hills to the north and northeast; but largest by far, occupying nearly one-sixth of the country, is the huge block-faulted plateau of the Massif Central, dominating the entire southeast. These highland areas were formed towards the end of the Palaeozoic era during the Hercynian period of mountain building and represent the first phase in the development of France's upland scenery.

Gaps between the highlands provide links between the Paris Basin and neighbouring lowland areas. The "gate of Poitou" gives access to the triangular basin of Aquitaine in the southwest, while similar gaps lead to the Flanders Plain, the North German Plain and the Rhône-Saone corridor. Beyond these outer lowlands lies a natural and imposing frontier – the much younger, more dramatic, glaciated mountains of the Pyrenees, the Alps and the Jura, which exemplify the country's second and much more recent period of mountain building. The Tertiary earth movements which produced these were also responsible for fracturing and dislocating the country's earlier mountain plateaux and, in the Massif Central, for volcanic activity that continued until comparatively recently.

The climate and natural vegetation of this large country are as varied as its natural regions. The north is typically oceanic, with warm summers and mild winters with much of its rainfall in autumn and early winter. The eastern regions are much more continental, with more summer rain and much lower winter temperatures, while the south has the typically Mediterranean climate of mild winter weather and very hot, dry summers. Lowland vegetation has been overtaken by agriculture over much of the country, but above the treeline there are extensive regions in the Alps and Pyrenees where the vegetation is little modified by man except for summer grazing. The mountain woodlands are well maintained as are most of France's forests, which cover a quarter of the land area.

PARK/RESERVE	SIZE (km²)	DESCRIPTION	MAP REF	PAGE NO.
CAP-SIZUN	0.5	Nature Reserve. Small coastal bird reserve. Large numbers of guillemots, razorbills, cormorants and kittiwakes.	A2	186
ARMORIQUE	650	Regional Park. Largest protected area in Brittany. Heathlands, moors, bogs and typical "bocage" landscape. Several offshore islands. Interesting mammal fauna, including common and grey seals.	A2	186
LES SEPT ILES	2.8	Nature Reserve. Group of small islands off the north Brittany coast. Important bird sanctuary.	A2	187
CAP FREHEL	4.0	Nature Reserve. Rocky, grass-topped promontory. Many cliff-nesting bird species.	A2	187
GOLFE DU MORBIHAN	15.0	Nature Reserve. Area of water with several islands. Large numbers of wintering wildfowl.	A2	188
BRIERE	400	Regional Park. Large area of marsh, lagoons and hay meadows. Interesting heathland and marsh plants.	A2	189
BAIE DE BOURGNEUF	42.0	Nature Reserve. Coastal reserve with sand, mud and rocky outcrops. Large wildfowl population.	A2	189
ST-DENIS-DU-PAYRE	2.07	Nature Reserve. Extensive wet meadow. Important bird nesting area. Rare plants.	B3	190
POINTE D'ARCAY	3.0	Nature Reserve. Outstanding wetland area within the Marais Poitevin Regional Park. Forested sandbar with heath and grassland.	B3	190
BAIE DE L'AIGUILLON	21.0	Nature Reserve. Large area of reclaimed marshland. Vast numbers of migrant and overwintering wildfowl.	B3	190
BANC D'ARGUIN	8.0	Nature Reserve. Low sandy island no more than 3 metres above sea level. Interesting bird fauna.	B3	190
MARQUENTERRE	23.0	Ornithological Nature Reserve. Region of saltings and brackish marshes. Important area for migrant birds.	B1	192
VALLEE DE LA GRANDE PIERRE ET DE VITAIN	2.96	Nature Reserve. Area of dense coppiced woodland and limestone grassland in valley of the River Cisse. Interesting flora and invertebrate fauna.	B2	192
LE LAC DE LA FORET D'ORIENT	23.0	Large artificial lake lying within Regional Park. Important resting and feeding area for migrant wildfowl.	C2	193
VOSGES DU NORD	1100	Regional Park. Partly cultivated, partly wooded hilly landscape. Areas of natural limestone grassland.	D2	193
VOLCANS D'AUVERGNE	2815	Regional Park. Remarkable area of old volcanic cones. Deciduous and coniferous forests.	C3	194
CEVENNES	840	National Park. Hilly region with deep gorges, limestone plateaux, crystalline rocks and forests.	C4	194
PYRENEES	457	National Park. Superb scenic mountain area on Spanish border. Extensive forests of beech and mountain pine. Many endemic plant species. Diverse mammal fauna including the brown bear.	B4	195
VILLARS-LES-DOMBS	2.43	Nature Reserve/Ornithological Park. Lakeland habitat of importance for aquatic plants and animals.	D3	196
PILAT	600	Regional Park. Landscape of wooded hills and heaths and granite outcrops. Large number of bird species.	C3	196
VERCORS	1350	Regional Park. Subalpine plateau with peaks, cliffs, gorges and forests. Rich mountain pasture.	D3	197
AIGUILLES ROUGE	32.8	Nature Reserve. Scenically beautiful and varied mountain terrain – glaciers, lakes, cliffs, high peaks and mountain forests. Typical alpine-bird and mammal species.	D3	198
MARAIS DU BOUT DU LAC D'ANNECY	0.84	Nature Reserve. Part of attractive mountain lake. Marsh, reed beds and open water. Several interesting nesting and wintering bird species.	D3	198
VANOISE	528.4	National Park. High alpine region. Complex geology of calcareous and crystalline rocks with contrasting floras. Extensive coniferous forest. Diverse mammal and birdlife. Interesting insect fauna.	D3	199
ECRINS	1080	National Park. Lakes, gorges, cirques and glaciers set in an area of outstanding alpine scenery.	D3	200
LUBERON	1200	Regional Park. Largely forested mountain ridge. Areas of maquis. Archaeological interest.	D4	200
MERCANTOUR	700	National Park. Strikingly diverse upland region with many endemic plants and insects.	D4	200
CAMARGUE	951.2	Regional Park/Nature Reserve. Internationally important wetland at mouth of River Rhône. Brackish lakes, riverine forest, dunes, sea shore and salt steppes. Many rare bird breeding species.	C4	202
PORT-CROS	15.9	National Park. Mediterranean Island with protected surrounding marine zone. Forest and maquis.	D4	204
CORSE	1500	Regional Park. Large part of central and western Corsica. Variety of mountain and coastal scenery. Many endemic plants. Birdlife contains locally occurring subspecies.	D5	205
SCANDOLA	16.7	Nature Reserve. Small rocky promontory within Corse Regional Park. Fine cliffs and interesting birdlife.	D5	205

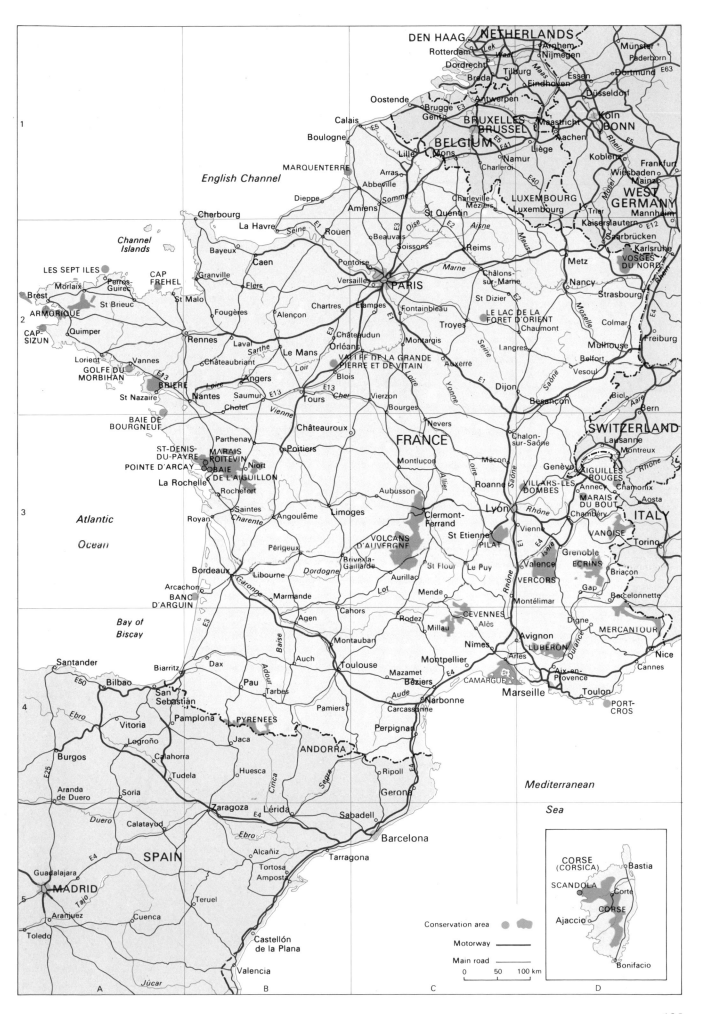

DEN HAAG   NETHERLANDS
                    Rotterdam   Lek   Arnhem   Münster
                    Dordrecht   Waal   Nijmegen   Paderborn
                Breda   Tilburg   Maas   Eindhoven   Dortmund   E63
        Oostende   Brugge E3   Antwerpen   Essen   Düsseldorf
    Calais   Gent   Maastricht   Köln   BONN
        Boulogne   BRUXELLES   Aachen
                            BRUSSEL   E41   Liège   Rhein
MARQUENTERRE   BELGIUM   Mons   Namur   Koblenz   Frankfurt
                    Lille   Charleroi   Wiesbaden
English Channel   Arras   LUXEMBOURG   Mainz   WEST
                    Abbeville   Charleville   Luxembourg   Trier   GERMANY
        Dieppe   Amiens   Somme   Mézières   Kaiserslautern   Mannheim
    Cherbourg   St Quentin   Saarbrücken   E12
        La Havre   Seine   Rouen   Oise   Reims   Metz   Karlsruhe
Channel   Bayeux   Beauvais   Aisne   VOSGES
Islands   Caen   Pontoise   Marne   Nancy   DU NORD
LES SEPT ILES   Flers   Versailles PARIS   Châlons-   Strasbourg
    Perros-   CAP   sur-Marne
Morlaix   Guirec   FREHEL   Granville   Etampes   Fontainebleau   St Dizier   LE LAC DE LA
Brest   St Malo   Chartres   Troyes   FORET D'ORIENT   Colmar
ARMORIQUE   St Brieuc   Fougères   Alençon   Chaumont   Mulhouse   Freiburg
CAP-   Quimper   Rennes   Laval   Châteaudun   Montargis   Langres   Belfort
SIZUN   Sarthe   Le Mans   Orléans   Vesoul
    Lorient   Vannes   Châteaubriant   Loir   VALLEE DE LA GRANDE   Auxerre
GOLFE DU   E13   Loire   PIERRE ET DE VITAIN   Dijon   Biel
MORBIHAN   BRIERE   Angers   Saumur   Blois   Yonne   Saône   Bern
    St Nazaire   Nantes   E13   Tours   Vierzon   Besançon   Aare
BAIE DE   Vienne   Cher   Bourges   SWITZERLAND
BOURGNEUF   Châteauroux   Chalon-   Lausanne
        Parthenay   Nevers   sur-Saône   Montreux
ST-DENIS-   MARAIS   Poitiers   FRANCE   Mâcon   Genève   AIGUILLES
DU-PAYRE   POITEVIN   Niort   Roanne   VILLARS-LES   ROUGES
POINTE D'ARCAY BAIE   Montluçon   Allier   DOMBES   Annecy   Chamonix
La Rochelle   DE L'AIGUILLON   Lyon   MARAIS   Aosta
        Rochefort   Aubusson   Rhône   DU BOUT
Atlantic   Saintes   Limoges   Clermont-   Chambéry   ITALY
    Royan   Charente   Ferrand   St Etienne   VANOISE
Ocean   Angoulême   VOLCANS   PILAT   Vienne   Torino
        Périgeux   D'AUVERGNE   Valence   Grenoble
            Brive-la-   St Flour   Le Puy   ECRINS
Bordeaux   Libourne   Gaillarde   VERCORS   Briançon
    Dordogne   Aurillac   Mende   Gap
Arcachon   Lot   Mende   Montélimar   Barcelonnette
BANC   Marmande   Digne
D'ARGUIN   Agen   Cahors   CEVENNES   MERCANTOUR
Bay of   Montauban   Rodez   Alès   Nice
Biscay   Baise   Millau   Nîmes   Avignon   LUBERON   Cannes
Santander   Auch   Toulouse   Arles   Aix-en-
    Biarritz   Adour   Montpellier   Provence
Bilbao   Dax   Pau   Béziers   CAMARGUE   Marseille
San   Tarbes   Mazamet   Toulon
Sebastián   Pamiers   Aude   Narbonne   PORT-
Vitoria   Pamplona   PYRENEES   Carcassonne   CROS
Ebro   Jaca   Perpignan
Burgos   Huesca   Mediterranean
Logroño   Cinca   ANDORRA
Aranda   Calahorra   Ripoll   Sea
de Duero   Soria   Segre
    Tudela   Gerona
Duero   Zaragoza   Lérida
SPAIN   Calatayud   E4   Sabadell
        Alcañiz   Barcelona
Guadalajara   Tortosa   Tarragona
MADRID   Amposta
Tajo   CORSE
Aranjuez   (CORSICA)   Bastia
    Cuenca   Teruel   SCANDOLA   Corte
Toledo   Castellón   Ajaccio   CORSE
        de la Plana
Júcar   Valencia
                Conservation area
                Motorway
                Main road
                0   50   100 km
                                        Bonifacio

PUFFIN A stocky sea-bird, easily recognized in summer by its black and white plumage and multi-coloured bill. In winter the bill is smaller and more yellow.

Cap-Sizun Nature Reserve

Situated on the north coast of Brittany, this small reserve was established in 1958 by the Société d'étude et de la protection de la nature en Bretagne. The rocky coast in this region is not well known, and although the birdlife of Cap-Sizun is similar to that of Les Sept Iles, the latter has attracted most of the attention. The reserve consists of two areas of coast. The larger area, containing a 4-kilo-metre-long offshore zone where hunting is forbidden and lying near the village of Kergulan, has large numbers of guillemots, razorbills, puffins, cormorants, kittiwakes, herring gulls, lesser and greater black-backed gulls as well as storm petrels and ravens. The smaller part of the reserve near the point and island of Milinou is a breeding site for choughs and fulmars.

Armorique Regional Park

The largest nature and landscape protection area in Brittany, Armorique Regional Park consists of several separate parts. The section south of Morlaix is mainly heathland, moors, bogs and "bocage", which is a landscape of small fields and hedgerows typical of the area. Smaller portions of the park are found farther to the west around the mouth of the River Aulne, on the Crozon peninsula and on a series of offshore islands, of which Ouessant is the largest. The park is crossed from south-west to northeast by the Montagnes d'Arrée, an impressive ridge, which is the region's most outstanding landscape feature.

The park is notable for its small colony of beavers, which were transplanted from the Rhône Valley to a small tributary of the River Aulne, where they have successfully estab-

ARMORIQUE

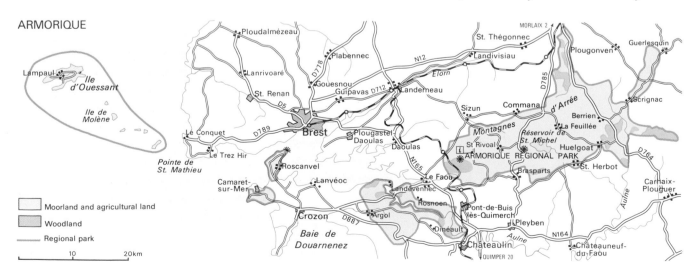

Moorland and agricultural land

Woodland

Regional park

10   20km

LES SEPT ILES *left* Ile Rouzic is the largest of the seven islands that make up this nature reserve lying off the north coast of Brittany. Twelve species of seabird, including the gannet, nest on the islands.

lished themselves. On the island of Ouessant there is a small protected breeding colony of grey seals, and common seals are also occasionally seen. Apart from local populations of wild boar and fallow deer there are few large terrestrial mammals, and birds of prey are also uncommon. Marsh and Montague's harrier are the most frequently seen species. The heaths and bogs which occur in the moorland areas are of considerable interest for plants and invertebrate life.

Les Sept Iles Nature Reserve

Of the nineteen nature or hunting reserves around the coast of Brittany, where wildlife is protected, Les Sept Iles, 7 kilometres off the northeast coast, is the most important. Established in 1976 it is managed by the Ligue Français pour la Protection des Oiseaux, and, apart from a lighthouse on the Ile aux Moines, it is uninhabited. Although the area of land above the high-tide level is only 40 hectares, a no-shooting zone around the islands enlarges the total protected area to 4000 hectares. The largest island, no more than 7.7 hectares, is of particular interest because of its twelve species of nesting seabirds and many land birds such as wrens, blackbirds, greenfinches, linnets, rock pipits, kestrels, ravens and starlings.

The most interesting seabird species found on the reserve is the gannet. Although it breeds nowhere else in France it has steadily increased on Les Sept Iles ever since it first bred here in 1939, and now numbers around 4500. Fulmars are a more recent acquisition. They did not nest on Les Sept Iles until 1960 but have now built up to a colony of 120. Among other species found on the reserve are shag, kittiwake, storm petrel, herring gull, greater and lesser black-backed gulls, common tern, razorbill, puffin and common guillemot. These last three, all species of auks, were severely affected by oil pollution from the wreck of the *Torrey Canyon* in 1967 and also by the even worse disaster of the *Amoco Cadiz* in 1978. The numbers of nesting pairs of puffins fell after the *Torrey Canyon* spill from 2000 to 240 and just as the population began to build up again the puffins were again severely affected by the *Amoco Cadiz* disaster, which destroyed nearly half the population.

Cap Fréhel Nature Reserve

Atop 20-metre cliffs, at the most northerly point of the rocky promontory that projects into the gulf of St Malo between the towns of St Malo and St Brieuc, lies Cap Fréhel Nature Reserve. In spring and summer the grasslands that cover the cliff tops are at their most attractive, with bluebells, Solomon's seal, daffodils and *Dianthus* species.

Cliff-nesting birds are the reserve's main attraction and the most numerous species are shags and herring gulls. Among others breeding in the area are oystercatcher, shag, lesser and greater black-backed gulls, puffin, fulmar, kittiwake and raven. The best seabird colonies are at Pointe du "Jas" a little to the west, Pointe de la Teignouse to the east and on the cliffs, west of the lighthouse which stands overlooking Cap Fréhel. Two offshore islets, Amas du Cap and La Fauconnière, also have large seabird populations.

BRIERE *above and right* Many waterfowl winter on the lakes and marshes of the central and southern parts of the Regional Park. The boats on the water channel *right* appear to have been used for the transport of reeds which are still cut in the area.

RED-BREASTED MERGANSER *left* This slender "sawbill" duck is found widespread throughout northern Europe nesting among rocks or heather.

BRIERE

- Meadow and agricultural land
- Marsh
- Woodland
— Regional park
-- Nature reserve

0   5   10km

VANNES 30
N165
La Roche Bernard
La Gouarais
Vilaine
Camoël
Férel
Missillac
Herbignac
La Chapelle des Marais
D33
Pontchâteau
Ste. Reine-de-Bretagne
Assérac
Crossac
St. Molf
D774
St. Lyphard
St. Joachim
Piriac-sur-Mer
BRIERE
Ile de Fédrun
Brivet
D773
REGIONAL PARK
La Turballe
D47
D51
Montoir-de-Bretagne
Guérande
La Grande Brière
N171
Bert
Trignac
Le Croisic
Marais Salants
St. André-des-Eaux
D99
St. Nazaire
Loire
N171
La Baule
Pornichet
D92
St. Brévin-les-Pins
Le Pouliguen
Ste. Marguerite
St. Marc
PORNIC 15

Golfe du Morbihan Nature Reserve

Managed as a marine hunting reserve by the Fédération Départementale des Chasseurs without as yet formal protection, official reserve status is currently being sought for both the water surface and the numerous islands of the Golfe du Morbihan. The gulf is sheltered on almost all sides and is protected from westerly gales by the Quiberon peninsula. The waters are therefore favoured winter quarters for many wildfowl and also attract numerous wildfowlers and punt-gunners. Although hunting is still permitted in certain areas, a large part of the gulf, adjacent to the south shore, has been set aside as a no-hunting area.

The list of overwintering and migrant birds recorded is considerable and the reserve's importance is primarily based on the large numbers of brent geese, which regularly visit the shallow waters to feed on eel-grass. Around 16,000 were seen at Morbihan during the winter of 1976–77. Among the other important species visiting the area are wigeon, teal, shelduck, golden-eye, red-breasted merganser, black-tailed godwit, grey plover, knot, great crested and black-necked grebes.

1 GOLFE DU MORBIHAN
Information : Société pour
l'étude et la protection de la
nature en Bretagne, Faculté des
Sciences, avenue Le Gorgeu,
29200 Brest
Access : from VANNES
Open : Unrestricted

2 BRIÈRE
Information : Maison du parc
naturel régional de Brière, 180
Ile de Fédrun, 44720 St-
Joachim
Access : from ST NAZAIRE
Open : Unrestricted
Facilities : Cultural centre and
museums within the park.
Animal park at St Malo de
Guersac. Nature trails

3 BAIE DE BOURGNEUF
Information : Delegation
régionale au Tourisme des pays
de la Loire, 3, place St-Pierre,
44000 Nantes
Access : from Bouin, 51km SW
of NANTES or Beauvoir-sur-Mer,
60km SW of NANTES
Open : Unrestricted

Three of the islands in the gulf are managed by the Société d'étude et de la protection de la nature en Bretagne. Er Lannic, on which breed common and Sandwich terns, is the most interesting.

Brière Regional Park
One of the largest areas of marsh and lagoons in inland France, La Grande Brière, totalling 7000 hectares, lies at the centre of this Regional Park, which is situated between the rivers Loire and Vilaine, close to St Nazaire.

The basin containing the marsh was formed by earth movements in the Tertiary which caused the underlying rocks to sink. Over millions of years the sea has penetrated the basin from time to time, laying down deposits of sediment. About eleven million years ago the basin was cut off from the sea by the formation of a littoral bar.

Although the marsh is a natural formation, its landscape has been greatly modified by human interference over the centuries – fishing, reed-cutting, grazing and hay-making – and it seems certain that, under natural conditions, woodland would have covered the drier land around it. On this area today is found a type of heath merging into boggy meadow that is inundated only during periods of high water. At the end of the summer, the fields are blue with heath lobelia.

Many birds are known to breed in the park, including the bearded tit, Cetti's warbler, Savi's warbler, grasshopper warbler, bluethroat, garganey and bittern. In the winter wild duck and geese visit the flooded areas.

Baie de Bourgneuf Nature Reserve
Lying south of the mouth of the Loire, Baie de Bourgneuf Nature Reserve consists of a stretch of coastline extending from close to Bourgneuf-en-Retz in the north to La Barre-de-Monts in the south. A low area of sand, sandy mud and rocky outcrops, with shallow water lying offshore, the reserve attracts many wildfowl but few breeding species. In autumn, winter and spring numbers of ducks, geese and waders may be very high, and waders, such as dunlin, curlew, oystercatcher, grey plover and avocet, may be present in their thousands. Brent geese have been recorded in numbers from 3000 to 5000 and normally there are many hundreds of teal, wigeon, pintail, scaup and shelduck.

St-Denis-du-Payré Nature Reserve

The Vendée, lying between Nantes and La Rochelle, is a fascinating area for the biologist; so much of the land bordering the sea consists of low-lying marshes or wet meadows which have been reclaimed from the sea or were formerly used as salt-pans.

The reserve is a vast meadow, the property of the commune of St Denis-du-Payré, and although it is marshy and badly drained in places and often flooded in the winter it is a valuable grazing area for the local farmers. This combination of conditions makes it an ideal habitat for wet-meadow birds, many of which are becoming increasingly rare in western Europe, where agricultural improvements have caused land to be drained whether or not it is fully exploited.

The meadow of St-Denis-du-Payré has never been ploughed, nor have fertilizers or herbicides been used, thus making it a valuable ecosystem in spite of its man-made origin. Cattle-grazing, its traditional use, has probably helped to maintain its value as a bird-nesting area as well as its floristic interest – it is one of the few places in western France where the butterfly iris is found. The water table has been carefully controlled so that a large shallow lake forms during winter and spring, which gradually dries out in summer.

In the winter of 1973 over 4000 duck, including 3000 teal, were recorded on the lake, which that year was 20 centimetres deep and covered 15 hectares. In 1975 redshanks, garganey, pintail, lapwing, black-winged stilts and black terns nested on the reserve and in the following year the breeding list included ruffs and black-tailed godwits as well as squacco herons and glossy ibis. White-winged black terns have also been seen during the summer months.

Pointe d'Arçay Nature Reserve

Regarded as one of the most important wetlands for waders and wildfowl on the Atlantic coast of France, Pointe d'Arçay Nature Reserve consists of a sand bar which has grown southwards across the estuary of the River Lay. The bar forms a series of ridges and is now mainly forested with maritime pine, although in some places there are areas of scrubby heathland and open grass. The whole reserve has become of considerable interest for plants and terrestrial birds as well as for wildfowl and waders, and is probably one of the few undisturbed terrestrial ecosystems on the Atlantic coast.

A few brent and greylag geese visit the reserve in the winter and there are considerable numbers of pintail, mallard, teal, shoveler, wigeon and shelduck. Spoonbills and avocets are also seen from time to time. The wading birds are particularly well represented: curlew, black-tailed and bar-tailed godwits, knots, grey plovers, redshank, dunlin, ringed plovers, Kentish plovers and whimbrel are all regularly seen.

Even in summer, when there are no migrants present, hoopoes and shrikes can be seen along the fringe of the woodland as well as many smaller birds of interest in scrubby areas. Since 1951, when it was first protected, much research has been carried out into the feeding behaviour of its migrant birds.

In 1979 the Pointe d'Arçay Reserve became part of the Regional Park of Marais Poitevin. This vast area of grassland, used mainly for cattle raising, is intersected by countless drainage channels, many of which are lined by oaks, willows, tamarisk and other shrubs, providing a habitat for numerous small birds.

The Regional Park also contains four outlying areas separated from the marshes and consisting mainly of woodlands – Mervent-Vouvart, de Chizé, d'Aulnay, de Chef-Boutonne, l'Hermitain and du Fouilloux.

Baie de l'Aiguillon Nature Reserve

North of La Rochelle, close to the Pointe d'Arçay, lies the Baie de l'Aiguillon, into which drain the waters of the Marais de la Sèvre – the largest area of reclaimed marshland in the Vendée. The northwest part of the bay forms a marine hunting reserve in which birdlife is protected.

On the seaward side of a bank, built along the shoreline to protect the grazing marshes from being flooded, the water is shallow and there is much fringing marshy vegetation, attractive to waterfowl. Of the migrant and overwintering wildfowl which congregate in the bay, ducks number between 30,000 and 40,000 and waders between 50,000 and 100,000. Among them are 4000 avocets (one of the largest winter concentrations in Europe) 6000 pintail, 6000 shelduck, four species of wild goose and many curlews and turnstones. The most abundant species are the dunlins (20,000 to 40,000), and the knots (5000 to 20,000). Marsh harriers and kestrels are the most numerous birds of prey.

The reclaimed marshland to the east of the bay forms the greater part of the recently established Regional Park of Marais Poitevin.

Banc d'Arguin Nature Reserve

This nature reserve, lying south of Cap Ferret, consists of a low, sandy island in the Arcachon basin at the northwesterly tip of the Landes de Gascogne Regional Park. On the island, which is nowhere more than 3 metres above mean sea level, the commonest dune plants are marram and sea couch grass. There is also an interesting associated flora, which includes sea bindweed, sea spurge, sea holly, and the toadflax *Linaria thymifolia*.

The reserve's main interest lies in its bird fauna. Species nesting on the island include the oystercatcher, crested lark, tawny pipit and Sandwich tern, a rare bird in France, of which over 2000 pairs breed in the region. The reserve is also an important overwintering area for such species as grey plover, bar-tailed godwit, dunlin and also for many gulls.

HOOPOE – an unmistakeable bird with prominent black-and-white winged bars over pink-brown plumage and a black-tipped crest.

MARAIS POITEVIN

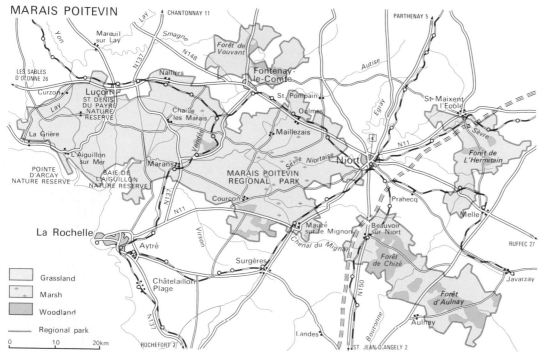

MARAIS POITEVIN *below* The Regional Park, in which lies the Pointe d'Arçay Nature Reserve, consists of four separate parts. The largest consists of an area of grassland traversed by drainage channels.

Marquenterre Ornithological Nature Reserve

Opened as a private reserve in 1973, this important wetland area, by the mouth of the River Somme on the Channel coast, is sometimes known as the "Camargue of the North". The whole of the Baie de Somme is a vast area of saltings and brackish grassland, which is inundated only at the highest tides, together with stretches of reclaimed land rather like those found in the Netherlands. In other areas dunes have been formed from sands exposed at low tide. They reach a height of 40 metres in places and are being driven inland by the prevailing winds. The vegetation consists mainly of marram grass, lyme-grass and sea buckthorn, and maritime pine has been planted in some areas to stabilize the sand.

The enormous area of saltings found in the Baie de Somme and in the adjacent reserve of Marquenterre attracts large numbers of wildfowl and other birds during migration periods, and over the winter months. Breeding species, not great in number include, however, the Kentish plover, greylag goose, black-headed gull, oystercatcher, little grebe and shelduck. Pintail and curlew have probably also nested in the area from time to time and avocets are frequently seen on passage. In 1975, thirteen avocet nests were counted and in the following years the number increased to thirty-five. Attempts to encourage the spoonbill and the white stork to breed have met with some success in the case of the latter, and in 1975 a pair of fan-tailed warblers nested for the first time. This species has been moving northwards in Europe for a number of years and now seems set to cross the Channel to Britain in the near future.

During migration many species of waders and wildfowl have been recorded in the area, including brent geese, bar-tailed godwits, scaup and grey plover. Among other migrants visiting the reserve are ospreys, little egrets and occasionally small numbers of snow geese. The mammal fauna includes the fox, polecat and muskrat, which is well established in the reserve's numerous waterways.

Vallée de La Grande Pierre et de Vitain Nature Reserve

A few kilometres north of Blois in the Loire Valley lies the most recently established State Reserve in France. It is situated in the valley of the River Cisse, where it is joined by the dry valley of the Grande Pierre and lies on Tertiary, calcareous rocks of hard limestone, which are mainly responsible for its interesting flora. Much of the site is covered by dense coppice woodland, but there are also many patches of calcicolous grassland, where most of the interesting plants and invertebrate animals are found. The dry valley of the Grande Pierre is thought never to have been cultivated or disturbed by quarrying and this factor greatly adds to its scientific interest.

Of the higher plant species 159 have been recorded, including the burnt and lizard orchids, the broomrape *Orobanche teucrium*, cut-leaved self-heal, large self-heal, white rockrose, the flax *Linum tenuifolium*, *Coronilla minima*, mountain germander and the rest-harrow *Ononis pusilla*.

The commonest grasses are heath false-brome and upright brome, but in many places their growth is sparse and open.

At the edge of the region of calcareous rocks there is a remarkable woody vegetation of downy oak, common juniper, box and St Lucie's cherry. Fifty-three species of birds, mostly fairly common, have been recorded nesting on the reserve.

MUSKRAT *above* A native of North America, the muskrat is well established in many parts of Europe.

MARQUENTERRE *above* Lying on the Channel coast, the reserve forms part of the Baie de Somme, a large area of dune, saltmarsh, mud flats and grassland important for overwintering and migrant birdlife.

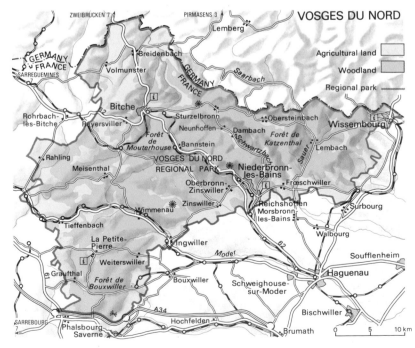

VOSGES DU NORD

Agricultural land
Woodland
Regional park

Le Lac de La Forêt d'Orient Nature Reserve

In a rolling landscape of valley pastures and low wooded hills La Forêt d'Orient Regional Park lies on the east side of the industrial city of Troyes, in the Champagne District, 180 kilometres southeast of Paris.

One of the park's principal features, a large artificial lake of 2300 hectares, popular for aquatic sports, has an ornithological reserve of 300 hectares on its northeast side. Here access is forbidden and wildlife is protected. The lake is particularly important as a resting and feeding area for both migrating and over-wintering wildfowl, and because it also supplies water to the Paris conurbation it fluctuates considerably in level – a factor that favours migrating birds in some instances. Of these species the common crane is perhaps the most remarkable. Many can be seen flying over the area in spring and autumn, some resting for a while in the vicinity of the lake during mild weather. In addition between 500 and 1200 bean geese have overwintered on the lake since 1969.

Each year counts are made of the wildfowl found on the reserve and on average a total of about 6000 birds from twenty-two species has been recorded. Six species which are rare in the region occur here each year: the shelduck, ruddy shelduck, ferruginous duck, scaup, smew and the goosander. Very occasionally red-breasted mergansers, eiders and long-tailed ducks are also seen. Large numbers of grebes and grey herons nest in the area and the marsh harrier frequently occurs, but as yet has not nested.

Perhaps the most extraordinary ornithological event in the region is the regular appearance in recent years of the sea eagle; the lakes of the Forêt d'Orient and of the Dur are the only known wintering quarters of this bird of prey in France, and two, three or even four birds at one time may be seen on each lake – a magnificent sight for the visiting naturalist.

Vosges du Nord Regional Park

Situated between the plain of the Rhine and the Lorraine plateau, the region of Vosges du Nord has been occupied by man for thousands of years; there are impressive Megalithic monuments, Roman remains and about forty chateaux built between the tenth and sixteenth centuries. Today it is a pleasant rural landscape, important for agriculture and forestry; 60,000 hectares of woodland lie in the heart of the park.

The landscape consists of three different types: the hills of the Piedmont Vosges in the east, the Lorraine plateau in the west and, lying between the two areas, a hilly region of Tertiary rocks. The Piedmont Vosges is a diverse landscape of fields and copses with an interesting geology; in the northern parts of the Saverne, the exposed faulted strata reveal different types of sedimentary rocks. The park's calcareous rocks are rich in fossils

and a special geological path has been laid out through the most exciting areas. The path climbs the hill of Basberg, which apart from its geology gives one of the most beautiful views in the north of Alsace and the Vosges.

The natural grassland flora of the region's calcareous soil has been mostly reclaimed for agriculture, but on Bastberg a little of the original vegetation, rich in limestone grassland plants, still survives. In the west small communal forests, dominated by oak and beech, alternate with grazed grasslands and hay meadows. Farmers are experimenting with new crops, particularly with cereals

VALLEE DE LA GRANDE PIERRE ET DE VITAIN

Grassland

Marsh

Woodland

Nature reserve

0   500m

and food plants which some people feel are not in keeping with the park's aim of retaining the traditional landscape.

The region's calcareous soils are generally fertile, but the sandy soils, originating from Rhine deposits found in other areas, are poor in nutrients and peat bogs have developed on them. In the valley of Schwartbach, near Neunhoffen, a fine bog has formed on the site of an artificial lake which has gradually become silted over.

The forests of the Vosges are of great importance to the park's fauna, particularly deer and other large mammals. In the past these woodlands were largely deciduous, but continuous felling and replanting with conifers has greatly changed their character and consequently the food supply for red deer, roe deer and wild boar has declined. To help visitors see the fauna at close hand an animal park has been built at Schwartzbach.

1 MARQUENTERRE
Information: Parc ornithologique du Marquenterre, St-Quentin-en-Tourmont, 80120 Rue
Access: from La Maye, 28km NW of ABBEVILLE
Open: April 1 to November 4 between 0930 and 1800
Facilities: Camouflaged paths. Observation hides

2 VALLEE DE LA GRANDE PIERRE ET DE VITAIN
Information: Office de Tourisme, Pavillon Anne de Bretagne, 3 avenue Jean-Laigret, 41000 Blois
Access: from Marolles, 8km N of BLOIS
Open: Unrestricted, but visitors must keep to footpaths

3 LE LAC DE LA FORET D'ORIENT
Information: Maison du parc naturel régional de la forêt d'Orient, 10200 Piney
Access: from TROYES
Open: Unrestricted except for the ornithological reserve to which access is forbidden
Facilities: Information centre. Marked footpaths within the park. Observation hides

4 VOSGES DU NORD
Information: Maison du parc naturel régional des Vosges du Nord, La Petite-Pierre, 67290 Wingen-sur-Moder
Access: from STRASBOURG
Open: Unrestricted
Facilities: Information centre. Geological trail. Marked footpaths within the park

FRANCE

Volcans d'Auvergne Regional Park

A large park, 120 kilometres from north to south, Volcans d'Auvergne has a remarkable landscape of extinct volcanoes, many of which have a perfectly preserved conical outline. The park is divided into five regions: Monts Dôme in the north; the Monts Dore, which contains the Puy de Sancy (1885 metres), the highest point; the immense pastures of the plateaux of Cézallier; the plateau of Artense and the Monts Cantal in the south.

A region of hard winters, abundant rainfall and warm summers, the pastures are green and the forests luxuriant. There are many lakes, several of which lie in volcanic craters, and many peat bogs which have developed on poorly drained acid soils. In general the forests consist of oak at low altitudes, sweet chestnut in the valleys, beech higher up on the hillsides and fir near the summits.

The flora is distinctive for the region, with carpets of daffodils turning the fields yellow in spring, an abundance of white narcissus and the red flowers of the dog's tooth violet. Wild orchids, particularly *Orchis provincialis*, colour the road verges yellow, and some fields appear blue with violets. Among the flowers which are seen later in the year, some of the less common ones are herb Paris, blue sow-thistle, Welsh poppy and red helleborine. Because of the considerable habitat diversity the birdlife consists of a great variety of species – and such birds of prey as the red kite, short-toed eagle, buzzard and goshawk nest in the area. The black woodpecker also occurs.

Cévennes National Park

Of the five National Parks on the French mainland, the Cévennes is the only one that is not a high mountain area. It is situated in the southern part of the Massif Central in a triangle between Mende, Alès and Millau, only two hours by car from Montpellier and the Mediterranean coast. Its distinctive landscape comprises deep gorges, green hills, forests and the wide open flat tops of the Causses, an area of stony waterless limestone plateaux with a rich and distinctive flora.

The highest mountains, Mont Lozère (1700 metres), Mont Bouges (1400 metres) and Mont Aigoual (1545 metres), are all composed of granite or schist and have a vegetation contrasting markedly with that of the Causses. Causse Méjean varies in altitude from 1000 to 1200 metres and although the summers are hot the area is high enough to suffer severe cold in the winter.

Life was hard in the Causses and few farms were established in the region, and although today, as in the past, the limestone grasslands and hills are grazed by many thousands of sheep, the shepherds live in the villages below. It is the milk from these flocks that is used to make the famous Roquefort cheese.

The central zone of the park has only 538 permanent inhabitants. The peripheral zone on the other hand is well populated, with over 41,000 people. In addition 60,000 tourists visit the park during the summer.

Forestry is an important occupation in the Cévennes. Extensive conifer plantations as

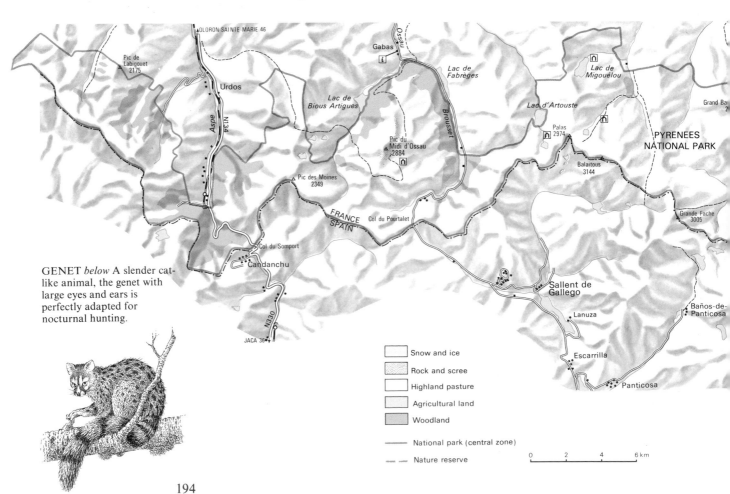

GENET *below* A slender cat-like animal, the genet with large eyes and ears is perfectly adapted for nocturnal hunting.

Snow and ice

Rock and scree

Highland pasture

Agricultural land

Woodland

National park (central zone)

Nature reserve

0   2   4   6 km

PYRENEES NATIONAL PARK

well as forests of oak, chestnut and beech are found on the granitic soils. The park's flora is of great interest. In spring a carpet of wild daffodils covers the mountain slopes, while in the forests and clearings can be seen the flowers of martagon lilies, the yellow pheasant's eye and *Arnica* species. The lady's slipper orchid is said to occur in the park as well as over forty other orchid species, many of which flower particularly abundantly after the scrub has been burnt.

On the Causses are found dwarf daffodils, pasque-flowers, wild tulips and the common feather-grass with its curious elongated flower heads. The birdlife includes eagle owls, which feed on rats inhabiting rubbish dumps outside towns, peregrine falcons, choughs, ravens, alpine swifts, rock thrushes, ortolan buntings, little bustards, stone curlews, hen-harriers and Montague's harriers.

Pyrénées National Park

Together, the French Pyrénées National Park and the Spanish park of Ordesa form a large single protected area of mountains, which is probably the finest in the whole region. It has superb scenery and offers enormous recreational potential – walking, horse-riding, rock-climbing and skiing.

The most striking feature of the Pyrénées National Park is the Cirque de Gavarnie, a huge glacial amphitheatre with a rock face beloved of climbers and with also one of the highest waterfalls (423 metres) in the Pyrénées. The larger Cirque de Troumouse to the

northeast of Gavarnie is not so striking, scenically, but with several lakes, rocky outcrops and a flat, grassy floor it is a fine place for birds and wild flowers.

Many plants which occur only in the Pyrénées are found in the park. Among the most beautiful are ramonda, Pyrenean pheasant's eye, yellow turk's-cap lily, Pyrenean gentian and the Pyrenean saxifrage with its long, white spikes. Beech trees, abundant in the valleys, were formerly even more widespread, but extensive grazing has prevented their regeneration. At higher altitudes mountain pine is the commonest tree and alpenrose forms a dwarf-shrub layer.

The park incorporates the nature reserves of Néouvielle, Mont Valier and Carlit. Within Néouvielle, which was created in 1935 by the Société Nationale pour la Protection de la Nature, mountain-pine forest grows to a height of 2400 metres and isolated trees grow up to 2600 metres, the highest in Europe.

In the forested zone of the park wild boars, genets, martens, foxes, badgers, and near streams, Pyrenean desmans, are found. The Pyrenean chamois, or isard, is well established and has a population of over 3000. However, the animal which all visitors would like to see is the brown bear. The best areas to see it are said to be the valleys of the Aspe and Ossau, although few now remain despite it being fully protected both inside and outside the park. Destruction and disturbance of its forest habitat are thought to be the main reasons for its decline.

1 VOLCANS D'AUVERGNE
Information: Maison du parc naturel régional des Volcans d'Auvergne, Château de Montlosier, Randanne, 63210 Rochefort-Montagne
Access: from CLERMONT-FERRAND, AURILLAC or ST FLOUR
Open: Unrestricted
Facilities: Information centres. Marked footpaths within the park. Guided walks during the summer

2 CEVENNES
Information: Parc National des Cevennes, Château de Florac, B.P. 4, 48400 Florac
Access: from MENDE, MILLAU or ALES
Open: Unrestricted
Facilities: Information centres within the park. Hotels and camp sites in the peripheral zone. Marked footpaths. Guided walks during the summer

3 PYRENEES
Information: Parc National des Pyrénées Occidentales, route de Pau, B.P. 300, 65013 Tarbes
Access: from PAU or TARBES
Open: Unrestricted
Facilities: Information centres and museums within the park. Botanical garden at Gavarnie. Hotels in the peripheral zone. Refuges in the central zone. Marked footpaths. Guided walks during the summer

PYRENEES

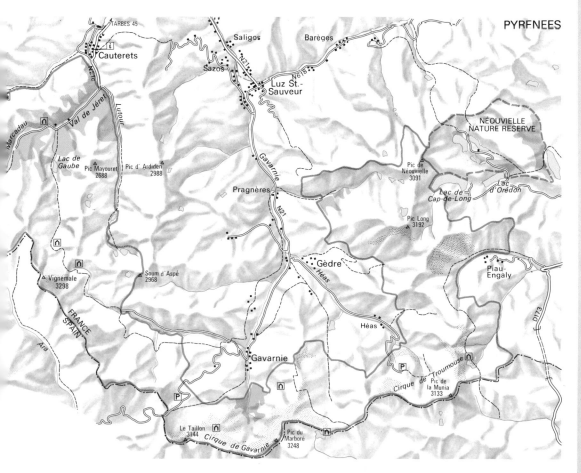

BLACK-NECKED
GREBE *left* This grebe,
distinguished in the
summer by its golden ear
tufts, breeds in temperate
and southern Europe on
well-vegetated lakes.

VERCORS *above* The
2086-m-high massif of
Mont Aiguille lies at the
southern end of a
magnificent 30-km-long
rocky escarpment on the
eastern side of the park.

Villars-les-Dombes Nature Reserve and Ornithological Park

Lying northeast of Lyon, near the town of
Villars-les-Dombes, this glacially formed
region of lakes is famous for its ornithological
park and botanical/zoological nature reserve.

The park, on the edge of one of the lakes, is
a place where visitors can see caged birds as
well as those flying free in their natural lakeland habitat, and in this sense it is similar to
the Zwin Reserve in Belgium. Of its 23 hectares,
9 hectares are water and there are about 300
species of birds on display.

The reserve of Les Dombes was established
in 1970 as a State Reserve specifically for
research into aquatic plants and animals.
Traditional use of the lakes for fish culture is
permitted and the land between the lakes is
farmed or used for commercial forestry. The
birdlife of the area is of particular importance
and has been carefully studied. Several rare
species breed here, among them the black-
necked grebe, whiskered tern and little egret.
The reserve is also important for wintering
wildfowl and for many migrant species.

Pilat Regional Park

Mont Pilat, rising from the centre of the
Regional Park, dominates this landscape of
wooded hills, heaths and granite outcrops,
known as chirats. On the east side, where the
park extends to the plain of the Rhône

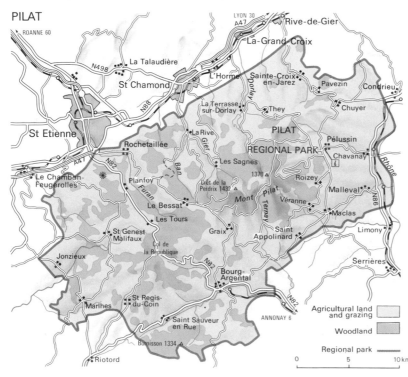

PILAT

Agricultural land
and grazing

Woodland

Regional park

0   5   10 km

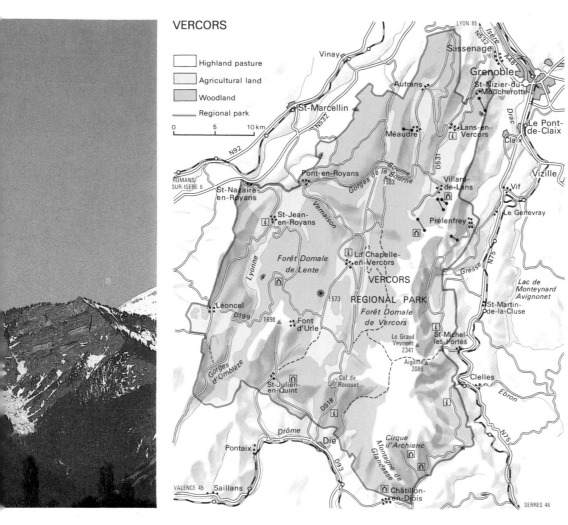

VERCORS

Highland pasture
Agricultural land
Woodland
Regional park

0 5 10 km

1 VILLARS-LES-DOMBES
Information: Parc
ornithologique départementale
de la Dombes, 01330 Villars-
les-Dombes
Access: from Villars-les-
Dombes, 33km NE of LYON
Open: Unrestricted except for
the botanical and zoological
reserve which is closed to
visitors. Permission may be
obtained from the director of the
park only for particular research.
Facilities: Information centre.
Aviaries within the park

2 PILAT
Information: Maison du parc
naturel régional du Pilat, Le
moulin de Virieu, 2 rue Benäy,
42410 Pelussin
Access: from ST ETIENNE
Open: Unrestricted except for
two "zones of silence" where
noise is forbidden
Facilities: Information centre.
Marked footpaths within the
park

3 VERCORS
Information: Maison du parc
naturel régional du Vercors,
Chemin des Fusillés, B.P. 14,
38250 Lans-en-Vercors
Access: from VALENCE or
GRENOBLE
Open: Unrestricted
Facilities: Information centres.
Marked footpaths within the
park. Mountain refuges

valley, the lower levels are patterned with orchards, market gardens and vineyards.

Between 400 and 800 metres altitude the park's forests consist of sweet chestnut, downy oak, ash and poplar. The mountain zone above, mainly pine, beech and fir, has an interesting flora of plants associated with the area's siliceous soils, which have been derived from the underlying granite – *Vaccinium*, *Aconitum*, *Arnica*, *Knautia* and *Alchemilla* species, together with orchids and daffodils.

More than a hundred species of birds have been recorded, including Bonelli's eagle, crag martins and the citril finch. The autumn migration of birds travelling south down the Rhône valley is a striking sight.

Red and roe deer have returned to the forests after a period of absence and wild boar can be found in the forests of Terrasse-sur-Dolay, de Pavezin and on the heights of de Pélussin and de Roizey. Fishing and hunting are regulated and visitors are asked not to collect plants or interfere with wildlife. In two areas "zones of silence" have been created, where noise is forbidden.

Vercors Regional Park

Between the towns of Grenoble, Valence and Die lies a magnificent subalpine region which has had Regional Park status since 1970. The area sits at an average altitude of 1200 metres and the greater part consists of a series of north-south ridges and valleys. Two separate levels can be distinguished – a lower plateau between 700 and 1200 metres, where the towns, villages and agriculture of the region are concentrated, and a wilder plateau above 1500 metres, with few inhabitants, culminating in the 2341-metre peak of Le Grand Veymont.

The park's calcareous rocks have been eroded into many strikingly beautiful formations – peaks, cliffs and gorges, and in one part an extensive series of caves and underground streams has been produced.

The vegetation shows a sharp contrast between north-facing slopes, where there are pines, spruce and beech, and south-facing aspects, which have drier, warmer soils and support a more open and poorer tree growth as well as pasture land near the valley floors. Downy oak and Scots pine are the commonest trees and at the foot of the slopes grow vines and lavender. Vercors is famous for its walnuts, and the oil is sold in the farms and towns nearby. The mountain pastures are rich in plants typical of the region – gentians, tulips, dog's tooth violet, martagon lilies and orchids, including the lady's slipper orchid.

The vertebrate fauna is rather poor, but there are wild boars, red and roe deer, chamois and the mouflon, which is an introduced species. Hunting is permitted throughout the park, for, unlike the French National Parks, there is no protected central zone.

Aiguilles Rouges Nature Reserve

North of Chamonix lies the massif of Aiguilles Rouges, separated by the valley of the River Arve from the massif of Mont Blanc. Aiguilles Rouges Nature Reserve, only 12 kilometres in length and not exceeding 4 kilometres in width, has wonderful mountain scenery with glaciers, lakes, rock cliffs, extensive moraines and peaks reaching nearly 3000 metres. It is composed of old rocks – schists, gneiss and granites – except for the Belvédère massif in the interior, which is made up of much younger sedimentary deposits that are usually calcareous and support a lime-loving flora. As the reserve varies in altitude from 1200 to 2965 metres all vegetation stages are therefore represented – subalpine, alpine and summit.

The forest ranges from spruce at the lower levels through larch on the higher slopes to alder. Alpenrose dominates the subalpine zone. Marmots are well established in the area, and chamois and ibex are also found. The ibex was reintroduced from the Gran Paradiso National Park in Italy and has now spread over about half of the reserve. The birdlife is typical of the central Alps – alpine swifts, alpine accentors, snow finches, alpine choughs, ravens and nutcrackers.

Marais du Bout du Lac d'Annecy Nature Reserve

The lake of Annecy, in the lovely mountain scenery on the north side of Les Bauges, has at its extreme southern end, at the tip of what is known as the Petit-Lac, the State Reserve of Marais du Bout du Lac d'Annecy. The reserve consists mostly of marsh, reed beds and a little open water, and in spite of the proximity of main roads and buildings provides shelter for some interesting nesting birds – the corncrake, water rail, garganey, teal, curlew and little bittern. During the winter months the number of wildfowl is increased by the arrival of dabbling ducks such as pintail and mallard and diving ducks such as goldeneye, goosander and scaup. There are also many swans.

SCARCE COPPER Common throughout central and Northern Europe, particularly in mountains, this butterfly is on the wing during July and August, and can be seen in meadows and alpine pastures.

VANOISE *below* The glacially-formed Lacs de Lanserlia lie on the western shoulder of the Grand Roc Noire in the south of the park.

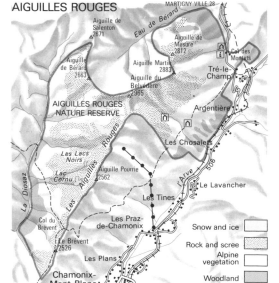

AIGUILLES ROUGES

MARTIGNY VILLE 28
Aiguille de Salenton 2671
Eau de Bérard
Aiguille de Mesure 2812
Col des Montets
Aiguille Martin 2883
Aiguille de Bérard 2663
Aiguille du Belvédère 2965
Tré-le-Champ
AIGUILLES ROUGES NATURE RESERVE
Argentière
Les Chosalets
Les Lacs Noirs
Lac Cornu
Aiguille Pourrie 2562
L'Arve
Le Lavancher
La Diosaz
Les Aiguilles Rouges
Les Tines
Col du Brévent
Les Praz-de-Chamonix
Le Brévent 2526
Les Plans
Chamonix-Mont-Blanc
SALLANCHES 26

Snow and ice
Rock and scree
Alpine vegetation
Woodland
Nature reserve

0   1   2   3 km

The Petit-Lac, itself a hunting reserve, has suffered from private building and tourist development along the shore line, which has undoubtedly detracted from its importance as a natural landscape.

Vanoise National Park

Established in 1963, Vanoise was the first National Park to be created in France and is perhaps today one of the most popular. It is situated in the central Alps between the high valleys of l'Arc and l'Isère and runs along the Italian border for 7 kilometres, where it abuts the Gran Paradiso National Park, Italy's most famous conservation area.

The central zone of the Vanoise is a region of high mountains, ranging from 1250 to 3852 metres and containing 107 summits exceeding 3000 metres. The incomparable mountain scenery, beautiful valleys and lakes, which, as well as their natural history interest, have facilities for walking and skiing, attract growing numbers of tourists and there is inevitably some conflict between the conservationists and the developers. Fortunately the central zone of the park proper has been able to resist these pressures and the roads, chair lifts and ski runs which would have otherwise penetrated inwards from the peripheral zone are absent.

The geology of the park is complex. The middle zone, in the region of the Col de la Vanoise, consists of calcareous rocks of the Triassic and Cretaceous periods with quartzites, schists and gypsum. In the north and south are wide zones of Permian metamorphic rocks and in areas of Triassic and Jurassic strata there are many famous sites for fossil fish and molluscs.

The forests are mainly coniferous, the tree species being determined by altitude, soil type and rainfall. Larch, firs, spruce, Scots pine, mountain pine and arolla pine are widespread, the last two extending up to the limit of tree growth. Among the plants typically found on the areas of quartzite and schist are wavy hairgrass, cowberry, blue-spiked rampion, rock campion and round-leaved restharrow. On the calcareous soils of the alpine zones there are many exciting plants ranging from crocuses, which appear in the meadows as the snow melts, to such glorious alpine plants as anemones, campanulas, cinquefoils, gentians and primulas.

A hundred or so years ago the bear, wolf, lynx, lammergeier and capercaillie were all found in the region of the park. Some disappeared only quite recently – the last bear was killed in 1921 not far from the park itself. Today the visitor can see the marmot, ibex, chamois, fox, badger, pine and stone martens as well as many smaller mammals. The typical mountain and forest birds, such as the golden eagle, buzzard, black grouse, ptarmigan, ring ouzel and nutcracker, are all present. Warm days in high summer provide an excellent opportunity to see the park's many beautiful species of butterflies, in particular the apollo, scarce copper, Cynthia's fritillary and mountain clouded yellow.

1 AIGUILLES ROUGES
Information: Office de gestion et Association des amis de la réserve des Aiguilles Rouges, 74400 Argentière
Access: from CHAMONIX
Open: Unrestricted
Facilities: Information point on the Col des Montets, open from June 1 to September 15. Mountain refuges within the reserve. Marked footpaths. Cable car to near the reserve's boundary from Les Praz-de-Chamonix

2 MARAIS DU BOUT DU LAC D'ANNECY
Information: Direction départementale de l'agriculture, Division de la protection de la nature, Cité administrative, rue Dupanloup, 74040 Annecy
Access: from ANNECY
Open: Unrestricted except during breeding season when visitors should not enter

3 VANOISE
Information: Parc National de la Vanoise, 135 rue du Docteur-Juilliand, B.P. 105, 73003 Chambéry cedex
Access: from Val d'Isère, 133km E of CHAMBERY
Open: Unrestricted
Facilities: Information centre at Lanslebourg-Mont-Cenis. Hotels in the peripheral zone. Refuges in the central zone. Marked footpaths. Guided walks from June to September

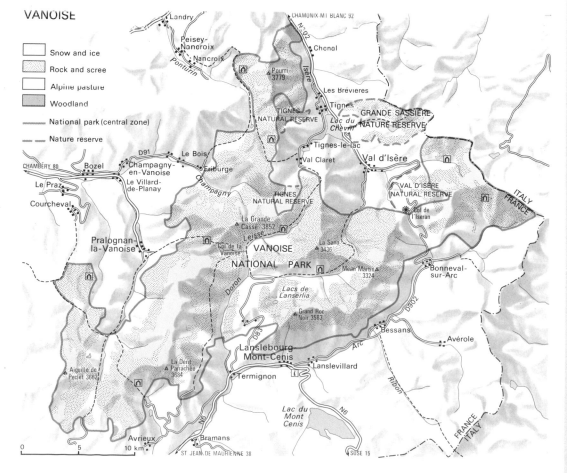

VANOISE

- Snow and ice
- Rock and scree
- Alpine pasture
- Woodland
- ——— National park (central zone)
- --- Nature reserve

Ecrins National Park

Established in 1973, ten years after its near neighbour Vanoise, Ecrins National Park is much less well known to the foreign visitor. It is the largest of the French National Parks and has superb alpine scenery as well as a rich fauna and flora. The centre of the park, dominated by four high peaks – Barre des Ecrins (4102 metres), La Meije (3983 metres), l'Ailefroide (3953 metres) and Pelvoux (3946

ECRINS

Snow and ice
Rock and scree
Alpine vegetation
Woodland
National park (central zone)

0   5   10km

LADY'S SLIPPER
ORCHID

metres) – is an area of lakes, gorges, cirques and glaciers and is forested extensively throughout by larch.

The park and its peripheral zone lie in a triangle formed by the towns of Briançon, Bourg d'Oisans and Gap. The Park proper has few inhabitants, but the peripheral zone, which is bounded by the lovely Durance, Drac and Romanche valley, contains a number of villages and small towns and has a total population of over 25,000. For some time the mountain valleys have had a declining population and have been losing their younger element to the towns in search of better opportunities. Recently, however the tourist trade has improved bringing greater prosperity to the region.

Except for the south, which is influenced by the Mediterranean climate, the animals and plants of the Ecrins massif are similar to other parts of the Alps. Ibex, although reintroduced in 1977 and 1978, are still scarce

and the visitor will more readily see chamois, marmots, the mountain hare and fox, as well as the golden eagle, capercaillie, rock partridge, ptarmigan, and many other typical alpine birds. Among the rarer plants are the orange lily *Lilium bulbiferum* ssp. *croceum*, the martagon lily, the queen of the Alps and the finest of all European wild orchids, the lady's slipper.

There are six nature reserves within the park, all in high valleys and established to protect particular aspects of the region's fauna and flora.

Lubéron Regional Park

Forming a crest of calcareous rocks no more than 1100 metres high, the mountains of Lubéron, 50 kilometres east of Avignon, form an impressive and imposing ridge on the north side of the Durance Valley. Most of the area is either forested or farmed and presents, like much of Provence, a most attractive rural landscape.

Vines, cereals, fruit trees and market-garden produce are the principal crops and the region is well known for its caves, steep-sided valleys and villages perched on rocky slopes, and is also of interest archaeologically. There are extensive oak forests, much of which have been coppiced, and on the ridge of the Petit Lubéron, where the forest road from Bonnieux to Cheval-Blanc runs, there is an area of large Atlas cedars planted in 1860, covering about 1000 hectares.

Being in a Mediterranean region the park has many typical plants of the maquis. These shrubs are particularly well developed in the combes, or dry valleys, making pathways difficult to follow in some places. The park's limestone terrain and rocky cliffs provide a habitat for Bonelli's eagle, short-toed eagle and the Egyptian vulture – all of which are now rare in France.

Mercantour National Park

Created in August 1979, Mercantour is the sixth and most recent of the French National Parks. The first proposals to protect this fine region were made fourteen years earlier, but agreement with the twenty-eight communes in the area proved difficult. Although it covers a large area the park is long and narrow and, apart from a region around St Etienne-de-Tinée, follows the frontier with Italy. As with other French National Parks, a peripheral zone has been created, the boundary of which is now being finalized.

The central zone, running from Col de Larche, in the north, to the Col de Brouis in the south, covers a large area, nearly 80 kilometres in length and, except for the northern and southern ends, no more than about 10 kilometres wide. As a consequence of its geographical extent the park is varied both in its geology and geography. The strong Mediterranean influences that can be seen in the area's flora contrast markedly with the

montane characteristics of the plantlife of the summits and with certain central European elements also found in the region because of its location.

There are three main landscape types: a region of gneiss and granite strongly eroded by glaciers in the east; a landscape of high sedimentary rocks in the centre between Tinée and Verdon and a beautiful lakeland area, where crystalline rocks reappear in the northwest, on the left bank of the high Tinée.

Mercantour is also the site of some remarkable Bronze-Age rock engravings which are found in the Val des Merveilles and the Fontanable cirque, and are said to be the best examples in Europe.

The park's geographical position, varied rocks and soils and climatic characteristics combine to support a remarkably rich flora with many plants found nowhere else in France. Probably the most famous species is a magnificent saxifrage, *Saxifraga floru-*

ECRINS *above* A beautiful alpine region in southeast France, the National Park encompasses the highest part of the Haut Daupine Mountains.

lenta, which has enormous spikes of rose-coloured flowers. Endemic to the region and found only in rocky places between 2500 and 3000 metres altitude, it is likely to become the emblem of the park. The insect fauna is equally interesting and also includes endemic species such as the larche ringlet and the lovely small apollo butterflies, both now much reduced by over-collecting. Among the park's mammals and birds are nearly all species found elsewhere in the Alps, including the ibex, which was reintroduced from Italy, and the mouflon, from Corsica. Chamois are numerous and all the region's smaller rodents and predators are found, including the wild cat, which is thought to be on the verge of extinction. The golden eagle, eagle owl, buzzard, sparrowhawk, as well as kites and harriers, all occur.

CAMARGUE

The region of marshes and lakes lying in the delta of the River Rhône, known as the Camargue, is one of the three most important coastal wetland areas in Europe. It is an area with a fascinating plant life and a bird life that is almost without equal – over 300 migrant species have been recorded in the region at some time. Only the Doñana on the Guadalquivir River in Spain and the Danube in Romania can rival the Camargue.

The Regional Park occupies the whole area south of the town of Arles, between the Petit and Grand Rhône. In the centre lies the vast Etang de Vaccarès, which, together with a region of lakes and marshes extending south to the sea, forms the State Nature Reserve. Two other reserves of importance lie in the area. One, known as the Imperial Reserve and sited on the west side of the State Reserve, is mostly water, and is managed by the municipality of Les Saintes-Maries-de-la-Mer. The other lies on the east side and is the location of the Biological Station of Tour du Valat, which is situated near Le Sambuc. The station is privately owned and has been responsible for much research on the biology of the Camargue, particularly with regard to its birdlife.

The ecology of the area is complex and the park contains brackish lakes, riverine forest, dunes, sea-shore and salt steppes (sansouire), with brackish pools and freshwater marshes in places. The beach, nearly 100 kilometres long, is composed of fine sand, and the dunes, on which are found groups of stone pines and Mediterranean shrubs as well as a typical dune vegetation, extend several kilometres inland in places.

The higher areas of salt steppe are generally drier than the surrounding land and have a vegetation of sea-lavender, the false brome *Brachypodium phoenicoides* and *Phillyrea angustifolia*. This is the main area for rearing the famous Camargue bulls and semi-wild white horses. Part of the steppes is also cultivated for rice, maize, wheat and vines and in places there are salt-pans and saline lagoons, where many rare birds breed – flamingos, slender-billed gulls, gull-billed terns, red-crested pochards, black-winged stilts and avocets. In the freshwater marshes there are bitterns, little bitterns, purple herons, night herons, squacco herons, cattle egrets, little egrets and marsh harriers. The reserve is also a breeding area for bee-eaters, rollers and great spotted cuckoos, among many other species.

The Camargue, without doubt one of the most important ornithological reserves in the whole of Europe, also has a fascinating fauna of amphibia, reptiles, including both snakes and lizards, as well as insects and other invertebrates.

GREATER FLAMINGO
The largest of all flamingo species, it is the only one to breed in Europe.

CAMARGUE

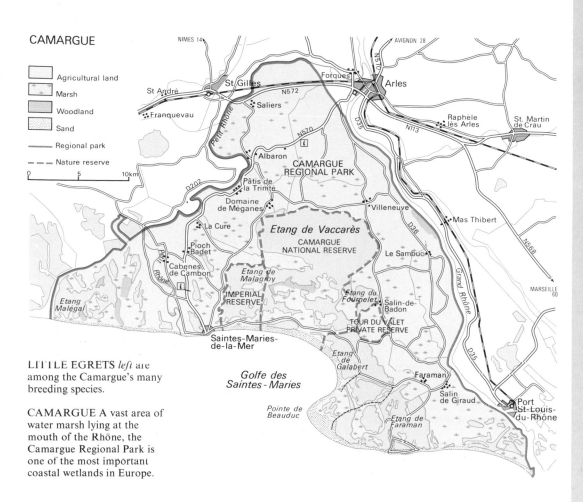

Legend:
- Agricultural land
- Marsh
- Woodland
- Sand
- ——— Regional park
- – – – Nature reserve

0 — 5 — 10km

NÎMES 14

AVIGNON 28

N570

St Gilles   Forques   Arles

St André   N572

Saliers

Franquevau   N570   D35   N113   Raphèle lès Arles   St. Martin de Crau

Albaron   [i]

CAMARGUE REGIONAL PARK

Pâtis de la Trinité

Domaine de Méganes   Villeneuve   Mas Thibert   N568

D202   Etang de Vaccarès   MARSEILLE 60

La Cure   CAMARGUE NATIONAL RESERVE

Pioch Badet   Le Sambuc

Cabanes de Cambon   [i]   Etang de Malagroy

Etang Malégal   IMPERIAL RESERVE   Etang du Fournelet   Salin-de-Badon

TOUR DU VALET PRIVATE RESERVE   Grand Rhône   D35

Saintes-Maries-de-la-Mer   Etang de Galabert   Faraman

Golfe des Saintes-Maries   Salin de Giraud

Pointe de Beauduc   Etang de Faraman   Port St-Louis-du-Rhône

LITTLE EGRETS *left* are among the Camargue's many breeding species.

CAMARGUE A vast area of water marsh lying at the mouth of the Rhône, the Camargue Regional Park is one of the most important coastal wetlands in Europe.

CAMARGUE
Information: Parc naturel régional de Camargue, Le Mas du Pont-de-Rousty, 13200 Arles
Access: from Arles
Open: Unrestricted
Facilities: Information centre – Le Centre d'Information de Ginès et Park Ornithologique, Pont de Gau, 13460 Les Saintes-Maries-de-la-Mer Musée Camarguais, Le Mas du Pont-du-Rousty, 13200 Arles Observation points throughout the park

203

CORSE

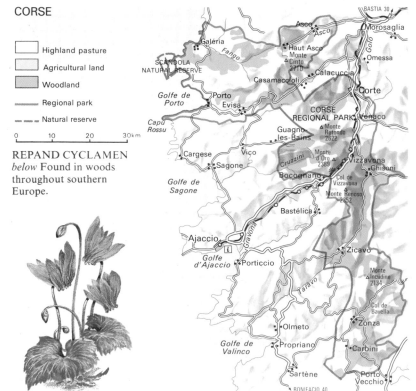

- ☐ Highland pasture
- ▨ Agricultural land
- ▨ Woodland
- —— Regional park
- --- Natural reserve

0   10   20   30 km

REPAND CYCLAMEN
below Found in woods
throughout southern
Europe.

[Map of Corsica with labels:] BASTIA 30, Asco, Asco, Morosaglia, Galéria, Fango, Haut Asco, Monte Cinto 2710, Omessa, Golo, SCANDOLA NATURAL RESERVE, Casamaccoli, Calacuccia, Corte, Golfe de Porto, Porto, Evisa, CORSE REGIONAL PARK, Venaco, Capu Rossu, Guagno-les-Bains, Monte Rotondo 2622, Cargese, Vico, Monte d'Oro 2389, Vizzavona, Cruzzini, Sagone, Bocognano, Ghisoni, Col de Vizzavona, Golfe de Sagone, Monte Renoso 2352, Bastélica, Ajaccio, Gravona, Zicavo, Golfe d'Ajaccio, Porticcio, Monte Incudine 2134, Taravo, Col de Bavella, Olmeto, Zonza, Golfe de Valinco, Propriano, Carbini, Sartène, Porto Vecchio, BONIFACIO 40

PORT-CROS *above* The Mediterranean Sea around
the island of Port-Cros forms one of the few protected
areas of sea-floor in Europe. The submarine zone is
famous for its marine life and rock formations.

Port-Cros National Park

The island National Park of Port-Cros is
exceptional in that more than half its total
area is under water and forms a marine zone
around the island in which the area's fascinating underwater life is protected from
collectors and exploiters.

Port-Cros and its larger neighbour Porque-
rolles lie less than 10 kilometres south of the
Côte d'Azur. Although Port-Cros is easily
reached by boat from Le Lavandou, the island
does not attract many visitors, because its only
beach is rather small. The village of Port-Cros
lies on the west side of the island in a bay
sheltered by the tiny islet of Bagaud, which is a
strict nature reserve to which no access is
permitted.

The climate is typically Mediterranean,
but is tempered by the sea, so that the
maximum temperature does not normally
exceed 27°C. The vegetation of Port-Cros is
quite remarkable: the island is one of the few
remaining places on the Mediterranean coast

where the area's original forest cover of evergreen trees still survives. The vegetation cover is dense and there are many holm oaks and Aleppo pines, as well as all the typical shrub plants of the maquis. There are few mammals on the island – only rabbits and some rodent species.

The insect fauna, however, is remarkably rich; there are 220 species of butterflies and moths, 600 species of beetles and the forests ring with the song of several different species of cicadas. The most striking butterfly is the two-tailed pasha, a woodland species which feeds on strawberry trees and produces two generations per year.

The fauna of the marine zone surrounding the island is in a better state than that of the littoral zone and there are many species such as groupers, eels, crayfish and lobsters among the rocks and aquatic plants off shore.

Six species of snakes, several lizards, one species of gecko and a number of amphibians are also found on the island. One particular amphibian, the Tyrrhenian painted frog, is found nowhere else in France. Because the island lies on a migration route, the birdlife is full of surprises. The park's breeding birds are also of interest and include two unusual seabirds, Cory's, or the Mediterranean, shearwater and the smaller eastern Mediterranean race of the Manx shearwater.

Corse Regional Park

Corsica is separated from Sardinia by only 12 kilometres. It is believed that both islands were once part of what is now southern France and that they gradually drifted south during the Tertiary period. As Corsica lies 160 kilometres from the coast of Provence and 82 kilometres from Tuscany, it is much nearer Italy than France and in fact the old Corsican dialect, still spoken in rural areas, is closer to Italian than it is to French.

The island is large, over 160 kilometres from north to south, and has an area of 8680 square kilometres. Most of the rocks are granitic and there are twenty peaks exceeding 2000 metres. The Regional Park occupies a large part of the centre of the island and a section of the rocky west coast on which the Scandola Nature Reserve is situated.

The whole region is one of great beauty and diversity, the character of which the park authorities are trying hard to preserve in the face of excessive hunting, forest clearance and frequent fires, which destroy the vulnerable maquis vegetation. Tourism is increasing rapidly, bringing additional problems of wildlife protection.

The vegetation has much in common with Sardinia, but the island's long period of isolation has permitted the development of many endemic plant species. About fifty-eight of these are recognized; 8 per cent of the island's total flora of higher plants.

In the past, extensive forests of conifers covered the mountain slopes, and although

areas still exist today they are much reduced. The finest forest tree is the Corsican pine. Growing to a height of 50 metres, it has been introduced all over Europe and is an important timber tree. Other widespread species include maritime pine, stone pine, Aleppo pine and silver fir. Evergreen oaks such as holm oak and cork oak are also common and in the maquis are found such typical Mediterranean bushes as strawberry trees, viburnums, myrtles and tree heaths.

In the spring many small plants flower along the coastal grasslands. There are two species of *Crocus*, both confined to Corsica and Sardinia, *Crocus minimus* and the larger *C. corsicus*. Very early in the year *Anemone stellata* is in flower and in March and April there is a glorious display of *Romulea* species, narcissi, orchids, of which fifty-one species have been recorded, and also of the beautiful repand cyclamen.

In its birdlife Corsica is notable for having most of the nesting lammergeiers and the only nesting ospreys in France. Both, although rare, are found in the Regional Park. Along the park's rocky coasts the most interesting seabird is the Cory's shearwater, which breeds in several localities. Many marshy areas, notably the lakes by the northeast coastline, where the purple heron, moustached warbler and marsh harrier occur, lie outside the park. These water bodies are important for wildfowl in the winter and during migration.

The most typical birds of the forest, maquis and hills are species such as the goshawk, red kite, rock sparrow, bee eater, alpine accentor and blue rock thrush. Many familiar European birds found on the island have evolved small local differences of plumage and are regarded as Corsican subspecies. Perhaps the most distinctive is the Corsican nuthatch, which has a white stripe over the eye and is found in coniferous forests between 700 and 1500 metres. Audouin's gull occurs much more locally: it nests on rocky coastal islands along the Corsican coast, but its numbers have declined considerably in recent years. Other rare birds include such species as the spotless starling and Marmora's warbler.

Scandola Nature Reserve

Lying within the Regional Park of Corsica, Scandola consists of a small rocky promontory on the north side of the Gulf of Porto. Its marine life and the wildlife on the adjacent land are of equal interest and, apart from Port-Cros National Park, it is the only marine nature reserve in France.

The coastline has impressive cliffs of granite porphyry and rhyolite and there are deep, colourful caves and basaltic columns. The birdlife is one of the chief interests of the coastline, where golden eagles, ospreys and Cory's shearwaters nest. The reserve also has a population of wild goats.

1 PORT-CROS
Information: Parc National de Port-Cros, 50 avenue Gambetta, 83400 Hyères
Access: by boat from Le Lavandou, 40km E of TOULON
Open: Unrestricted except for Bagaud which is closed to visitors
Facilities: Marked footpaths throughout the island

2 CORSE
Information: Maison du parc naturel régional de Corse, Palais Lantivy, B.P. 417, 20184 Ajaccio cedex
Access: from AJACCIO or CORTE
Open: Unrestricted
Facilities: Marked footpaths within the park

3 SCANDOLA
Information: Maison du parc naturel régional de Corse, Palais Lantivy, B.P. 417, 21084 Ajaccio cedex
Access: from Porto, 83km N of AJACCIO
Open: Closed to visitors: may only be viewed from reserve boundary

SPAIN

Anyone who travels across Spain from the Pyrenees to the southwest will readily appreciate what a large country it is; with an area of 502,000 square kilometres it is second only in size to France. On the other hand, the population density, averaging about 64 per square kilometre is low in comparison with, say, the Netherlands, which at 413 persons per square kilometre is Europe's most densely populated country. Spain, therefore, as might be expected, still has many remote and wild areas, and a most interesting wildlife.

The Pyrenees form a natural barrier, isolating the Iberian Peninsula from the rest of Europe; remarkable differences in vegetation exist between its northern and southern sides. Climatic and ecological conditions in Spain range between Atlantic, continental and Mediterranean, the vegetation of the last type having a close affinity with the fauna and flora of North Africa in a way not represented elsewhere in Europe.

The interior of Spain consists of a vast plateau, the Meseta, which, with an average height of between 600 and 700 metres, is crossed by several mountain chains or sierras. Numerous groups of mountains lie throughout Spain: the Pyrenees, rising to over 3600 metres, the Cantabrians in the northwest, which are generally lower and are influenced by the oceanic climate and the Atlantic, and the massif of the Sierra Nevada in the south, where the highest peak found in mainland Spain, Mulhaceñ, rises to over 3478 metres. There are also several important rivers, such as the Guadalquivir, which rises in the mountains of Sierra de Cazorla and whose delta is partly within the famous nature reserve of the Coto Doñana.

Spain is still mainly agricultural and its olive plantations, vineyards and orange groves are an integral part of the landscape. In the southeast other crops such as cotton, sugar cane and even rice are important. There are few large water bodies in the interior, but during the last thirty years many reservoirs, some of them of considerable size, have been constructed on the larger rivers for irrigation purposes. In addition thirteen wetlands of international importance for wildfowl have been identified and include such famous sites as the National Park of Tablas de Daimiel, the lagoons of Villafafila, in the province of Zamora, and Gallocanta in the provinces of Zaragoza and Teruel. The Fuenta de Piedra lagoon in Málaga province is the only place in Europe where the flamingo nests, apart from the Camargue. But perhaps the most important wetland in Spain, and in the whole of southwest Europe, is the largely intact ecosystem of the Guadalquivir marismas, of which 35,000 out of a total of 250,000 hectares lie within the National Park of Doñana.

The forest area of Spain is now much reduced and occupies only about 10 per cent of the land surface. Formerly, however, it is likely that at least two-thirds of the peninsula were covered with forests of holm oak and associated tall shrubs such as viburnums and *Arbutus* species. Very little of this remains and most of the existing forest is found in mountainous areas, where apart from hunting, fishing and grazing alternative forms of land use are not viable. In the lowlands around the Mediterranean the forest has virtually disappeared and been replaced by maquis – woody evergreen shrubs which probably provided the understory of the original primeval forest.

The flora of Spain, one of the richest in Europe, exceeds 5000 species and is second only to the Balkans. The North African element in the Spanish flora is of particular importance and accounts for a considerable proportion of the plants found in the southwest. 400 species of plants are endemic to Spain, and this is again close to the total found in the Balkans. Unfortunately quite a number of the endemics are rare because of landuse changes, grazing, or, in a few cases, overcollecting.

Nature conservation began in Spain in 1918, when the Covadonga and Ordesa National Parks were established, but progress to strengthen legislation has been slow; the last law was passed in 1975. This act established four categories of protected area – Strict Nature Reserves, National Parks, Natural Places of National Interest and Natural Parks. The last two categories combine natural history and aesthetic values and are perhaps more concerned with landscape beauty and traditional ways of life than wildlife protection. There are five National Parks in mainland Spain, and four others in the Canary Islands. In addition there are nineteen sites of National Interest and one Natural Park. There are also thirty-six National Game Reserves which, although managed only for game species, provide a habitat for many other forms of wildlife.

The Ministry of Agriculture is the government's chief agency for nature conservation, and acts through a section known as ICONA (Instituto Nacional para la Conservación de la Naturaleza). ICONA is divided into four sub-directorates dealing with fires and ecology, renewable natural resources, national forests and administration. The sub-directorate of renewable natural resources is divided into two services, one for game and one for parks and reserves. It is only this last sub-division which is concerned with National Parks.

In addition to ICONA, the Superior Council for Scientific Investigation (CSIC), which is the main state research organization, has a scientific advisory committee for nature protection. It is also responsible for the biological station and integral reserve of the Marismas, which lie within the National Park of Doñana. There is also a Spanish branch of the World Wildlife Fund (ADENA) and a few voluntary bodies, of which the most influential is the Spanish Association for the Management of the Environment (AEORMA). The Spanish

National Ornithological Society has also some influence on policy and on public opinion.

Although interest and concern for the environment and nature conservation is increasing, public support still lags a good way behind that in other countries and this is no doubt the reason for the low level of resources provided by the government.

Spain still retains most of its vertebrate fauna and indeed it claims to have lost only the beaver since the Middle Ages. The Spanish wolf occurs in several places and is still not a protected animal; the lynx is known in some forested regions, includ-ing the Coto Doñana. Spain has not lost any of its large birds of prey, although a number have become very scarce, including the magnificent imperial eagle, the lammergeier and black vulture. Spain also has an extremely rich invertebrate fauna, particularly of butterflies, which have been well studied, and it was the first European country to produce a Red Book of endangered species of Lepidoptera (butterflies and moths).

CAÑADAS DEL TEIDE   The 3718-metre-high volcanic cone of Mount Teide in the centre of the island dominates the National Park.

PARK/RESERVE	SIZE (km²)	DESCRIPTION	MAP REF.	PAGE NO.
ANCARES	79.8	National Reserve. Small area in the Cordillera Cantabrica with extensive coniferous and deciduous woodland.	A1	210
COVADONGA	169.3	National Park. Superb mountain region with beech and oak forest, heath and grassland.	B1	210
SAJA	181.9	National Reserve. Largely forest-covered area in the Cordillera Cantabrica. Interesting mammal fauna	B1	211
PICOS DE EUROPA	76.3	National Reserve. Rugged mountain landscape with jagged peaks and scree slopes in region of weathered limestone rocks. Area of alpine pasture on morainic deposits.	B1	212
LAGO DE SANABRIA	50.3	Natural Park. High plateau with lakes and mountain streams. Extensive forests and rich shrub flora.	B1	213
SIERRA DE LA DEMANDA	738.2	National Reserve. Part of extensive mountain range reaching to over 2000 metres. Many game animals.	C1	213
ORDESA	157.1	National Park. Spectacular mountain area comprising four river valleys. Limestone topography with waterfalls, gorges and cliffs. Exciting flora. Several large mammal species. Interesting birdlife.	C1	214
AIGÜES TORTES Y LAGO DE SAN MAURICIO	224.0	National Park. Glaciated valleys, lakes, cirques and hanging valleys. Large coniferous forests. Many birds of prey. Interesting mammal and reptile fauna.	D1	214
TORTOSA Y BECEITE	292.9	National Reserve. Low mountain area with varied scrub and forest vegetation.	D2	215
DELTA DEL EBRO	640.0	Largely unprotected wetland in eastern Spain. Important bird wintering and breeding ground.	D2	215
LAS BATUECAS	209.8	National Reserve. Beautiful mountain region lying west of Madrid. Well known for game animals.	B2	216
GREDOS	228.2	National Reserve. Beautiful mountain region lying west of Madrid. Well known for game animals.	B2	216
MONFRAGUE	178.5	Natural Park. Large stretch of the Tajo valley in Extremadura region. Many birds of prey.	B2	217
HAYEDO DE TEJERA NEGRA	13.9	Natural Park. Mountainous region of dark-grey Silurian slates and quartzites. Forests of beech, oak, yew, mountain ash and pine.	B2	218
TABLAS DE DAIMIEL	18.1	National Park. Shallow inland lake with both fresh- and brackish-water plants. Numerous small islands. Important breeding and overwintering area for wildfowl, especially duck.	B2	218
CAZORLA Y SEGURA	764.5	National Game Reserve. Landscape of peaks, valleys, gorges and cliffs. "The Spanish Switzerland."	C3	218
SERRANIA DE RONDA	219.6	National Reserve. Rugged limestone mountains. Ancient relict woodland.	B3	219
DOÑANA	757.7	National Park. Wetland of European importance. Dune heath, cork-oak forest, pine woods and brackish marshes. Fine mammal and reptile fauna. Diverse birdlife with many rare species.	A3/B3	220
CAÑADAS DEL TEIDE	135.7	National Park. Volcanic caldera surrounding 3719-metre Pico del Teide. Lava flows, rocky outcrops with areas of sand and ash. Interesting endemic flora.	C4	222
CALDERA DE TABURIENTE	46.9	National Park. Enormous steeply rimmed volcanic crater. Pine forest and sub-alpine flora.	C4	223
GARAJONAY	39.7	National Park. Remarkable forest of laurel trees on volcanic terrain. Lush vegetation.	C4	223
TIMANFAYA	51.1	National Park. Portion of volcanic island of Lanzarote. Sparse vegetation contains several endemic species.	D4	223

CAZORLA Y SEGURA A beautiful mountain reserve in Southern Spain containing the headwaters of the Guadalquivir. Earth movements and erosion through wind and rain have endowed its limestone topography with many spectacular cliffs and gorges.

The dominant landform of the Iberian peninsula is the meseta, a massive block of ancient rocks faulted into a series of plateaux averaging some 600 metres above sea level. A central mountain chain, formed by the Sierra de Gredos and the Sierra de Guadarrama, separates the higher northern plateaux from the slightly lower southern blocks. In the south the meseta is flanked by a long, narrow fertile plain, open to the Atlantic and drained by Spain's only navigable river, the Guadalquivir, while to the northeast the broad triangle of the Ebro Valley forms an arid lowland tract between the meseta and the foot-hills of the Pyrenees.

The hinterland of the meseta is barren, inaccessible and sparsely populated – a harsh and heavily eroded landscape characterized by flat-topped or rounded hills and broken-up plateau regions, quite unlike the sharp angular features of the Alps and best described by the Spanish term *muela*, meaning shaped like a molar tooth.

The Spanish climate is generally continental in character, but even so the country has great climatic variation. The mild, humid northwest is heavily forested, while the rest of the country, particularly the Ebro basin and the extreme southeast, receives only a modest winter rainfall and is parched throughout the summer months. The kermes Oak and stone pine are the most common trees, but more typical still is scrubby vegetation of the maquis with stunted oaks, wild thyme and lavender. In the extreme southeast, even this is replaced by the low bushes, lichens and drought-resistant grasses of the *calvero*, the esparto grasslands that flower briefly in spring and autumn. The animal life, predominantly European in the north, contains representatives of Africa'a fauna in the south. The peninsula forms a crucial link in many bird-migration routes.

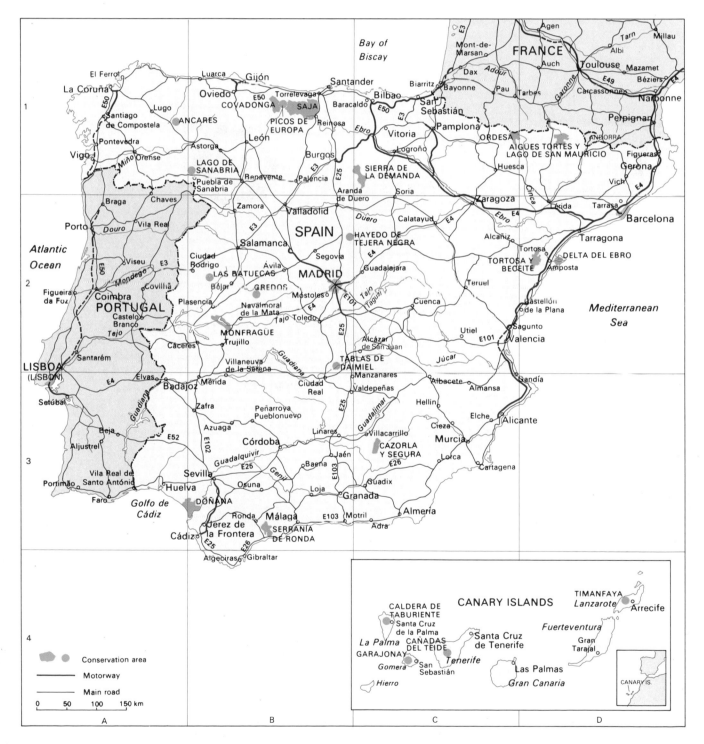

209

SPAIN

Ancares National Reserve

On the northwest slope of the Sierra de las Ancares lies one of the smallest of a series of National Reserves which extends the length of the Cordillera Cantabrica from Santander to Lugo. Two thousand hectares are planted with conifers, particularly with Scots pinc, a tree that is not indigenous to the area.

Natural deciduous woodlands of oak, beech, holly, alder, hazel and birch are found on the slopes of the Sierra Agulleiro and Barreira and in the Valle de Peñarrubia. The relatively cool, damp climate encourages a lush vegetation and on some of the higher areas peat bogs have developed. Above the tree line there are extensive areas of natural mountain pasture.

Although there are several small villages in the reserve, the brown bear is said to survive as well as the wolf, though in small numbers. Apart from the main game animals – red deer, roe deer, hares and rabbits – the mammal fauna includes wild cats, genets, foxes and red squirrels. A small population of capercaillie lives in the forest; this important game bird is not hunted at present in Spain because its numbers have fallen in recent years.

Covadonga National Park

Established in 1918, this, Spain's first National Park, is situated on the beautiful western flank of the Picos de Europa at the highest point of the Cordillera Cantabrica. It extends eastwards from Covadonga in Oviedo Province to the Rio Cares in León province. The rocks, mostly of Carboniferous limestones, create a typical karst landscape, however, schists and sandstones occur in some areas and the whole of this northerly region is one of considerable ecological diversity.

Covadonga National Park is an area of outstanding scenic beauty with high peaks, reaching 2400 metres or more, clear lakes of glacial origin, dark forests of beech and oak and extensive green pastures. The famous Cantabrican mists enhance the mysterious enchantment of the region. Although there are no permanent inhabitants, there is, however, a pastoral tradition and sheep, goats, pigs, horses and cattle graze widely, maintaining the green swards and also preventing forest regeneration. The tree cover, formerly much more extensive, is predominantly of beech at higher altitudes and the pedunculate, sessile and Pyrenean oaks at lower levels. Yew still occurs in shady, dry valleys, but is less widespread than in the past.

Throughout the beech woods there are many interesting plants, particularly spurge laurel, green hellebore, bilberry and kidney saxifrage. Bulbous corydalis, dog's tooth violet, *Narcissus* species, Pyrenean squill and oxlip occur in woods at higher altitudes. Forest clearance has resulted in areas of heath-covered leached soils on which grow gorse and several *Genista* and *Erica* species, together with bilberry, heather and the attractive Saint Dabeoc's heath. The grasslands consist of low-level hay meadows, highland summer pastures and pre-alpine grassland, known as Rocailles. Depending on their aspect and the amount of grazing they are subjected to, all these areas can have a rich flora.

The fauna of the park, especially the vertebrates, is well known. Formerly the bear and wolf, both regarded as Spanish subspecies of the European forms, inhabited Covadonga and are said still to occur nearby in the Picos de Europa. The fox, wild cat, genet, badger, otter, pine marten, polecat, garden dormouse, European mink and the wild boar are all found in the park. Chamois, now said to number several thousands, occur on the higher slopes.

The birdlife ranges from the larger predatory species such as the golden eagle, griffon vulture, buzzard, sparrowhawk and goshawk to small passerines such as Bonelli's warbler, pied flycatcher, rock thrush, black-eared wheatear, black redstart and several species of larks, pipits and buntings. Common and alpine choughs are frequent; the latter have been seen feeding on scraps left by visitors in the car park at Lake Ercina. The bee-eater, wallcreeper, Egyptian vulture, hen-harrier and Montagu's harrier, capercaillie, black woodpecker and short-toed eagle are also found in the region.

Several proposals have been made for enlarging the park, particularly on the east side and on the south boundary, to ensure protection for woodlands on the other side of the Dobra valley. This would make good sense ecologically because at present the boundaries are arbitrary.

ST DABEOC'S HEATH – An evergreen undershrub with purple flowers, it is found on heaths and in open woods.

COVADONGA

Llerices
Covadonga
Sierra de Covadonga
La Trapa
Comeya
Casaño
Dobra
Fana
Lago de Enol
Pelabarda
Pomperi
Osu
Minas de Buferrera
Buferrera
Lago de la Ercina
Llorosos 1792
San Roman
Primiello 1228
Cien
Amieva
Junjumia
Stella
Pico Robecas 1663
Majada de Ario
Cares
COVADONGA NATIONAL PARK
Torre Blanca 2290
San Ignacio
La Jocica
Caín
Biamon
Peña Santa 2596
Troba
Sierra Caballo
Corona
Cordiñanes
Cares
Posada de Valdeon
Los Llanos
Prada

Rock and pasture
Agricultural land
Woodland
National park

0   2   4 km

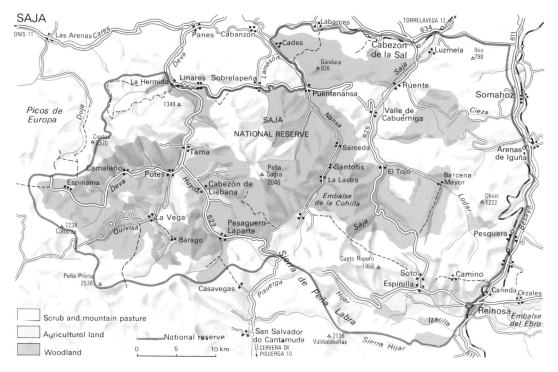

SAJA

ONIS 11 · Las Arenas Cares · Panes · Cabanzon · Labarces · Cabezón · TORRELAVEGA 12 634

Cades · Gándara 926 · Cabezón de la Sal · Luzmela · Ibio 798

La Hermida · Linares · Sobrelapeña · Puentenansa · Ruente · Somahoz

Picos de Europa · 1349 · SAJA NATIONAL RESERVE · Valle de Cabuérniga · Cieza

Conter 2370 · Tama · Peña Sagra 2046 · Sarceda · Arenas de Iguña

Camaleño · Potes · Cabezón de Liébana · Santotis · El Tojo · Barcena Mayor

Espinama · La Lastra · Embalse de la Cohilla · Obios 1222

Deva · 2234 Coriscao · Quivisa · La Vega · Pesaguero-Laparte · Saja · Pesquera

Bárago · Peña Prieta 2536 · Cueto Ropero 1958 · Soto · Camino

Casavegas · Pisuerga · Sierra de Peña Labra · Espinilla · Cañeda · Orzales

San Salvador do Cantamuda · 2136 Valdecebollas · Sierra Hijar · Izarilla · Reinosa · Embalse del Ebro

CERVERA DE PISUERGA 10

☐ Scrub and mountain pasture
☐ Agricultural land
☐ Woodland

National reserve

0   5   10 km

Saja National Reserve

On the east side of the Picos de Europa and extending as far as the vast Embalse del Ebro is the largest National Reserve in Spain. It occupies the northern slopes of the Cordillera Cantabrica and covers practically the whole of the western half of Santander Province apart from the coastal fringe. About two-thirds of the area is controlled by ICONA (the nature conservation section of the Ministry of Agriculture) and the Spanish Forest Service; the remainder is private property. There are many peaks over 2000 metres, the highest being Pico de Peña Prieta at 2536 metres. Several rivers run through the reserve, including the Saja, which drains north to the Bay of Biscay and the Ebro, which rises in the reserve and crosses the country to the Mediterranean. The abundance of water has created numerous marshes and bogs.

Most of the reserve is covered with beech and oak forest. Beech grows particularly well on Saja mountain, while the pedunculate oak is more extensive in the north, growing mainly between 600 and 700 metres, but in places extending to 1000 metres. Some beech trees reach an enormous size, occasionally up to 30 metres in height. The famous Cubilón oak in the valley of Cabuérniga is 27 metres high and more than 3 metres in diameter. However, the forest cover is very varied, as one would expect in such a large area, with cork oaks, chestnuts and a rich shrub layer of hazel, holly, blackberry, broom and *Erica* species.

In spite of the presence of a considerable human population and many villages, the brown bear survives on Monte Palombera and Híjar, and the wolf, which, it is claimed, attacks sheep in the autumn and winter, is said to be increasing in spite of hunting. The red deer – reintroduced in the 1950s – roe deer, wild boar, chamois, badger and wild cat occur in various parts of the reserve, mainly in forested areas. The capercaillie is found in small numbers and is, at present, a protected species.

Industry, apart from a small mine and a hydroelectric installation on the Nansa River, is virtually absent. Farming is the most important activity, particularly grazing of domestic stock and growing grapes, wheat, maize, rye and potatoes.

SAJA Although largely covered by vegetation, the now tilted bedding plains along which the Cantabrican limestones were laid down, can here be clearly seen.

1 ANCARES
Information: Delegacion Provincial de Turismo, Avenida García Portela 7, Lugo
Access: from Beccerea, 43km SE of LUGO
Open: Unrestricted except during the hunting season
Facilities: Wardens on site

2 COVADONGA
Information: Oficina de informacíon del Parque Nacional de Covadonga, Servicio Provincial de ICONA, calle Uría 10, Oviedo
Access: from Covadonga, 85km E of OVIEDO
Open: Unrestricted
Facilities: Information centre at Oviedo. Refuges within the park. Nature trails. Wardens on site

3 SAJA
Information: Delegacion Provincial de Turismo, Plazo Velarde 1-1°, Santander
Access: from SANTANDER, OVIEDO or REINOSA
Open: Unrestricted
Facilities: Wardens on site

211

Picos de Europa National Reserve

A superb mountain area in the Cordillera Cantabrica, the Picos de Europa lies south-east of the Covadonga National Park. The landscape of the reserve is as grandiose as its name implies and consists of the Los Urrieles Massif, the steepest and most rugged of the Cantabricans. The highest points are the peaks of Naranco de Bulnes (2516 metres) and Torre Cerredo (2648 metres).

At these heights the winters are long and cold, and snow lies on the ground from December to May or for even longer in some areas. As in the Covadonga Park humid winds, blowing in from the Bay of Biscay, often bring cloud and mist into the reserve. Nevertheless it is frequently possible to climb above the cloud layer and emerge into brilliant sunshine.

The Picos are composed of hard pale-coloured limestones dating from the lower Carboniferous. The stone has weathered and fragmented to form extensive scree slopes in many places. Huge morainic deposits at 1700 metres near Peña Vieja form a flat area of

alpine pasture, on which the Aliva Refuge is situated. In this area and close to the Parador there are numerous orchids, among them the man orchid, fragrant orchid, fly orchid, early spider orchid, burnt orchid and black vanilla orchid: gentians, saxifrages and narcissi are also common. Most of the reserve is too exposed for tree growth, but in sheltered valleys willows, hazels and maples form a scrubby growth. Where trees are able to grow, the commonest species are Pyrenean oak, beech, birch, ash, alder and the large-leaved lime.

The fauna was formerly much richer than it is today and the reserve used to be one of the best localities in northern Spain for bears and wolves. The former animal is protected by law, but the latter is regarded as a game species in some places. The populations of both these species, and of the roe deer, are now much reduced; the chamois, however, is still relatively common. The Spanish ibex has disappeared and plans have been made for its reintroduction. Some limited hunting by local villagers is permitted.

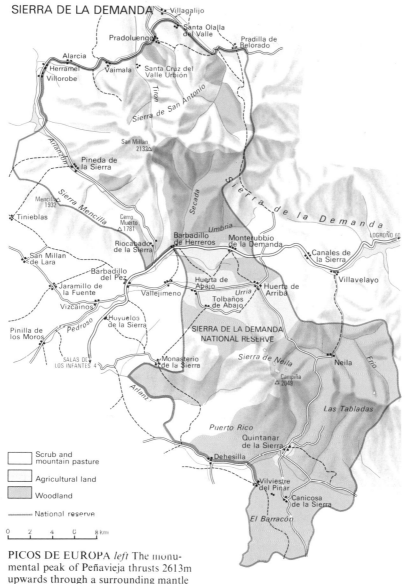

SIERRA DE LA DEMANDA

Scrub and mountain pasture

Agricultural land

Woodland

National reserve

0 2 4 6 8km

PICOS DE EUROPA *left* The monumental peak of Peñavieja thrusts 2613m upwards through a surrounding mantle of weathered debris.

1 PICOS DE EUROPA
Information: Delegacion Provincial de Turismo, Plaza Velarde 1-1º, Santander
Access: from Espinama, 127km SW of SANTANDER or Portilla de la Reina, 115km NE of LEÓN
Open: Unrestricted
Facilities: Refuge within the park. Cable car to the cliff tops from the Parador Fuente De

2 LAGO DE SANABRIA
Information: Delegacion Provincial de Turismo, Avenida de Italia 11, Zamora
Access: from Ribadelago, 18km NW of PUEBLA DE SANABRIA
Open: Unrestricted

3 SIERRA DE LA DEMANDA
Information: Delegacion Provincial de Turismo, Plaza Alonso Martínez 7, Burgos
Access: from Salas de los Infantes, 47km SE of BURGOS
Open: Unrestricted except during the hunting season
Facilities: Wardens on site

Lago de Sanabria Natural Park

In the high plateau of the Segundera massif lies the Lago de Sanabria Natural Park, an area of lakes and mountain streams. The River Tera, the largest in the park, has its source at the foot of the 2124-metre Peña Trevinca and, before entering Lago de Sanabria at the centre of the park, flows underground through the Cueva de San Martín – a cave which has been scheduled as a site of natural interest. In dry, hot summers some sections of the river dry out, but in winter, when rainfall is plentiful, the total water surface increases and many temporary pools form.

In the surrounding area there are extensive forests of deciduous trees – oaks, sweet chestnuts, birches, poplars, alders and ash trees, as well as Scots pines, yews and several other species. The shrub flora is rich and contains five species of *Genista* and four of *Erica*. The game fauna includes roe and fallow deer, wild boars, partridges, wolves, rabbits and hares. The wild cat and both the pine and beech marten inhabit the woodlands.

The birdlife includes eagles, vultures, kites and the eagle owl.

Sierra de la Demanda National Reserve

The Sierra de la Demanda form part of an extensive mountain range southeast of Burgos. The reserve is contiguous with the National Reserves of Cameros, Urbión and the Coto Nacional de Ezcaray, which together total 275,000 hectares. Three peaks in the northwestern part of the reserve are over 2000 metres, Triguera, San Millan and Cabeza Aguilez. There are several lakes, six of which have been constructed by the Forest Service to improve facilities for anglers.

The forests, particularly those containing Scots pine, beech and the Pyrenean oak, are an important natural resource. As it is chiefly a hunting reserve, game animals are plentiful and include many species. Roe deer and wild boar are the most numerous; some red deer and a few wolves are also found. The birdlife includes among other species eagle owls, golden eagles, goshawks, sparrowhawks and griffon vultures.

213

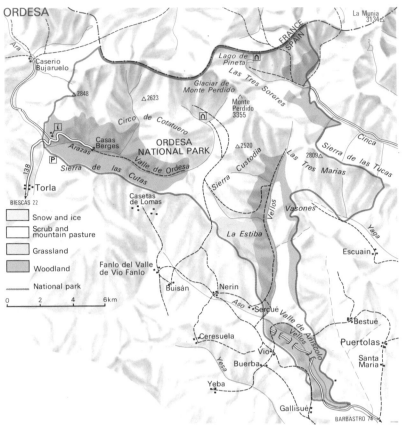

ORDESA

Snow and ice
Scrub and mountain pasture
Grassland
Woodland
National park

0 2 4 6km

Ordesa National Park

Established in 1918, Ordesa is one of the two oldest National Parks in Spain and has probably the most magnificent scenery of any. It is situated in the central Pyrenees and adjoins the French Pyrenees National Park; the whole area forms the largest and finest protected area in these mountains.

For about sixty years Ordesa National Park was much smaller than it is today, only 2046 hectares, and consisted mainly of a single valley, 15 kilometres in length with steep, rocky sides, towering 1000 metres above the River Arazas, and largely forest covered. From Monte Perdido (3355 metres), on the east side of the area, four valleys descend to the west and south. The most spectacular is the Ordesa valley, the original heart of the park. In 1978 three other valleys, Añisclo, Pineta and Gargantas de Escuaín were added, increasing the area to its present 15,709 hectares. The variety of landscapes derived from Tertiary and Cretaceous limestones is remarkable — waterfalls, gorges, immense rock cliffs, forests and glaciers.

Four tree species, Scots pine, mountain pine, beech and common silver fir dominate the forests of the park. Scots pine, widespread on the northern slopes, is replaced by the mountain pine above 1700 metres. Although there are extensive stands of beech, many of the finest trees have been felled. Associated tree species include yew, aspen, birch, alder, goat willow, and Italian maple.

The flora is rich and exciting; striking plants such as the yellow turk's-cap lily, the globe flower, the magnificent endemic Pyrenean saxifrage with its broad flower spikes, sometimes reaching nearly one metre in length, can all be seen. In the area's wet flushes smaller saxifrages grow together with numerous other plants such as primulas, gentians, the Pyrenean aquilegia, the alpine and large-flowered butterworts and the tiny German asphodel.

The fauna, of considerable interest, includes the chamois, roe deer, fox, wild cat, genet, badger, polecat, wild boar, otter and Pyrenean ibex. Among the small mammals found here are the red squirrel, pine marten, edible dormouse, garden dormouse, and the Pyrenean desman — a curious mole-like creature which hunts in streams. A large number of bird species have been recorded in the area. Of special interest are the golden eagle, lammergeier, an endangered bird of prey which is still said to nest in the park, the goshawk, peregrine falcon, rock nuthatch, rock sparrow and alpine chough.

Aigües Tortes y Lago de San Mauricio National Park

Located in a high-altitude region in the east central Pyrenees, on the west side of Andorra, this park was established in 1955. It was not included in the 1971 United Nations List of National Parks, however, because extensive forest exploitation and the presence of huge hydroelectric installations prevented it from meeting the protection criteria required. Since then the boundary of the park has been changed, more than doubling the area, and its protection status is under review.

Dominated by the massif of Els Encantats (2747 metres), the park consists of two glaciated valleys, one draining east and the other west, together with a large number of lakes, hanging valleys and spectacular cirques. Extensive forests of conifers cover large tracts of the mountain side. The common silver fir and the Scots pine are the commonest trees at middle altitudes, while in the high mountain zone, between 1700 metres and 2000 metres, the mountain pine dominates. The herbaceous plants include such beautiful species as martagon lily, yellow turk's-cap lily, alpine gentian, *Gentiana nivalis, Gentiana burseri* and yellow mountain saxifrage.

The birdlife is particularly noted for large birds of prey such as golden eagles, buzzards, honey buzzards and red kites. Black woodpecker and capercaillies are found in the forests: wallcreepers, snow finches and rock thrushes occur in open rocky habitats.

Chamois and wild boar are the only large mammals found in the park. The curious, mole-like Pyrenean desman and the Pyrenean brook salamander inhabit river margins. This salamander, known only from these mountains, prefers cold, clear waters, where temperatures do not exceed 15°C and is most abundant at about 2000 metres altitude. Most are dull-coloured with a rough skin and some have pale markings along the back.

Tortosa y Beceite National Reserve

Inland from the hot and crowded Costa del Azahar and just west of the great delta of the River Ebro are the low-altitude mountains of Puertos de Tortosa and Beceite – an area of peaks, ravines and shady forests. The highest points in the reserve are Barcina (1360 metres) and Monte Caro (1447 metres), which rises almost vertically from the littoral plain on the southeast side.

Spiny shrubs, particularly hedgehog broom and *Genista scorpius*, grow at the highest levels, above 1300 metres. Lower down, the lovely snowy mespilus and rosemary are common. Yew has established itself on the upper parts of the steep ravines, while the kermes and Portuguese oaks dominate the lower regions. Three isolated and almost pure patches of beech surrounded by pine forest occur between 1000 and 1250 metres at Tortosa, Rocquetas and La Cenia. The commonest pines are Aleppo, black and Scots.

The varied forest and scrub vegetation provides an excellent habitat for wildlife and wild boar and Spanish ibex are common; mouflon, wild cats, genets and foxes may also be seen. The birdlife includes the rare black vulture, golden eagles, sparrowhawks, goshawks, red kites and owls.

Delta del Ebro

The east coast of Spain has few wetlands of any size, but the delta of the River Ebro, 70 kilometres southwest of Tarragona, is an exception. However, apart from one or two small areas this wetland, although of international importance for wildfowl, is not yet fully protected.

About two-thirds of the total area – a huge "fan" projecting into the Mediterranean – is now cultivated and planted mainly with rice. On the remainder a vast holiday development of hotels, apartments and marinas was proposed, but, after many protests, the government refused permission for its construction. Marshes and saline, or brackish, lagoons cover about 5200 hectares, and dunes, together with other uncultivated ground, make up a further 2850 hectares. In places there are reedbeds and other aquatic and marsh vegetation. About 1227 hectares form part of a National Game Reserve for wildfowl.

In spite of extensive reclamation the delta is still important for wintering birds such as wigeon, shoveler, mallard, teal and pochard, with total numbers sometimes reaching 35,000. The salt pans south of the Los Alfaques Peninsula attract flamingos and many waders, gulls and terns.

1 ORDESA
Information: Parque Nacional de Ordesa, Servicio Provincial de ICONA, General Las Heras 8, Huesca
Access: from Torla, 90km NE of HUESCA
Open: Unrestricted
Facilities: Information centre. Hotel, camp site and refuges within the park. Nature trails. Wardens on site

2 AIGÜES TORTES Y LAGO DE SAN MAURICIO
Information: Parque Nacional de Aigües Tortes y San Mauricio, Servicio Provincial de ICONA, calle del General Yagüe 37, Lerida
Access: from Bohi, 135km N of LERÍDA or ESPOT, 170km NE of LERÍDA
Open: Unrestricted
Facilities: Nature trails. Wardens on site.

3 TORTOSA Y BECEITE
Information: Delegacion Provincial de Turismo, Rambla del Generalisimo 25-2°, Tarragona
Access: from TORTOSA
Open: Unrestricted except during the hunting season
Facilities: Footpaths within the reserve. Wardens on site.

4 DELTA DEL EBRO
Information: Delegacion Provincial de Turismo, Rambla del Generalísimo 25-2°, Tarragona
Access: from AMPOSTA
Open: Unrestricted

PYRENEAN DESMAN *above* A mole-like creature which lives in riverbank burrows, the desman is easily identified by its unique spatulate muzzle and long tail.

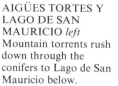

AIGÜES TORTES Y LAGO DE SAN MAURICIO *left* Mountain torrents rush down through the conifers to Lago de San Mauricio below.

215

Las Batuecas National Reserve

Situated in the sparsely populated Extrema-dura region, Las Batuecas National Reserve lies south of Salamanca and northwest of the Sierra de Gredos. At the heart of the region is the mountain of Peña de Francia (1723 metres); the Peña de Francia range forms the northern side. The mountains are wild and lonely with deep, narrow valleys, numerous springs and forests. In the north and north-east the main trees are oaks, sweet chestnuts, yews and hollies with the occasional beech, while to the south cork oak and strawberry tree predominate. Some trees, particularly oak, strawberry tree and holly, grow to a great size. Alongside steams in sheltered valleys, alder, ash and willows occur. The species most frequently found in the shrub layer are Mediterranean mezereon, *Genista scorpius*, narrow-leaved cistus, the lavender *Lavandula stoechas* ssp. *pedunculata*, mastic tree, terebinth, *Lygos sphaerocarpa*, *Rubus ulmifolius* and rosemary.

The animal life was formerly much richer, and included bears, wolves, black storks, imperial eagles and black vultures, but all have long since disappeared. On the other hand a few lynx survive and the roe deer and Spanish ibex have been reintroduced. Two pairs of golden eagles and about thirty pairs of griffon vultures inhabit the reserve.

In addition to its landscape and wildlife, Las Batuecas is well known for its caves and Neolithic cave paintings, particularly for those found at Canchal del Zarzalón, Ermita de Cristo, Canchal de las Cabras Pintadas and Risco del Ciervo.

Gredos National Reserve

The great capital of Madrid, with nearly four million inhabitants, is fortunate in having the beautiful Sierra de Gredos lying about 120 kilometres to the west. This region, in central Spain, has a continental climate with cold winters and warm, dry summers. Snow, on the northern slopes, may lie for five to six months of the year.

The rocks are of granite, gneiss and Silurian slate. On the south side of the reserve, where steep slopes descend to the Tietar valley, there are many waterfalls and deep torrent beds. Close to the 2692-metre Pico Almanzor, the most prominent feature on the reserve, lies the spectacular north-facing Cirque de Gredos, with its extensive area of erratics and other glacial phenomena.

Maritime pine is the most widespread tree in the central region of the reserve, while Scots pine predominates in the northwest. Mere remnants of formerly extensive forests of cork oak and sweet chestnut still exist. On the higher slopes there are many alpine flowers such as gentians, narcissi, paeonies and numerous *Genista* species. The beautiful yellow flowers of the alpine anemone *Pulsatilla alpina* ssp. *apiifolia* cover extensive areas of north-facing slopes in May.

The reserve is well known for its game species, the most numerous animal being the Spanish ibex, of which there are about 3000. The centre of the reserve, in the vicinity of Pico Almanzor, forms a protected zone in which the shooting of ibex is prohibited. This is the best place to view the ibex because here they have become accustomed to visitors and do not run away. In the summer the ibex keep to a zone between 1800 and 2400 metres, but in winter they descend about 1000 metres. The "Plataforma", at 1800 metres, which can be reached by car, is also an excellent ibex-observation point. There is competition for the pastures, however, because most of the local people are pastoralists and keep herds of cattle – the most common domestic animal.

The visitor can see Egyptian, black and griffon vultures, golden eagle, red and black kites, honey buzzard, alpine chough, stork, firecrest, crossbill and rock bunting.

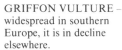

GRIFFON VULTURE – widespread in southern Europe, it is in decline elsewhere.

SPANISH LYNX Depicted here pouncing on its prey, the lynx is declining in Spain.

Monfragüe Natural Park

In the Extremadura region of southwestern Spain is an area of high mountains roughly the size of Switzerland, which has been very little disturbed by man and retains much of its original vegetation. The hillsides are clothed with primeval cork oak and holm oak woodland, a favoured breeding site for many birds of prey. After a long campaign by conservationists, the Monfragüe Natural Park, a 30-kilometre stretch of the Tagus valley, was established in 1979 to preserve the area's unique character. The area is increasingly threatened by reafforestation with eucalyptus plantations, in which the native fauna and flora cannot live – one-fifth of the park has already been replanted – and is confronted with the construction of hydroelectric works along the course of the River Tagus. In addition to these problems a nuclear power station began operating upstream in 1980, discharging waste water into the river just before it enters the protected area.

The birdlife in this region is an ornithologist's dream. It has one of the largest known colonies of black vultures, about sixty pairs, large numbers of griffon vultures as well as Egyptian vultures, golden, Bonelli's, booted, imperial and short-toed eagles, peregrine falcons, eagle owls, buzzards, goshawks, black and black-shouldered kites and marsh harriers. Both white and black storks nest in the ancient forests. The river, which is dammed in two places within the park, attracts many birds of passage, such as little and cattle egrets, grey and night herons, spoonbills and greylag geese.

With so many birds of prey present it is not surprising that the mammal fauna is also rich in species. Twenty-six are recorded, including red deer, mouflon, pardel lynx, genet, mongoose, rabbit, hare, otter, fox, badger, polecat, beech marten, wild cat and wild boar. In addition nineteen species of snakes and lizards breed either in the park itself or in adjacent areas.

1 LAS BATUECAS
Information: Delegacion Provincial de Turismo, Gran Via 9-1°, Salamanca
Access: from SALAMANCA or CIUDAD RODRIGO
Open: Unrestricted except during the hunting season
Facilities: Wardens on site

2 GREDOS
Information: Delegacion Provincial de Turismo, Alfonso Montalvo 2 prpal., Avila
Access: from Arenas de San Pedro, 140 km W of MADRID
Open: Unrestricted except during the hunting season
Facilities: Refuges within the park. Wardens on site

3 MONFRAGÜE
Information: Director conservador del Parque Natural de Monfrague, Servicio Provincial de ICONA, calle General Primo de Rivera 2, Cáceres
Access: from CACERES or NAVALMORAL DE LA MATA
Open: Unrestricted

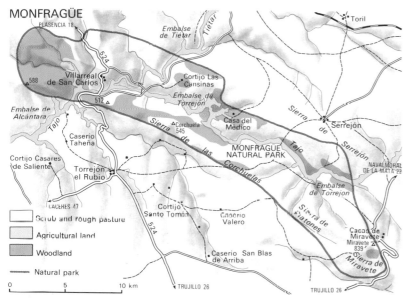

MONFRAGÜE

Scrub and rough pasture

Agricultural land

Woodland

Natural park

0   5   10 km

BLACK VULTURE
above This large bird of prey is now considered an endangered species.

GREDOS *below* The sierras are tinged with yellow in early summer.

217

Hayedo de Tejera Negra Natural Park

On the Silurian slates and quartzites of the Sierra de Riaza, which forms the provincial boundary in the northwest corner of Guadalajara, lies the Hayedo de Tejera Negra Natural Park, an attractive area of impressive beech-woods. The ash grey- and black-coloured rocks of the vicinity give the park its name. The area is contained within the northern part of the much larger National Reserve of Sonsaz, a region known for its severe winters,

TABLAS DE DAIMIEL

Agricultural land

Marsh and reeds

National park

0   1   2 km

where snow sometimes remains on the higher parts for six or seven months. The highest peak in the park is Butrera (2046 metres). The park's two rivers, the Lillas and Zarza, flow through a well-developed forest of beech, oak, yew and mountain ash. Scots pine has been planted in several places.

With such species as roe deer, wild boar, golden eagle, goshawk and red kite, the fauna is similar to that of many other Sierras in central Spain.

Tablas de Daimiel National Park

About 30 kilometres northeast of the provincial capital of Ciudad Real lies the wetland area of Tablas de Daimiel. It was created in 1973 to save it from extensive drainage and land reclamation, a threat which has not entirely disappeared; the surrounding area is intensively cultivated with vines and cereals and adequate protection from disturbances is therefore difficult to attain.

"Tablas" are areas of shallow water. In the Tablas de Daimiel the water fluctuates widely in level from year to year and derives from two rivers of very different origins, the River Cigüela, which brings brackish water from the high moorland of Cabrejas, and the River Guadiana, which rises 15 kilometres to the

south and carries fresh water into the park. In the floodplain of Tablas de Daimiel, the water from both rivers mingles, creating a distinctive hydrosere in which both fresh- and brackish-water plants are found; the reed *Phragmites australis* is the most favoured species in freshwater areas and the cut-sedge is the commonest in brackish water – the Tablas are said to have the most extensive areas of cut-sedge in Europe.

In the marshes there are numerous islands, the largest covering 30 hectares. Around the margins of the park are groups of *Tamarix gallica*, the only tree species on the Tablas. The mammal population consists mainly of smaller European species, such as polecat, otter, water vole, stoat, rabbit and hare, but in recent years the wild boar has considerably increased in numbers.

The Tablas de Daimiel was established primarily to protect its birdlife and is regarded as an area of national importance for breeding and overwintering ducks. More than 1000 pairs of red-crested pochards breed here, forming the most important colony of these birds in Europe. Among other breeding species are mallard, gadwall, garganey, shoveler, marbled teal, pochard, black-necked grebe, night heron, little egret, bittern and purple heron. Smaller marsh birds of interest are the bearded tit and Savi's warbler. In addition there are large populations of wading birds such as black-winged stilts, avocets, redshanks, ruffs and Kentish plovers.

Cazorla y Segura National Game Reserve

Of the ten National Game Reserves in Spain, the Sierras of Cazorla and Segura are probably the most beautiful and yet one of the least known to foreign visitors. Situated in southern Spain, about 325 kilometres south of Madrid, the reserve includes the upper reaches of the River Guadalquivir, together with a vast reservoir built for hydroelectric power and extensive mountains and forests. The landscape is a mosaic of peaks, valleys, rocky gorges and vertical cliffs and displays many typically karst limestone phenomena.

The two sierras are part of a great mountain massif, which, because of its magnificent scenery, has been called the "Spanish Switzerland". There are several peaks over 1800 metres; Empañadas, at 2106 metres, is the highest. The reserve has extensive upland coniferous forests of black pine, maritime pine and Aleppo pine. On the lower slopes and in the valleys there are broad-leaved woodlands containing holm oak, Portuguese oak, kermes oak and *Quercus lusitanica* as well as narrow-leaved ash, black poplar, strawberry tree, box and numerous scrub species. The flora is extremely rich and between 1200 and 1300 species have been recorded here. Many are either rare or endemic to the region, such as the beautiful Cazorla violet, which has intensely coloured crimson-carmine flowers with long, slender

1 HAYEDO DE TEJERA NEGRA
Information: Delegacion Provincial de Turismo, Travesía Beladiez 1, Guadalajara
Access: by forest road from Cantalojas, 70km SE of ARANDA DE DUERO
Open: Unrestricted

2 TABLAS DE DAIMIEL
Information: Parque Nacional de las Tablas de Daimiel, Servicio Provincial de ICONA, Avenida de las Mártines 31, Ciudad Real
Access: from Daimiel, 30km NE of CIUDAD REAL
Open: Wednesday to Sunday between 0900 and 2000 in the summer and 1000 and 1700 in the winter
Facilities: Information centre. Nature trails within the park. Warden on site. Observation towers

3 CAZORLA Y SEGURA
Information: Delegacion Provincial de Turismo, Reyes Católicos 1-1°, Jaén
Access: from Cazorla, 38km S of VILLACARRILLO
Open: Unrestricted except during the hunting season
Facilities: Refuges within the park. Wardens on site

4 SERRANÍA DE RONDA
Information: Delegacion Provicincial de Turismo, Puerta del Mar 12-2°, Málaga
Access: from RONDA or Coín, 33km W of MÁLAGA
Open: Unrestricted

spurs. Other plants of interest include a butterwort *Pinguicula vallisneriifolia* which catches insects on long, strap-shaped sticky leaves, and two lovely endemic *Narcissus* species, one tiny, growing near melting snow at the highest altitudes, and the other a trumpet daffodil, which grows 1.5 metres tall.

Since this is a hunting reserve, game animals such as the ibex, mouflon, fallow and red deer, wild boar and red-legged partridges are important, and the preservation of their habitats has enabled many other wildlife species to survive. There are about five pairs of both golden and Bonelli's eagles, as well as many peregrine falcons, goshawks, red kites, buzzards, griffon and Egyptian vultures. In the mountains the alpine accentor, rock thrush, blue rock thrush, wallcreeper, ortolan bunting and alpine chough are found, while the reservoir has attracted black-winged stilts, gull-billed terns, little terns and occasionally pratincoles as breeding species.

Serranía de Ronda National Reserve
Only two hours' drive from the crowded holiday beaches of the Costa del Sol is a wonderful region of wild, rugged limestone mountains, which, apart from the attractive town of Ronda, is rarely visited.

CAZORLA Y SEGURA The River Borosa waterfall lies in the eastern part of the reserve.

The forests in the National Reserve have been greatly depleted by overgrazing, fires, charcoal burning and felling, and the once magnificent holm-oak forests are now reduced to garrigue – a form of open scrub. In some areas, above an altitude of between 1750 and 1800 metres, a relict woodland, known as quejigal, can be found, composed mainly of oak with some maple. The trees, stunted, with short massive trunks and much-decayed wood, are several centuries old. At lower altitudes the most characteristic tree is the Spanish fir, which bears big purple cones.

In the early spring the road to Ronda is enlivened by a glorious display of *Iris planifolia*, a vigorous plant with lovely blue flowers, and by white splashes of the small, but large-flowered, hoop petticoat daffodil, which grows in rock crevices. The sweetly scented, paper-white daffodil, a characteristic plant of the region, is widely distributed.

Apart from the Spanish ibex, large game animals are not abundant in this reserve and shooting is therefore limited. The reserve has an exciting birdlife; golden, Bonelli's and booted eagles and eagle owls are all present.

DOÑANA

One of the finest wetlands in Europe occurs in the delta of the River Guadalquivir just north of Cadiz on the southwest coast of Spain. The area, a fascinating blend of marshland, woodland and dune habitats, is world famous for its birdlife, which includes almost every known European wildfowl species.

EGYPTIAN MONGOOSE – a small weasel-like mammal.

Doñana was first protected in 1969 and was as late as the early 1960s, so isolated that no road approached its borders and visitors had to travel by horse from the nearby village of El Rocío to gain access. Soon afterwards, however, an asphalt road was built along the edge of the marshes to the impressive Palacio de Doñana in the centre of the park and today a new coast road has brought extensive holiday development right up to the borders of the area.

Unfortunately this remarkable ecosystem faces several other threats. A proposal has been made to build a motorway through the park to the port of Cadiz; intensive rice cultivation in other parts of the delta disturbs the water regime and there is the danger of pollution from excessive use of insecticides and fertilizers.

For centuries Doñana was a royal hunting reserve and has never had any permanent settlements. This is probably why so much of the heathland, coastal dunes and marshes has survived, relatively unspoilt. The Palacio, built in the seventeenth century as a hunting lodge, is the only substantial building in the park and is now a biological research station.

Although the whole area, except for the coastal dunes, is flat, it embraces a variety of biologically diverse habitats; dune heath, pine woods, remnants of cork-oak forest and brackish marshes, or marismas, together with natural transition zones. Ancient arms of the Guadalquivir form canal-like depressions in the marshes and there are several shallow lakes that retain water even when the rest of the marismas dry out in late summer. In the spring, when water levels are at their highest, small elevated islands known as vetas stand out above the flooded delta. The marshes are dominated by glasswort, shrubby glasswort, *Arthrocnemum glaucum* and *Limoniastrium monopetalum*. The sandy heaths are shrub-covered, principally by *Halimium halimifolium* and green heather, and have extensive forests of stone pine and support many flowering plants.

Doñana is famous for its mammal fauna – fallow and red deer, lynx, mongoose, wild

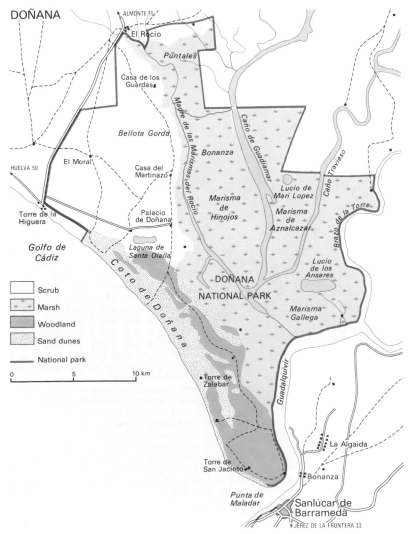

DOÑANA

Scrub
Marsh
Woodland
Sand dunes

National park

0   5   10 km

boar, wild cat, otter, polecat, fox, genet, red squirrel and badger. Its reptile fauna of snakes and lizards is one of the richest in Spain, and in addition there are two species of terrapin as well as the spur-thighed tortoise.

The National Park is perhaps best known for its birdlife – the magnificent imperial eagle, the flamingos on the lakes and the large breeding colonies of egrets, spoonbills and herons found in the cork oaks. Vast flocks of wildfowl are present in winter and during migration periods. Rarities such as the white-headed duck, marbled teal and ruddy shelduck all breed in the park. The purple gallinule, seldom seen in Spain, breeds in the marismas and, in summer, when the marshes are dry, the collared pratincole, stone curlew and pin-tailed sandgrouse may be seen. Black-winged stilts and the crested coot, one of Europe's rarest birds, also breed in Doñana.

DOÑANA
Information: Sr A. Camoyan, ICONA, Plaza de España, Sector IV, Seville
Access: from SEVILLA or JEREZ DE LA FRONTERA
Open: Permission to visit the Park must be obtained from: Estación Biológica de Doñana, c/Paraguay Nº 1, Sevilla
Facilities: Nature trails and footpaths within the park but visitors must be accompanied by a guard. Wardens on site Observation tower

DOÑANA Stretching over hundreds of square kilometres, Doñana's vast marismas form one of Europe's finest wetlands. At the edges *above* dry sandy heathland has in places been colonized by bracken.

221

CAÑADAS DEL TEIDE

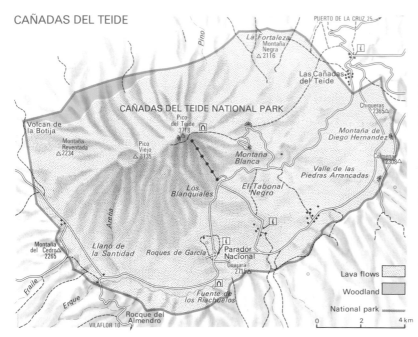

CAÑADAS DEL TEIDE The remnant of a 15km-wide volcanic crater in the centre of the Island of Tenerife marks the boundary of the National Park.

"TEIDE" PANSY

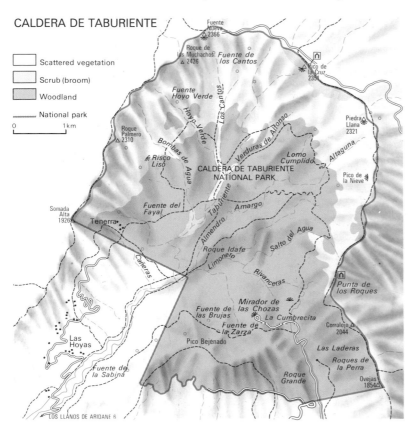

Cañadas del Teide National Park

The island of Tenerife is dominated by the volcanic cone of Pico del Teide (3718 metres), Spain's highest mountain. The gigantic caldera, 75 kilometres in circumference, lying at an average altitude of 2100 metres, forms the National Park. The landscape consists of lava flows, extensive plains of sandy erosion material, derived from the walls of the caldera – Los Roques de García – and gorges which were formed by eruptions after the main caldera had appeared. The gorges, known as the Cañadas del Teide, were used by the "guanche" shepherds for grazing sheep in the summer. (Guanche is the name given to the original inhabitants of the Canary Islands, who may have come from North Africa.)

The lava flows, some black and others reddish, stand out against the coarse yellow sands and volcanic ash, and, together with the spectacular rocky outcrops, give an impression of a lunar landscape. These inhospitable grounds are known as "mal país", or badlands and at first sight seem to be entirely devoid of vegetation. However, numerous plants, some brightly coloured, grow wherever the soil has been able to accumulate. The flora consists mainly of endemic plants, many of which are found only in this area of Tenerife. Two common shrubs, the strongly scented, white-flowered Las Cañadas broom and the sticky, yellow-flowered *Adenocarpus viscosus*, grow on the wide areas of pumice and volcanic debris. In flat areas and sheltered depressions several other shrubby plants occur, such as *Pterocephalus lasiospermus*, *Nepeta teydea*, *Micromeria julianoides*, *Scrophularia glabrata* and *Tolpis webbii*. At the Parador Nacional it is possible to see one of the park's most spectacular plants, the giant red-flowered *Echium wildpretii*, which grows to a height of 2 metres. Yellow-flowered *Centaurea arguta* and the lovely *Cistus osbeckifolius*, which has large pink flowers, are both local rarities. La Fortaleza and the southern cliffs of Montaña de Diego Hernández, which have been described as natural rock gardens, are particularly rich in flowers, found only locally. The higher reaches of Montaña Blanca and Pico del Teide have only a single species of flowering plant – a tiny, sweet-scented endemic pansy *Viola cheiranthifolia*.

Some prickly junipers and Canary Island pines occur in the area, but because the best pine forests lie outside the park, the most famous Tenerife bird, the blue chaffinch – a coniferous forest-dweller, does not occur within the protected area. The birdlife is in fact rather poor, consisting of peregrine falcon, kestrel, sparrowhawk, barbary partridge, raven, great grey shrike, canary, blue tit, the endemic canary pipit and the plain swift. Likewise there are few mammals or reptiles, and only the rabbit, a few mouflon – survivors of twelve introduced in 1970 – the vagrant hedgehog and a lizard *Lacerta galloti* are found.

Caldera de Taburiente National Park

The small island of La Palma is also known as "Isla Verde" – the Green Island – because of its extensive forests of Canary Island pine, the laurel *Laurus canariensis* and evergreen shrubs such as *Myrica faya*, tree heath and *Ilex canariensis*. In many areas, however, the forest has been cleared for growing fruit, vines, vegetables and tobacco.

The National Park consists of the enormous crater of an extinct volcano, about 10 kilometres in diameter, which dominates the centre of the island. The floor of the crater, lying between 600 and 900 metres above sea level, is surrounded by a steep-sided rim which exceeds 2000 metres in places and culminates in the Roque de los Muchachos (2426 metres). Located in the interior of the caldera is the Roque Idafe, which was sacred to the original inhabitants of the island.

Much of the park area is covered by pine forest. Above 200 metres the vegetation is more open and is dominated by a yellow-flowered shrub, *Adenocarpus viscosus* which forms vast carpets and fills the air with a sweet, sickly scent. In this zone there is a well-developed subalpine flora similar to that found on Tenerife. *Adenocarpus* species, together with *Nepeta teydea* and prickly juniper, occur on both Tenerife and La Palma, several species such as *Echium gentianoides*, *Viola palmensis*, *Cerastium sventenii*, *Tolpis calderae* and *Pterocephalus porphyranthus* are only found on La Palma, particularly on the highest ground.

The fauna is very poor: an endemic wild goat formerly inhabited the caldera, but is now extinct. Today it is populated by a few rabbits, several lizards and the small stripeless tree frog. The birdlife includes Canary Island races of species which are common and widespread elsewhere, such as the kestrel, raven, rock dove, rook, blue tit and black cap.

Garajonay National Park

La Gomera is one if the least disturbed of the Canary Islands. It has few roads, no airport and limited facilities for the tourist. Although the island is volcanic in origin, no eruptions are known to have taken place since the beginning of the Quaternary, about one million years ago. It is therefore probable that the vegetation has evolved naturally since then. The park encompasses about 10 per cent of the island. Within its boundaries are the highest point, the peak of Garajonay (1484 metres), and a small plateau lying

between 800 and 1400 metres above sea level. In the northeast, humid Atlantic winds often produce a cloud cap over the mountains, bringing moisture to the forests.

The main reason for establishing the National Park is to protect its remarkable forest of laurisilva, a type of vegetation which has virtually disappeared from the other islands. Laurisilva is an unusual type of woodland, confined to the Canary Islands, in which various species of laurel tree dominate. The forest of El Cedro at the head of the Hermigua Valley is probably the richest of this type on the island. It is characterized by *Laurus azorica*, *Ilex canariensis*, *Myrica faya*, *Arbutus canariensis*, *Persea indica* and *Salix canariensis*. Some of the laurels are very old and have enormous trunks.

Whereas on other islands exploitation of ground water to meet the demands of new developments has dried out the surface water, on Garajonay the woodlands are characterized by numerous streams, wet banks and rock faces, with a lush vegetation, notably of ferns, making them especially attractive. Mosses and lichens cover the trunks of many of the trees and, with the mists which are commonplace, give the forest the atmosphere of a tropical jungle. The insect fauna, particularly the beetles, is rich in endemic species. The laurel pigeon and the long-toed pigeon, both now rare species, are found on Garajonay exclusively in the laurisilva.

Timanfaya National Park

On the west coast of Lanzarote, a triangle of land lying below 510 metres is protected as a National Park. The entire island is volcanic and more than twenty-five craters occur in its 20,000 hectares of lava fields. Volcanic activity was recorded in the eighteenth and nineteenth centuries and although the last eruption took place in 1824 even now soil temperatures below the surface can be remarkably high as, for instance, on the ash cone of Islote de Hilario, where 140°C was recorded at a depth of 10 centimetres.

The park receives very little rainfall, only about 60 millimetres per annum, and consequently vegetation is sparse. However, moist air from the Atlantic has enabled a rich lichen-flora to develop and over twenty species are known, several of which are found nowhere else. Few flowering plants occur within the reserve itself and most of Lanzarote's endemic species, notably *Odontospermum intermedium*, *Echium pitardii* and *Polycarpea robusta* are found in the Famara district, at the north of the island.

There are few vertebrate animals; the most interesting is the lizard *Lacerta atlantica*, which grows to about 35 centimetres in length. It is very dark in colour – some specimens are almost black – an obvious adaptation to life in a desert landscape of volcanic ash and lava. It feeds on insects and vegetation and is sometimes found scavenging around villages.

1 CAÑADAS DEL TEIDE
Information: Parque Nacional del Teide, Servicio Provincial del ICONA, Avenida de los Reyes Católicos 31, Santa Cruz de Tenerife
Access: from Vilaflor, 77km SW of SANTA CRUZ DE TENERIFE
Open: Unrestricted
Facilities: Information centres. Refuges within the park. Nature trails. Cable car to Pico de Teide. Wardens on site

CALDERA DE TABURIENTE
Information: Parque Nacional de la Cáldera de Taburiente, Servicio Provincial del ICONA, Avenida de los Reyes Católicos 31, Santa Cruz de Tenerife
Access: from La Cumbrecita, 31km NW of SANTA CRUZ DE LA PALMA
Open: Unrestricted
Facilities: Refuges by park boundary. Nature trails. Wardens on site

3 GARAJONAY
Information: Parque Nacional de Garajonay, Servicio Provincial del ICONA, Avenida de los Reyes Católicos 31, Santa Cruz de Tenerife
Access: from El Rejo, 17km NW of SAN SEBASTIÁN
Open: Unrestricted
Facilities: Forest trail within the park

4 TIMANFAYA
Information: Parque Nacional de Tinanfaya, Servicio Provincial de ICONA, Avenida Marítima del Nortes, Las Palmas
Access: from Tinajo, 10km NW of ARRECIFE or Yaiza, 12km W of ARRECIFE
Open: Unrestricted
Facilities: Nature trail from the ash cone of Islote de Hilario

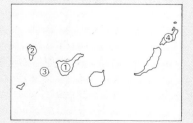

PORTUGAL

With forests, agricultural land and fisheries as its chief resources, and an economy largely based on exporting sardines, port wine and forest products such as cork, Portugal is not over developed industrially. Although it has a population of nine and a half million there are only three towns, Lisbon, Oporto and Coimbra, of over 50,000.

The north of the country, influenced by the Atlantic climate, has plentiful rainfall and is fertile and well populated, whereas, south of the River Tejo, there are vast heathland areas which in the summer are hot and dry. There are also many forests of pines and oaks, cork-oak plantations and shrub vegetation of the maquis type. Trees cover about 30 per cent of the total area, greatly in excess of the proportion in Spain. In the southernmost part of the country, the Algarve – one of the most popular tourist areas – winters are wet and summers dry. The vegetation is of a Mediterranean type with the addition of many Atlantic plant species. Its wildlife communities are distinctive, and include some which are peculiar to the southwestern part of the Iberian peninsula.

Although the flora is not as rich as Spain's, – about 3000 species of flowering plants of which about 65 are endemic – Portugal nevertheless has some extremely important botanical regions. The Algarve, which is one of these, has a wide range of habitats ranging from the treeless, windswept heathlands of Sagres and Cape St Vincent to wide dunes and coastal marshes farther to the east. Even the roadside verges in this area are marvellous places for plants, where in spring the visitor may see several species of *Narcissus*, asphodels, *Gladiolus*, *Iris*, *Erica* and *Cistus*. Around Monte Gordo the stone pine woodlands are bright with the whiteflowered broom, which is often accompanied by a carpet of *Narcissus bulbocodium*.

Although much of the original oak forests of *Quercus canariensis* and *Q. faginea* have long since disappeared, the Serra de Monchique is still one of the classic botanical localities of the Algarve. The limestone ridge of the Serra de Arrábida is also an important area, and over 1000 species of plants have been recorded.

To the birdwatcher the fauna is of particular interest. In addition to impressive birds of prey, such as red and black kites and three species of harriers, there is also the rare black-shouldered kite. Only the size of a kestrel, it is confined to central and southern Portugal, and relatively few pairs are known. The golden, imperial, bonelli's and booted eagles occur in the mountains and ospreys, which also breed here, are often seen on migration.

In the interior of southern Portugal, the mostly cultivated plateau land of Alentejo provides a suitable habitat for great and little bustards, and also for black-bellied and pin-tailed sandgrouse.

Pratincoles and black-winged stilts are also well known and nest along the Tejo valley and in the marshes of the Algarve. The pinewoods of the south are good places to see azure-winged magpies, and the marshes along the rivers have many interesting warblers, such as the great reed, cetti's and fan-tailed. Sardinian warblers are resident and both local and rufous bush chats may be seen in a few areas south of the River Tejo.

Portugal has a number of wetlands of international importance as feeding areas for wintering and migrating aquatic birds. The Ria d'Aveiro, about 60 kilometres south of Oporto, has 6000 hectares of lagoons and salt pans which provide a favourable habitat for waders and gulls.

The Tejo estuary, close by Lisbon, forms a vast intertidal zone of mudflats at low tide, bordered by saltmarshes and rice fields, where many interesting wading birds and duck can be seen. Farther up the Tejo near Golega lies the nature reserve of Paul do Boquilobo, which was established on a temporary

basis a few years ago and has a fine freshwater marsh and lake. It has a heronry, which, with several different breeding species, is the most important in Portugal. The Sado estuary, 50 kilometres southeast of Lisbon, is also important for migrant birds and the coastal strip of sandy islands, marshes and mud-flats of the Algarve is an excellent area for aquatic species. Many of the birds in this area seem to have become used to the noise of aircraft from Faro Airport, which lies nearby.

Seventy kilometres north of Lisbon there are important colonies of cliff-nesting birds, and the Island of Berlengo, situated about 12 kilometres offshore, is a breeding locality for Cory's shear-water and the razorbill. South of Lisbon the coast between Sesimbra and Setubal, declared a Natural Park in 1977, has calcareous cliffs with nesting ledges for guillemots and a rich maquis-type flora.

There is one National Park, in the north, and seven other protected areas, either Natural Parks or nature reserves. On the Portuguese Atlantic Islands there is a nature reserve on Madeira and two on the Azores. A further nine have been proposed for mainland Portugal and two more for the islands. The Department for the Environment is the govern-ment body responsible for nature conservation and works through the National Service for Parks, Reserves and Heritage Landscapes. In addition the forest service has a department dealing with parks and reserves and also a section concerned with the protection of game species. There is a small voluntary society for the protection of nature, with 1600 members and a Portuguese ornithological society, both of which have some influence on policy. Local conservation groups have also been formed in Oporto and Braga. However, the total resources devoted to nature conservation are not great and much more could be achieved given more support from the government and the general public.

ALGARVE The popular southern coast of Portugal contains several of the country's nature reserves and offers a variety of marsh and duneland scenery as well as spectacular cliff topography.

PORTUGAL

The principal elements of the Portuguese landscape are the westernmost extremities of the major structural features that dominate the Iberian peninsula, modified somewhat as they fall away to a broad, and geologically much younger, coastal plain. The north of the country consists of a heavily forested mountain plateau, between 1000 and 150 metres high and deeply dissected by narrow valleys, many of which have cut down through the rock to less than 300 metres above sea level. North of the Douro estuary the plateau falls steadily towards the coast, but south of that river a major fault scarp separates the highlands from a broad, marshy plain. The centre of the country is marked by east-west mountain ridges – the westward extension of the sierras running across the Spanish meseta, but here less dramatic, rising to 500 metres in the west and to a maximum of 2000 metres in the east, in the Serra da Estrêla. All of the country's major rivers flow over the meseta in a series of narrow gorges and valleys. Gently undulating lowlands characterize the Tejo valley and the marshy plains of the Sado basin, separated from the south coast by the ridge of the Algarve mountains.

Mild, damp winters and hot, dry summers are typical of the predominantly Mediterranean climate, but the effect of the Atlantic is readily apparent, particularly in the north, where rainfall is everywhere greater than 900 millimetres and locally in excess of 2500 millimetres. However, in the east and south of the country conditions are very different: winter rains amount to little more than 635 millimetres anywhere and summer months are arid. Elm and poplar flourish in the dense forests of the northern plateaux, but are replaced by cork oak and chestnut in the central ridges. Pines are common in the coastal lowlands, but of greater significance here is the remarkable intermingling of plant species from northern Europe and the Mediterranean zone.

PARK/RESERVE	SIZE (km²)	DESCRIPTION	MAP REF.	PAGE NO.
PENEDA GERÊS	600	National Park. Horseshoe-shaped region of mountains and valleys. Variety of vegetation types.	C1	228
PATEIRA DE FERMENTELOS	14.9	Nature Reserve. Marshland area in Ria d'Aveiro. Vegetation dominated by rushes and eelgrass. Important wintering area for migrant water birds. Algae growth in lagoons, harvested for fertilizer.	B2	228
SERRA DA ESTRÊLA	522.2	Nature Park. Region of rounded grass-topped mountains, glacial lakes and deep valleys. Rich shrub and herbaceous flora.	C2	228
PAUL DO BOQUILOBO	3.93	Nature Reserve. Lake with surrounding marsh in Tejo valley. Willows, poplars and extensive sedge beds. Several heron species.	B3	230
ESTUÁRIO DO TEJO	228.5	Nature Reserve. Saline lagoons, marshes and mudflats. Outstanding area for aquatic bird life. Many breeding species. Rich dune and marshland flora.	B4	230
ARRÁBIDA	108.2	Nature Park. Rocky limestone ridge with extensive maquis vegetation. Over 1000 plant species.	B4	230
SERRA DE MONCHIQUE	c 130	Nature Reserve (Proposed). Mountain region with forest and heath.	B5	230
PONTA DE SAGRES	c 60	Nature Reserve. Plateau area of hard dolomitic rocks. Distinctive herbaceous flora.	B5	232
RIA FORMOSA	105.0	Nature Reserve. Coastal region of marshes, mudflats and sandbars. Important wildfowl feeding ground	C5	232
CASTRO MARIM	c 80	Nature Reserve. Series of shallow lakes and saline lagoons attracting large numbers of migratory water birds.	C5	233

CATTLE EGRET *above*
This egret may often be seen on grassland, where it typically feeds among grazing livestock.

ESTUÁRIO DO TEJO
One of Europe's finest wetlands lies virtually on the outskirts of Lisbon. It is exceptionally important for migrating wildfowl.

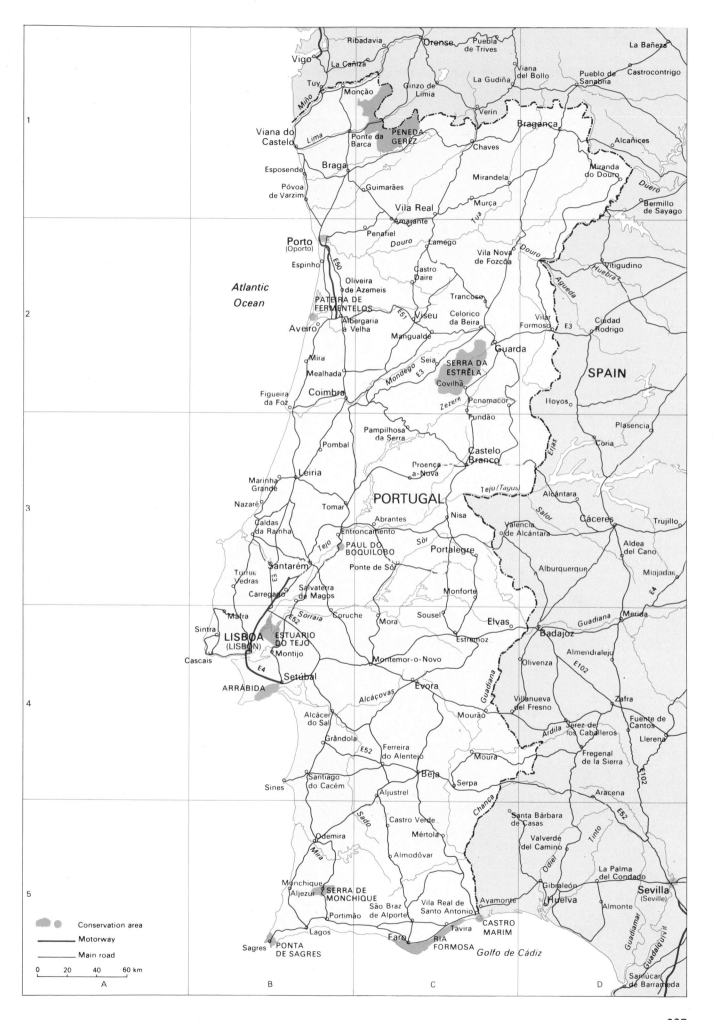

Vigo
Ribadavia
Orense
Puebla de Trives
La Bañeza
Castrocontrigo
La Cañiza
Tuy
Monção
Ginzo de Limia
Viana del Bollo
Pueblo de Sanabria
Alcañices
Viana do Castelo
Lima
Ponte da Barca
PENEDA GERÊZ
Verin
Bragança
Esposende
Braga
Chaves
Miranda do Douro
Duero
Póvoa de Varzim
Guimarães
Mirandela
Bermillo de Sayago
Vila Real
Murça
Tua
Porto (Oporto)
Amarante
Penafiel
Lamego
Douro
Espinho
Castro Daire
Vila Nova de Fozcôa
Douro
Vitigudino
Huebra
Atlantic Ocean
Oliveira de Azemeis
Trancoso
PATEIRA DE FERMENTELOS
Viseu
Celorico da Beira
Vilar Formoso
Agueda
E3
Ciudad Rodrigo
Aveiro
Albergaria a Velha
Mangualde
Guarda
SPAIN
Mira
Seia
SERRA DA ESTRÊLA
Mealhada
Mondego
Covilhã
Figueira da Foz
Coimbra
Zezere
Penamacor
Hoyos
Plasencia
Fundão
Pampilhosa da Serra
Coria
Pombal
Castelo Branco
Proença a-Nova
Erjas
Leiria
Tejo (Tagus)
Alcántara
Marinha Grande
Salor
Cáceres
Trujillo
Nazaré
Tomar
Abrantes
Nisa
Valencia de Alcántara
Aldea del Cano
PORTUGAL
Caldas da Rainha
Entroncamento
Sôr
Portalegre
Alburquerque
Miajadas
E4
Santarém
Tejo
PAUL DO BOQUILOBO
Ponte de Sôr
Torres Vedras
Salvaterra de Magos
Monforte
Carregado
Sorraia
Coruche
Mora
Sousel
Guadiana
Merida
Mafra
Sintra
LISBOA (LISBON)
ESTUARIO DO TEJO
Montijo
Cascais
Montemor-o-Novo
Estremoz
Elvas
Badajoz
Olivenza
Almendralejo
Setúbal
E4
ARRÁBIDA
Évora
Alcáçovas
Villanueva del Fresno
Zafra
Alcácer do Sal
Mourão
Guadiana
Fuente de Cantos
Grândola
Ferreira do Alentejo
Ardila
Jerez de los Caballeros
Llerena
E52
Moura
Fregenal de la Sierra
Santiago do Cacém
Beja
Serpa
Sines
Aljustrel
Aracena
E102
Castro Verde
Chança
Santa Bárbara de Casas
Odemira
Mértola
Almodôvar
Valverde del Camino
Tinto
Odiel
La Palma del Condado
Mira
Sado
Gibraleón
Monchique
Aljezur
SERRA DE MONCHIQUE
São Braz de Alporte
Vila Real de Santo Antonio
Ayamonte
Huelva
Sevilla (Seville)
Almonte
Portimão
Lagos
Faro
Tavira
CASTRO MARIM
Guadiamar
Sagres
PONTA DE SAGRES
RIA FORMOSA
Golfo de Cádiz
Sanlúcar de Barrameda

Conservation area
Motorway
Main road
0   20   40   60 km

227

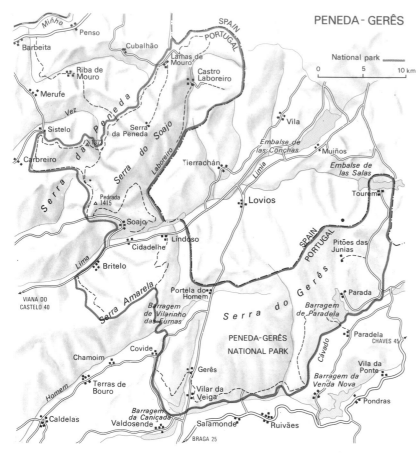

PENEDA - GERÊS

National park ———

0   5   10 km

SCHREIBER'S GREEN
LIZARD Slightly smaller
than the common green
lizard, this species is
confined to Portugal and
northwest Spain.

GUM CISTUS
An aromatic shrub
growing on dry hills in
south-west Europe.

Peneda-Gerês National Park

A region of immense valleys, mountain torrents, crystal-clear water, peaks and granite escarpments, Peneda-Gerês is situated along the northern frontier of Portugal and has long been famous for the beauty and grandeur of its scenery. The park forms a horseshoe-shaped area of mountains and valleys crossed by the River Lima and bounded by the River Cávado in the south and southeast. It was declared a National Park in 1970 and includes a large part of the mountain chains of Peneda, Amarela and Gerês, which are extensions of the Spanish Cordillera Cantabrica. The mountains, of moderate height, reach their highest point at Mt Nerosa (1545 metres). Three large reservoirs lie within the park, two of which are in the valley of the River Cávado. In addition a wolfram mine is sited within the boundaries; unfortunately the waste ensuing from it is dumped within the park.

The mean annual rainfall in this part of Portugal is comparatively high, about 1600 millimetres, and supports rich and varied vegetation. Much of the forest of pine and oak is extremely old and some trees have a trunk diameter of 2 metres. Among the flowering plants are eighteen species confined to the region of the park, and a notable rarity, *Iris boissieri*, is found only above 600 metres.

The fauna was formerly rich in large vertebrates, such as bears, wolves, wild goats and the lynx. However, although wolves are still not uncommon, the bears and goats became extinct in the last century and the lynx is very scarce and may have disappeared altogether.

Roe deer and wild boar still remain, but in small numbers, and a herd of small feral horses also occurs. Golden and booted eagles breed here, but would appear to be rare, and both the black-shouldered kite and Montagu's harrier can be seen. The reptile fauna is particularly interesting because of the presence of Schreiber's green lizard, which, in Europe, is confined to this corner of Iberia.

Pateira de Fermentelos Nature Reserve

About 60 kilometres south of Porto, where the River Vouga empties into an extensive estuary near the town of Aveiro, lies the Pateira de Fermentelos Nature Reserve, an area of marshland and reed beds within the 6000-hectare Ria d'Aveiro. The lagoons and marshes of the Ria have a vegetation dominated by rushes and eel-grass and are internationally famous for wintering and migrating aquatic birds. Saltpans in the north provide a habitat for waders and gulls, and there is a heronry of little and cattle egrets in the maritime pines around São Jaointo.

Although the lagoons are full of fish, extensive algal growth prevents large-scale fishing; the algae, however, are harvested and used as a fertilizer. Much of the area is greatly disturbed by hunters, and consequently fewer birds breed here than formerly. The establishment of the nature reserve, it is hoped, will provide adequate protection for the remaining species.

Serra da Estrêla Nature Park

High in the Serra da Estrêla, this nature park lying between the towns of Covilha and Gouveia in central Portugal contains the highest mountain (1991 metres) in the country. The terrain is composed of old crystalline and Palaeozoic rocks and the peaks have rounded, grassy summits. There are several glacial lakes, deep valleys and extensive moraines.

Because of the high rainfall the park has a variety of vegetation, ranging from Mediterranean to montane in character. Between 800 and 1500 metres there are fine forests of pedunculate oak, chestnut and pine, with understories of ericaceous shrubs, and, near Poco do Inferno at 1000 metres, relic forests of Pyrenean oak.

The shrub and herbaceous flora is rich in species, including several interesting endemics, and forms a plant community distinctive of the central Portuguese mountains. At fairly high altitudes the shrubs *Echinospartum lusitanicum*, *Halimium alyssoides*, *Genista florida* and *Cistus purgans* are found. Most of these plants have yellow flowers adding colour to what otherwise appears to be a barren landscape. A closer inspection reveals a great many delightful herbaceous plants – *Silene elegans*, the daisy-like *Phalacrocarpum oppositifolium*, the bellflower, the curved sandwort and the tiny *Jasione crispa*. In damp grassland at 1800 metres the large blue trumpets of the marsh gentian appear in late summer.

1 PENEDA-GERÊZ
Information: Parque Nacional
da Peneda-Gerêz, Rua de Santo
Geraldo 29, 4700 Braga
Access: from BRAGA or
PONTE DA BARCA
Open: Unrestricted
Facilities: Camp sites within
the park. Marked footpaths

**2 PATEIRA DE
FERMENTELOS**
Information: Serviço Nacional
de Parques, Reservas e
Patrimonio Paisagístico, Rua da
Lapa 73, 1200 Lisboa
Access: from AVEIRO
Open: Unrestricted

3 SERRA DA ESTRÊLA
Information: Serviço Nacional
de Parques, Reservas e
Patrimónío Paisagístico, Rua da
Lapa 73, 1200 Lisboa
Access: from GUARDA,
COVILHÃ or SEIA
Open: Unrestricted

BOOTED EAGLE A small eagle, easily confused with the rough legged buzzard; it has two distinct plumage phases. It is found mainly in hilly, forested country and breeds in southern and central Europe. Despite the introduction of protective laws in some countries, it is, however, still considered to be rare.

Paul do Boquilobo Nature Reserve
With a total of 2000 nests, Paul do Boquilobo Nature Reserve, a freshwater marsh in the valley of the River Tejo north of Santarem, has the most important heronry in Portugal. The reserve consists of a lake surrounded by marsh, with much submerged and emergent vegetation and willows and poplars on firmer ground. Its extensive sedge beds are grazed by horses and cattle, and some parts are cut by the local farmers. Night heron, squacco heron, little egret and cattle egret are among the principal heron species and about 2500 duck, mainly mallard, pintail, gadwall, shoveller and teal winter here.

Estuário do Tejo Nature Reserve
A complex of saline lagoons, marshes and mudflats, which is said to constitute one of the ten most important wetlands in Europe, the nature reserve stands on the eastern and southern shores of the Tejo estuary, just south of the bridge at Vila Franca de Xira.

RHODODENDRON Widely naturalized throughout western Europe.

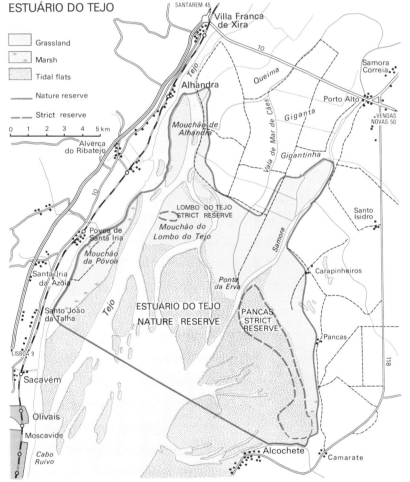

many breeding birds found both in the wetlands and on the drier surrounding areas are purple heron, marsh harrier, avocet, black-winged stilt and collared pratincole.

The dunes, damp hollows and marshlands, which are found in association with the wetlands, have a rich flora.

Arrábida Nature Park
An isolated outcrop of limestone on the coast of Portugal, southeast of Lisbon, the Serra da Arrábida lies between the towns of Setubal and Sesimbra. The mountain ridge, reaching to no more than 500 metres, with steep, scrub-covered slopes falling down to the sea, runs parallel to the coast. The extensive maquis scrub, the best of its type in Portugal, is the park's most interesting feature.

The vegetation is dominated by the kermes oak and such typically Mediterranean shrubs as Phoenician juniper, *Genista tournefortii*, strawberry tree and wild jasmine. In rock crevices and in the shelter of the scrub cover grow anemones, orchids, squills, *Fritillaria lusitanica* and wild tulips. Dense forests of Portuguese oak and, in its shade, the Spanish bluebell and the coral-pink western peony are found in sheltered valleys. Over 1000 species of plants have been recorded along the 55 kilometres of the Serra da Arrábida.

Among the birds found in these mountains are eagle owls, blue rock thrushes, black-eared wheatears and black redstarts. Many sea birds, including the common guillemot, breed within the park, on a group of offshore rocks which forms a zoological reserve.

Being close to the large urban centres of Lisbon and Setúbal, the Serra da Arrábida is a popular recreation area and attracts a great many visitors. Quarrying and second home development are, alas, degrading some areas.

Serra de Monchique Nature Reserve (Proposed)
The beautiful Serra de Monchique separates the southern Portuguese provinces of Alentejo and Algarve. Its rocks produce acid soils and the area's high rainfall gives rise to perennial springs and irrigated terraces. The village of Monchique, lying at 460 metres between the twin peaks of Foia (902 metres) and Picota (744 metres), is famous for its camellia trees.

The Algerian and Portuguese oaks, which formerly made up the mountain forests, have been almost entirely replaced with Eucalyptus plantations, maritime pines, cork oaks and olive groves. Picota, the most interesting area for plants, has some strikingly attractive species such as western peony, *Rhododendron ponticum* (here in its native habitat), two separate species of white heather, the strawberry tree, common primrose, the squill *Scilla monophyllos, Romulea bulbocodium* and the Spanish bluebell. The rare tree, *Myrica faya,* can be found, usually near streams.

Both Bonelli's and booted eagles are said to breed and it is believed that the lynx occurs.

The reserve is an excellent roosting and feeding area for many species of migrant and wintering aquatic birds. Waders number up to 70,000 and an estimated 75 per cent of the European avocet population winters here. Other species commonly occurring are grey plover, ringed plover, dunlin, redshank, curlew and whimbrel. The greater flamingo, greylag goose and spoonbill are also regularly seen. Among the

ARRÁBIDA

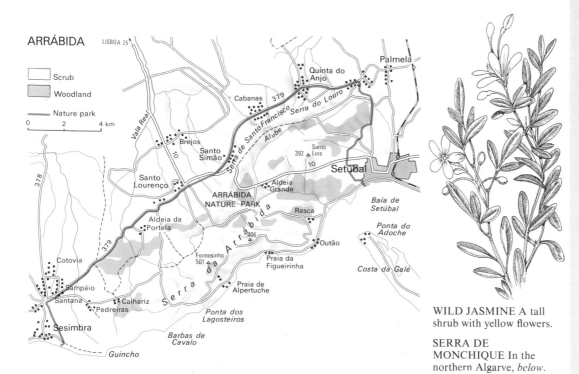

- Scrub
- Woodland
- Nature park

0   2   4 km

LISBOA 25
Vala Real
378
10
379
Brejos
Santo Simão
Santo Lourenço
Cotovia
Sampáio
Santana
Pedreiras
Calhariz
Sesimbra
Guincho
Barbas de Cavalo
Aldeia da Portela
Formosinho 501
Serra de Santo Francisco
Cabanas
379
Alube
392 Santo Luis
Serra do Louro
Quinta do Anjo
Palmela
Setúbal
10
ARRÁBIDA NATURE PARK
Aldeia Grande
Rasca
Ponta dos Lagosteiros
Serra da Arrábida
406
Praia da Figueirinha
Praia de Alpertuche
Outão
Baía de Setúbal
Ponta do Adoche
Costa da Galé

WILD JASMINE A tall shrub with yellow flowers.

SERRA DE MONCHIQUE In the northern Algarve, *below*.

1 PAUL DO BOQUILOBO
Information: Serviço Nacional de Parques, Reservas e Património Paisagístico, Rua da Lapa 73, 1200 Lisboa
Access: from SANTARÉM
Open: Unrestricted

2 ESTUÁRIO DO TEJO
Information: Serviço Nacional de Parques, Reservas e Património Paisagístico, Centro de Estudos de Migracões e Protecção de Aves, Rua de Lapa 73, 1200 Lisboa
Access: from LISBOA or MONTIJO
Open: Unrestricted except for two protected areas which are closed to visitors
Facilities: Observation tower at Pancas

3 ARRÁBIDA
Information: Serviço Nacional de Parques, Reservas e Património Paisagístico, Rua da Lapa 73, 1200 Lisboa
Access: from SETÚBAL
Open: Unrestricted

4 SERRA DE MONCHIQUE
Information: Serviço Nacional de Parques, Reservas e Património Paisagístico, Rua Justino Cumaro 4, 1° Dto, 8000 Faro
Access: from MONCHIQUE
Open: Unrestricted

CASTRO MARIM

Grassland and agricultural land

Marsh

Woodland

Nature reserve

0   1   2 km

PONTA DE SAGRES
above Erica species are
seen here in flower on a
cliff-top limestone
pavement.

Ponta de Sagres Nature Reserve

The extreme southwestern corner of the
Algarve is well known not just for its treeless
heaths and windy weather; the Ponta de
Sagres and Cape St Vincent are familiar to
the navigator because of their conspicuous
limestone cliffs and the bird-watcher also
knows it as a place to find the peregrine
falcon, chough and alpine swift. This region,
because of its hard calcareous dolomitic
rocks, which form a karst-like plateau with
very little soil, is one of the less fertile parts
of the Algarve. Its flora of low shrubs, bulbous
plants and herbs is quite distinctive. The
dominant shrub, *Cistus palhinhae*, has sticky
leaves and pure white flowers. Four other
Cistus species as well as many other scrub
species are found throughout. In spring spiny
thrift, the spiny shrub *Astragalus massiliensis*
and the orange flowers of *Calendula suffruti-
cosa* add colour to the heaths.

Ria Formosa Nature Reserve

The town of Faro on the coast of the Algarve
overlooks the Ria Formosa, a remarkable
area of marshes, mudflats, lagoons, saltpans

RIA FORMOSA

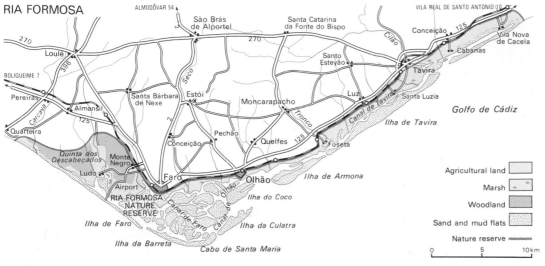

1 PONTA DE SAGRES
Information: Serviço Nacional de Parques, Reservas e Património Paisagístico, Rua Justino Cumaro 5, 1° Dto, 8000 Faro
Access: from SAGRES
Open: Unrestricted

2 RIA FORMOSA
Information: Serviço Nacional de Parques, Reservas e Património Paisagístico, Rua Justino Cumaro 5, 1° Dto, 8000 Faro
Access: from FARO or TAVIRA
Open: Unrestricted
Facilities: Marked footpaths within the reserve

3 CASTRO MARIM
Information: Reserva Natural do Sapal de Castro Marim, Vila Real de Santo António
Access: from VILA REAL DE SANTO ANTONIO
Open: Unrestricted
Facilities: Marked footpaths within the reserve. Observation hides

Agricultural land

Marsh

Woodland

Sand and mud flats

Nature reserve

0   5   10 km

PIN-TAILED SANDGROUSE *above*
This is the only species of sand grouse which nests in Europe.

RIA FORMOSA *left*
Cliffs define the rocky coastline of the Algarve, south of the town of Faro, close to the reserve.

and sand bars. The nature reserve extends from a point 15 kilometres west of Faro, eastwards beyond Tavira, for a distance of about 60 kilometres and is subjected to much human interference. Apart from a small section, the Ludo Game Reserve, which is protected except for fishing, the marshland and mudflat shellfish fauna is intensively exploited. The western part of the main reserve lies in the flight path of Faro airport and is close to farmland and an area of rapidly expanding urban development. In addition some of the offshore sand-bars are crowded with holiday homes, a problem that the National Service for Parks and Reserves is trying to prevent from spreading to hitherto unspoilt areas.

In spite of this activity on its doorstep the reserve is still recognized as a wildfowl feeding ground of international importance for such species as the greater flamingo, spoonbill and avocet, as well as for numerous ducks and waders. Breeding birds are also important, of which the little egret, grey heron, stork, black-winged stilt, Kentish plover and redshank are the most common species. The gull-billed tern, purple gallinule and pin-tailed

sandgrouse also breed on the reserve, but are rare. In warmer, sheltered localities, a Mediterranean-type flora has developed on drier coastal areas.

Castro Marim Nature Reserve
This nature reserve takes its name from a small town close to the mouth of the River Guadiana, which separates Portugal from Spain. It is almost entirely of ornithological interest and consists of a series of shallow lakes and lagoons, many of which are still exploited commercially for salt. Like most such wetlands lying in coastal areas, it is used by large numbers of water birds on migration and by many others as a wintering area. Twenty-three species of waders have been recorded overwintering here and the reserve also has an impressive breeding population. Castro Marim claims to have the largest colony of black-winged stilts in the country and for this reason the species has been chosen as the reserve's emblem. Also breeding in the area are the Kentish plover, black-tailed godwit, redshank, avocet, white stork and marsh harrier.

233

ITALY

Italy is known throughout the world for its historic and cultural treasures, but far fewer visitors are aware of its rich and diverse landscapes and wildlife. A magnificent alpine zone lies in the north, sweeping from west to east in a wide arc over 950 kilometres long; to the south is the arid limestone area of Calabria, and linking the two are the Apennines, the mountain chain which forms the backbone of Italy.

Three thousand years of settlement have greatly altered the natural vegetation of Italy and perhaps nowhere more so than in the coastal lowlands, where the once extensive forests have been either replaced by an open scrubby vegetation known as maquis, or planted with such tree crops as olives, figs and almonds. The former extensive wetlands have also disappeared, the last, the Pontine Marshes south of Rome, were drained between 1932 and 1934.

Although there are at present few National Parks and only four with adequate staff and management, numerous reports, studies and proposals have been presented concerning nature conservation over a period of many years.

In 1971 proposals were published for the creation of six new National Parks and various other categories of protected areas, including forty-one nature reserves and twenty-eight Regional Natural Parks.

So far the greatest progress has been made in the establishment of reserves in State Forests, and by 1980, 101, including six in National Parks, had been set up. Regional Forestry Departments in northern Italy have established fifteen other reserves, and six Regional Parks are protected by local authority legislation. There are, in addition, six important reserves – Wildlife Refuges and Protection Oases – managed by the Italian WWF. This organisation and Italia Nostra are the most active private associations in the country.

The importance of large numbers of effectively protected sites is underlined by the weakness of Italian law concerning hunting. The large number of hunters in Italy and the long season when game may be shot is well known and the toll taken of migratory birds has led to much international effort directed at persuading the Italian government that protection should be extended to more species and legislation be made more effective.

The bear, wolf, monk seal, ibex and chamois are protected, although in the case of the wolf enforcement is very difficult, particularly because of the illegal use of poison. All birds of prey, owls, storks, cranes, the flamingo and small birds, such as swallows, martins, tits, and warblers, are on the protected list, but many birds of passage protected in other countries may be shot.

GRAN PARADISO One of Europe's most famous National Parks. It was instrumental in saving the alpine ibex from extinction.

235

Italy consists of a narrow finger of land extending south from the Alps towards the continent of Africa, and the mountainous islands of Sicily and Sardinia. The Italian Alps form a crescent of mountains running along the northern border of the country from the high Graian Alps in the west to the Dolomites in the east. South of the Alps lies the great Padanovenetian Plain, which accounts for more than half Italy's lowland area. It was formed between two and three million years ago from material washed down by glacial meltwater and is still being built out eastwards by the Po and its tributaries.

The Italian Peninsula arose during the folding of the Apennines in the late Tertiary and early Quaternary. The mountains, forming a complex system of separate chains, are narrow in the north and south and broad in the centre – in the Abruzzi, where lies the Gran Sasso (2814 metres), the highest peak on the peninsula. In the central Apennines, limestone predominates at the highest levels and water is scarce except on the lower slopes. The southern Apennines are composed largely of limestones and clays giving way in the south to the granites of the La Sila and Aspromonte mountains.

The islands are of contrasting structure and geology. Sicily is a continuation of the Apennines, with calcareous rocks, whereas Sardinia is largely granitic and is a remnant of an extensive landmass that formerly existed in the Tyrrhenian Sea.

Italy has a wide variety of climates. The alpine region has a typical montaine regime with high precipitation and large seasonal and diurnal temperature ranges. The plain to the south also has a high annual temperature range and has normally no less than 1000 millimetres precipitation per annum. The climate of the southern peninsula and islands is Mediterranean, modified by the region's maritime position.

GENNARGENTU A beautiful and unspoilt mountain area on the eastern side of Sardinia. Despite its outstanding scenery, its National Park status is only "proposed".

PARK/RESERVE	SIZE (km²)	DESCRIPTION	MAP REF	PAGE NO.
ALPE VEGLIA	39.3	Natural Park. Typical alpine area with extensive pastures and larch forests.	A1	238
STELVIO	1370	National Park. Large mountain area containing the largest glacier in Italy. Forests and alpine meadows with	B1	238
ADAMELLO-BRENTA	4.36	Natural Park. Magnificent mountain area with only alpine population of brown bears in the Alps.	B1	238
PANEVEGGIO-PALE DI SAN MARTINO	158	Natural Park. Beautiful region of forests, mountains, lakes and waterfalls on dolomitic limestone rocks. Remarkable for its beautiful forests of firs and pines.	B1	239
FUSINE	0.45	Natural Park. Small but beautiful mountain region in the Julian Alps.	C1	239
GRAN PARADISO	730	National Park. Former royal hunting reserve on the French frontier. Famous for the ibex. Outstandingly beautiful alpine pastures. Complex metamorphic geology. Alpine botanical garden.	A1	240
MONTE DI PORTOFINO	12	Natural Park. Part of a rocky peninsula in NE Italy with fine maquis vegetation. Beautiful rocky coast.	A2	242
PUNTE ALBERETE	3	Wildlife Oasis. Marshland area with willows, poplars and elms in the Po Delta. Nesting populations of herons.	B2	242
VAL DI FARMA	c 45	Forest Reserve. Unspoilt watercourse through forests with both northern and Mediterranean tree species.	B2	243
ABRUZZO	400	National Park. Wooded mountain region in central Italy, famous for Apennine wolves and brown bears.	C3	243
BOLGHERI	21.8	Wildlife Refuge. Coastal cattle-grazed marshlands attracting large numbers of wildfowl and wading birds.	B2	244
MAREMMA	70	Regional Park. Unspoilt stretch of coastline south of Grosseto. Rocky outcrops, brackish marsh and woodland. Rich fauna, including the crested porcupine and several snakes and lizards. Important bird breeding locality.	B3	244
ORBETELLO	8	Nature Reserve. Series of tidal lagoons forming the most important breeding site for migrant birds in Italy.	B3	245
LAGO DI BURANO	3	Wildlife Refuge. Coastal lake attracting large numbers of waterfowl and waders.	B3	245
CIRCEO	74.5	National Park. Lowland area with woodlands and interesting coastal flora. Contains important Roman archaeological site.	C3	246
UMBRA	100	Forest Nature Reserve. Remnant oak and beech woodlands. Interesting variety of birds of prey.	D3	247
SALINA DI MARGHERITA	37	Nature Reserve. Large tract of salt lands attracting thousands of waterfowl. Both fresh- and brackish-water habitats. Rich flora of rushes and sedges.	D3	247
POLLINO	500	National Park (Proposed). Region of forests and streams in the highest part of the southern Apennines.	D4	247
CALABRIA	170	National Park. Beautiful montane area largely forested. Widely varied fauna.	D4	248
GENNARGENTU	1000	National Park (Proposed). Impressive wilderness landscape of rolling hills, rocky peaks and cliffs. Large areas of both woodland and maquis. Thriving population of mouflon.	A3/A4	248
ETNA	500	National Park (Proposed). Volcanic mountain with remarkable flora and fauna, including several endemic species.	C4	248

Belfort
Basel
Schaffhausen
Winterthur
St Gallen
GERMANY
Salzburg
Bad Ischl
Selzthal
Wiener Neustadt
Gyor
BUDAPEST
Biel
Solothurn
Zürich
Feldkirch
Wörgl
Kitzbühel
Salzach
Enns
Leoben
Raba
Szombathely
Székesfehérvár
Neuchâtel
Aare
Luzern
Landeck
Innsbruck
AUSTRIA
Judenburg
HUNGARY
Nagykanizsa
Kaposvár
BERN
Thun
Andermatt
Rhein
LIECHTEN-
STEIN
Lienz
Graz
Mur
Pécs
Lausanne
SWITZERLAND
Merano
Bressanone
Villach
Klagenfurt
Maribor
Varazdin
Balaton
Brig
ALPE
VEGLIA
St Moritz
Adige
Bolzano
Drau
Celje
Koprivnica
Drava
Osijek
Martigny
Domodóssola
Bellinzona
Locarno
STELVIO
Tirano
ADAMELLO-
BRENTA
PANAVEGGIO-PALE
Belluno
Trento
Udine
FUSINE
Ljubljana
Sava
Zagreb
Bjelovar
Virovitica
Aosta
Aronao
Varese
Como
Bérgamo
Lago di
Garda
Brenta
Treviso
Trieste
Karlovac
Sisak
Kutina
GRAN PARADISO
Milano
(Milan)
Brescia
Verona
Vicenza
Venezia
(Venice)
Rijeka
Kupa
FRANCE
Novara
Pavia
Oglio
Nogara
Adige
Poreč
Pula
Karlovac
Prijedor
YUGOSLAVIA
Torino
(Turin)
Po
Piacenza
Cremona
Mantova
Krk
Banja
Luka
Tuzla
Asti
Alessandria
Parma
Ferrara
Cres Rab
Bihac
Una
Urbas
Bosna
Cúneo
Tanaro
Génova
(Genoa)
Réggio
nell' Emila
Módena
Bologna
PUNTE ALBERETE
Ravenna
Karlobag
Pag
Gospić
Gračac
Jajce
Zenica
Travnik
Bugohno
Sarajevo
Savona
MONTE DI PORTOFINO
Forlì
Reno
Zadar
Knin
La Spézia
Pistóia
Rímini
Pésaro
Sinj
Goražde
Impéria
Pisa
Arno
Firenze
(Florence)
SAN
MARINO
Šibenik
Cetina
Nice
Ligurian Sea
Livorno
VAL DI
FARMA
Siena
Arezzo
Ancona
Porto Recanati
Split
Mostar
Cécina
Sansepolcro
Macerata
Brač
Hvar
Avtovac
BOLGHERI
Follónica
Elba
Grosseto
Perúgia
Todi
Folígno
Áscoli Piceno
Vis
Neretva
Kórčula
Mljet
Trebinje
MAREMMA
Orbetello
ORBETELLO
Viterbo
Terni
Rieti
Pescara
Ortona
Dubrovnik
CORSE
(CORSICA)
Bastia
Calvi
Golo
Corte
Aleria
LAGO DI BURANO
Tarquinia
L'Aquila
Adriatic Sea
Ajaccio
Taravo
Sartène
Civitavecchia
ITALY
ROMA
(ROME)
Avezzano
ABRUZZO
Vasto
Térmoli
UMBRA
Vieste
Bonifacio
Velletri
Latina
Sacco
Isérnia
Campobasso
Manfredónia
SALINA DI MARGHERITA
Porto Tórres
Tempio Paus
Olbia
CIRCEO
Fórmia
Cápua
Benevento
E56
Andria
Barletta
Molfetta
Bari
Sássari
Siniscola
Terracina
Cáserta
Avellino
Altamura
Brindisi
Macomer
Nuoro
Orosei
GENNARGENTU
Arbatax
Napoli
(Naples)
Salerno
Sele
Otranto
Basento
Potenza
Agri
Táranto
Lecce
Alghero
Tirso
Tyrrhenian Sea
Sapri
Lauria
Golfo di
Taranto
Gallípoli
Otranto
Oristano
Flumendosa
SARDEGNA
(SARDINIA)
Belvedere
Marittimo
POLLINO
Castrovillari
Gúspini
Carbónia
Cágliari
Rossano
Cosenza
CALABRIA
Catanzaro
Lipari Islands
Palmi
Vibo Valentia
Locri
Trapani
Palermo
Cefalù
Messina
Réggio di Calabria
Marsala
Alcamo
SICÍLIA
(SICILY)
Taormina
ETNA
Catánia
Castelvetrano
Caltanissetta
Platani
Salso
Agrigento
Salso
Gela
Siracusa
Sicilian Channel
Licata
Ragusa
Pantelleria

Malta Channel

MALTA

Conservation area

Motorway

Main road

0   50   100 km

A   B   C   D

237

Alpe Veglia Natural Park

Situated on the Swiss frontier, Alpe Veglia, one of Italy's newest natural parks, lies close to the Simplon Pass, where Monte Leone divides Italy from Switzerland. The park consists of the high part of the Valle Cairasca and is surrounded on three sides by mountain crests and ridges. On the south side is the Val Divedro, through which runs the main road from the Rhône Valley into Italy.

The region is typically alpine; there are extensive areas of pasture and, at high altitude forests of larch. Large expanses of creeping azaleas, primulas, crocuses, orchids, saxifrages, campanulas, gentians, snowbells, *Arnica* and edelweiss carpet the hillsides.

Marmots are plentiful and chamois, beech marten, ermine, polecat, mountain hare, fox, squirrel and possibly the wild cat can all be found. The birdlife is typically alpine, with raven, ring ouzel, alpine chough and ptarmigan all present. Unfortunately birds of prey are seldom seen because they have been so severely persecuted by hunters in the past.

Stélvio National Park

This area, the largest of the Italian National Parks, and big even by European standards, reached its present size of 137,000 hectares in 1976. It lies in the northern part of the Italian Alps adjacent to the Swiss National Park and embraces a mountainous area varying in altitude from 350 to 3905 metres. There are fourteen main valleys and the park contains the largest of the Italian glaciers, the Ghiacciaio dei Forni. Stélvio was established in 1935 when it was already a very popular tourist area. Hotels, ski lifts and other forms of development continued to flourish within its boundaries until the middle 1960s. Since then greater control over development and more effective management has slowed down the rate of commercial exploitation.

The park has fine forests of larch and Norway spruce and at higher altitudes arolla pine. Except at the highest altitudes, where there is very little vegetation, there are extensive alpine pastures. The park's flora has three endemic plants of considerable interest – *Primula daonensis*, *Saxifraga vandellii* and *Astragalus venostanum*. The fauna includes a large herd of red deer, about 2000 roe deer and a small herd of ibex introduced from the Gran Paradiso. One hundred and thirty species of birds have been recorded, including the capercaillie, the black grouse, ptarmigan, rock partridge, alpine chough, golden eagle, eagle owl and black woodpecker.

Adamello-Brenta Natural Park

A large and magnificent area in the Trentine Alps of northern Italy, Adamello-Brenta Natural Park includes three groups of mountains, the Adamello, Presanella and Brenta range. The steep slopes, forested with spruce, rowan, birch and alder, rock cliffs and peaks make much of the area relatively inaccessible and consequently some of Italy's least-disturbed mountain forests are found here. It is also one of the most popular tourist areas in the country; there has been considerable pressure to build ski-lifts and hotels for winter sports. The Stélvio National Park, which is only a few kilometres to the north, has probably had more than its fair share of tourist development, and Italian conservationists would like to preserve the Adamello-Brenta region from a similar fate.

BROWN BEAR Much persecuted in the past, the brown bear is now protected in many European countries.

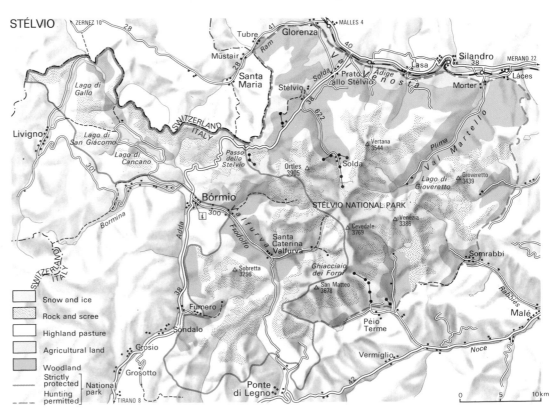

238

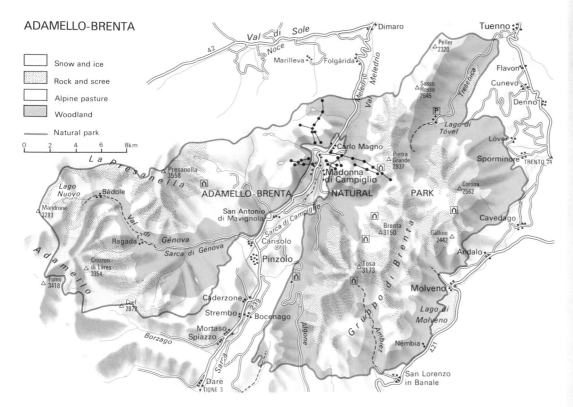

ADAMELLO-BRENTA

Snow and ice
Rock and scree
Alpine pasture
Woodland
Natural park

0 2 4 6 8km

1 ALPE VEGLIA
Information: Ente Provinciale
Turismo, Corso Cavour 2,
Novara
Access: from main road to
Simplon Pass, N of
DOMODÓSSOLA
Open: Unrestricted

2 STÉLVIO
Information: Direzione del
Parco Nazionale, Bórmio,
(Sondrio)
Access: from TIRANO or
MERANO
Open: Unrestricted
Facilities: Park centre in
Bórmio. Hotels and tourist huts
within the park

3 ADAMELLO-BRENTA
Information: Ente Provinciale
Turismo, Corso 3 Novembre 132,
Trento
Access: from the Val di Sole,
W of BOLZANO
Open: Unrestricted
Facilities: Hotels at Madonna
di Campiglio and camp site at
San Antonio. Climbers' huts
within the park. Cable cars

**4 PANEVEGGIO-PALE DE
SAN MARTINO**
Information: Ente Provinciale
Turismo, Corso 3 Novembre 132,
Trento
Access: from Predazzo, 5Gkm
SE of BOLZANO
Open: Unrestricted, but visitors
must keep to footpaths
Facilities: Hotel, visitor centre
and information office at
Paneveggio. Nature trails

5 FUSINE
Information: Regione
Autonoma Fruili Venezia Guilia,
Azienda delle Foreste, Via
Manzini 41, 33100 Udine
Access: from Fusine, 9km E of
TARVISIO
Open: Unrestricted
Facilities: Refuges within the
park

Faunistically, Adamello-Brenta is perhaps best known for the small number of brown bears which are still said to live in the region, the only population still surviving in the Alps outside Yugoslavia. It is difficult to get recent information about the bear population and its conservational status is uncertain.

In the Brenta region there are very few roads which penetrate far into the mountains. Lago di Tóvel, famous for an algal growth that turns it red at certain times of the year, is situated in one of the areas that can be easily reached. In the Adamello range the road through the Val di Génova provides easy access for the visitor. It has numerous parking places, and several signed footpaths lead from the road through the spruce forest into the higher valleys. The footpaths through the forest in the Sacra Valley pass by areas of moss- and fern-covered stones, and carpets of bilberry and cowberry.

Paneveggio-Pale di San Martino Natural Park

The dolomitic landscape of the eastern Italian Alps, characterized by high peaks, rocky cliffs and pinkish rocks that turn almost red in the evening sun, is the setting for the Paneveggio-Pale di San Martino Natural Park, a remarkable area of forest, mountain lakes and waterfalls that has been designated a natural park to give some protection to the region. The park includes three state forests and lies mainly on dolomitic limestone rocks.

The area's 3500 hectares of forest, still relatively untouched, and containing magnificent firs, Scots and arolla pines, are the park's most important biological characteristics. Among the park's endemic plants are *Saxifraga depressa*, Dolomites bellflower, Dolo-

mites primrose, *Primula minima* and several rarities, including *Papaver rhaeticum*, the edelweiss and lady's slipper orchid. In the alpine meadows, gentians, primulas and orchids are found as well as the globe flower and the alpine aster.

Until the early part of this century bears, wolves and vultures were found within the park. Today the chamois, red deer, roe deer and marmot are well established and there are several pairs of golden eagles and some capercaillie, black grouse and ptarmigan.

Fusine Natural Park

A small, attractive montane region centred on two small mountain lakes, the Fusine Natural Park is situated high in the Julian Alps close to the Austrian and Yugoslav frontiers. The lakes occupy an amphitheatre that was carved out by ice action during the last glaciation and subsequently dammed by moraines. Above, and partly encircling the lakes, towers the majestic dolomitic massif of Margant, soaring to 2677 metres at its highest point. The park is part of the 50,000-hectare Tarvisiano Forest, one of the largest state forests in Italy and itself a protected area. Proposals have been made to give "park status" to the whole forest.

On both sides of the River Falla, lying to the west of Tarvisio, are extensive areas of woodland consisting of red fir, beech, white fir, larch, Scots pine, black pine, bird cherry and hazel. The understorey vegetation is varied and supports a rich fauna of roe deer, red deer, chamois, hares, foxes and martens. Bear footprints have been seen, which probably belong to immigrants from Yugoslavia. The park's bird population includes the capercaillie, black grouse, eagle owl, golden eagle and black woodpecker.

239

GRAN PARADISO

To say that without the Gran Paradiso National Park the alpine ibex would have become extinct is no exaggeration. At a time when the ibex had been eliminated from all other parts of Europe by uncontrolled hunting, the Gran Paradiso formed the ibex's last refuge. The establishment of the National Park has effectively saved them from disappearing altogether and they now number about 3000 individuals.

Gran Paradiso lies between 1200 and 4000 metres in the Graian Alps, adjacent to the French Vanoise National Park. It became a hunting reserve in 1851 and in 1856 was declared a private hunting area for the Italian royal family. In 1922 it was presented to the nation and became Italy's first National Park.

The Italian conservation efforts regarding the ibex have been so successful that it has been possible to reintroduce small groups into other parts of the Italian, Swiss, French and Austrian Alps. Even so, fears for their survival within Gran Paradiso itself still remain. The National Park is bordered on the western, northern and southern sides by three major valleys. Unfortunately the bottoms of these valleys are not within the park area, so that when the ibex descend to lower levels in winter, they pass beyond its boundaries and many are shot despite a law that purports to protect them wherever they are. Hunting pressures around the park are considerable and poaching is perhaps the wardens' most difficult problem.

As well as being hunted for their beautiful horns, the ibex were thought to be able to cure all manner of illness, from cancer to calluses. Their blood, heart and even the hair balls from their stomach were thought to have magical properties.

The best time to see the ibex is in the evening or early morning; ibex normally live above 3000 metres, but descend to lower slopes during hours of darkness.

Geologically the area is a complex of schists, calcareous slate, gneiss and mica, fissured and veined with quartz and iron-rich seams. Within the park the mountain valleys are green and well wooded up to 2300 metres and the most widespread tree is larch. There are forests of arolla pine and Norway spruce, which, where the trees do not grow too closely together, have a shrub layer of juniper, rhododendron, bilberry and elder. Rowan and bearberry grow principally under the Norway spruce canopy. The alpine meadows are particularly beautiful in July when covered in flowers and many Apollo butterflies flutter over the open blooms. At the head of the Valnontey valley there is an interesting alpine botanical garden, "Paradisia", where many of the plants found in the park can be seen growing together.

Wolves, brown bears, lynx and the lammergeier were all former inhabitants of the area, but were killed off during the period that the park was used as a hunting reserve. Today there are foxes, mountain hares, brown hares, chamois, marmots and over eighty species of birds, including the golden eagle and the eagle owl. The ptarmigan and the alpine chough are widespread.

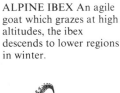

ALPINE IBEX An agile goat which grazes at high altitudes, the ibex descends to lower regions in winter.

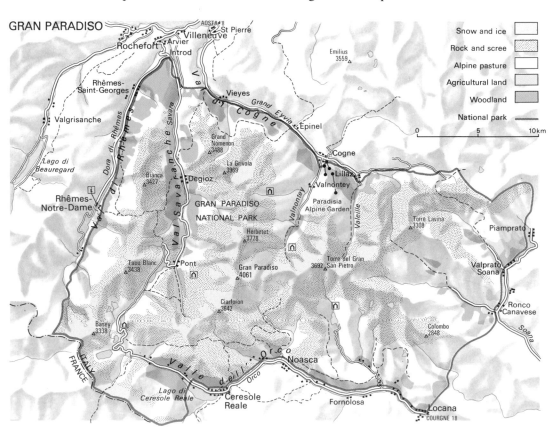

GRAN PARADISO

Snow and ice
Rock and scree
Alpine pasture
Agricultural land
Woodland
National park

GRAN PARADISO
A glacial stream,
banked by boulders
brought down by the
spring melt-waters,
rushes down from
high alpine peaks.

GRAN PARADISO
Information: Ente Autonomo
Parco Nazionale Gran Paradiso,
Via Della Rocca, 47; 10123
Torino
Access: from AOSTA or Pont
Carnavese, 50km N of TORINO
Open: Unrestricted
Facilities: Display centres at
the villages of Rhêmes Notre
Dame and Valsavarenche, open
July to August. Mountain
refuges and climbers' huts
within the park. Wardens on site

OCELLATED LIZARD
Principally a ground
lizard, it feeds on large
insects, other lizards and
even small mammals. It
can grow to 80 centi-
metres in length.

Monte di Portofino Natural Park

In the Gulf of Genoa few areas of coastline have escaped development for tourism, and although the seafront around Portofino, about 30 kilometres east of Genoa, is no exception, the rugged promontory on which it lies has resisted change more successfully. The creation of the Natural Park in 1935 not only gave the area protection from hunting but also from commercial development. In spite of this, poaching is prevalent and illegal building and new roads have begun to encroach on previously unspoilt areas.

The approach to Portofino town, which runs along an attractive stretch of rocky coastline, flanked by wooded hills and dotted with many small villages, draws large numbers of tourists. Beyond the public roads where few tourists venture is a fine area of macchia vegetation with *Cistus* species, tree heath, mastic tree, juniper, strawberry tree and myrtle. Aleppo pine is found on the lower slopes and maritime pine occurs higher up. There are also forests of chestnut and hornbeam. Among the less-common plant species recorded in this area are royal fern, *Pteris cretica, Orchis brevicornis, Limonium cordatum,* and *Asplenium petrarche.*

The most interesting animal found within the park is the ocellated lizard, which is the largest European species of the genus *Lacerta.* Although it is common throughout Spain, southern France and northwest Africa, the ocellated lizard is found in no other part of Italy excepting the extreme western part of Liguria. The park is also the western limit of the Italian wall lizard.

Punte Alberete Wildlife Oasis

Within the delta of the Po, one of the great rivers of Europe, lie extensive areas of marsh-land and coastal lagoon, which, although of supreme natural value, are used in most cases for commercial fishing and wildfowl shooting. Although comprehensive proposals for the establishment of a "Delta National Park" have been made, so far only one small site, at Punte Alberete, has been put aside and is managed as a nature reserve. This wetland reserve created by the Italian World Wildlife Fund in 1969 is, because of its magnificent birdlife, recognized to be of international status. It lies to the north of Ravenna and is divided into separate northerly and southerly parts by the River Lamone. On the eastern edge of the reserve is the Pineta San Vitale, the last littoral forest surviving on the Italian Adriatic coast.

The marsh woodland of willows, poplars and elms found within the reserve provides a nesting area for egrets and herons and is one of the few surviving examples of this habitat in Italy. The little egret population varies from 500 to 1000 pairs. There are about 50 pairs of night herons, 50 to 200 pairs of squacco herons, many grey herons and up to 10 sporadically breeding pairs of glossy ibis on the reserve. The duck species found breeding here include mallard, garganey, shoveler and ferruginous. In addition, the locally occurring penduline tit also nests.

The marsh vegetation, second only as an attraction to the birdlife, includes the rare greater water-parsnip. Jersey orchid and field gladiolus are found growing in wet meadows.

ABRUZZO *left* Hilltop villages are a characteristic feature of the central Apennines. Beech forests stop abruptly a few hundred metres short of the mountain summits.

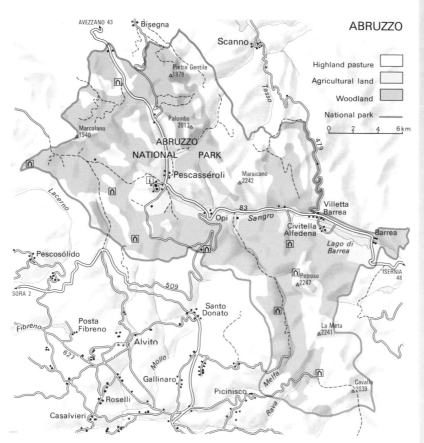

APENNINE WOLF *below* This rare wolf survives as a remnant population in central and southern Italy and is now fully protected.

ABRUZZO

Highland pasture
Agricultural land
Woodland
National park

0 2 4 6km

1 MONTE DI PORTOFINO
Information: Ente Provinciale Turismo, Via Roma 11-4, 16121 Genova
Access: from Santa Margherita, 32km E of GENOVA
Open: Sunrise to sunset

2 PUNTE ALBERETE
Information: WWF Italia, Sezione Emillia-Romagna, Via Cartoleria 17/2, 40124 Bologna
Access: from RAVENNA
Open: Public allowed along perimeter bank between sunrise and sunset. For groups of more than 10 people permission to enter reserve must be obtained through WWF Ravenna, Via Mentana 19, 48100 Ravenna
Facilities: Observation tower. Wardens on site

3 VAL DI FARMA
Information: WWF Italia, Sezione di Siena, Piazza San Agostino 14, 53100 Siena
Access: by track from Lamalasa, 35km S of SIENA
Open: Unrestricted

4 ABRUZZO
Information: Ente Autonomo Parco Nazionale d'Abruzzo, Via Livorno 15, Roma
Access: from Pescasséroli, 65km NW of ISÉRNIA
Open: Unrestricted
Facilities: Information centre and museum within the park. Mountain refuges. Wardens on site

Val di Farma Forest Reserve

The Farma valley, well known to Italian naturalists and local people as a beauty spot, is one of the few water courses in southern Tuscany which is still in its natural state. The forests lying on either side of the valley contain many Mediterranean tree species. On south-facing slopes there are pines, holm oaks, strawberry trees, cork oaks and mastic trees. The north-facing slopes of the valley have a different vegetation – one that is more characteristic of northern regions, with chestnut, holly, oak, hazel, hornbeam, maple and poplar growing through an understorey of shrubs, ferns, mosses and lichens. Beech, lime and yew trees are also found throughout. The yews are interesting, as they occur in few other areas of peninsular Italy and their presence in this forest was only discovered a few years ago. In a small, deeply shaded pond is found the alpine newt, an unusual amphibian which occurs here in its most southerly position in Italy.

Abruzzo National Park

Probably the most famous of the Italian National Parks, Abruzzo is situated in the central Apennines, at an altitude of between 700 and 2200 metres. After the Second World War the park went through a difficult period without effective protection and faced numerous problems related to speculative building and commerce. These have now largely been solved and the park's recent history is a model of how problems of maintaining the integrity of such areas can be overcome.

The park's mountain slopes are clothed in the rich green of ancient beech forests, which stop short of the rocky, relatively barren summits. Many other trees, including two species of maple, the flowering ash, and a local race of pine, the black pine, grow within the forests. Dwarf mountain pine and common juniper are found at higher altitudes.

Above the woodland a region of grassland contains bilberry, bearberry and several endemic plants, including a newly discovered species of iris, *Iris marsica*. On the lower slopes the scrub vegetation provides berries and fruits for both birds and the brown bear, of which the park has a population of between 70 and 100, a higher concentration than anywhere else in Europe apart from the Balkans. In addition there is a small population of Apennine wolves, a sub-species of *Canis lupus* – now a very rare animal indeed. The wolves can be seen at Civitella Afedena, where some are kept in a special enclosure to study their behaviour. Wild cats, squirrels, snow voles, pine martens, and a large population of foxes are also found. Red deer and roe deer, both formerly native to the park, have recently been reintroduced.

One of the park's most interesting animals is the Apennine sub-species of the chamois, which differs in its winter coat from the alpine variety, and has longer horns. Between 350 and 400 specimens live within the park, and are generally easily seen – in the absence of hunting they are relatively tame. The golden eagle, rock partridge, eagle owl and raven, alpine chough, common chough and the rare white-backed woodpecker all form part of the interesting bird fauna.

Bolgheri Wildlife Refuge

On the initiative of its owner, Marquese Mario d'Incisa della Rocchetta, the Bolgheri Wildlife Refuge was established in 1962 so that hunting rights could be terminated. In 1970 the reserve was transferred to the auspices of the Italian World Wildlife Fund.

Situated on the coast the reserve consists largely of cattle-grazed marsh grassland lying at about sea level and subject to flooding in winter. The marshland, of value because it is attractive to wildfowl, has been extended by a series of ditches along which water is pumped. A pathway nearly 2 kilometres long and fenced on either side enables this area to be reached without disturbance to the birdlife.

A long list of wildfowl and wading birds visiting the reserve in both the winter months and during migration seasons has been compiled. Osprey, lesser spotted eagle, black stork, crane, western bluethroat and Blyth's reed warbler have all been seen. In summer the meadows provide nesting sites for black-winged stilts and lapwings. The refuge is the most southerly lapwing-nesting locality in Italy. The night heron and purple heron are known to breed in wooded areas.

As well as marshy meadowland the reserve also has a sandy littoral zone of maquis-type vegetation, plantations of conifers and areas of ash and elm woodland. Apart from birds, the reserve's principal animals are crested porcupine, roe deer, pine marten, wild boar, otter and both terrestrial and aquatic tortoises.

Maremma Regional Park

To the visitor who has seen the intensive development that has taken place along the Italian Mediterranean coast, this remarkably unspoilt area in the vicinity of Grosseto is something of a surprise. Maremma Regional Park, established in 1975, has survived undisturbed because the public have never had traditional right of entry and there is no public road along this part of the coastline.

The park consists of a series of rocky spurs overlooking areas of cattle-grazed brackish marshes, stone pine and juniper woodland and a series of low dunes on which grow marram grass, sea daffodil, asphodel, yellow horned poppies and a maquis-type scrub vegetation. The ruins of the Torre di Collelungo on the coast, southeast of Marina di Alberese, is an excellent viewpoint from which to survey both the coast and the woods that stretch inland across the limestone hills of Monte dell'Uccellina. The forests, formerly important as sources of cork and charcoal, contain few large trees today. The holm oak, strawberry tree, tree heath, turkey oak, hop-hornbeam and service tree are all commonly found within the park, depending on aspect and situation.

In the dykes draining the wet meadows and along the River Ombrone there is a rich fauna of snakes and lizards. The park's larger mammals include the wild boar, fox, roe deer, fallow deer, badger, wild cat, pine marten and a well-established population of crested porcu-

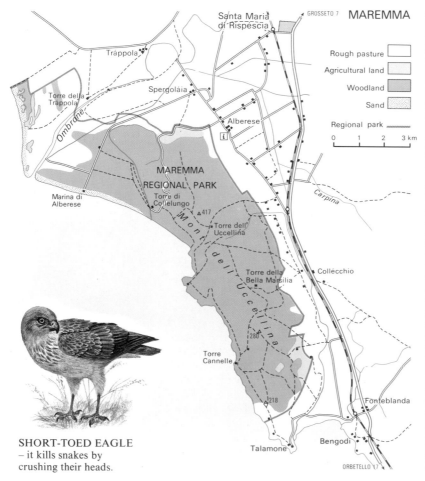

SHORT-TOED EAGLE
– it kills snakes by
crushing their heads.

244

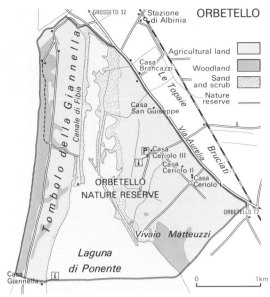

ORBETELLO

Legend:
- Agricultural land
- Woodland
- Sand and scrub
- Nature reserve

Labels on map: GROSSETO 32, Stazione di Albinia, Casa Brancazzi, Le Topaie, Casa San Guiseppe, Via Aurelia, Bruciati, Casa Ceriolo III, Casa Ceriolo II, Casa Ceriolo I, ORBETELLO NATURE RESERVE, ORBETELLO 12, Vivaio Matteuzzi, Laguna di Ponente, Casa Giannella, Tombolo della Giannella, Canale di Fibia

0   1km

BLACK-WINGED STILT *left* An elegant wading bird, the stilt is readily identified by its extremely long legs and straight bill.

MAREMMA *below* Stone pines and clumps of rushes border one of Maremma's many man-made drainage ditches.

pine. A striking aspect of the area's animal life is the local breed of white, broad-horned cattle which are ranched over the meadows.

Protection from shooting has provided a breeding refuge for birds such as the peregrine falcon, hobby, short-toed eagle, kingfisher, oystercatcher, wryneck, hoopoe and many more. Numerous migrants visit the park, including the osprey and dotterel.

Orbetello Nature Reserve

Situated about 20 kilometres north of Lago di Burano, Orbetello reserve consists of a series of tidal lagoons which form the northern part of the larger lagoon of Ponente. The reserve, established by the Italian World Wildlife Fund in 1972, and the area to the south are of great ornithological interest and form perhaps the most important region for migrant birds in Italy. Within the reserve boundary lies a mixture of habitats – low dunes covered with maquis, brackish lakes, freshwater ponds, cultivated fields and strips of woodland consisting of ash, poplar, elm and eucalyptus.

The black-winged stilt, which has been adopted as the reserve symbol, nests locally as well as Montague's harrier, stone curlew, several species of duck and probably also the great spotted cuckoo. The bee-eater is known to nest on flat, sandy areas. During the migration season great concentrations of duck and waders can be seen. Flamingo, osprey, spoonbill, white stork, several species of terns, avocet and the collared pratincole can all be seen. It is claimed that if one visits the reserve often enough one will eventually see almost every species of European water bird in existence.

Lago di Burano Wildlife Refuge

Lying on the south side of the province of Grosseto, Lago di Burano is a famous site for observing the movements of migrant birds along the Mediterranean coast of Italy. The lake provides shelter and rest for large numbers of water birds during migration when elsewhere there is much disturbance from hunters. The list of species is long and includes a wide variety of waterfowl and waders. Among the migrants are the rare great spotted cuckoo, the hoopoe, the great white heron and the glossy ibis. Before the reserve was created in 1967 about 6000 birds were killed annually by hunters. Commercial fishing is permitted on the lake, but there is a complete ban on hunting within the boundaries of the reserve. On the seaward side of the lake there is an extensive area of maquis-covered dunes containing several species of oak, the mastic tree, juniper, myrtle and broad-leaved mock-privet. In addition to a rich variety of plants the reserve has a diverse animal population, including the terrestrial tortoise, polecat, weasel, badger and the crested porcupine, which has long been resident in Italy and was probably introduced by the Romans.

1 BOLGHERI
Information: WWF Italia, Delegazione per la Toscana, Via San Gallo 32, 50129 Firenze
Access: from CÉCINA
Open: Tuesday and Friday, November to March only by previous arrangement with WWF
Facilities: Observation tower

2 MAREMMA
Information: Conzorzio del Parco Naturale della Maremma, 58010 Alberese, Località Pianacce
Access: from GROSSETO
Open: All public holidays, Saturday, Sunday and Wednesday, 0900 to one hour before sunset. June 15 to September 30, 0700–1600. Ticket required from park office or local post office, limited number of tickets sold each day
Facilities: Signposted nature trails

3 ORBETELLO
Information: WWF Italia, Delegazione per la Toscana, Via San Gallo 32, 50129 Firenze
Access: from Albinia railway station, 32km S of GROSSETO
Open: Thursday and Sunday, October to April. Two hours per day at 1000 and 1300 by warden on site. Visits at other times by arrangement with WWF
Facilities: Information caravan. Observation hide and tower. Warden on site

4 LAGO DI BURANO
Information: WWF Italia, Delegazione per la Toscana, Via San Gallo 32, 50129 Firenze
Access: from Capalbio railway station, 49km S of GROSSETO
Open: Thursday and Sunday, September to May, at 1000 and 1300. Visits at other times by arrangement with WWF
Facilities: Nature trail. Observation hide and field station. Warden on site

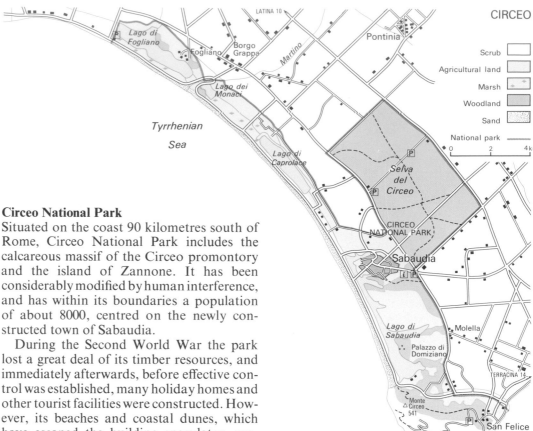

Scrub
Agricultural land
Marsh
Woodland
Sand
National park

Circeo National Park

Situated on the coast 90 kilometres south of Rome, Circeo National Park includes the calcareous massif of the Circeo promontory and the island of Zannone. It has been considerably modified by human interference, and has within its boundaries a population of about 8000, centred on the newly constructed town of Sabaudia.

During the Second World War the park lost a great deal of its timber resources, and immediately afterwards, before effective control was established, many holiday homes and other tourist facilities were constructed. However, its beaches and coastal dunes, which have escaped the building speculator, preserve an interesting vegetation of Mediterranean plants such as *Thymelaea hirsuta*, Phoenician juniper and prickly juniper. On the calcareous Circeo headland there are cork oaks, holm oaks, and dwarf fan palms.

The State Forest of Circeo lies farther inland on an area of drained marshland which was formerly part of the notorious Pontine marshes, the cause of communication and health problems for over two thousand years. There were many attempts to drain the marshes and it was not until the 1930s that this was successfully accomplished. The forest today is composed of two species of oaks,

Hungarian oak and pedunculate oak, together with Caucasian ash, common alder and English elm. Unfortunately a number of exotic trees have also been introduced, such as eucalyptus, false acacia and pine, which have altered the forest's original character.

Wild boar are well established throughout the park, and foxes, pine martens, beech martens, weasels and brown hares can be seen in certain areas. The Indian grey mongoose introduced into the park some years ago has now become such a pest that steps have been taken to reduce its numbers. The lakes are

CIRCEO Large parts of the National Park, which contains a State Forest, are wooded, mainly with evergreen oak.

particularly important for aquatic birdlife – mainly migratory and over-wintering species. In the last few years more than 220 species have been recorded.

The park is also of considerable archaeological interest. The palace of the Roman emperor Domician, built in the first century AD on the shores of Lago di Sabaudia, is now being excavated. The site lies in the forest of Sabaudia and covers about 40 hectares. In the numerous caves on Monte Circeo, there is powerful evidence of occupation by prehistoric man. The oldest relic is a skull of Neanderthal Man, dating from the mid-Palaeolithic period (190,000 to 90,000 years ago), which was discovered in 1939.

Umbra Forest Nature Reserve
In 1886 the Forest of Umbra, lying on the Gargano promontory, was recognized to be of special public interest and was given to the Italian Forestry Administration to conserve and manage for posterity. Today, conservation is an important part of its work, and two strict nature reserves lie within its limits. The flora is very rich and 2000 different species have been recorded, including several found nowhere else. Beech woodland, containing hornbeam, field maple, flowering ash and yew trees, covers about 2500 hectares in the southern part of the area. Some of the yew trees are thought to be over 600 years old. The forest has many interesting plants, notably sowbread, which grows in carpets on the forest floor.

The hillsides of the Gargano promontory were once extensively covered with forests of oak at an altitude of between 300 and 600 metres. The total area is much reduced and numerous other trees are found growing with the oaks – three species of hornbeam, flowering ash, *Sorbus* species, butcher's broom, *Cistus* species, spindle-tree, laurel, clematis, *Viburnum*, mastic tree and *Phyllerea*.

There are few large trees left in the oakwoods. Most were taken, before the area was protected, to be made into railway sleepers, barrels and to provide charcoal. Among the interesting birds of prey found in the area are buzzards, red kites, and owls. The mammal fauna includes the edible dormouse.

Salina di Margherita di Savoia Nature Reserve
This vast area of government-owned salt lands, situated immediately northwest of the town of Barletta, has through the efforts of the Italian World Wildlife Fund, become a no-shooting area, transforming the birdlife of the region. Thousands of geese are usually found on this reserve and a recent mid-winter census recorded 19,000 wigeon, 10,000 coot, 2200 shelduck, 2100 pintail, 1700 shoveler, 310 pochard and 150 teal. In addition there were numerous avocets, egrets, grey herons, cormorants, curlew and little stints.

The reserve includes areas of fresh, brackish and salt water and has a rich flora of rushes and sedges, Chenopodiaceae and aquatic algae. Frogs and toads are abundant and provide food for many birds.

Pollino National Park (Proposed)
The Pollino massif, a region of forests, streams and gorges at the highest part of the southern Apennines, has since 1971 had the status of a proposed National Park.

The wolf, wild boar, otter, wild cat and crested porcupine inhabit the area and the roe deer, which has virtually disappeared from the rest of southern Italy, still survives here. Several thousand fine examples of the Bosnian pine, a glacial relic species mainly confined to Greece and the southern Balkans, and rare in Italy, are found in Pollino. Its birdlife is especially noted for the birds of prey which inhabit the magnificent gorge of Raganello in the southern part of the proposed park.

1 CIRCEO
Information: Ministero dell'Agricoltura e della Foreste, Parco Nazionale del Circeo, Ufficio Amministrazione di Sabaudia, 04016 Sabaudia
Access: from LATINA
Open: Most of the forest area is a closed nature reserve, permission to visit must be sought from the park office
Facilities: Reception centre and museum at Sabaudia

2 UMBRA
Information: Ufficio Amministrazione Foreste Demaniali del Gargano, 71030 Foresta Umbra (Foggia)
Access: from MANFREDÓNIA
Open: Unrestricted except for the strict reserve, which may not be entered without a guide
Facilities: Visitor centre. Camp site

3 SALINA DI MARGHERITA DI SAVOIA
Information: Ufficio Amministrazione Foreste Demaniali del Gargano, 71030 Foresta Umbra (Foggia)
Access: from MANFREDÓNIA or BARLETTA
Open: The reserve may only be entered with a guide
Facilities: Observation huts

4 POLLINO
Information: Ufficio Amministrazione Foreste Demaniali della Calabria, Via Bagnano, Castrovillari
Access: from Mormanno 28km NW of CASTROVILLARI
Open: Unrestricted

POLLINO

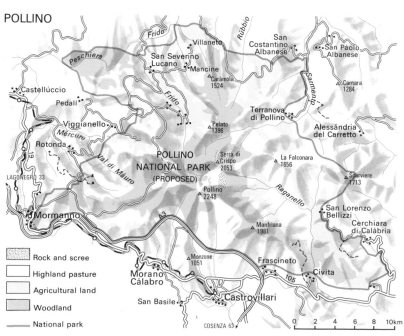

BOSNIAN PINE Found throughout southeastern Europe from Italy to Bulgaria, this pine has silver-grey bark and a dark purple cone which later ripens to pale brown.

Rock and scree
Highland pasture
Agricultural land
Woodland
National park

Calabria National Park

Situated in the most southerly province of mainland Italy, this National Park is composed of three separate mountain regions, the Sila Grande, the Sila Piccola and Aspromonte. All the areas are the responsibility of the State Forest Department and although the park was established in 1968 it was another ten years before the boundaries were defined.

The attractive mountain scenery, lying between 1200 and 1400 metres on the Calabrese plateau and covered for the most part by Corsican pine, beech, white fir, maple, oak, aspen and chestnut, has many plants of

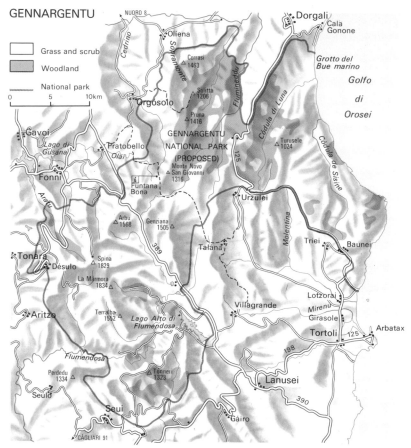

GENNARGENTU

☐ Grass and scrub
▨ Woodland
— National park
0   5   10km

interest, including the needle furze, a species typical of Atlantic heathlands.

The forests provide shelter for wild cats, otters, martens and southern red squirrels. A small number of Apennine wolves, the most important group of this rare animal in southern Italy, are found within the park. There are also a few roe deer and the wild boar is common. The forest dormouse is the rarest animal and is elsewhere confined to eastern Europe. The most striking species of birds are Bonelli's eagle, short-toed eagle, Egyptian vulture, goshawk, sparrowhawk, peregrine falcon, eagle owl, black and red kites and black woodpecker. Reptiles include the asp viper and the locally occurring spectacled salamander, *Salamandrina terdigitata,* found only in Italy.

Gennargentu National Park (Proposed)

Somehow Sardinia has so far escaped the

excesses of the developer and building speculator and still retains many remarkable areas of wild country. None is more impressive for its size than the unspoilt landscape of the proposed park of Gennargentu – claimed to be the finest wilderness area in Italy. The main part, lying south of Nuoro and Dorgali, is centred on the mountain massif of Gennargentu. For the most part it has a rolling rather than rugged landscape with numerous rocky crests, peaks, cliffs and, on the eastern side, spectacular valleys and gorges running down to the sea. Much is forest covered with holm oak or has been replanted with *Pinus nigra.* There are also vast areas of maquis in which *Cistus* species, the strawberry tree and the tree heath are common. From time to time large areas of heathland are burnt by shepherds in an attempt to improve the grazing, a practice that has progressively degraded the soil.

Limestone "islands" within areas of coarse granitic rock have made an important contribution to the variety of the vegetation in the region. The limestone peak of Monte Novo San Giovanni has numerous endemic species; some are confined to rock crevices, but others, such as the sea lavender *Limonium morisianum,* and the thrift *Armeria sardoa,* are more extensive.

The area's principal faunal interest lies in its native population of mouflon, a species of wild sheep that has suffered greatly in the past from over-hunting. Gennargentu's population is protected within a 5000-hectare fenced area, which the mouflon can leave or enter at will, but from which the local domestic sheep are excluded. Although groups are found elsewhere in Sardinia, they do not receive this kind of protection and have to compete with sheep for food. Captive mouflon can be seen in the enclosure at the Forest House in Funtana Bona.

Birds of prey are less common than formerly. Golden eagle, buzzard, peregrine falcon, kestrel and goshawk are known still to breed, but because poison has been used extensively to control the large fox population, the griffon vulture, black vulture and lammergeier are seldom seen.

There is a well-established breeding colony of Eleanora's falcon and both Manx and Cory's shearwaters breed in the coastal cliffs. Until 1967 the monk seal, which is found only in the eastern Mediterranean, bred on the Sardinian coast, particularly at Grotta del Bue Marino. Today, however, because the small beaches and caves which it favours are no longer free from human interference, it has largely disappeared.

Etna National Park (Proposed)

One of the most spectacular of Europe's volcanoes, Mount Etna, was given great publicity when in 1979 a small amount of lava flowed down the south side, cut through a road and damaged several buildings and vineyards.

About ninety eruptions have been recorded in historical times. Mount Etna, snow-capped for much of the year and frequently hidden in cloud, reaches to over 3300 metres and is the tenth largest volcano in the world. It has one immense crater and a number of subsidiary cones which give the volcano a lunar-landscape appearance. It is a remarkable area for wildlife, particularly plants. Its lower slopes, close to the sea, are favourable for the cultivation of olives, oranges, figs, vines and carobs. Higher up there are oaks, sweet chestnut and extensive plantations of hazel. Above the cultivation zone are forests of black pine, oak and sweet chestnut. At an altitude of between 1800 and 1900 metres the pine thins out and is replaced, in places, by beech and the Etna birch, whose autumn colours – yellow leaves against white bark – contrast so beautifully with the dark green of the pines. Above the tree line and growing up to 2500 metres in altitude on lava fields, a native species of milk-vetch, the Sicilian milk-vetch, covers the ground with spiny hummocks.

Due to uncontrolled shooting the fauna is not very rich and consists mainly of rabbits, the rock partridge and a few golden eagles which are now rare. Vultures and both roe and fallow deer were once frequent, but have now disappeared. The eastern orange-tip butterfly has been seen in the area and the reptile fauna is of particular interest.

As far back as 1969 the Italian conservation association, Italia Nostra, worked out a conservation plan for Mount Etna, but so far nothing has been done to implement its proposals and the area continues to be spoiled by speculative building, new roads, hunting and the over-exploitation of its remaining forests.

1 CALABRIA
Information: Ministero dell'Agricoltura e delle Foreste, Parco Nazionale della Calabria, Ufficio Amministrazione di Cosenza, 87100 Cosenza
Access: from COSENZA, RÉGGIO DI CALABRIA and CATANZARO
Open: Unrestricted except during winter. Best visited in late spring and autumn

2 GENNARGENTU
Information: Ente Provinciale Turismo, Piazza Italia 9, Nuoro
Access: from Orgósolo 20km S of NÚORO
Open: Unrestricted
Facilities: Information point at Funtana Bona

3 ETNA
Information: Ente Provinciale Turismo, Largo Paisiello 5, 95124 Catánia
Access: from Linguaglossa 50km N of CATÁNIA
Open: Unrestricted
Facilities: Mountain refuges within the park

MOUFLON *above* They were originally introduced to central and southern Europe as game. Mature males have heavy horns, which form a near circle.

ETNA *below* Solitary pink patches of Sicilian soapwort here grow on Etna's volcanic soils.

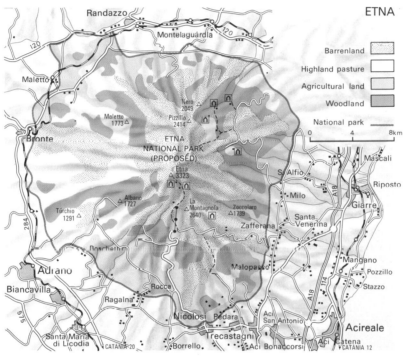

ETNA

Barrenland
Highland pasture
Agricultural land
Woodland
National park

0 4 8km

YUGOSLAVIA

Situated on the Balkan Peninsula, Yugoslavia with its remarkable landscape of mountains, valleys, plains and dissected coastline and more than 1200 islands is of outstanding interest to both naturalist and conservationist. Its flora, which is one of the richest in Europe, is determined by its diverse geography: the Alps in the northwest, the Mediterranean zone of the southern Karst, the northern plains – part of the large Pannonian Plain of central Europe – and the eastern territories, which are typically Balkan and have many relict and endemic species.

One of the most remarkable features of Yugoslavia's landscape and wildlife is the Karst – an area of limstone mountains, stony plateaux, canyons, gorges and vertical rock cliffs with innumerable springs, underground rivers, caves, and lakes. Its cave fauna of blind amphibia, bats, insects and spiders is probably the most remarkable in Europe.

The mountainous character of much of the country has preserved extensive forests, partly because they have an economic importance, as timber production is the only possible form of land use, and partly because steep slopes have prevented exploitation in many places so that primeval forest has survived.

Wildlife protection in Yugoslavia is organized on a republic level, with an institute for nature protection in each of the six Autonomous Republics. The institutes are usually staffed by biologists, geographers and lawyers, with a Director who may be either a civil engineer or a forester.

The main part of the conservation effort is the care of the sixteen National Parks. These are wild areas in the true wilderness sense and are usually of considerable size. In some cases, however, commercial development related to tourism has been extensive, for example at the Plitvice Lakes National Park in Croatia, where 1300 people employed in hotels, restaurants, camp sites and other services live in the park, and at the Triglav National Park in Slovenia, where there is much less development but a large number of visitors.

The most recent National Park, the Kornati Islands in Croatia, established in August 1980, has no staff at present and there are no permanent inhabitants. It consists of 140 islands, together with the sea between them, and is as important for its marine wildlife as for its land plants and animals.

Apart from the National Parks there are numerous other categories of protected areas, from strict nature reserves – some of which lie within National Parks – to Regional Parks, Protected Landscapes and arboreta. Nature reserves at present total about 170 and many more are planned.

PLITVICE LAKES The most popular of National Parks in Yugoslavia, it is chiefly known for its series of beautiful waterfalls.

251

PARK/RESERVE	SIZE (km²)	DESCRIPTION	MAP REF.	PAGE NO.
TRIGLAV	20.0	National Park. Picturesque part of the Julian Alps. Rich flora on limestone terrain.	A1	254
POSTOJNA, PIVKA & PLANINA CAVES		System of caves and underground rivers southwest of Ljubjana. Many thousands of rock chambers, some more than 100 m long. Superb limestone formations. Unusual cave fauna.	A1	254
RIŠNJAK	30.1	National Park. Forested mountain in magnificent karst landscape. Extensive mixed forest, some in a virgin state.	A2	254
PLITVICE LAKES	193.8	National Park. Series of sixteen lakes and waterfalls surrounded by extensive area of forests and meadows. Numerous rare plants. Interesting birdlife and mammal fauna.	A2	255
PAKLENICA	36.2	National Park. Region of high beech-clad valleys, in southern Velebit Mountains. Remarkable endemic flora.	A2	256
RIJEKA KRKA	140.0	Natural Reserve. 7.5-kilometre stretch of Krka River-valley gorge with lakes and waterfalls.	B2	256
HUTOVO BLATO	37.3	Natural Reserve. Part of the Neretva River-delta marshlands. Important for migratory and overwintering birds.	B3	256
MLJET	31.0	National Park. Area of maquis and forest at western end of the island of Mljet. Typical Mediterranean flora. Interesting insects, particularly butterflies.	B3	256
FRUŠKA GORA	273.0	National Park. Lowland area at edge of Panonian Plain with forest and steppe vegetation. Several rare plants. Historical and cultural interest.	C2	258
DJERDAP	821.2	National Park. Protected area lying along the Danube, partly in Yugoslavia and partly in Romania. Oak woodland. Large artificial lake. Several rare and endemic plants.	D2	258
SUTJESKA	172.5	National Park. Fine virgin forest containing both deciduous and coniferous woodland. Many rare tree and shrub species.	C3	258
DURMITOR	320	National Park. Mountain massif and river gorge. Alpine lakes forests and mountain pastures with rich flora.	C3	259
BIOGRADSKA GORA	34.0	National Park. River valley and mountain region. More than half covered by virgin forest.	C3	259
LOVĆEN	20.0	National Park. Mountain area in southeastern Dinaric Alps. Karst landscape with forest and grassland.	C3	260
MAVROVO	730.9	National Park. Mountain area with forest and alpine pasture. Wide variety of scenery and vegetation with endemic species. Bears, wolves and lynx. Large number of predatory bird species.	C3/C4	260
GALIČIA	237.6	National Park. Unique mountain area with diverse flora. Important wildfowl-breeding area.	C4/D4	261
PELISTER	120.0	National Park. Alpine pasture and large expanse of forest in southern mountain area. Rich birdlife.	D4	261

TRIGLAV The fast flowing Dolinka River carries meltwater away from the snows of the Triglav Massif. The National Park is situated in the magnificent Julian Alps in the extreme northwest of the country, adjacent to the Italian frontier.

Yugoslavia's enormous variety of rock types and complex geological structure bear witness to a violent past in which sedimentary deposits were crushed, folded and thrust up into mountain ranges, while elsewhere massive subsidence was taking place. Wind, ice and water have since combined to create a land of wild contrasts – in an area still prone to the destructive violence of earthquakes.

The northern plains of the Danube basin consist of relatively young deposits, seldom forming features much more than 400 metres high, but this uninspiring lowland is flanked by spectacular mountain scenery. In the extreme northwest lies a small Alpine zone consisting of part of the Julian and Karawanken Alps, among whose jagged ridges and deeply glaciated valleys rise Yugoslavia's highest peaks, Triglav (2864 metres) and Grintavec (2558 metres). In the south of the country, in Macedonia

and southern Serbia, massive limestones and crystalline rocks interspersed with sediments have given rise to a mountain wilderness, the karst landscape of Croatia and Slovenia – a bleak limestone plateau pockmarked with sink-holes and riddled with cave systems – contrasting with the rugged uplands of eastern Yugoslavia with their more rounded hills and deep river valleys.

No other country in Europe has such great climatic variation in relation to its size, the effects of the various mountain ranges and interior basins giving rise to widely varying local regimes of temperature and rainfall. Vegetation is similarly varied with pines and evergreen shrubs typical of the Mediterranean zone; scattered beechwoods and scrub clothing the limestone uplands, and oak and beech forests giving way at higher altitudes to coniferous forest in the eastern highlands.

Conservation area

Motorway

Main road

0   50   100 km

Triglav National Park

The most northerly of the Yugoslav National Parks, Triglav lies not far from the Italian and Austrian frontiers in a most picturesque part of the Julian Alps. The boundary originally extended from the Savica waterfall up into a high valley containing seven lakes, surrounded by peaks and ridges that reach to nearly 2400 metres in places. Triglav Mountain (2864 metres), the highest in Yugoslavia, lies just to the north. In June 1981 Triglav was enlarged to 84,000 hectares and now includes the entire Yugoslav portion of the Julian Alps. The underlying Triassic limestone is responsible for the area's typical karst landscape, on which a rich flora of alpine plants with many native Illyrian species occurs.

The lower regions of the park consist mainly of beech forest, while on the steep rocky slopes of Komarča, which are especially warm and dry, a community of sub-Mediterranean plants has developed. These slopes represent an alpine karstic oasis for many plants which need warm conditions, notably hop-hornbeam, flowering ash, wig tree, snowy mespilus, whitebeam, *Cythisanthus radiatus* and winter savory.

On the higher mountain slopes spruce dominates and near the limit of tree growth, in the Seven Lakes Valley, there are large areas of larch and mountain pine. Above the tree line lie extensive alpine pastures, rocks and scree slopes with many rare alpine species. A complete collection of Julian Alps plants can be seen in the beautiful alpine garden of "Juliana" in the nearby Trenta valley.

Postojna, Pivka and Planina Caves

Highly complex systems of caves and underground rivers have evolved in many parts of Yugoslavia's extensive karst landscape, and although only a small proportion of the many thousands of caves in existence have been studied, it is clear that they contain a specialized fauna of great scientific interest. Probably the most popular caves are those at nearby Postojna.

Postojna Cave, 16.5 kilometres long, was discovered in 1818 and opened to the public the following year. The cave system has several immense chambers, including one in which was held the opening session of the 1965 International Speleological Congress. One particular chamber, known as the Beautiful Cave, is around 500 metres long and is especially noted for its marvellous stalagmite and stalactite formations.

Pivka Cave, lying 4 kilometres from Postojna, was formed by the Pivka River, a watercourse which travels 7 kilometres underground from Postojna Cave before reappearing on the surface in a 60-metre-deep bowl-shaped depression.

Of equal interest and less commercialized is the Planina Cave, 10 kilometres from Postojna. The path through the cave system leads to the Chamber of the Giants, where on one side the stalactites are 10 metres long.

To the biologist these caves are of special interest: the olm, a cave amphibian, which, apart from an isolated colony in northern Italy, is confined to Yugoslavia, was first discovered here. Whitish in colour, with pink gills, it has small eyes and legs and sometimes reaches an overall length of 30 centimetres. Its method of reproduction is quite extraordinary and depends on the water temperature.

The cave also contains several species of crustacea such as *Troglocaris schmidti*, *Asellus cavernicolus*, *A. carniolicus* and *Titanethes albus*. There is in addition a cave harvestman *Nelima troglodytes*, several cave spiders and two species of moths.

Outside, especially in the valley of the River Rak, lie extensive meadows which are cut for hay and have remained unchanged for many centuries. In some parts, areas of uncut vegetation mark places where winter rains sink through the limestone to replenish the underground rivers. These beautiful permanent pastures are rich in plants and are particularly attractive in early summer.

Rišnjak National Park

Situated in the most westerly part of the Dinaric mountain range, the Rišnjak National Park is essentially a forested mountain reaching to a height of 1528 metres. Its limestone and dolomitic rocks form a magnificent

TRIGLAV The 2864m-high Triglav mountain soars above the Vrata valley in the Julian Alps.

karst landscape in which plants of both northern-continental and southern-sub-Mediterranean origin are found; around thirty different plant communities have been described. Much of the lower slopes are covered with mixed beech and fir forest, while above 1200 metres a characteristically alpine form of beech forest, containing *Fagus erraticum subalpinum*, is found. These forests have never been extensively exploited, and unaltered virgin forest can still be found in many places. For this reason the National Park has the status of a strict nature reserve.

A 200-metre-deep, funnel-shaped hole known as Viljska Ponikva is Rišnjak's most striking karstic feature. Local influences produce a temperature inversion inside the hole which influence the zoning of its plant life.

Growing on the alpine pastures above the tree line are numerous scarce plants such as hairy alpenrose, black vanilla orchid, edelweiss, false bellflower, heart-leaved saussurea, *Gentiana symphyandra*, orange lily, queen of the Alps and the large yellow ox-eye.

Plitvice Lakes National Park

A unique area, Plitvice Lakes is the most famous of the Yugoslav National Parks and is visited by nearly a million people each year. It is a United Nations World Heritage Site and combines nature preservation with a highly organized and profitable tourist de-velopment in a way which is probably unrivalled elsewhere.

The main feature of the park is a series of sixteen lakes of varying sizes, linked together by waterfalls The falls are formed by the deposition of a material known as travertine, a rock-like substance composed mainly of calcium carbonate, filtered from the water by the aquatic mosses *Cratoneuron commutatum* and *Bryum pseudotriquetrum*. The travertine gradually builds upwards and outwards, increasing in height until the falls eventually collapse under the weight of water.

Away from the lakes there are fine beech and fir forests and alpine meadows and, in one part, a virgin forest of beech, fir and spruce – one of several strictly protected areas. The park has numerous rare plants such as *Daphne blagayana*, lady's slipper orchid, orange lily, *Lilium carniolicum*, martagon lily, *Paeonia mascula*, *Primula auricula*, *P. kitaibeliana*, Wulfen's primrose and large butcher's broom.

Despite the tourist development the wild boar is on the increase and about fifty bears live in unfrequented parts of the park and surrounding area. Otters are very scarce. The rivers and smaller lakes have only two native species of fish, of which the common trout is the more abundant. They sometimes reach 1 metre in length and up to 11 kilograms in weight. In the two largest lakes, the rainbow trout has been introduced.

1 TRIGLAV
Information: Planinska zveza Slovenije, Dvoržakova 9, 6100 Ljubljana
Access: from BLED
Open: Unrestricted
Facilities: Refuges within the park. Marked footpaths

2 POSTOJNA, PIVKA & PLANINA CAVES
Information: (Postojna and Pivka) Postojnska jama, Jamska 30,.66230 Postojna (Planina) Turistično društvo Planina, 66232 Planina pri Rakeku
Access: from LJUBLJANA or TRIESTE
Open: (Postojna) May 1 to September 30.
(Pivka) May 1 to June 30 and September 1 to 30
(Planina) unrestricted
Facilities: Hotel and camp site at Postojna and camp site near Pivka. All caves have guided tours

3 RIŠNJAK
Information: Turistički savez Hrvatske, Amruševa 8, 41001 Zagreb
Access: from Crni Lug, 55km NE of RIJEKA
Open: Unrestricted

4 PLITVICE LAKES
Information: Nacionalni Park Plitvice, 48231 Plitvička Jezera
Access: from KARLOVAC or BIHAĆ
Open: Unrestricted except for the strict nature reserve which may not be entered
Facilities: Information centre at Plitvička Jezera. Hotels and camp sites within the park

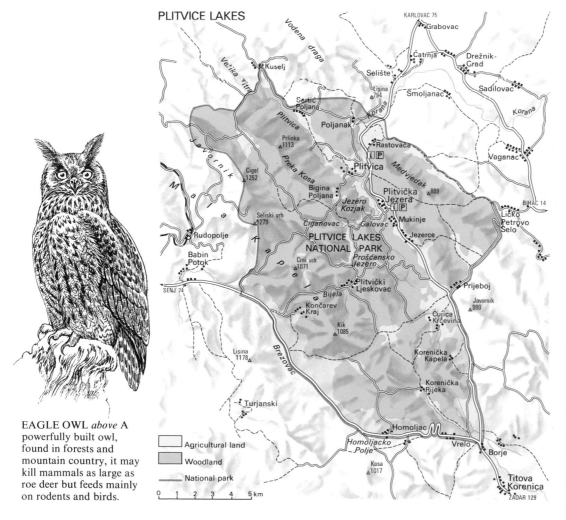

PLITVICE LAKES

EAGLE OWL *above* A powerfully built owl, found in forests and mountain country, it may kill mammals as large as roe deer but feeds mainly on rodents and birds.

Agricultural land

Woodland

National park

0 1 2 3 4 5 km

Paklenica National Park

The only National Park on the Dalmatian coast of mainland Yugoslavia, Paklenica lies in the southern part of the Velebit mountain range and is known both for its beauty and remarkable endemic flora. The park consists largely of several high beech-clad valleys surrounded by rocky limestone peaks. Two gorges, of which the larger and more westerly is the main access route, lead into the valleys from the coast. These magnificent ravines are walled largely by limestones and dolomites and rise to 400 metres of vertical rock in places. There are numerous caves, of which Manita Peč and Jama Vodarica are the most interesting.

About half the area of the park consists of beech and black-pine forest. Much of the lower rocky slopes are covered by a scrub vegetation of downy oak, ash, hornbeam, juniper and littoral beech, which has suffered greatly from fires. Several Velebit mountain endemic plants, such as *Campanula velebitica*, *Saxifraga velebitica*, *Aubretia croatica* and *Aquilegia kitaibelli*, occur in the park.

The rock nuthatch, black redstart, wallcreeper, blue rock thrush, griffon vulture, golden eagle and eagle owl are all found here. The brown bear is rare and the visitor is more likely to see the wild boar, roe deer or fox.

COMMON VIPER
Found mainly on heaths, dunes and grassland, the viper, the commonest poisonous snake in Europe, has a preference for moist habitats.

Rijeka Krka Natural Reserve

Although Rijeka Krka is described as a "managed natural reservation", all activities within its boundaries are regulated and it successfully combines the provision of tourist facilities with the protection of its forests and wildlife. The reserve consists of a 75-kilometre-long portion of the Krka River valley, with its majestic gorge, lakes and waterfalls. The rocky sides of the gorge vary from 60 to 100 metres in height and where the valley widens several lakes have formed. The largest, Lake Visovačko, is 9 kilometres in length and varies between 150 and 1500 metres in width. The waterfalls are formed by deposits of calcium carbonate, which gradually increase in height and width in the same way as those at Plitvice. Skradinski waterfall, although not the highest, is probably the most beautiful. It is 500 metres wide and has seventeen cascades, falling through a total of more than 45 metres.

The lower part of the valley has a Mediterranean-type vegetation characterized by the holm oak and at higher altitudes the oriental hornbeam. Even though the flora has not been intensively studied, so far 173 species of plants have been recorded. The fox, pine marten, polecat and otter are found in the reserve; the latter, however, is very rare. The birds of prey are said to include the golden eagle, Egyptian vulture and lesser kestrel. An endemic species of trout *Salmothymus obtusirostris krkensis* lives in the lakes and rivers.

Hutovo Blato Natural Reserve

Although only part of the vast marshlands that make up the Neretva River delta is protected by Hutovo Blato Natural Reserve, the whole area is important for both migratory and wintering birds. The delta, several kilometres in diameter, is criss-crossed by channels through which the people who inhabit the marshland gain access. Much of the area has been reclaimed and there is considerable evidence of exploitation.

The delta is probably best seen from the road which runs along the south side and there are extensive areas of reed beds and several small pools which are easily accessible to the bird-watcher. During the rainy season, from November to May, the delta water level rises and the greater part of the protected area is transformed into a sheet of water. The flora includes about 165 species and subspecies of such primitive plants as fungi, lichens, mosses and ferns and over 500 flowering plants. Even though 235 species of birds have been recorded the birdlife, which consists mainly of wintering and migratory species, is not as rich as it was before the marshes were so intensively exploited. The list of species includes the pygmy cormorant, purple, squacco and night herons, spoonbill and the great white egret.

Mljet National Park

The island of Mljet must be regarded as one of the most idyllic spots on the Adriatic coast. The National Park is situated at the western end of this forest- and maquis-covered island, and although it has been established for over twenty years it has survived without major tourist development. The park's main feature comprises two connected, deep, enclosed bays with rocky shores, the Veliko and Malo Jezero. The bays have a maximum depth of 46 metres. Like much of Yugoslavia's Dinaric coastline the island consists of Cretaceous limestone and dolomite with deposits of terra rossa, an iron-rich residual soil.

The vegetation is typically Mediterranean and includes such trees and shrubs as holm oak, strawberry tree, tree heath, carob, myrtle, mastic tree, laurel and junipers, including the prickly juniper.

Although there is no published information, the insect life is clearly rich because of the numerous plants and shrubs found in the park. A visit in September 1980 recorded several common species of butterfly such as the southern white admiral and the Cleopatra butterfly, as well as many other interesting invertebrates.

The reptile fauna is said to have been much reduced by the introduction of the Egyptian mongoose at the beginning of the century. Nevertheless the Turkish gecko, the sharp-snouted rock lizard and Dahl's whip snake still inhabit the area. Until recently Mljet was one of the few surviving sites for the monk seal in the Adriatic, but its breeding areas have been disturbed and there seems to be no real evidence that this rare animal has occurred here in recent years.

MLJET

Woodland

National park

0   2   4km

RIJEKA KRKA *below*
The waterfalls on the
Krka River are formed
of a type of limestone
deposited by aquatic
mosses. The falls are
constantly changing –
new ones building up
while old ones collapse.

1 PAKLENICA
Information: Turistički savez
Hrvatske, Amruševa 8, 41001
Zagreb
Access: from Starigrad-
Paklenica, 46km NE of ZADAR
Open: Unrestricted

2 RIJEKA KRKA
Information: Turistički savez
Hrvatske, Amruševa 8, 41001
Zagreb
Access: from ŠIBENIK
Open: Unrestricted but visitors
must keep to footpaths
Facilities: Camp site within
the reserve. Marked footpaths by
the waterfalls

3 HUTOVO BLATO
Information: Turistički savez
Bosne i Hercegovine, Titova
80/1, 71001 Sarajevo
Access: from Čapljina, 14km N
of METKOVIĆ
Open: Unrestricted

4 MLJET
Information: Turistički savez
Hrvatske, Amruševa 8, 41001
Zagreb
Access: by boat from Trstenik
on the Pelješac peninsula,
95km NW of DUBROVNIK or by
boat from DUBROVNIK
Open: Unrestricted
Facilities: Hotels and camp
site within the park

257

Fruška Gora National Park

Unlike most Yugoslav National Parks which are situated in mountainous districts, Fruška Gora lies in an area of lowland on the border of the wide Pannonian Plain. It follows the River Danube for about 80 kilometres and consists of meadows, cornfields, vineyards and orchards. There are about sixty villages and sixteen monasteries in the area, some of which are very old and of great historical and cultural interest. Throughout the greater part there are scattered areas of forest and steppe vegetation, wherein lies the park's principal conservation interest. Among the many rare steppe plants found in this area are such species as *Amygdalus nana,* the pasque-flower *Pulsatilla grandis, Ranunculus illyricus, Salvia nutans, S. austriaca,* the scabious *Scabiosa ucranica,* feather-grass, *Tragopogon floccosus,* and the seakale *Crambe tataria.*

Djerdap National Park

The biggest canyon in Europe lies within Djerdap National Park, an internationally protected territory partly in Yugoslavia and partly in Romania. The park extends along the Danube from near the town of Golubac, about 100 kilometres due east of Belgrade, downstream to Tekija, almost opposite the Romanian town of Orsova. At its narrowest point in Djerdap the Danube is only 150 metres broad and is bordered by rock walls 300 metres high. The park contains the largest artificial lake in Yugoslavia and Europe's greatest hydroelectric works.

BUZZARD *above* The most widespread of the larger European raptors.

A number of rare plants have been recorded here, several of them endemic to the region. In addition as many as ten species of oak are known to grow in the area. Among the park's most typical plants are walnut, nettle tree, Turkish hazel and lilac. The vast canyon is at its most beautiful in spring, when the lilac flowers on the mountain slopes and in the surrounding beech woods. In the autumn the cliffs are tinged with the red and orange foliage of the wig tree.

Within the Yugoslav part of the park there are five strict nature reserves, a Neolithic settlement, eight historical monuments of the Roman or medieval period and over a hundred separate geological, geomorphological or botanical nature monuments.

Sutjeska National Park

Peručica, one of the best-known virgin forests in Europe, forms a strict nature reserve of 1434 hectares within Sutjeska National Park. The vegetation within the reserve is beautifully zoned altitudinally and ranges from oak woods on the lower slopes to scrubby mountain pines at the upper limit of tree growth. It is claimed that the best parts of the virgin forest have over 1000 cubic metres of timber per hectare. There are twelve species of conifers and 143 species of broadleaved trees and shrubs, including such rarities as yew, *Spiraea chamaedryfolia, Cerasus mahaleb,* Tatarian maple and the endemic species of Greek maple *Acer heldreichii,* subsp. *visiani* and *Petteria ramentacea.* On the alpine pastures

and rocks above grow *Aubretia croatica*, Monte Baldo anemone, *Daphne malyana*, Dinaric pansy, *Iris bosniaca* and *Achillea lingulata,* as well as many other beautiful plants of interest.

In other parts of the National Park, which takes its name from the Sutjeska River, the forest cover has suffered greatly from fire damage and it is thought that above the tree line, the alpine meadows have suffered as a result of intensive grazing.

Among the park's attractions are several glacial lakes and a monument commemorating the victories of the partisan fighters during the Second World War. The bear, wolf, chamois and eagle are notable members of the area's animal life.

Durmitor National Park

Durmitor, a United Nations World Heritage Site, consists of two parts, a mountain massif, with the highest peak reaching 2522 metres, and a 30-kilometre stretch of the magnificent Tara River Gorge. The gorge is 1000 metres deep in places and its steep, forested sides are virtually untouched because human settlement has not been possible.

Both in summer and winter the alpine lakes on the Durmitor massif, especially Crno Jezero (the Black Lake) which is the largest, are favourite spots with visitors. Around this lake and on the lower slopes of the mountains lies a splendid forest of fir, spruce and beech. At higher levels there are extensive alpine pastures and rock cliffs in the midst of a

typical karst landscape. The flora is very rich, with many relict and endemic species, for example, *Trifolium durmitoreum*, *Verbascum durmitoreum*, *Carum velenovsky*, *Edraianthus glisicii* and *Saxifraga preuja*. The vegetation is clearly zoned with altitude.

Until recent years the park was not well regulated and illegal hunting reduced the game animals to a low level. This situation is now improving and populations of chamois, bear, eagle, capercaillie, black grouse, rock partridge and many other birds are expected to increase in the future. Most of the pastures are grazed by sheep and cattle. The herdsmen and their families, however, occupy these high levels only during the summer, moving their stock and homes to Žabljak in the winter.

Biogradska Gora National Park

The valley of the Biogradska River and much of the surrounding Bjelasica mountains, including three peaks of over 2100 metres, lie within the Biogradska Gora National Park. The park, which is over 66 per cent tree-covered, has been described as one of the finest virgin forests in Yugoslavia. Around Biogradsko Lake, the best known and most easily reached of the area's five natural lakes, lies a forest of beech, ash, sycamore and fir with many magnificent trees, some reaching a height of 60 metres. The trees are moss- and lichen-covered, and both fallen and standing dead timber is unusually abundant, creating an attractive environment for fungi and invertebrate animals, such as wood-boring beetles. In all sixty-four species of trees and shrubs occur in the park. The Montenegro beech is most characteristic of the area and the rare maple, *Acer heldreichii* subsp. *visiana*, is found near the tree line.

The animal life includes the red deer, roe deer, chamois, bear, wolf, golden eagle, and buzzard as well as many other birds, woodpeckers in particular.

1 FRUŠKA GORA
Information: Turistički savez Srbije, Dobrinjska 11, 11001 Beograd
Access: from NOVI SAD
Open: Unrestricted

2 DJERDAP
Information: Turistički savez Srbije, Dobrinjska 11, 11001 Beograd
Access: from TURNI-SEVERIN or POŽAREVAC
Open: Unrestricted
Facilities: Hotel within the park

3 SUTJESKA
Information: Turistički savez Bosne i Hercegovine, Titova 80/1, 71001 Sarajevo
Access: from Tujentište, 40km N of AVTOVAC
Open: Unrestricted
Facilities: Hotel and camp site within the park

4 DURMITOR
Information: Turistički savez Crne Gore, Bulevar Lenjina 2/1, 81001 Titograd
Access: from Žabljak, 63km SW of PLJEVLJA (no easy access from the south)
Open: Unrestricted
Facilities: Hotels and camp sites within the park. Marked footpaths

5 BIOGRADSKA GORA
Information: Turistički savez Crne Gore, Bulevar Lenjina 2/1, 81001 Titograd
Access: from Mojkovac, 93km N of TITOGRAD
Open: Unrestricted
Facilities: Camp site within the park. Marked footpaths. Warden on site

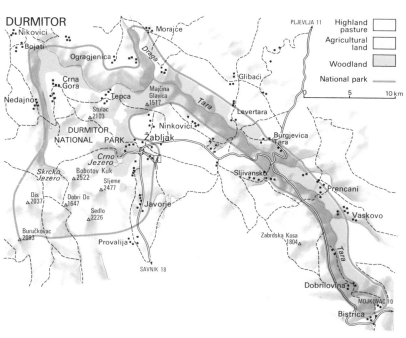

DURMITOR *left* A total of eighteen glacial lakes lie in the beautiful countryside of the Durmitor massif, at the heart of the National Park. These lakes, particularly the largest, are favourite tourist spots.

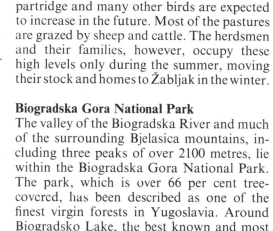

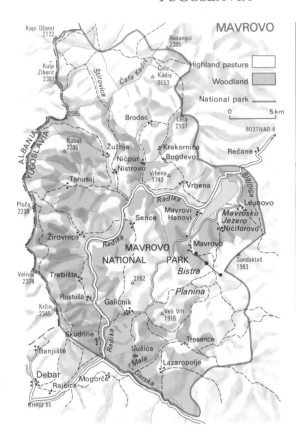

MAVROVO

Highland pasture
Woodland
National park
0   5 km
BOŠTIVAR 0

MAVROVO *right* A dome-topped cliff projects upwards from scree and forest – the park is renowned for its wealth of remarkable geological and landscape features.

Lovćen National Park

The smallest of the Yugoslav National Parks, Lovćen is situated west of the town of Cetinje in the Lovćen mountain massif. It forms part of the southeastern Dinaric mountain chain and was established in 1952. From Štirovnik (1749 metres), the highest peak, there is a magnificent view of the beautiful fjord-like Boka Kotovska on the Adriatic coast. The mountain, consisting of Triassic and Jurassic limestones and dolomites, lies close to the sea and receives rather more rainfall than areas farther inland. Even so its karst landscape has no permanent surface water. However, temporary pools form during the rainy season between November and December.

The hop-hornbeam and downy oak dominate the lower regions of the park, while over 1100 metres there is a forest zone of beech with the moor grass *Sesleria autumnale*. The flora consists of about 1200 different kinds of plants from 95 families. Among the rare plants which are endemic to the area are *Lamium lovcenicum*, *Berteroa gintlii*, and *Endraianthus lovcenicus*. In addition there is *Petteria ramentacea*, *Moltkea petraea*, *Amphoricarpus neumayeri*, Balkan pine, *Viburnum maculatum*, *Centaurea nicolai* and *Dianthus nicolai*. Less is known about the fauna, but the beech marten and fox are

known to be widespread; wolves and wild cats, however, are rare. The birdlife includes the rock partridge, raven, Imperial eagle, buzzard, griffon vulture and peregrine falcon.

The mausoleum of Njegoš, the most celebrated ruler of Montenegro and a distinguished poet, lies within the park boundaries and attracts many visitors.

Mavrovo National Park

Lying between 600 and 2700 metres on the Bistra Planina, to the east of the Albanian frontier, Mavrovo, the largest of the Yugoslavian National Parks, has more than fifty peaks over 2000 metres. About half the area is forested and a further 29,000 hectares, lying mostly above the tree line, are covered with alpine pasture. The park has a striking variety of scenery; dome-like summits, gentle slopes and rock cliffs are essential elements of the area's peculiar beauty.

Most characteristics of a typical Macedonian flora and fauna are represented in the area – Mediterranean, continental and subalpine. In the extensive beech and fir forests there are about 120 bears; wolves and lynx, however, are less numerous. The wolf is not protected because it preys on the sheep which graze in the park. Where the wolves are a menace, they are shot or caught and sent to

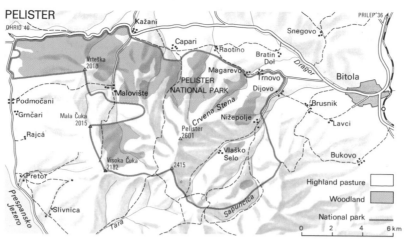

PELISTER

OHRID 40 · Kažani · Capari · Raotino · Snegovo · PRILEP 36 · Vrteška 2010 · Magarevo · Bratin Dol · Dragor · Bitola · Malovište · PELISTER NATIONAL PARK · Trnovo · Dijovo · Crvena Stena · Podmočani · Grnčari · Mala Čuka 2015 · Rajcá · Pelister 2601 · Nižepolje · Brusnik · Lavci · Visoka Čuka 2182 · Vlaško Selo · 2415 · Bukovo · Pretor · Prespansko Jezero · Slivnica · Sapunčica · Tara

Highland pasture
Woodland
National park

0   2   4   6 km

RED KITE an elegant raptor, it is found in wooded hill country.

zoos. Bears also sometimes kill sheep, but in these cases compensation is paid to the farmer and an animal is destroyed only if it is particularly troublesome.

The birdlife includes a wide range of birds of prey – the golden, Imperial, spotted and booted eagles, the griffon and Egyptian vultures, the lammergeier, osprey, goshawk, common and rough-legged buzzards and the eagle owl. The peregrine falcon is numerous and both red and black kites can be seen in the park. The smaller birds and the flora have now been studied in detail, but this work has not yet been published.

Galičica National Park

Situated between the two large lakes of Prespa and Ohrid, the Galičica National Park is a unique area in Yugoslavia. It forms the southern part of the Dinaric mountain range and combines both southern and northern elements in its flora as well as species characteristic of the east and of the Mediterranean. The list of woody plants includes about 150 species, a higher number than for any other National Park in Yugoslavia. An abundance of Grecian juniper, which here grows to the size of a large tree, and several species of oak, of which the Macedonian oak is one of the most interesting, give the forests their dis-

tinctive appearance. The forests are famous for the rare tree *Celtis caucasicas*.

Within the park, on Lake Prespa, lies the small island of Golem Grad, known for its snakes and lizards. Two species of tortoise, both numerous, are found on the island and in one group of Grecian junipers there is a colony of nesting cormorants.

Lake Prespa and Ohrid are of outstanding importance as wildfowl refuges and perhaps comprise the most important wetland area in southern Europe. Both lakes are free from pollution, especially Lake Prespa, which is remarkable for its breeding colony of Dalmatian pelicans. Parts of the lakes lie in Albania and rely on international co-operation for their preservation.

The fauna of the Galičica forests includes the bear, a few wolves, the wild boar and numerous species of birds of prey. The alpine pastures are grazed by sheep and cattle which sometimes fall prey to either bears or wolves.

Pelister National Park

Pelister and nearby Galičica, which both lie near the Greek Frontier, are the most southerly National Parks in Yugoslavia. Pelister is remarkable for its large forest of Macedonian pine, a rare species which is confined to the mountains of the central Balkans. The Macedonian pine here forms two distinct associations, one with bracken and the other with bilberry. On the lower slopes it grows into a fine tall tree, but where it reaches the tree line it sometimes has a bushy appearance like the dwarf mountain pine. The cone is quite distinctive – long, narrow and rather soft to the touch.

Most of the Baba Mountains, with several peaks over 2000 metres of which Pelister (2601 metres) is the highest, lie within the park. Magnificent mountain pastures extend above the tree line and there are two glacial lakes. Many of the mountain rivers are rich in trout. The bear is the most notable member of the fauna; the wolf is rare and the lynx was formerly found here. The bird fauna, which is being studied at present, is known to be extremely rich. Details however, are not yet available.

1 LOVĆEN
Information: Turistički savez Crne Gore, Bulevar Lenjina 2/1, 81001 Titograd
Access: from KOTOR
Open: Unrestricted
Facilities: Mountain refuges within the park

2 MAVROVO
Information: Turistički savez Makedonije, Maršala Tita 39, p.fah 25, 91001 Skopje
Access: from DEBAR or GOSTIVAR
Open: Unrestricted
Facilities: Hotels within the park. Cable-car to Mount Bistra from Mavrovo. Marked footpaths

3 GALIČICA
Information: Turistički savez Makedonije, Maršala Tita 39, p.fah 25, 91001 Skopje
Access: from OHRID
Open: Unrestricted
Facities: Camp sites within the park

4 PELISTER
Information: Turistički savez Makedonije, Maršala Tita 39, p.fah 25, 91001 Skopje
Access: from BITOLA
Open: Unrestricted
Facilities: Mountain hut within the park

261

GREECE

Despite its small size – half the area of Great Britain – Greece has a remarkable range of landscapes and wildlife habitats and contains a few wild and remote areas that are still largely unspoilt. It has a vast number of islands and a coastline of over 15,000 kilometres, one of the longest in Europe.

Although official statistics claim that 19 per cent of Greece is forest-covered the impression gained by the visitor is of extensive areas of mountain and hill country which appear to be in a condition of semi-desert, even though trees once grew there in the past. The maquis-type vegetation is kept in its present condition by sheep and goat grazing and frequent fires. Forest still survives in remote areas, on steep slopes and at high altitudes, and at least one area of virgin forest has survived and is to be protected.

A conservationist would be both delighted and perplexed by the things he sees in Greece. It has the richest flora of any country in Europe – over 6000 species – and the largest number of endemic plants, about 685 species. The glorious display of spring flowers on the hillsides and also on the famous archaeological sites has often been described, and delights all visitors, whether or not they are interested in natural history.

The fauna is also remarkably rich and includes numerous large birds of prey, which are rare in many other countries of western Europe. The wolf and jackal are widespread and the brown bear, although uncommon, still survives.

This remarkable wildlife heritage, together with a climate of warmth and sunshine for most of the year, makes Greece one of the most wonderful places for the visiting naturalist in Europe.

However in contrast to the country's cultural heritage of art and history, a source of great pride to the Greek people, the exceptional value of its natural history – which, surely, is an equally important part of its national heritage – is largely ignored. Organized nature conservation work in Greece is very recent and development of public interest is likely to be slow.

At present Greece is one of the few European countries without a national ornithological or entomological society and no National Appeal of the World Wildlife Fund. It does, however, have the small but excellent Hellenic Society for the Protection of Nature, with nearly a thousand members. It was founded in 1951 and does magnificent work in promoting the cause of nature conservation, although it does not own any nature reserves. The Goulandris Natural History Museum at Kifissia near Athens, a privately run organization, provides a most valuable educational service for school-children in enabling them to understand and appreciate the value and importance of wildlife and its environment. At a local level, the Zagorian Research

Centre in northwest Greece, in Ioannina and Kipi, is actively promoting a sense of pride in the environment of one of the most interesting and beautiful parts of the country. The State Forest Service has responsibility for conservation work, and has a section to deal specifically with National Parks and other protected sites.

The first Greek National Park, Mount Olympus, was created in 1938 and the second, Mount Parnassos, later in the same year. There are now ten sites throughout the country known as National Parks, with a total area of 70,000 hectares, but only one has staff and active management. Even Mount Olympus still has no full-time staff.

All the National Parks contain areas of considerable natural history interest, but Mount Parnis, on the north side of Athens, and Sounion, at the southernmost tip of the peninsula, south of Athens, have so much tourist and other commercial development that perhaps they should be regarded as Regional Parks with the primary purpose of providing recreational facilities. They are not described here and additional sites have been inserted instead, which are of greater natural value even if their protected status is still largely theoretical rather than enforced in practice.

The National Parks have both an inner, or nucleus, zone and an outer zone. In the nucleus all wildlife and landscape features are protected – although there are no means of enforcement – but in the outer zone, which may be considerably larger, tourist development, hunting and commercial activities may be permitted.

In addition to National Parks, there are nineteen conservation sites known as Aesthetic Forests, eleven Protected Wetlands and thirty-two Natural Monuments, which are usually small sites designed to protect particular features of interest. Because so many marshes have been drained for agricultural or other development most of the protected wetlands are important sites internationally. But as with the National Parks, the Forest Service, which is the controlling body, lacks staff and funds, and regulation of activities on the protected wetlands is virtually non-existent.

Tourist development is proceeding at a great rate in many areas, particularly on the island of Crete, which is probably the most famous botanical region of Greece. The popular Samaria National Park in western Crete regulates tourist activities, but at the extreme eastern tip the delightful Aesthetic Forest of Vai, which protects a small area of endemic palm trees, is suffering because of uncontrolled tourist pressure. The National Parks Service is aware of these problems, but as its resources are very small in relation to its responsibilities, progress is sometimes slow. In spite of this it is striving to make the nature conservation policy in Greece more effective.

VIKOS-AOOS The spectacular gorge of the River Voidomatis, seen here from near the village of Monodendrion, at the park's centre.

GREECE

Large-scale earth movements have shaped much of the Greek landscape, and even today the region suffers continuing geological instability. In the east and northeast of the country, hard crystalline rocks have been fractured into a series of upland blocks: the Aegean islands are all that remains of this same land surface drowned in the neighbouring zone of subsidence. The west and south of the country are formed of much younger rocks that have been heavily folded. The sharp ridges and valleys of the countryside are a simple reflection of the geology – alternating sequences of hard limestone and marble and softer sandstones and shales.

Limestone completely dominates the scenery. Much of Greece is a rugged, wild and sparsely vegetated land characterized by steep slopes, ravines, caves and faults – one of the largest and most dramatic having produced the impressive escarpment in east Thessaly, rising from the surrounding countryside near sea level to the 2917-metre summit of Mount Olympus.

Though the land was formerly well wooded, forest clearance, fire and centuries of overgrazing by sheep and goats have created vast areas of scrub and semi desert. Nevertheless the vegetation of Greece is still one of great variety and complexity, having been influenced by plant migration from adjacent land masses. During the Tertiary period the Balkans formed a peninsula joined with what is now Turkey and many plants originating from Asia Minor and Iran were able to move in. Today the vegetation ranges from the alpine plants of the high peaks to the evergreen woods of the Mediterranean and the scorched, dry phrygana – a dry stick-like vegetation– of the Greek islands. Nearly one-third of the land comprises lowland plains, valleys and foothill country, generally fertile and productive – the hillsides being planted with vines, olives and other fruits, while the lowlands, especially in Macedonia, yield good pasture and a variety of crops, including wheat, cotton and tobacco, among those of commercial importance.

SAMARIA GORGE
"One of the seven natural wonders of Europe". It is encased by sheer rock walls 600 metres high and only 3.5 metres apart at the narrowest point.

PARK/RESERVE	SIZE (km²)	DESCRIPTION	MAP REF.	PAGE NO.
LAKE MIKRÍ PRESPÁ	194.7	National Park. Southern part of Lake Préspa with shallow lagoons and large areas of reed swamp. Important bird-breeding locality. Many rare aquatic birds. Especially well known for pelicans.	A1	266
LAKE KERKÍNI	c 60	Protected Wetland. Wetland area in the valley of the River Strimón. Outstanding birdlife.	B1	266
RODOPI	5.0	National Monument. Untouched forest of beech fir and spruce. Rich flora and fauna. Many large mammals.	C1	266
EVROS DELTA	—	Protected Wetland. Extensive area of marsh and lagoons on the Turkish frontier. Large and varied birdlife.	C1	267
MOUNT OLYMPUS	40.0	National Park. Mountain of legendary fame with maquis and forest. Unique floristic interest, several endemic species.	B2	267
VIKOS AOÖS	34.12	Magnificent river gorge with superb views and exciting birdlife.	A2	268
PINDUS	101.4	National Park. Remote mountain area with extensive forests. Important for birds of prey.	A2	269
GULF OF ARTA	c 180	Protected Wetland. Extensive marshland attracting many water birds.	A2	269
CEPHALONIA	28.6	National Park. Beautiful forested limestone area in vicinity of Mount Aínos.	A3	269
MOUNT OETI	72.1	National Park. Forested area in the Gíona range. Rich flora with several endemic orchids.	B2	270
MOUNT PARNASSOS	35.1	National Park. Mountains with forests, alpine pastures and rocky limestone cliffs.	B2	270
SAMARIA GORGE	48.5	National Park. Spectacular rocky gorge with 600-metre-high sides. Remarkable endemic flora.	C4	270
VÁI	0.09	Aesthetic Forest. Small coastal area of endemic palms of unique scientific importance.	D4	271

Lake Mikrí Préspa National Park

For centuries Lake Mikrí Préspa, together with Lakes Ohrid and Great Préspa, which all lie in an area on the borders of Greece, Yugoslavia and Albania, were almost inaccessible to the outside world, partly because of political tensions and partly because the access roads were few and badly maintained. Mikrí Préspa's exciting birdlife was "discovered" in 1967, when two French ornithologists found an important breeding colony of pelicans on the lake. In the succeeding years intensive work revealed the lake's extraordinarily rich bird fauna, and showed the area to be among the finest in Europe.

The National Park was established in 1971 and has a 4815-hectare nucleus zone, which includes the total water surface and a 200-metre strip around the lake shore, where wildlife is totally protected. The water is relatively shallow, only 14 metres deep, and there are large areas of reedswamp and shallow lagoons at the northern end, down the eastern shore and at the southern end, which stretches into Albania. Most of the lake's rare aquatic birds breed in these parts.

The nesting colonies of Dalmatian and white pelicans are the most famous wildfowl features of the lake. They are both large, magnificent birds, and very rare in Europe – the total world population of the Dalmatian pelican is thought to be only between 700 and 1100 breeding pairs, although numbers fluctuate from year to year. Other breeding birds include the spoonbill, common and pygmy cormorants, grey and purple herons, squacco heron, night heron, little bittern, glossy ibis, great white and little egrets, goosanders (the most southerly colony in Europe) and black-necked grebe.

Although the mammals have not been so intensively studied there is evidence that the brown bear, wolf, jackal, otter and the coypu, which has recently been introduced for commercial purposes, live in the region of the lake. The coypu is unfortunately destroying the reeds and is probably discouraging some birds from nesting in the area.

Lake Kerkíni Protected Wetland

The works of man have made Lake Kerkíni one of the finest wetland areas in Greece. The lake lies in the valley of the River Strimón, which flows south, close to the Bulgarian border, into the Aegean Sea, and at one time contained extensive areas of marsh. About 30 years ago a bank was built for irrigation purposes, flooding the area around the lake. Silt carried down by the river quickly collected behind the bank, creating an area of shallow water and low islands. The subsequent development of marsh vegetation and woodland has enticed many species of birds to these parts. Despite Kerkíni's internationally recognized status its boundaries are still provisional and the protection of its birdlife is not yet enforced. The whole area is, moreover, threatened by a proposal to raise the water level by 10 metres, thus submerging all important nesting areas. At present the lake has all the waterfowl recorded for Greece, including the pelican.

Rodopi Virgin Forest National Monument

Rodopi is a fine example of virgin forest, a natural feature that, except in Yugoslavia and the countries to the east, has practically disappeared throughout Europe. The forest, which is probably larger than anything found farther west, is mainly of beech, fir and spruce and contains many massive trees; some beech and fir trees have 14-metre girths. When its scientific status was assessed jointly by the International Union for the Conservation of Nature and a team of Greek biologists, one of the party described his first visit in 1975 to this forest of soaring trees and silence as "like entering a cathedral". At that time there were no roads or any other evidence of man's intrusion. However, since then a number of roads have been built and some trees felled.

The three climatic types represented in the region – continental, Mediterranean and oceanic – have contributed to the forest's remarkably rich fauna and flora. Many of the bird species are central European and nineteen reach their southernmost limit in the forest. Most of the Greek woodpeckers – three-toed, black, white-backed, great spotted and green – have been recorded. Many large mammals, particularly the brown bear, wolf, lynx, red deer, roe deer and chamois, live within the protected area. As some of these animals often wander great distances, it has been proposed that the whole region between the rivers Charadra Thermion and Pharasinu Potami should be a no-hunting zone.

LAKE MIKRÍ PRÉSPA

YUGOSLAVIA
GREECE

Megáli Préspa
(Great Préspa)

ALBANIA
GREECE

Mirtsa Rema

Laimos
Áyios Yermanós
Miliónas
Faradhes
Plati
△2117
Gelé 1360
LAKE MIKRÍ PRÉSPA
NATIONAL PARK
Kallithéa
Áyios Akhíllios
Lefkónas
△1676
Áyios Dhimitrios
Mikrí Préspa
Rékata
FLÓRINA 32
Varnitsite
1434
Osova
Kariaí
Trigonon
Pixos
Dhaseri
Mikrolímni
Vronderón
Tsoutsouli 1457
Raista 1145
Oxiá
Tirnoven
Biological station
KASTORIA 30
Kraniés
Rakickë
Angathotón
Sfika
Shyec

Pasture
Agricultural land
Marsh
Woodland
National park

0 1 2 3 4 5 km

DALMATIAN
PELICAN *above* A rare
European species.

MOUNT OLYMPUS
below The "Throne of
Zeus" lies on the
southwest face.

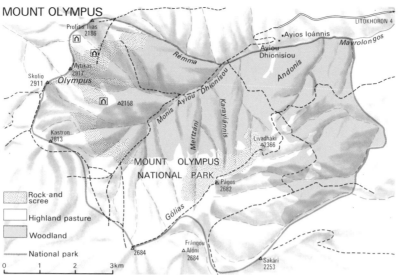

MOUNT OLYMPUS

LITÓKHORON 4

Profítis Ilías
2186

Mytikás
2917
Olympus
Skólio
2911

Ayios Ioánnis

Ayiou
Dhionisíou
Mavrolongos

Rémma

Andonis

△2158

Monís Ayiou Dhionisíou

Meritzáni

Karayiánnis

Kastron
2813

Livadháki
△2366

MOUNT OLYMPUS
NATIONAL PARK

Págos
2682

Gólias

Rock and
scree

Highland pasture

Woodland

National park

2684

Frángou
△ Alóni
2684

Sakári
2253

0   1   2   3km

Evros Delta Protected Wetland

At the mouth of the River Evros, which
forms the frontier between Greece and
Turkey, lies an extensive area of marsh and
lagoons. The Greek side of the delta has long
been known as a remarkable area for waterfowl and, together with the adjacent forests of
Calabrian pine and black pine, which have
more large birds of prey than any other
comparable region in Greece, forms an area
of the highest international importance. However, despite its value the proposed boundary
of the protected zone has not yet been fixed
by the Forest Service, the responsible
authority, and such activities as illicit road
construction and unregulated hunting still
take place.

The spur-winged plover, a primarily North
African and Asiatic species, and also the
avocet, although its nests are often destroyed
by cattle, still breed in this wetland but in
reduced numbers. The islands have remained
undisturbed and are excellent breeding sites
for gull-billed terns, common and little terns
and Sandwich terns – the only colony in
Greece. In addition collared pratincoles and

redshanks are numerous. The neighbouring
coniferous forest regularly provides nesting
sites for such predatory species as black
vultures, golden eagles, imperial eagles and
sea eagles. The Turkish side of the border is
also interesting ornithologically; less reclamation work has been done there.

Mount Olympus National Park

Established in June 1938 as the first National
Park in Greece, Mount Olympus, "the
dwelling place of the Gods", combines the
fascination of Greek legend with a unique
flora, fauna and landscape. The great massif
of Olympus (2917 metres) – the highest Greek
mountain – dominates the central eastern
coastline and attracts a great many visitors.
Its slopes, rising almost straight out of the
Aegean Sea, have a clearly zoned vegetation.
The lower zones are covered with maquis, as
is common throughout much of Greece,
followed, between 800 and 1800 metres, by
forests of beech and pine, mainly black pine.
The Balkan pine forms the tree line, which
reaches 2500 metres in places.

As most of the mountain consists of
Triassic and Jurassic limestones, surface
water is scarce and the soils are usually dry.
The flora has been well studied and about
1500 species of flowering plants and ferns
have been recorded, including nineteen species
which are endemic to the mountain. Among
them are the conspicuously large blue-
flowered *Campanula oreadum*, found in rock
crevices between 2000 and 2900 metres;
Viola striis-notata, confined to mobile screes
between 2400 and 2900 metres, and the
bluish-lilac, bell-flowered *Jankaea heldreichii*, which is typical of shady crevices in
beech forest and one of the finest of the
Olympus endemics. *Saxifraga spruneri*, which
is endemic to the central part of the Balkan
Peninsula, from northern Albania to central
Greece, has white flowers and is the commonest saxifrage above 2600 metres. About
half of the 150 species recorded above 2400
metres are endemic to the Balkan Peninsula.

1 LAKE MIKRÍ PRÉSPA
Information: Tmima Dason, I
Arti 42, Flórina
Access: from FLÓRINA or
KASTÓRIA
Open: Unrestricted except for
western shore for which a
military permit is required
Facilities: Small hotels in
Laimos and Mikrolimni. Marked
trails. Observation tower

2 LAKE KERKÍNI
Information: Ministry of
Agriculture, General Directorate
of Forests and Forest
Environment, Section of
National Parks and Aesthetic
Forests, 3–5 Ippokratous Street,
Athens
Access: from
SIDHIRÓKASTRON or SÉRRAI
Open: Unrestricted

3 RODOPI
Information: Ministry of
Agriculture, General Directorate
of Forests and Forest
Environment, Section of
National Parks and Aesthetic
Forests, 3–5 Ippokratous Street,
Athens
or Ministry of Co-ordination,
1 Syntagma Square, Athens
Access: from DRÁMA
Open: Military permit required.
Advice from either of the two
addresses above

4 EVROS DELTA
Information: Ministry of
Agriculture, General Directorate
of Forests and Forest Environ-
ment, Section of National Parks
and Aesthetic Forests, 3–5
Ippokratous Street, Athens
Access: from
ALEXANDROÚPOLIS
Open: Military permit required.

5 MOUNT OLYMPUS
Information: Diefthensi
Dason, Kioutaxias 1, Kateríni
Access: from Ayiou
Dhionisiou, 7km W of
LITÓKHORON
Open: Unrestricted
Facilities: Greek Alpine-Club
refuges within the park

267

PINDUS

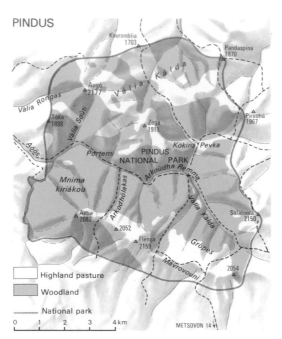

Highland pasture

Woodland

National park

0   1   2   3   4 km

MÉTSOVON 14

Vikos-Aóös Gorge National Park

Near the border with Albania, in the little known mountains of central Greece, lies one of the country's most striking natural features – the gorge of the River Voidomatis at Vikos. The gorge, which takes its name from a local village, lies in the nucleus zone of the National Park and can be approached at the upper end along a path leading from Monodendrion past the old monastery at Oxya. Fortunately the best views of the gorge can be had from near this point, for a little further on the path degenerates into a cliff ledge which becomes progressively narrower and more dangerous.

Where the gorge sides are less precipitous, and in the countryside nearby, there are forests of beech, fir, bosnian pine and black pine. The cliffs are the breeding haunts of griffon vultures, golden and Bonelli's eagles and peregrine falcons. Mammals such as bears, wolves and jackals live in the region.

Pindus National Park

The Pindus range of mountains lies in one of the least accessible regions of northern Greece. The park, created in 1966, is situated north of the main road between Ioánnina and Tríkala, not far from where it reaches an altitude of 1700 metres, higher than any other asphalt road in Greece. Within the park, which ranges in altitude between 1200 and 2177 metres, are two important rivers, the Vàlia Kàlda and the Aóös, and extensive forests of common beech, black and Bosnian pine, hornbeam and hop-hornbeam as well as oak and fir.

The fauna is not well known, but certainly includes the brown bear, wolf and jackal. The more familiar species found in the area are the roe deer, chamois and wild boar. The Pindus range is important ornithologically, particularly for birds of prey. Precisely which species are to be found is as yet unknown; their status is being studied at present.

JACKAL *above* The slightly built European jackal spends the day in dense cover and hunts at night. It is found mainly in Greece.

CEPHALONIA *left* The island, of which the National Park forms a small part in the region of Mount Ainos, lies off the west coast of Greece.

Gulf of Árta Protected Wetland

The most important wetland on the west coast of northern Greece is the Gulf of Árta, an enormous, almost enclosed, shallow bay southwest of the town of Árta. Silt deposited by two rivers, the Loúros and the Árakhthos, has created an extensive area of marshland and reedswamp, which originally measured about 30 by 10 kilometres, but has now largely been reclaimed and cultivated. The marsh remaining along the gulf's wide margins, together with the islands, sand-bars and lagoons, attract many water birds for breeding, roosting, and overwintering.

The gulf is of special international importance because it is one of only two sites in Greece where the Dalmatian pelican, a species now on the endangered list of European birds, is known to breed. Isolated specimens of the white pelican are often seen in summer, but breeding has not yet been proved. Numerous other marsh birds, notably the purple heron, little egret, little bittern, glossy ibis, squacco heron and white stork regularly visit the reserve. Wading birds such as the Kentish plover, redshank and black-winged stilt breed in the wetland and the stone curlew and collared pratincole nest on the dry saltings. In the area adjacent to the marshes the bee-eater, roller, short-toed lark, crested lark, red-rumped swallow, golden oriole, penduline tit and short-toed treecreeper are among the species of particular interest.

Cephalonia National Park

Cephalonia, one of the largest islands off the west coast of central Greece, has the distinction of being the type locality for the Greek fir. This tree, widespread throughout Greece, mainly above 800 metres, was first described from the forest, which now forms the National Park. Scenically it is a very beautiful limestone area with Mt Aínos (1628 metres) forming the centrepiece. Apart from the fir forest, rocky ground and mountain meadowland make up much of the park.

GULF OF ÁRTA

[Map legend: Agricultural land; Marsh; Sand; Protected wetland]

IOANNINA 65 · Khalkiádes · Árta · Loúron · Pétra · Nea Kerasous · Kostakioi · Rákhi · Gavriá · Kolomodhia · Kombóti · Polidhroson · Aneza · Limnothálassa · Pakhikálamos · Sampsous · Vigla · Mitikas · Loutrótopos · AMFILOKHIA 26 · Flambóura · GULF OF ÁRTA PROTECTED WETLAND · Kommëno · Salaóra · Koronisia · Peranisi · Ormos Salaóras · PREVEZA 3 · Loúros · Arakhthos · 0 2 4 6 km

1 VIKOS-AÓÖS
Information: Ministry of Agriculture, General Directorate of Forests and Forest Environment, Section of National Parks and Aesthetic Forests, 3–5 Ippokratous Street, Athens
Access: from Kónitsa, 65km N of IOÁNNINA
Open: Unrestricted
Facilities: Marked trails and footpaths within the park

2 PINDUS
Information: Diefthensi Dason, Ipiresia Georgias, Grevená
Eccess: from Métsovon, 58km E of IOÁNNINA or Krania, 15km SW of GREVENÁ (access roads not asphalted)
Open: Unrestricted

3 GULF OF ÁRTA
Information: Hellenic Republic Natinnal Tourist Organisation, Information Department, B/2, 2 Amerikis Street, Athens 133
Access: from ÁRTA
Open: Unrestricted

4 CEPHALONIA
Information: Tmima Dason, Diad, Constantinou, Argostólion, Cephalonia
Access: from ARGOSTÓLION or SÁMI
Open: Unrestricted

269

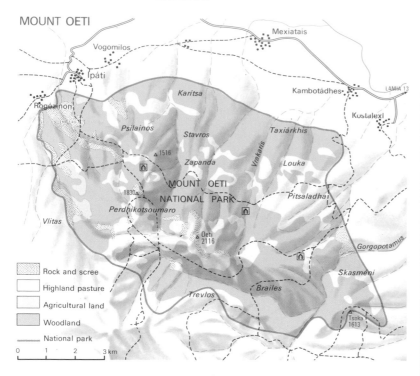

MOUNT OETI

Rock and scree
Highland pasture
Agricultural land
Woodland
National park

0   1   2   3 km

AGRIMI *below* A wild goat, possibly introduced to Crete in antiquity, now confined to this Gorge.

VAI *right* The remarkable palms of Vai, known to occur in only one other place in Crete, form an oasis of green at the arid eastern tip of the island. Here their fronds project above the pink flowers of the oleander.

Mount Oeti National Park

Between the altitudes of 600 and 1900 metres, the National Park extends over most of Mount Oeti, a peak in the Gíona range. Its picturesque slopes are extensively forested with oak, beech, sweet chestnut, black pine and Greek fir and the park's rich flora includes a number of endemic orchids. Most of the large mammals typically found in Greek forests inhabit the area except the bear. The "Oeti wild goat" occurs in the park.

Mount Parnassos National Park

Established in 1938, Mount Parnassos National Park is situated in central Greece, just east of Delphi, overlooking the Gulf of Corinth. It consists of a mountain region varying in altitude from 1100 to 2000 metres, with rocky limestone cliffs, attractive open valleys and an extensive forest of Greek fir. In many places growth is poor and the foliage is festooned with lichens. The stony limestone soil supports little vegetation under the canopy. Other species of tree, including hop-hornbeam, hornbeam and the shrubby prickly juniper, occur but in isolated pockets. Extensive alpine pastures lie at higher altitudes and many plants of special interest, both rare and endemic, have been recorded in the area. Several species of crocus, together with *Colchicum catacuzenium*, appear as the snows melt in spring and the delicate blue flowers of *Anemone blanda* and alpine squill can be seen at the edge of the forest.

Within this mountain complex, which includes the deep valleys, peaks and rock

cliffs of nearby Delphi, the birdlife is particularly exciting. The most impressive species are the large birds of prey – golden and Bonelli's eagles, griffon, black and Egyptian vultures and the lammergeier. In the fir forests white-backed and black woodpeckers are found, while at higher altitudes rock and ortolan buntings, rock partridges, shore larks, rock thrushes, black redstarts and alpine accentors can be seen. The rock cliffs, and especially the famous archaeological site of Delphi, ring with the lovely song of the rock nuthatch.

Samaria Gorge National Park

Crete holds a special place in the natural history of Greece because of its geographical position, between the mainland and the north African coast, and its large number of endemic plants and interesting fauna. It also has the distinction of having one of the most spectacular National Parks in Greece, which in 1979 won the Council of Europe "European Diploma". The gorge, which can justifiably be called one of the "seven wonders of Europe" is situated in the mountains of western Crete south of the town of Khaniá and begins abruptly at Xilóskala on the south side of the plain of Omalós. From this point, 1200 metres high, a path descends steeply into the gorge, continuing for 16 kilometres until it reaches the sea at Ayía Roúmeli. The main gorge, only 3.5 metres wide at its narrowest point, is contained by red and grey rock walls which tower to a height of 600 metres. This gorge and the several smaller ones which adjoin it form the National Park.

1 MOUNT OETI
Information: Dasarxeio
Forestry Department, Ipsilantou
16, Lamia
Access: from Ipáti, 25km W of
LAMÍA
Open: Unrestricted
Facilities: Marked trails.
Greek Alpine-Club refuges within
the park

2 MOUNT PARNASSOS
Information: Dasonomio
Forestry Department, Ámfissa
Access: from Arákhova, 10km E
of DELFI or Eptálofon, 53km S of
LAMIÁ
Open: Unrestricted
Facilities: Greek Alpine-Club
refuge close to park boundary

3 SAMARIA GORGE
Information: Ipiresia Georgias,
Tmima Dason, Periduu 22,
Khaniá, Crete
Access: from Xilóskala, 42km S
of KHANIÁ
Open: May to November,
between 0600 and 1500. After
1500 until sunset visitors
allowed only 2km into park
Facilities: Information point
and tourist pavilion at the
entrance to the park.
Information point at Ayia
Rouméli. Marked trails.
Wardens on site

4 VÁÏ AESTHETIC FOREST
Information: Hellenic Republic
National Tourist Organisation,
Information Department B/2,
2 Amerikis Street, Athens 133
Access: from Váï, 26km NE of
SITÍA
Open: Unrestricted
Facilities: Observation tower
within the park

In much of Crete the landscape is dry and relatively barren, but here there are mountain streams and springs, and forests of the local Calabrian pine and a subspecies of the funeral cypress endemic to Crete cover the slopes. Deciduous trees such as Cretan maple, kermes oak, oriental plane, olive, as well as shrubs such as tree heath and prickly juniper are also widespread. The flora of the gorge is especially noted for its fourteen endemic species, of which *Paeonia clusii* is the most beautiful. It flowers in spring and is covered in large white blossoms.

Among the larger animals and birds are the beech marten and badger, golden eagle, griffon vulture, Egyptian vulture, lammergeier, raven, common and alpine choughs and chukar partridge. The best-known animal is, however, the Agrimi or Cretan wild goat, an ancient species with ibex-like horns. A relict population of about 300 animals lives in the gorge.

Váï Aesthetic Forest

At the extreme eastern end of Crete lies a remarkable, small forest consisting almost entirely of the endemic palm *Phoenix theophrastii*. The forest stands just inland from a sandy beach, behind a string of dunes. Although the palms often grow to a height of about 15 metres, many are short and almost bush-like. The fruit resembles a date and is produced in large clusters on a central stem. Beneath the canopy there are large stands of rush tussocks, grasses and other plants, while close to the sea, sea-lavenders prevail.

Phoenix theophrastii is the only "tree" palm in Europe and is known to occur in only one other place, in an inaccessible cove on the south side of Crete, where two or three of the trees can be found growing. Looking like a scene from North Africa, Váï Forest is both astonishing visually and scientifically unique.

Although nothing is known about the invertebrate fauna it is probably of considerable interest. The bay at Váï is very popular and much illegal camping takes place among the palms next to the beach.

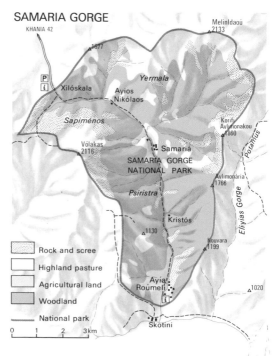

SAMARIA GORGE

Rock and scree
Highland pasture
Agricultural land
Woodland
National park
0 1 2 3km

GLOSSARY

biotope The environment in which a creature lives.

bunter The earliest part of the Triassic period, a zone within the geological time scale that lasted from 225 to 195 million years ago.

calcicolous (of vegetation) Preferring or confined to calcareous soils.

caldera Large volcanic crater, often formed by the collapse of surface rocks.

cirque Large, glacially eroded armchair-shaped hollow on the side of a mountain.

dolomite A form of limestone consisting of at least 15 per cent magnesium carbonate.

endemic (of plants and animals) Native only to a particular area or country.

erratic A rock or stone that has been moved away from its place of origin. The term usually implies glacial transportation.

esker A long, sinous ridge of sand and gravel deposited beneath a glacier by meltwater.

Europa-Reserve A nature reserve (in Germany) that has been recognized by the German Section of the International Council for Bird Protection to be of ornithological importance, particularly for migrants.

feral (of animals) Having reverted to a wild state after being domesticated.

fumarole A vent on the side of a volcano or on a lava flow which emits hot gases.

greywacke A hard, mid-grey sandstone, usually devoid of bedding planes.

halophyte An organism adapted to living in a salt environment.

hydrosere The succession of plants and animals in an aquatic environment.

IUCN International Union for the Conservation of Nature.

karst landscape A form of limestone topography, typified by caves and underground rivers, produced by the action of ground water (water within the rocks themselves) rather than by surface erosion. The name derives from the Karst district of Yugoslavia.

kettle hole A depression formed in glacial deposits after a block of ice melted.

moraine Material deposited by glacier ice. Moraines can occur at the "snout", beneath or at the margins of a glacier.

plant succession The progressive changes that take place in the colonization of an area by a group of plants, from bare earth to climax community.

puntgun A large-bored gun used for shooting wildfowl from a punt.

Ramsar Convention Abbreviation for the International Conference on the Conservation of Wetlands and Waterfowl, held at Ramsar, Iran, in 1971.

Raptor A bird of prey.

Roche moutonnée Literally a "sheep rock". Roches moutonnées have been worn smooth on one side and plucked and shattered on the other by the action of glacier ice. The smooth side faces the direction from which the ice came.

Slack A damp or wet depression in a coastal sand dune system, often with interesting plants and animals.

UN World Heritage Site A site of "Universal Value" established under the provisions of the UNESCO 1972 International Convention concerning the Protection of World Cultural and Natural Heritage.

vascular plant All higher plants: they are distinguished from others by the possession of a system of cells through which nutrients are transferred to all parts of the organism.

WWF World Wildlife Fund.

MAP KEY

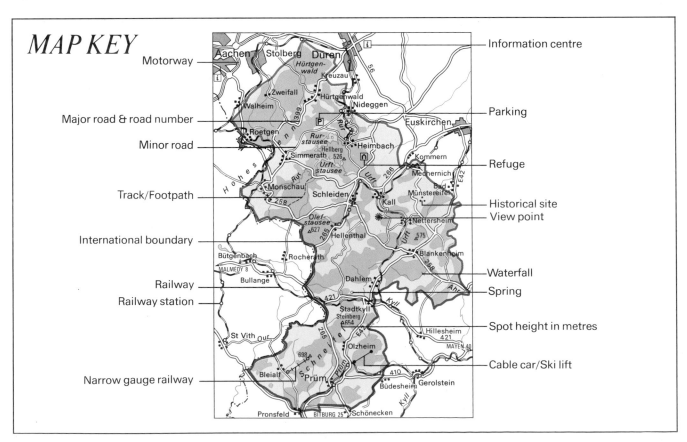

Motorway

Major road & road number

Minor road

Track/Footpath

International boundary

Railway

Railway station

Narrow gauge railway

Information centre

Parking

Refuge

Historical site

View point

Waterfall

Spring

Spot height in metres

Cable car/Ski lift

INDEX TO PLANTS AND ANIMALS

References in *italics* refer to the illustrations

283

GENERAL INDEX

Page numbers in *italics* refer to the illustrations

ADDRESSES OF CONSERVATION ORGANIZATIONS

Federation of European Nature and National Parks
Föderation der Natur- und Nationalparke Europas, Guldenhagen 23, 3400 Göttingen, West Germany
International Council for Bird Preservation, British Museum (Natural History), London SW7, United Kingdom
International Union for Conservation of Nature and Natural Resources (IUCN), Gland 1196, Switzerland
International Water Fowl Research Bureau, The Wildfowl Trust, Slimbridge, Gloucestershire, United Kingdom
World Wildlife Fund (WWF) International, Avenue de Mont Blanc, Gland 1196, Switzerland
NORWAY
National Council for Nature Protection
Statens Naturvernrånd, Myntgt. 2, Oslo
Norwegian Union for Nature Protection
Norges Naturvernforbund, Akersgaten 63, Oslo
ICELAND
Forestry Service
Skograekt Ríkisins, Ranarg 18, Reykjavík
Nature Conservation Council
Náttúruverndarráð, Hverfisgötu 26, Reykjavík
SWEDEN
National Environment Protection Board
Statens Naturvårdsverk (SNV), Nature Conservation Division, Box No. 1302, 171 25 Solna
National Forest Service
Domänverket, Pelle Bergs Backe 3, 79181 Falun
Swedish Society for the Conservation of Nature
Svenska Naturskyddsföreningen, Kungsholmstorg 125, 1121 Stockholm
FINLAND
Forest Research Institute, Unionkatu 40A, 00170 Helsinki 17
Office for National Parks, National Board of Forestry, Box 233, 00121 Helsinki 12
DENMARK
Danish Nature Conservation Society
Danmarks Naturfredningsforening, Frederiksberg Runddel 1, 2000 København F
Forest Service
Skovstyrelsen, Miljøministeriet, Slotsholmsgade 12, 1216 København K
Nature Conservation Board
Fredningsstyrelsen, Miljøministeriet, Slotsholmsgade 12, 1216 København K
WEST GERMANY
Bavarian League for Nature Protection
Bund Naturschutz in Bayern, Schönfeldstrasse 8, 8000 München
German League for Bird Protection
Deutscher Bund für Vogelschutz, Favoritepark 2, 7140 Ludwigsburg
German WWF
Umweltstiftung WWF, Bockenheimer Anlage 38, Frankfurt am Main
National Protection Society for Nature Conservation and Land Ecology
Bundesforschungsanstalt für Naturschutz und Landschaftsökologie, Konstantinstrasse 110, 5300 Bonn 2
AUSTRIA
Austrian Alpine Society
Österreichischer Alpenverein, Renngasse 4, 1190 Wien
Austrian Friends of Nature
Österreichische Naturfreunde, Untere Alpe Donau 51, 1220 Wien
Austrian League for Nature Protection
Österreichischer Naturschutzbund, Messeplatz 1, 1070 Wien
Austrian WWF
WWF/Österreich, Ottakringerstrasse 120, 1162 Wien
SWITZERLAND
Swiss League for the Protection of Nature, Wartenbergstrasse 22, Postfach 73, 4020 Basel
NETHERLANDS
Nature Conservation Council
Natuurbeschermingsraad, Maliebaan 12, 3581 CN Utrecht
Society for the Protection of Nature
Vereniging tot behoud van Natuurmonumenten in Nederland, Schaep en Burgh, Noordereinde 60, 1243 JJ 's-Graveland
Research Institute for Nature Management
Rijksinstituut voor Natuurbeheer, Kemperbergerweg 67, 6818 RM Arnhem
BELGIUM
Ardenne et Gaume, rue Marie de Bourgogne 41, 1040 Bruxelles
Association of Nature and Bird Reserves of Belgium
Les Réserves Naturelles et Ornithologiques de Belgique, rue Vautier 31, 1040 Bruxelles
Council for Nature Conservation
Le Service de la Conservation de la Nature auprès de l'Administration des Eaux et Forêts, boulevard Bischoffsheim 32, 1000 Bruxelles

National Union for the Protection of Nature
Entente Nationale pour la Protection de la Nature, rue Perk 16, 1960 Sterrebeek *and* Walenstrasse 27, 2000 Antwerpen
Superior Council for Nature Reserves and Nature Conservation
Le Conseil Supérieur des Réserves Naturelles et de la Conservation de la nature, Administration des Eaux et Forêts, boulevard Bischoffsheim 32, 1000 Bruxelles
De Wielewaal, Graatakker 13, 2300 Turnhout
LUXEMBOURG
Luxembourg League for the Study and Protection of Birds
Ligue Luxembourgeoise pour l'Etude et la Protection des Oiseaux, 32 rue de la Forêt, Luxembourg
Service for Nature Conservation
Conseil Supérieur de la Conservation de la Nature, Administration des Eaux et Forêts, avenue de la Porte-Neuve 34, Luxembourg
UNITED KINGDOM
Countryside Commission, John Dower House, Crescent Place, Cheltenham GL50 3RA
Countryside Commission for Scotland, Battleby, Redgorton, Perth PH1 3EW
Forestry Commission, 231 Corstorphine Road, Edinburgh EH1 7AT
National Trust, 42 Queen Anne's Gate, London SW1H 9AS
National Trust, Committee for Northern Ireland, Rowallane House, Saintfield, Ballynahinch, Co. Down BT24 7LH
National Trust for Scotland, 5 Charlotte Square, Edinburgh EH2 4DU
Nature Conservancy Council, 19 Belgrave Square, London SW1X 8PY
Royal Society for Nature Conservation, The Green, Nettleham, Lincoln LN2 2NR
Royal Society for the Protection of Birds, The Lodge, Sandy SG19 2DL
EIRE
National Trust for Ireland 126 Lower Camden Street, Dublin 2, Eire
FRANCE
Federation of French Nature Parks
Fédération des Parcs Naturels de France, 45 rue de Lisbonne, 75008 Paris
Federation of Nature Protection Societies
Fédération Française des Sociétés de Protection de la Nature (FFSPN), 57 rue Cuvier, 75005 Paris
French League for the Protection of Birds
Ligue Française pour la Protection des Oiseaux, BP 263, La Corderie Royale, 17305 Rochefort cedex
National Society for the Protection of Nature
Société National de Protection de la Nature (SNPN), 5 rue Cuvier, 75005 Paris
Society for the Study and Protection of Nature in Brittany
Société pour l'Étude et la Protection de la Nature en Bretagne, Faculté des Sciences, avenue le Gorgeu, 29200 Brest
SPAIN
National Institute for Nature Conservation
Instituto Nacional para la Conservación de la Naturaleza (ICONA), Subdirección general de Recursos Naturales Renovables, Gran Vía de San Francisco 35, Madrid
Spanish WWF
Asociación Defensa de la Naturaleza (ADENA), Santa Engarcia 6, Madrid
Superior Council for Scientific Investigation
Consejo Superior de Investigaciónes Científicas (CSIC), Serrano 117, Madrid
Spanish National Ornthological Society
Sociedad Española de Ornitolgía, Museo Nacional de Ciencias Naturales, Castellano 80, Madrid 6
PORTUGAL
League for the Protection of Nature
Liga para a Protecção da Natureza, Faculdade de Ciéncias, R. Escola Politécnica, 1200 Lisboa
National Service for Parks, Reserves and Heritage Landscapes
Serviço Nacional de Parques, Reservas e Património Paisagístico, Rua da Lapa 73, Lisboa 2
ITALY
Associazione "Italia Nostra", Corso Vittorio Emanuele 287, 00186 Roma
Italian Alpine Club
Club Alpino Italiano (CAI), Via Ugo Foscolo 3, 20121 Milano
Italian Botanical Society
Instituto di Botanica, Universita di Roma, Piazzale Aldo Moro 7, 00100 Roma
Italian National Research Council
Consiglio Nazionale delle Ricerche, Piazzale Aldo Moro 7, 00100 Roma
Italian WWF
WWF/Italia, via P.A. Micheli 50, 00197 Roma
YUGOSLAVIA
Nature Conservancy (for Bosnia & Herzegovina)
Zavod za zaštitu spnmenika kulture, Leninova 14B, Sarajevo
Nature Conservancy (for Croatia)
Republički Zavod za zaštitu pirode, Ilica 44, Zagreb
Nature Conservancy (for Macedonia)
Zavod na zastita na prirodata na S.R. Makedoniju, Skopje
Nature Conservancy (for Montenegro)
Republički Zavod za zaštitu prirode, Ilije Milacica 22, Titograd
Nature Conservancy (for Serbia)
Republički Zavod za zaštitu prirode, III Bulevar 106, Beograd
Nature Conservancy (for Slovenia)
Zavod za spomeniško varsto, Pleclikov trg 2, Ljubljana
GREECE
Hellenic Society for the Protection of Nature, 9 Kydathineon Street, Athens
Ministry of Agriculture, General Directorate of Forests and Forest Environment, Section for National Parks & Aesthetic Forests, 3-5 Ippokratous Street, Athens

BIBLIOGRAPHY

GENERAL

A Directory of Western Palaearctic Wetlands, IUCN (Gland, 1980)
Dupont, P., *373 Parcs Nationaux et Réserves d'Europe*, Fayard (Paris, 1976)
Ferguson-Lees, J., *et al.* (eds.), *A Guide to Bird-Watching in Europe*, Bodley Head (London, 1975)
Garms, H., *The Natural History of Europe*, Paul Hamlyn (London, 1976)
Les Parks Nationaux, *Proceedings of the International Colloquium on European National Parks* (Paris, 15-17 June, 1970)
Polunin, O., *Flowers of Europe*, University Press (Oxford, 1969)
Poore, D., & Gryn-Ambroes, P., *Nature Conservation in Northern and Western Europe*, IUCN (Gland, 1980)
Smit, J. C., & van Wijngaarden, A., *Threatened Mammals in Europe*, Council of Europe Nature & Environment Series, No. 10 (Strasbourg, 1976)
United Nations List of National Parks and Equivalent Reserves, Hayez (Brussels, 1971)
Wirth, H. (ed.), *Nature Reserves in Europe*, Edition Leipzig (Leipzig, 1979)
World Wildlife Fund Yearbook 1980-81, WWF (Gland, 1981)
Zimmerman, G., *et al.*, *Natur als Erlebnis: Die Nationalparke in Mittleuropa*, DRW-Verlag (Stuttgart, 1979)

NORWAY

Holt-Jensen, A., *The Norwegian Wilderness: National Parks and Protected Areas*, Tanum-Norli (Oslo, 1978)

ICELAND

Einarsson, E., Flora and Vegetation, *Iceland: country and population*, Central Bank of Iceland (Reykjavik, 1975)
Jonasson, P., *Ecology of Eutrophic Subarctic Lake Mývatn and the River Laxá*, Icelandic Literature Society (Copenhagen, 1980)

SWEDEN

Ahlén, Ingemar, *Faunavård: Om bevarande av hotade djurarter i Sverige*, Statens Naturvårdsverk (Stockholm, 1978)
Larsson, T., *Demarcation and Description of Swedish Wetlands of International Importance*, Bulletin SNVPM 1262E, Statens Naturvårdsverk (Solna, 1980)

FINLAND

Bestimmungen für die Nationalparks, National Board of Forestry (Helsinki, 1979)
National Parks of Finland, National Board of Forestry (Helsinki, 1975)

DENMARK

Dahl, K., *Kort over Danmark. Tekst og detailkort over fredede områder*, Geodaetisk Institut (Copenhagen, 1979)

GERMANY

Ant, H., & Engelke, H., *Die Naturschutzgebiete der Bundesrepublik Deutschland*, Bundesanstalt für Vegetationskunde, Naturschutz und Landschaftspflege (Bonn-Bad Godesberg, 1973)
Erz, W., *Katalog der Naturschutzgebiete in der Bundesrepublik Deutschland*, Institut für Naturschutz und Tierökologie (Bonn, 1979)
Erz, W., *Nationalpark Wattenmeer*, Paul Parey (Hamburg & Berlin, 1972)
Erz, W., *Naturschutz-Grundlagen, Probleme und Praxis, Handbuch für Planung, Gestaltung und Schutz der Umwelt*, Kilda-Verlag (Greven, 1980)
Haarmann, K., & Pretscher, P., *Die Feuchtgebiete internationaler Bedeutung in der Bundesrepublik Deutschland*, Kilda-Verlag (Greven, 1976)
Heintze, G., *Landschaftsrahmenplan Naturpark Meissner-Kaufunger Wald* (Darmstadt, 1966)
Meister, G., *Nationalpark Berchtesgaden, Begegnung mit dem Naturparadies am Königssee*, Kindler Verlag (München, 1976)
Offner, H., *Unsere Naturpark: Gepflegte Landschaften und Stätten der Erholung, Band 1: Schleswig-Holstein, Hamburg, Niedersachsen, Nordrhein-Westfalen*, DRW-Verlag (Stuttgart, 1976)
Offner, H., *Unsere Naturpark: Gepflegte Landschaften und Stätten der Erholung, Band 2: Rheinland-Pfalz, Saarland, Hessen, Bayern, Baden-Württemberg*, DRW-Verlag (Stuttgart, 1977)
Runge, F., *Die Naturschutzgebiete Westfalens und des Regierungs-Bezirkes Osnabrück*, Aschendorff (Munster, 1978)
Wadensee, Natuurmonumenten ('s-Graveland, 1977)

AUSTRIA

Machura, L., *Naturschutz in Österreich*, Österreichisches Naturschutzbund (Graz, 1970)
Wolkinger, F., *et al.*, *Die Natur und Landschaftsschutzgebiete Österreichs Vol 7*, Österr. Ges. für Natur-und Umweltschutz (Vienna, 1981)

SWITZERLAND

Antonietti, A., *et al.*, *Naturlehrpfad am Monte S. Giorgio*, Ente Ticinese per il Turismo (Bellinzona, 1980)
Becherer, A., *Führer durch die Flora der Schweiz*, Schwabe (Basel/Stuttgart, 1972)
Burckhardt, D., *et al.* (eds.), *Schweizer Naturschutz am Werk*, Verlag Paul Haupt (Bern, 1960)
Burckhardt, D., *Die schönsten Naturschutzgebiete der Schweiz*, Ringier (Zürich/München, 1980)
Lüps, P., *et al.*, Die Vogelwelt des Kantons Bern, *Der Ornithologische Beobachter*, 75 (1978)
Willi, P., Phanologie der selteneren Wasservögel auf dem Klingnauer Stausee. *Der Ornithologische Beobachter*, 70 (1973)

NETHERLANDS

Handboek van Natuurreservaten en Wandelterreinen in Nederland, Natuurmonumenten ('s-Graveland, 1980)
Hesse, J., *Mécanismes Institutionnels et économiques de la Conservation des éspaces naturels aux Pays-Bas*, Ecole Polytechnique (Paris, 1981)

Den Houte de Lange, S. M. (ed.), *Rapport van het Veluwe-Onderzoek*, Pudoc (Wageningen, 1977)
Westhoff. V., *et al.*, *Wilde Planten*, 3 vols, Natuurmonumenten ('s-Graveland, 1970)

BELGIUM

Colloquium Laagveengebieden, 25 Jaar "De Zegge", Antwerp Zool. Soc. (Antwerp, 1978)
Kesteloot, E., *Parcs Nationaux et Réserves naturelles en Belgique*, Le Patrimoine de l'institut royal des Sciences naturelles de Belgique (1962)
Noirfalise, A., *et al.*, *Les Réserves Naturelles de la Belgique*, L'Administration des Eaux et Forêts, Ministère de l'Agriculture (Bruxelles, 1970)
Schumacker, R., & Noirfalise, A., *Les Hautes Fagnes*, A.S.B.L. Parc-Naturel Hautes Fagnes-Eifel et Federation du Tourisme de la Province de Liège (1976)

UK & EIRE

Angel, H., *et al.*, *The Natural History of Britain and Ireland*, Michael Joseph (London, 1981)
Countryside Commission Annual Report, HMSO (London)
Dartmoor National Park, Guide No. 1, HMSO (London, 1979)
Exmoor National Park, Guide No. 8, HMSO (London, 1979)
Hickin, Norman, *Irish Nature*, O'Brien Press (Dublin, 1980)
Lake District National Park, Guide No. 6, HMSO (London, 1979)
Nature Conservancy Council Annual Report, HMSO (London)
Peak District National Park, Guide No. 3, HMSO (London, 1971)
Ratcliffe, D. A., *A Nature Conservation Review*, 2 vols., University Press (Cambridge, 1977)
Sheaie, John, *Nature in Trust: The history of Nature Conservation in Britain*, Blackie (Glasgow, 1976)
Snowdonia National Park, Guide No. 2, HMSO (London, 1980)
Stamp, Dudley, *Nature Conservation in Britain*, Collins (London, 1969)
Wildlife in Britain, AA (London, 1976)

FRANCE

Association des Amis du Parc National du Mercantour, *Le Massif du Mercantour et des Alpes Maritimes*, Serre (Nice, 1978)
Atlas des Réserves d'Avifaune Aquatique, Ministère d l'Environment et du Cadre de Vie (Nevilly/Seine, 1979)
Le Conseil d'Administration du Parc National de la Vanoise et son Comité Scientifique (ed.), *Le Parc National de la Vanoise*, Les Imprimeries Reunies de Chambéry (Chambéry)
Derenne, P., *Guide du Naturaliste dans les Alpes*, Delachaux et Niestlé (Paris, 1972)
Etchekopar, R. D., *Réserves Françaises d'Oiseaux de Mer et de Marais*, Union des Fédérations départementales côtières des chasseurs (Paris, 1961)
Harant, H., & Jarry, D., *Guide du Naturaliste dans le Midi de la France*, Delachaux et Niestlé (Paris, 1973)
Schaer, J. P., *et al.*, *Guide du Naturaliste dans les Alpes*, Delachaux et Niestlé (Paris, 1972)

SPAIN

Aritio, L. B., *Los Parques Nacionales Españoles*, Incafo (Madrid, 1979)
Bramwell, D., & Bramwell, Z., *Wild Flowers of the Canary Islands*, Stanley Thornes (London, 1974)
Kunkel, G. (ed.), *Biogeography and Ecology of the Canary Islands*, Junk (Den Haag, 1976)
Medina, F. O., & de la Peña, J., *Reservas y Cotos Nacionales de Caza I. Región Pirenaica*, Incafo (Madrid, 1976)
Medina, F. O., & de la Peña, J., *Reservas y Cotos Nacionales de Caza II. Región Cantábrica*, Incafo (Madrid, 1977)
Medina, F. O., & de la Peña, J., *Reservas y Cotos Nacionales de Caza III. Región Central*, Incafo (Madrid, 1978)
Medina, F. O., & de la Peña, J., *Reservas y Cotos Nacionales de Caza IV. Región Mediterránea*, Incafo (Madrid, 1979)
Mountford, G., *Portrait of a Wilderness, The Story of the Coto Doñana Expeditions*, Hutchinson (London, 1958)
Stocken, C. M., *Andalusian Flowers and the Countryside*, E. M. Stocken (Thurlestone, 1969)
de Viedma, M. C. (ed.), *Fauna de Cazorla, Vertebrados, Monographiás 19*, ICONA (Madrid, 1978)

PORTUGAL

de Saeger, H., Au Portugal. Le Parc National de Gerêz *Ardennes et Gaume No. 27* (1972)

ITALY

Cassola, F., & Tassi, F., Proposta per un sistema di Parchi e Riserve Naturali in Sardegna, *Bollettino della Societa Sardu di Scienze Naturali Vol. 13* (1973)
Farneti, G., Pratesi, F., & Tassi, F., *Guida alla Natura d'Italia*, Mondadori (Verona, 1975)
Pedrotti F. (ed.), *S.O.S. Fauna Animali in Pericolo in Italia*, Associazione Italiana per il W.W.F. (Roma, 1976)
Pratesi, F., *Parchi Nazionale e Zone Protette d'Italia*, Musumeci (Aosta, 1977)
Tassi, F., I. Parchi Nazionali, *Urbanistica Informazioni*, No. 1 (1978)

GREECE

Bauer & Miller, Proposals for Nature Conservation in Northern Greece, *IUCN Occ. Paper* No. 1 (1971)
Bohr, M. J., The need for the protection of the virgin forest of Rodopi, *Proceedings of the Conference on the Protection of the Flora, Fauna & Biotopes in Greece* (1979)
Gorge of Samaria National Park, Greece, European Diploma series 19, Council of Europe (Strasbourg, 1980)
Huxley & Taylor, *Flowers of Greece and the Aegean*, Chatto & Windus (London, 1977)
Strid, A., *Wild Flowers of Mt Olympos*, Goulandris Natural History Museum (Kifissia, 1980)

ACKNOWLEDGEMENTS

Editor James Somerville
Art Editor John Pallot
Cartographic Editor Caroline Simpson
Assistant Editor Barbara Westmore
Picture Researcher Marilynn Zipes
Production Manager Ken Cowan
Production Editor Fred Gill
Index prepared by Richard Bird

Harrow House Editions would also like to thank Celia Dearing, Sue Gallacher, Jane Greening and Grace Sadd for their help and support.

The author would like to express his gratitude to the large number of individuals and organizations who, in addition to the consultants listed earlier, gave valuable assistance in the compilation of the book.

Dr Rudolf Berndt
Dr Hermann Blindow
Peter Broussalis
Gisli Gislason
Ingo Hausch
H. R. Henneberg
Jacques Hesse
International Union for the
  Conservation of Nature and
  Natural Resources (IUCN)
Dr A. Brenk Kostič
Wilfried Ludwig
C. Marshall
Richard Nairn

Nature Conservancy Council
E. O'Connor
H. O. Rehage
Dr Josef H. Reichholf
Royal Geographical Society
Malcolm Rush
Dr Helmut Schenk
Dr F. R. Thiele
Dr Thiessen
Michael Tigges
Gwynne Vevers
Richard Weyl
I. A. Wörnle

The author also wishes to pay special tribute to his wife, Rita Duffey, without whose help, particularly in the translation of scientific papers, the work could not have been completed.
Special thanks are due to the Winston Memorial Trust, whose fellowship awarded in 1980 enabled the author to visit many protected areas in Yugoslavia, Greece and Italy.

CARTOGRAPHERS

Maps of parks and reserves prepared by **Clyde Surveys Ltd.**, Reform Road, Maidenhead, Berkshire
Route maps by **Eugene Fleury**
Maps on pages 8–9, 10–11, 12–13 by Berry Fallon Design
Map on pages 16–17 by Product Support (Graphics) Ltd.
Maps on pages 164–177, Crown Copyright Reserved

ARTISTS

All birds and plants by **John Barber**
All insects and mammals by **Norman Weaver**
All flags by Jeremy Banks

PICTURE CREDITS

A: Above B: Below L: Left R: Right C: Centre
1, 2–3: Duscher/Bruce Coleman Ltd; 7: R. Claquin/Explorer; 8 (AL): Peter Jackson/Bruce Coleman Ltd; (BR): Claude Pissavini/Jacana; 9 (AR): Hans Reinhard/Bruce Coleman Ltd; 10 (AL): Jim Grant (AR): Charlie Ott/Bruce Coleman Ltd; 11 (CL): Leonard Lee Rue III/OSF/AA (BR): Rod Williams/Bruce Coleman Ltd; 12 (CL): M. Fogden/Bruce Coleman Ltd (BR): Jean-Paul Ferrero; 13 (AR): Zepf Bregenz/NHPA (BR): L. R. Dawson/Bruce Coleman Ltd; 18–19 Fabius Henrion/Explorer; 20 (AR): Heather Angel; 23 (AR): C & M Moiton/Explorer; 25: Wayne Lankinen/Bruce Coleman Ltd; 26: Richard Vaughan/Ardea; 29: Pål Hermansen/Naturfotografenes Billedbyrå; 30: Bengtson/Naturfotografenes Billedbyrå; 33 (AR): Vulcain/Explorer; 32–33 (BR): Claye/Explorer; 134: Heather Angel; 36–37: Olsson/Bildhuset; 42–43: Nilsson/Naturfotografernas Bildbyrå; 44: Gustav Hansson/Bildhuset; 45: Gustav Hansson/Bildhuset; 47: Robert Gillmor/Bruce Coleman Ltd; 48: Gustav Hansson/Bildhuset; 50: Johanson/Naturfotografernas Bildbyrå; 52–53: Luonnonkuva-Arkisto; 54 (BR): Luonnonkuva-Arkisto; 56: R. Volot/Explorer; 58–59: Martin-Guillou/Explorer; 60–61: Luonnonkuva-Arkisto; 62–63: Fahn/Schapowalow; 64 (BR): Ellen Thoby; 66–67: Schapowalow; 69: Brian Hawkes/NHPA; 70: Jen & Des Bartlett/Bruce Coleman Ltd; 72–73: Ole Malling; 75: Lars Jarnemo/Naturfotografernas Bildbyrå; 76: Bormann/Schapowalow; 80: Meyer/Photo Center; 82: Meyer/Photo Centre; 85: Bormann/Schapowalow; 86: Meyer/Photo Center; 88–89: Hans Reinhard/Bruce Coleman Ltd; 92: Bormann/Schapowalow; 94: Jacana; 96: Fritz Prenzel; 97 (AR): Gunter Ziesler; 98–99: M. Thonig/ZEFA; 100–101: Robert Harding Picture Library; 103: Ian Beames/Ardea; 104: Peter Baker; 106–107: Veiller/Explorer; 108–109: Gunter Ziesler; 111: Dr H Jungius; 112–113: Paolo Koch/Vision International; 114: Dr E. Duffey; 117: Duscher/Bruce Coleman Ltd; 118: John Gerlach/OSF/AA; 119: W. Zepf/NHPA; 121: Fritz Vollmar/Bruce Coleman Ltd; 122–123: Pierre Tetrel/Explorer; 124: Dr E. Duffey; 125: Ian Beames/Ardea; 126–127: J. A. L. Cooke/OSF; 129: Jan Van de Kam; 130 (AR): Jan Van de Kam; 132: Hug/Explorer; 135: Heather Angel; 136: Adrian Davies/Bruce Coleman Ltd; 139: J. L. G. Grande/Bruce Coleman Ltd; 141: Jan Van de Kam; 143: Jan Van de Kam; 144–145: A. Pelletier/Explorer; 146: Louis-Yves Loirat/Explorer; 149: Louis-Yves Loirat/Explorer; 150: K. Desender/J. Hublé; 152–153: A. Bailey/Ardea; 153: C. R. Dawson/Bruce Coleman Ltd; 154–155: D. Clément/Explorer; 156: A. Saucez/Explorer; 158–159: Malcolm Aird; 163: Robin Fletcher/Vision International; 164–165: M. Fogden/Ecology Pictures; 166: BTA; 167: BTA; 168–169: Brian Hawkes; 170: P. H. Evans/Bruce Coleman Ltd; 172–173: Malcolm Aird; 174–174: Robin Fletcher/Vision International; 178–179: The National Trust (Northern Ireland); 181: Colin Molyneux; 182–183: Gerard Sioen/CEDRI; 186–187: C. Delu/Explorer; 188: Brevelay/Explorer; 188–189: S. Marmounier/CEDRI; 191: H. Veiller/Explorer; 192: Anderson-Fournier/Explorer; 196: Eric Andersson/Fotogram; 198: A. Arnaud/Fotogram; 201: Denis Hughes-Gilbey; 202: Boet/Jacana; 202–203: Christian Sappa/CEDRI; 204: Claude Rives/CEDRI; 207: Robert Estall; 208: Blassi/ICF; 211: Blassi/ICF; 212–213: Blassi/ICF; 215: Blassi/Firo-Foto; 217: J. L. G. Grande/Salmer; 219: Blassi/ICF; 220–221: Blassi/ICF; 221: Dr E. Duffey; 222: Brian Hawkes; 224–225: Louis-Yves Loirat/Explorer; 226: Louis-Yves Loirat/Explorer; 229: J. L. G. Grande/Bruce Coleman Ltd., 231: J. Allan Cash Ltd; 232: Dr E. Duffey; 233: Eric Saint-Servan/Explorer; 234–235: Dr E. Duffey; 236: John Simms; 241: Jacques Brun/Explorer; 242: Melinda Berge/Bruce Coleman Ltd; 244–245: Foto Fabio Cassola; 246: Fritz Vollmar; 249: Foto Fabio Cassola; 250–251: Dr E. Duffey; 252: Peter Ward/Nat. Science Photos; 254: Peter Ward/Nat. Science Photos; 257: Robert Harding Picture Library; 258–259: Dr E. Duffey; 250–261: Roy/Explorer; 263: C. M. Dixon; 264: Lelievre/Explorer; 267: C. M. Dixon; 268–269: Paul M. Tatopoulos/Explorer; 270–271: D. Clément/Explorer.